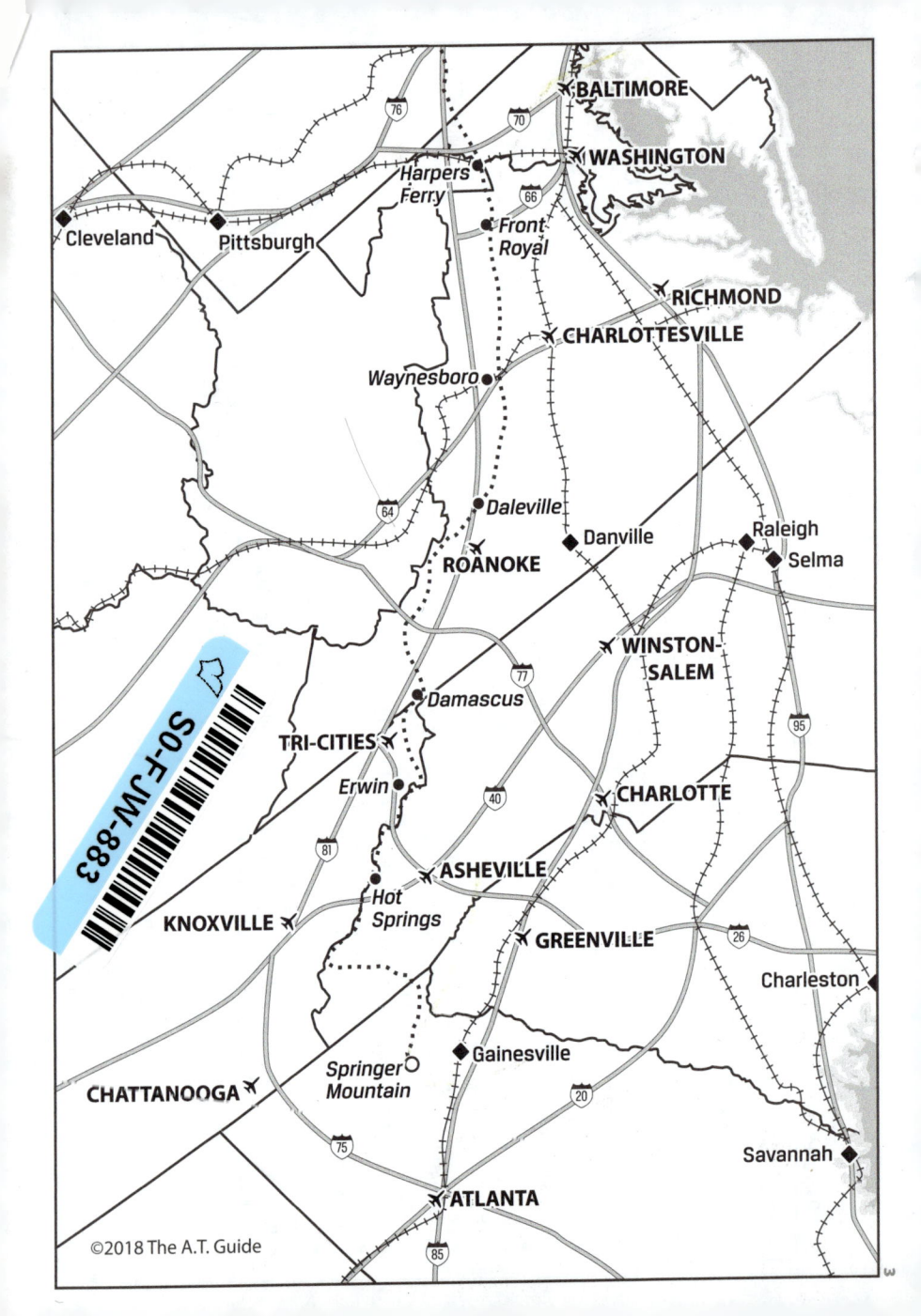

©2018 The A.T. Guide

Maildrop Guidelines

Packages sent to PO:	Packages sent to businesses
John Doe C/O General Delivery Trail Town, VA 12345 Please hold for AT hiker ETA May 16, 2018	John Doe C/O Hiker Hostel 2176 Appalachian Way Trail Town, VA 12345 Please hold for AT hiker ETA May 16, 2018

▼ Use your real name (not a trail name) as some Post Offices and businesses require photo ID in order to retrieve your package. Be sure to include an ETA & return address.

▼ Only send "General Delivery" mail to a Post office.

▼ FedEx and UPS packages cannot be addressed to PO boxes.

▼ USPS will forward unopened general delivery mail for free if it was shipped by Priority Mail.

▼ Be prepared to show an ID when you retrieve your mail.

▼ The "C/O" name is essential when mailing to a business's PO Box; without it, they may not be able to retrieve your mail.

▼ When sending mail somewhere other than a PO, it's best to call first.

▼ Hostels & outfitters go out of business. Consider adding your phone number or email so they have a way to contact you about your mail.

▼ Send maildrops to a lodging facility only if you plan to stay there. If your plans change, offer to pay for the service of holding your mail.

▼ Many outfitters hold maildrops. Although none have rules about what you send, it's bad form to buy from an on-line retailer and have it shipped to a store where you could have bought it.

Maildrop services: These businesses offer small quantities of typical resupply items, packaged and mailed to you on the AT:

⊕ ✉ **Zero Day Resupply** Maildrop resupply service for thru-hikers. No sales tax or handling fee, next day shipping.(ZeroDayResupply.com)

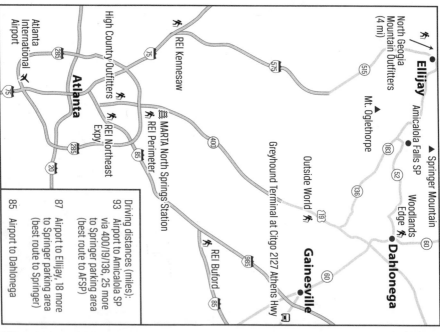

Driving distances (miles):
93 Airport to Amicalola SP via 400/19/136, 25 more to Springer parking area (best route to AFSP)

87 Airport to Ellijay, 18 more to Springer parking area (best route to Springer)

85 Airport to Dahlonega

Getting to Springer Mountain

The southern terminus of the AT on Springer Mountain is accessible only by foot. The 8.8-mi. Approach Trail originating at the Visitor Center in Amicalola Falls SP is one means of getting there. Or you can drive to Springer Parking area on USFS 42, a dirt road passable by most vehicles unless there is bad-weather washout. From the parking area, hike south 1 mi. on the AT to Springer Mtn. Your hike would begin by retracing your steps. (See Start of Trail map pg.10)

The closest major city is Atlanta, GA, 82 mi. south. If you fly or take AMTRAK into Atlanta, take the MARTA rail system to the North Springs Station; shuttlers pickup from there. There is also Greyhound bus service to Gainesville, GA, 38 mi. from the park.

Shuttle Services

☎ ⬤ **A.T. Survivor Dave's Trail Shuttle** 678.469.0978 (No texts please) Affordable shuttle service to/from Atlanta Airport & North Springs MARTA Station to Amicalola Falls SP, Springer Mountain, & all trailheads up to Fontana Dam. Will stop at outfitter and/or supermarket for supplies (time permitting). Stove fuels avail on-board. Well behaved dogs welcome. Will respond promptly to phone messages.⟨atsurvivordave.com⟩

☎ **Appalachian Adventure Company** 706.265.9454, 865.456.7677 thomasbazemore@icloud.com Shuttles, slackpacking, guided hikes, tours for GA, NC, TN. Will p/u-d/o ATL, AVL, or TYS airports, bus or Amtrak. Fees based on length, accessibility & # of passengers. Max 10 hikers w/gear. Pet friendly. ⟨fb.com/appalachianadventureco⟩

☎ ⬤ **Ron Brown** 706.669.0919 hikershuttles@outlook.

com Flat rate shuttles to/from the AT or trail towns up to Fontana, incl Amicalola Falls SP, Atlanta airport, & Gainesville, GA. Dogs welcome. Extra stops ok. Fuel on request.⟨fb.com/Rons-Appalachian-Trail-Shuttle-1742702761404⟩

☎ **Subman Shuttles** 706.889.7044 2003 & 2016 Thru-hiker provides shuttles from Atlanta to start of trail.

Outfitters Near the Southern Terminus

🥾 **Half Moon Outfitters** 404.249.7921 Open 10-5, 363 days a yr (closed Easter & Christmas). Full svc outfitter, fuel/oz, ask about shuttles. 36 N Park St, Dahlonega, GA 30533.

🥾 **High Country Outfitters** 404.814.0999 Roswell Rd. #B, Atlanta, GA 30306

🥾 ⬤ **Mountain Crossings** 706.745.6095 See info at Neel Gap, US 9.

🥾 **Outside World Outfitters** 706.265.4500 471 Quill Dr, Dawsonville, GA 31534. Conveniently located en route to Springer from major area transits. Carries TSA regulated items incl canister fuel, stoves, & trekking poles.⟨outsidegeorgia.com⟩

🥾 **REI Atlanta Area** REI Five Atlanta Area Stores:
- ▲ 1800 Northeast Expy NE, Atlanta, GA 30329 404.633.6508
- ▲ 1165 Perimeter Ctr W Ste 200, Atlanta, GA 30338, 770.901.9200
- ▲ 740 Barrett Pkwy, Ste 450, Kennesaw, GA 30144, 770.425.4480
- ▲ 1600 Mall of Georgia Blvd, Buford, GA 30519, 770.831.0676
- ▲ 7531 North Point Pkwy, Alpharetta, GA 30022, 770.998.2622

🥾 ⬤ **Woodlands Edge** 706.864.5358 Open M-Sa 10:30a-5p, Su 11a-5p, 363 days a yr (closed Easter & Christmas Day). Full svc outfitter, fuel/oz, ask about shuttles. 36 North Park St, Dahlonega, GA 30533.

🥾 ⬤ **North Georgia Mountain Outfitters** (22.9W) 706.698.4453 travis@hikenorthgeorgia.com Full svc outfitter. Tu-Sa 10-6.⟨hikenorthgeorgia.com⟩

Stay Up to Date on all Updates, Advisories & Trail Information

A.T. Guide - Updates...TheATGuide.com/updates
A.T. Guide - Report a Change or Suggestion.................TheATGuide.com/contact
ATC Trail Camping & Fire Updates (pg. 61).....................appalachiantrail.org/camping
ATC Trail Widwide Updates (pg. 61)......appalachiantrail.org/home/explore-the-trail/trail-updates
Baxter State Park (pg. 224)...baxterstateparkauthority.com
Shenandoah National Park (SNP) (pg.88)...nps.gov/shen

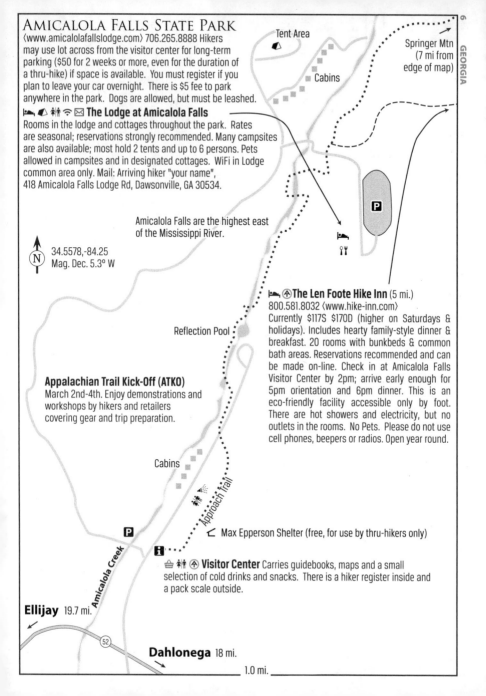

AMICALOLA FALLS STATE PARK

〈www.amicalolafallslodge.com〉 706.265.8888 Hikers may use lot across from the visitor center for long-term parking ($50 for 2 weeks or more, even for the duration of a thru-hike) if space is available. You must register if you plan to leave your car overnight. There is $5 fee to park anywhere in the park. Dogs are allowed, but must be leashed.

The Lodge at Amicalola Falls
Rooms in the lodge and cottages throughout the park. Rates are seasonal; reservations strongly recommended. Many campsites are also available; most hold 2 tents and up to 6 persons. Pets allowed in campsites and in designated cottages. WiFi in Lodge common area only. Mail: Arriving hiker "your name", 418 Amicalola Falls Lodge Rd, Dawsonville, GA 30534.

Tent Area

Cabins

Springer Mtn (7 mi from edge of map)

GEORGIA

6

Amicalola Falls are the highest east of the Mississippi River.

34.5578,-84.25
Mag. Dec. 5.3° W
N

Reflection Pool

Appalachian Trail Kick-Off (ATKO)
March 2nd-4th. Enjoy demonstrations and workshops by hikers and retailers covering gear and trip preparation.

The Len Foote Hike Inn (5 mi.)
800.581.8032 〈www.hike-inn.com〉
Currently $117S $170D (higher on Saturdays & holidays). Includes hearty family-style dinner & breakfast. 20 rooms with bunkbeds & common bath areas. Reservations recommended and can be made on-line. Check in at Amicalola Falls Visitor Center by 2pm; arrive early enough for 5pm orientation and 6pm dinner. This is an eco-friendly facility accessible only by foot. There are hot showers and electricity, but no outlets in the rooms. No Pets. Please do not use cell phones, beepers or radios. Open year round.

Cabins

Approach Trail

Max Epperson Shelter (free, for use by thru-hikers only)

Visitor Center Carries guidebooks, maps and a small selection of cold drinks and snacks. There is a hiker register inside and a pack scale outside.

Ellijay 19.7 mi.

Amicalola Creek

52

Dahlonega 18 mi.

1.0 mi.

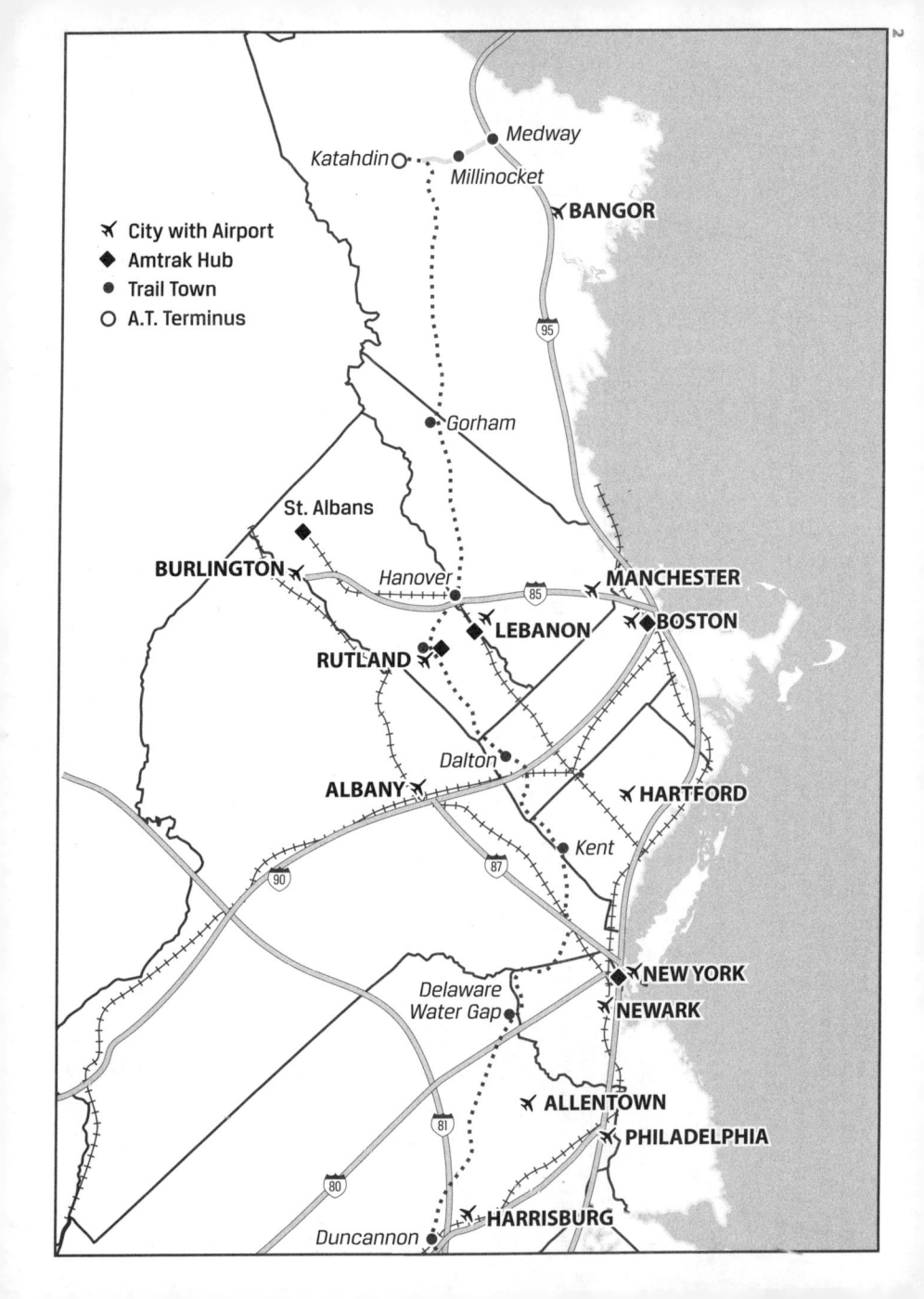

2

Legend:
- ✈ City with Airport
- ◆ Amtrak Hub
- ● Trail Town
- ○ A.T. Terminus

Katahdin ○ ┄ ● *Medway*
Millinocket
✕ **BANGOR**

95

● *Gorham*

St. Albans ◆
BURLINGTON ✈ *Hanover* ●
85
MANCHESTER ✈
✕ ◆ **BOSTON**
RUTLAND ● ◆ ✈ ◆ **LEBANON**

● *Dalton*
ALBANY ✕
✕ **HARTFORD**

● *Kent*

90
87

◆ ✕ **NEW YORK**
Delaware Water Gap ●
◆ **NEWARK**

81
✈ **ALLENTOWN**
✕ **PHILADELPHIA**

80
✈ **HARRISBURG**
Duncannon ●

About this Book

The A.T. Guide is an on-trail reference, so its size is constrained. Information that can be researched before the hike is not included. Descriptions are terse. Tips and items of interest are scattered throughout where space is available.

Book Organization - A spread is the pair of pages seen when the book is laid open. The A.T. Guide contains a spread of trail data followed by a spread of services available to hikers within that section. Occasionally there are back-to-back spreads of the same type.

Data Spreads have landmarks, mileages and elevations. Every spread covers approximately 39.8 miles of trail (19.9 miles per page). An elevation profile is "watermarked" on the data. Lines of text that describe landmarks are spaced so that they intersect the profile map at the approximate location of each landmark. Small triangular pointers below the profile line identify shelter locations. The vertical exaggeration of the profile maps is 7.6:1.

Services Spreads provide resupply information for towns that the trail passes through or near. Businesses are selectively included, and maps may only show a portion of town closest to the trail. Places of business that appear to be adjacent may be separated by one or more unspecified buildings or roads. When a map is provided, post office information will be on the map. Information presented in the map is not repeated in the text unless more elaboration is needed. The width of the mapped area is at the bottom or top of the map.

Prices are listed as given in fall of 2017. No one is obliged to maintain these prices. Lodging prices are dynamic, but most facilities listed will do their best for hikers. Let them know if you are thru-hiking; there may be a "thru-hiker rate."

2018 is expected to be a popular year for hiking the A.T. Most thru-hikers travel north, starting in Georgia in March or April. Other plans lessen impact on the trail and may better suit hikers seeking a more secluded experience or a longer window of mild weather. Learn more about alternative hikes and the benefits here: ⟨http://appalachiantrail.org/home/explore-the-trail/thru-hiking/alternative⟩

Miles from Katahdin   Miles from Springer   Elevation profile & elevation in feet.

1966.9 222.2 **Tri-Corner Knob Shelter** . . . . ☽ ◗ ◖ ⊏ (12) 5897
20.1◀12.6◀5.2◀▶7.7▶14.8▶25.3 Cables.

The next 3 shelters to the north are 7.7, 14.8 and 25.3 miles from this shelter. (5.2, 12.6, and 20.1 to the south).

There is a privy, water source, and shelter (capacity 12) at this location.

How to Read Directions in this Book

North/South: At many points along the trail, a northbound hiker will be heading some direction other than compass north, but this book will always refer to "north" as the direction on the AT that ultimately leads to Katahdin. When reference is made to the true bearing, the word "compass" will precede the direction. (e.g., "compass south"). If the trail joins a section of road, enters a park, or enters a town, the "south" end is where a northbound hiker first arrives, and the "north" end is where he/she leaves.

East/West: "East" is to the right of the trail for a northbound hiker and "west" is to their left, regardless of the compass reading. Most east-west directions are abbreviated along with a distance in miles. For example, three-tenths of a mile east is written "0.3E."

Left/Right: If a road leads to a town that is to the west, then a northbound hiker would go to their left, and the southbound hiker to their right. Once on the road both hikers are headed in the same direction, so any additional directions are given using the words "left" and "right." "Left" and "right" are also used to describe features near a shelter, from the perspective of a person outside of the shelter looking in.

SoBo	NoBo	**The Approach Trail**	Elev
8.8	0.0	**Amicalola Falls State Park,** archway behind Visitor Center . . . . . . ⊛⊕ ♐♦	1800
8.7	0.1	**Max Epperson Shelter,** for thru-hiker use only . . . . ♐ ⚟ ♦ ⊏ (12)	1858
8.4	0.4	Reflection Pond at base of falls	2003
8.1	0.7	Staircase - 604 steps to the top of the Falls	2216
7.7	1.1	Parking, side trail to Lodge . . . . 🅿 ♐	2639
7.6	1.2	Lodge Road (lodge to east)	2642
7.5	1.3	Trail to **Len Foote Hike Inn** (5.0E) blazed lime-green . . . . (pg. 6)	2656
7.3	1.5	USFS Road 46, steps on north side	2584
5.6	3.2	High Shoals Road	2841
4.0	4.8	Frosty Mountain. Spring (0.2E) is unreliable. . . . . ⬠	3384
3.7	5.1	Frosty Mountain Road, USFS Road 46	3178
3.4	5.4	Trail to **Len Foote Hike Inn** (1.0E) blazed lime-green . . . . (pg. 6)	3353
3.1	5.7	Woody Knob.	3406
2.8	6.0	Nimblewill Gap, USFS Road 28	3100
2.6	6.2	Spring (left of trail), unreliable . . . . ⬠	3419
1.5	7.3	**Black Gap Shelter** (0.1W) . . . . ⬠♦⬤(6) ⊏ (7)	3300
		Spring is on opposite side of the Approach Trail (0.1E).	
0.0	8.8	Springer Mountain . . . . 🅿	3782

2190.9	0.0	**Springer Mountain southern terminus**, register on back of rock with plaque . 📷	3782
2190.7	0.2	**Springer Mountain Shelter** (0.2E) Tent pads . . . . 🌙◑⚠(18)⊏(12)	3720
		►2.6►7.9►15.5 150 yards north, Benton MacKaye Trail to east.	
2189.9	1.0	Big Stamp Gap, USFS 42 . . . . 34.6376,-84.1954 🅿	3350
2188.9	2.0	Benton MacKaye Trail.	3268
2188.2	2.7	Footbridge, stream . . . . ◑	2918
2188.1	2.8	**Stover Creek Shelter** (0.1E) (2006) . . . . 🌙◑⚠(3)⊏(14)	2916
		2.6◄►5.3►12.9►24.8	
2188.0	2.9	Footbridge, stream . . . . ◑	2873
2187.5	3.4	Stream. . . . . ◑	2693
2186.7	4.2	Benton MacKaye / Duncan Ridge Trail to east	2586
2186.6	4.3	Three Forks, USFS 58, footbridge	2530
2185.7	5.2	Benton MacKaye / Duncan Ridge Trail to west . . . . ◑	2800
		Trail to Long Creek Falls	
2184.7	6.2	Dirt road, 0.2W to Hickory Flats Cemetery, pavilion. . . . . 🌙	3081
2183.5	7.4	Hawk Mountain campsite (0.2W) 30 designated tent pads . . . . . 🌙🌙⚠(30)	3220
2182.8	8.1	**Hawk Mountain Shelter** (0.2W) (1993) . . . . 🌙◑⊏(12)	3194
		7.9◄5.3◄►7.6►19.5►20.6 Water south on AT and 0.1 mile behind shelter.	
2182.3	8.6	Hightower Gap, junction USFS 42 & 69 . . . . 34.6635,-84.1297 🅿	2854
2180.4	10.5	Horse Gap	2681
2179.4	11.5	Sassafras Mountain	3347
2178.7	12.2	Cooper Gap, USFS 15, 42 & 80 . . . . 34.653,-84.0846 🅿	2929
2178.2	12.7	Justus Mountain	3219
2177.4	13.5	Dirt road.	2752
2176.6	14.3	Justus Creek. Use designated campsites north of creek, to west . . . . . ◑⚠(6)	2589
2176.0	14.9	Stream. . . . . ◑	2636
2175.5	15.4	Blackwell Creek . . . . ◑	2656
2175.2	15.7	**Gooch Mountain Shelter** (0.1W) (2001) Water behind shelter . . 🌙◑⚠(6)⊏(14)	2789
		15.5◄12.9◄7.6◄►11.9►13►22.1 Designated tentsites, cables.	
2174.2	16.7	Spring to the east . . . . ◑	2831
2173.9	17.0	Gooch Gap, USFS 42 (gravel). . . . . 34.6521,-84.0323 🅿◑	2824
		Suches, GA (2.7W - see Woody Gap entry) water north of rd 0.1E on marked trail	
2173.0	17.9	Roadbed.	2939
2172.8	18.1	Liss Gap	3052
2172.2	18.7	Ramrock Mountain . . . . 📷	3222
2171.0	19.9	Seasonal springs. . . . . ◌	3208

| 2170.6 | 20.3 | Woody Gap, GA 60 . . . . 34.6777,-84.0000 🅿 🏛 🏕 💧 (pg. 11) | 3196 |

Suches, GA (2.0W); spring north of road 0.2W.

2169.7	21.2	Preaching Rock, view to east. Woody Lake in Suches in view to west. . . . . . 📷	3593
2169.4	21.5	Big Cedar Mountain, rock ledges and views. . . . . 📷	3737
2169.2	21.7	Spring to west . . . . 💧	3659

| 2168.3 | 22.6 | Spring to west . . . . 💧 | 3325 |

| 2167.4 | 23.5 | Dockery Lake Trail. . . . . | 3050 |
| 2167.0 | 23.9 | Lance Creek, camp in designated sites north of footbridge . . . . 💧 🔺 (6) | 2865 |

| 2166.3 | 24.6 | Henry Gap (unmarked) is 70 yards west on side trail, woods road to GA 180.. . 🅿 | 3083 |

🐻 A hard-shell bear-resistant canister is required for hikers overnighting between Jarrard Gap and Neel Gap from Mar 1 - Jun 1. No fires (year-round) from Slaughter Creek Trail to Neel Gap.

| 2164.8 | 26.1 | Jarrard Gap, dirt road. . . . . 💧 (0.3W) (pg. 11) | 3250 |
| 2164.6 | 26.3 | Gaddis Mountain . . . . | 3402 |

| 2163.4 | 27.5 | Turkey Stamp . . . . | 3742 |
| 2163.3 | 27.6 | **Woods Hole Shelter** (0.4W) 24.8◄19.5◄11.9◄►1.1►10.2►15.0 . . .) 💧 🔺 ⊏ (7) | 3662 |

Bird Gap, Freeman Trail east bypasses Blood Mtn & rejoins AT at Flatrock Gap

2163.0	27.9	Slaughter Creek Trail, spring on AT, campsite 0.1 North on AT . . . . 💧 🔺 (8)	3800
2162.6	28.3	Duncan Ridge Trail, Coosa Trail to west	4168
2162.2	28.7	**Blood Mountain Shelter** (1934) 20.6◄13◄1.1◄►9.1►13.9►21.2. . . . . 📷) ⊏ (8)	4457

Privy 50 yards south. No fires. Stream (0.8S). Many views from AT North of shelter

| 2160.9 | 30.0 | Flatrock Gap, Freeman Trail east bypasses Blood Mtn; west. . . . . 🅿 💧 (0.2W) | 3487 |

to Byron Reece parking area. Balance Rock 150 yards north.

| 2159.8 | 31.1 | Neel Gap, US 19 . . . . 34.7411,-83.9206 🅿 (pg. 11) | 3125 |

| 2158.7 | 32.2 | Bull Gap, spring 0.1W. 💧 🔺 | 3685 |

| 2158.1 | 32.8 | Levelland Mountain, view . . . . 📷 | 3870 |

| 2156.9 | 34.0 | Swaim Gap, spring to west. . . . . 💧 | 3536 |

| 2156.2 | 34.7 | Wolf Laurel Top, views to east . . . . 📷 | 3780 |

� Mayapple – White flower ball dangling under an umbrella of broad leaves. Plant is about a foot tall.

| 2154.8 | 36.1 | Cowrock Mountain . . . . 📷 | 3842 |

2153.8	37.1	Tesnatee Gap, GA 348, Russell Hwy . . . . 34.7262,-83.8476 🅿 (pg. 11)	3138
2153.3	37.6	Wildcat Mountain. . . . . 📷	3637
2153.1	37.8	**Whitley Gap Shelter** (1.2E) Spring 0.3 mi. behind shelter.. . . 📷) 💧 🔺 (3) ⊏ (7)	3625

22.1◄10.2◄9.1◄►4.8►12.1►20.2 Campsite 0.1F with view just beyond.

| 2152.9 | 38.0 | Hogpen Gap, GA 348, Water S of rd, E of AT . . . . 34.7250,-83.8399 🅿 💧 (pg. 11) | 3444 |
| 2152.0 | 38.9 | White Oak Stamp . . . . | 3470 |

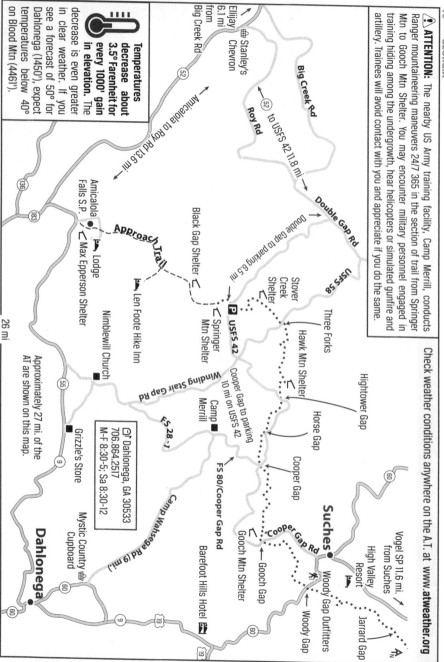

⚠️ **ATTENTION:** The nearby US Army training facility, Camp Merrill, conducts Ranger mountaineering maneuvers 24/7 365 in the section of trail from Springer Mtn to Gooch Mtn Shelter. You may encounter military personnel engaged in training hiking among the undergrowth, hear helicopters or simulated gunfire and artillery. Trainees will avoid contact with you and appreciate if you do the same.

Check weather conditions anywhere on the A.T. at www.**atweather.org**

🌡️ Temperatures decrease about **3.5° Farenheit for every 1000' gain in elevation.** The decrease is even greater in clear weather. If you see a forecast of 50° for Dahlonega (1450'), expect temperatures below 40° on Blood Mtn (446)1').

Elijay 6.1 mi from Big Creek Rd

⌖ Stanley's Chevron

Big Creek Rd

Roy Rd

(52)

(52)

Amicalola to Roy Rd 13.6 mi →

to USFS 42 11.8 mi →

Double Gap Rd

Double Gap to parking 6.5 mi →

(136)

(183)

Amicalola Falls S.P. ●

Approach Trail

Black Gap Shelter

Len Foote Hike Inn

⌂ Lodge
⌂ Max Epperson Shelter

Nimblewill Church

Winding Star Gap Rd

Springer Mtn Shelter

🅿 USFS 42

USFS 58

Stover Creek Shelter

Three Forks

Hawk Mtn Shelter

Hightower Gap

Horse Gap

Cooper Gap to parking 10 mi on USFS 42

Cooper Gap

(60)

Vogel SP 11.6 mi from Suches

High Valley Resort

Suches ●

Woody Gap Outfitters

Jarrard Gap

Aᴺ

26 mi

(55)

Camp Merrill

FS 28-1

Grizzle's Store

Camp Wahsega Rd (9 mi.)

FS 80/Cooper Gap Rd

Gooch Mtn Shelter

Gooch Gap

Cooper Gap Rd

Woody Gap

Approximately 27 mi. of the AT are shown on this map.

☎ Dahlonega, GA 30533
706.864.2517
M-F 8:30-5; Sa 8:30-12

Mystic Country Cupboard

Dahlonega ●

(60)

(9)

(9)

(19)

(19)

(60)

Barefoot Hills Hotel 🏨

20.3 WOODY GAP, GA HWY 60

Jeff Moon Shuttle Service 706.994.2307 ripplerider8@aol.com North Springs MARTA Station to Fontana Dam NC. Always willing to extract customers if things aren't going well.

Suches Hiker Shuttles 678.967.9510 24/7. Dogs/Groups ok. Range: ATL airport to Fontana Dam

Wes Wisson 706.747.2671, 706.781.4333 Covers N Georgia paved rds only.

Barefoot Hills Hotel (6.6E) 770.312.7342 Open yr-round. Bunks, pvt rooms & pvt cabins for up to 2-3 people. Check web, text, call for pricing & avail. Shuttles can be arranged for a fee. Laundry, Computer w/WiFi. Shuttles can be arranged for a fee. Laundry, canister fuel & limited gear avail for purchase.(barefoothills.com)

» Suches, GA 30572 (2W)
⊙706.747.2611, M-F 12:15-4:15 (pronounced "such-is")

Wildcat Lodge and Campground (7.5W) 706.973.0321 $15 Bunkroom, $12 camping. Lodge room sleeps 8: $100D, $25EAP. Camp store has Coleman & canisters. Diner serves B/L.

26.1 JARRARD GAP

Lake Winfield Scott Recreation Area (1.7W) 706.747.3816 Tent sites $18 for up to 5 persons. Showers & bathrooms. Leash dogs.(recreation.gov)

31.1 NEEL GAP, US 19

Mountain Crossings 706.745.6095 Full-svc outfitter, full resupply, gear shakedown, expert shoe & pack fitting. Alcohol/oz. Bunkroom $20PP incl shower w/towel. No Pets. Ask about shuttles. Outgoing shipping avail. Mail (USPS/UPS/FedEx) held for 2 wks, $1 fee at p/u: 12471 Gainesville Hwy, Blairsville, GA 30512.(mountaincrossings.com)

Blood Mountain Cabins (0.4E) 706.745.9454 Thru-hiker rate $72. Cabin w/kitchen, sat TV, holds 4 adults 2 kids under age 13. Laundry free w/stay. WiFi at lodge. No pets. Pizza & wings in store.(bloodmountain.com)

Vogel State Park (2.8W) 706.745.2628 Primitive tent sites $26-$32 (+ tax), cabins for 2-10 persons $120-$250. $2 Shower for tenters & visitors. $5 fee/vehicle/stay.(gastateparks.org)

Goose Creek Cabins (3.3W) 706.781.8593 Cabins & shuttles avail, call for details.

Jim's Smokin' Que (7.5W) 706.835.7427 Th-Sa 11a-8p, phone orders 8a-11a.

» Blairsville, GA 30514 (14W)All major services.

Misty Mtn Inn (10.4W) 706.745.4786 at@ mistymtninn.com Pet-friendly cabin $90+$10/bed incl free thru hiker shuttle from Neels, Tesnatee, Hogpen & Unicoi. $30/Bed group cabins during bubble. GA - NC shuttle, slackpack, trail-side resupp'ly, parking & amenities avail yr-round. Pizza & other delivery avail.(mistymtninn.com)

Blairsville Hikes & Bikes (13.1W) 706.745.8141 M-Sa 10-5:30. Hiking essentials incl poles, fuel & hiker food.

» Dahlonega, GA 30533 (17E)All major services.

37.1 ★ TESNATEE GAP, GA 348 (RUSSELL HWY)
38.0   HOGPEN GAP, GA 348

» Blairsville, GA 30514 (14W)(services above)

48.3 RED CLAY GAP

Enota Mountain Retreat (1.4W) 706.893.9966 No sign & trail not blazed; be certain of location if you walk. Marked on some maps by its previous name "Camp Pioneer." Trail is downhill to Joel's Creek & follows creek into camp. Driving from Unicoi Gap: 2.4W on Hwy 17, then left 2.4 mi on Hwy 180. Tentsites & cabins - check rates online. Beautiful waterfall, trout pond, Laundry. Store w/snacks & small game items. WFS possible on organic farm. Mail (guests/free, non-g.est/$15): 1000 Hwy 180 Hiawassee, GA 30546.

⚠️

Water Sources

Be aware of trail conditions before heading out, and tune in to advice from outfitters and other hikers. The trail gets rerouted, springs dry up, streams alter their course. Be prepared to deal with changes, particularly late in the season. Never carry just enough water to reach the next spring.

| 2150.9 | 40.0 | Poor Mountain . . . . | 3620 |

> ⚠ Get the most out of your guidebook: pay attention to lines that end with a page number. The page that is referenced will list the services avail at or near the trailhead.

2149.2	41.7	Sheep Rock Top	3558
2148.3	42.6	**Low Gap Shelter** 15◄13.9◄4.8◄►7.3►15.4►22.8 . . . . ☽ ♦ 🌢 (4)⌐ (7)	3024
		Water 30 yards in front of shelter. Cables. Privy on steep hill beyond shelter.	
2147.9	43.0	Stream. . . . . ♦	3183
2146.9	44.0	Poplar Stamp Gap, spring 0.1E, gap and side trail unmarked. . . . . ♦ 🌢	3345
2146.2	44.7	Spring to west . . . . ♦	3550
2144.9	46.0	Stream with cascade, several streams in area . . . . ♦	3464
2144.4	46.5	Cold Springs Gap	3495
2143.3	47.6	Chattahoochee Gap, Jacks Gap Trail to west, spring 0.5E . . . . ♦	3584
2142.6	48.3	Red Clay Gap . . . . (pg. 11)	3485
2142.0	48.9	Site of former Rocky Knob Shelter . . . . ♦	3630
2141.7	49.2	Spring west of trail down slope . . . . ♦	3606
2141.0	49.9	**Blue Mountain Shelter** 21.2◄12.1◄7.3◄►8.1►15.5►23.6 . . . . ☽ ♦ 🌢 (4)⌐ (7)	3880
		Bear cables. Spring on AT (0.1S), camping west of AT, south of shelter.	
2140.1	50.8	Blue Mountain	4025
2138.6	52.3	Unicoi Gap, GA 75, **Helen, GA** (9.0E) . . . . 34.8017,-83.7428 🅿 (pg. 14)	2949
		Hiawassee, GA (12.0W)	
2137.9	53.0	Stream. . . . . ♦	3502
2137.7	53.2	Rocky Mountain Trail to west . . . . ♦	3715
2137.2	53.7	Rocky Mountain, views from AT 0.1 north of summit . . . . 📷 🌢	4017
2135.9	55.0	Indian Grave Gap, USFS 283 . . . . 34.7927,-83.7143 🅿	3113
		Andrews Cove Trail to east.	
2135.2	55.7	Tray Mountain Rd (gravel), USFS 79, piped stream east on road. . . . . ♦	3480
2134.9	56.0	Cheese factory site, water (0.1W) on blue-blazed trail . . . . ♦ 🌢	3579
2134.2	56.7	Tray Gap, Tray Mountain Rd, USFS 79 . . . . 34.7993,-83.691 🅿	3847
2133.4	57.5	Tray Mountain. . . . . 📷	4430
2132.9	58.0	**Tray Mountain Shelter** (0.2W) . . . . ☽ ♦ 🌢 (3)⌐ (7)	4193
		20.2◄15.4◄8.1◄►7.4►15.5►22.8 Spring 0.1 mile behind shelter. Cables.	
2131.7	59.2	Wolfpen Gap	3550
2131.2	59.7	Steeltrap Gap, water 0.5E . . . . ♦	3448

| 2130.6 | **60.3** | Young Lick Knob . . . . | | 3748 |

2130.6	60.3	Young Lick Knob	3748
2129.3	61.6	Swag of the Blue Ridge.	3451
2128.2	62.7	Sassafras Gap, water 0.2E on steep blue-blazed trail ♦⌂	3500
2127.3	63.6	Addis Gap,. . . . . ♦⌂	3304
		Campsite 0.5E down old fire road, stream to right of campsite.	
2126.3	64.6	Kelly Knob, trail skirts summit	4126
2125.5	65.4	**Deep Gap Shelter** (0.3E) 22.8◄15.5◄7.4◄►8.1►15.4►20.3. . . ☽♦⌂(4)⌐(12)	3554
		Water 0.1 before shelter.	
2124.4	66.5	"Vista" blue-blaze leads 0.1E to campsite. . . . . ⌂	3886
2124.1	66.8	Powell Mountain	3850

.ıll No phone signal at Dicks Creek Gap. If you need ride, call from Shelter or Powell Mtn.

2122.9	68.0	Moreland Gap, water to east. . . . . ♦	3015
2121.9	69.0	Dicks Creek Gap, US 76 . . . . 34.9121,-83.6188 ⛺🅿 ◊ (pg. 14)	2675
		Water, picnic tables at the gap, **Hiawassee, GA** (11.0W)	
2120.9	70.0	Campsite, 200 yards to water . . . . ♦⌂	3177
2120.1	70.8	Cowart Gap . . . . ♦	2900
2118.7	72.2	Buzzard Knob	3679
2118.6	72.3	Bull Gap	3541
2117.9	73.0	Spring . . . . ♦	3317
2117.4	73.5	**Plumorchard Gap Shelter** (0.2E) Privy 0.2 mi down steep trail . ☽♦⌂(6)⌐(14)	3144
		23.6◄15.5◄8.1◄►7.3►12.2►19.8 Creek on trail to shelter & spring (0.1W) of AT.	
2116.7	74.2	As Knob	3460
2116.2	74.7	Blue Ridge Gap, dirt road (no longer passable by car).	3090
2115.2	75.7	Spring to west, campsite. . . . . ♦⌂	3403
2114.5	76.4	Rich Cove Gap.	3532
2114.3	76.6	Rocky Knob	3574
2113.0	77.9	**GA-NC** border	3821
2112.9	78.0	Bly Gap, signed spring 30 ft east of A.T. located between . . . . . . ♦⌂	3840
		GA-NC border & Bly Gap. Old and twisted tree often photographed. Signed	
		camping area on blue blazed trail 100yds north of Bly Gap.	
2111.6	79.3	Courthouse Bald, summit 0.1W	4708

52.3   UNICOI GAP, GA 75

🏕️ **Enota Mountain Retreat** (4.8W) (see info above)

» **Helen, GA 30545** (9E), ☎706.878.2422, M-F 9-12:30 & 1:30-4, Sa 9-12, tax 15%. Tourist town with many hotels, restaurants, gift shops, river rafting & tubing rentals. Visitor Center on Bruckenstrasse (near the PO) has info about places to stay & a free phone for making reservations.

🛏️ **Helendorf River Inn** (9.3E) 800.445.2271 visitus@helendorf.com Prices 1 or 2 persons Su-Th; Nov-May $44, Apr-May $54, Jun-Aug $84, +tax, +$10EAP. Wkend rates higher. Incl c. b'fast. Pets $20. Visa/MC/Disc ok.

🛏️ **Riverbend Motel and Cabins** (9.3E) 706.878.2155 Downtown Helen convenient to amenities, pet friendly - $20 pet fee.

🛏️ **Surestay Motel** (9.4E) 706.878.291 Ask for hiker room $55+tax for 1 or 2 persons, no pets. Ask about shuttles.

🛏️ **Baymont Inn & Suites** (9.6E) 706.878.2111 Q beds $65 + tax, 1 K bed $75+tax any day, full b'fast buffet. Occasional shuttle svc avail.⟨wyndhamhotels.com⟩

🛏️ **Country Inn & Suites** (9.6E) 706.878.9000 Call for rates, hiker discount (seasonal), incl full hot b'fast, indoor pool & hot tub.

🛏️ **Econo Lodge** (10.4E) 706.878.8000 Wkdays $60, wkends higher, incl c. b'fast. Pets under 20 lbs w/$20 fee.

🏪 **Betty's Country Store** (12E)(see Dicks Creek Gap)

69.0   DICKS CREEK GAP, US 76

» *Hiawassee, GA 30545* (12E)(see Dicks Creek Gap)

🚕 **Affordable Taxi** 706.970.0794 Based in Hiawassee w/service to/from Dicks Creek Gap & Unicoi Gap; longer shuttles can be arranged.

🛒 **Top of Georgia Hiking Center** (0.7W) 706.982.3252 Open yr-round 7-7. Street sign w/arrow marks easy half mile downhill rd walk to TOG (trail west from gap). Full svc discount outfitter specializes in thru-hiker gear. Full resupply. Bunk & shower $30 & pvt 2 bed cabins $70. Both incl free c. b'fast & use of full hostel kitchen w/stay. Advance reservations avail but not req'd. Free yr-round daily shuttles for overnight guests to Hiawassee, Dicks Creek Gap & Unicoi Gap. Shuttles as far south as Atlanta Marta, North Spgs Station, & N to Fontana for fee. Long term parking-fee. Pizza & snacks avail. Laundry $5/load (we do it for you) w/ free hospital scrubs provided. Computer, free Wi-Fi. Print your Smoky Mtn Permits here. Fun morning seminar, "10 Keys for a Successful Thru-Hike" Pet friendly. Separate suite for hikers w/pets. No alcohol/drugs. Mail ($2 fee) held for 21 days. ID req'd to p/u packages: 7675 US Hwy 76 E, Hiawassee GA 30546. ⟨topofgeorgiahikingcenter.org⟩

🛏️ **Henson Cove Place B&B w/Cabins** (5.8W) 706.896.6195 relax@henson-cove-place.com Cabin for 1-6 persons, full kitchen, 3BR, 1.5BA. $100 for 3, $135 for 4-5, $150 for 6. B'fast $8PP. Standard B&B rooms $100D, b'fast incl. All stays w/free ride to/from AT from Dick's Creek Gap or Unicoi Gap, or into town for provisions. Free laundry & internet. Slackpacking, CC & well behaved pets ok. Shuttles, parking for section hikers. Mail: 1137 Car Miles Rd, Hiawassee, GA 30546.

» *Hiawassee, GA 30546* (10.6W) **Hiker Fool Bash** *Mar 30-Apr 1, info at Budget Inn. Food, fun & games* ⟨hikerfoolbash.com⟩

🛏️ **Budget Inn** (10.1W) 706.896.4121 $39.99S, $5EAP, pets $10, coin laundry. Free ride for guests to/from Dick's Creek Gap or Unicoi Gap (9 & 11a) Mar-Apr. Non-guest shuttles for a fee. ♿**Mountain Crossings Outfitter Satellite** on-site. Visa/MC ok. Complimentary guest maildrop transfer to Baltimore Jack Place Hostel in Franklin. Mail: 193 South Main St, Hiawassee, GA 30546.

🛏️ **Mull's Inn** (10.7W) 706.896.4195 $55/Up, no pets, shuttles by arrangement. Guest Mail: 213 N Main St, Hiawassee, GA 30546.

🛏️ **Holiday Inn Express** (10.9W) 706.896.8884 $79/ Up, CC ok. Full b'fast incl. Laundry, indoor pool, hot tub. No pets. Mail: 300 Big Sky Dr, Hiawassee, GA 30546.

🍴 **Lake Chatuge Lodge** (11.9W) 706.896.5253 reservations@lakechatugelodge.com $89/up incl c. b'fast. **Hawg Wild BBQ & Catfish House** on site.

🛒 **Mountain Roots Outfitters** (10W) 706.896.1873 M-Sa 11-5. Canister fuel, freeze-dried meals, small gear items.

🛒 **Ingles** (10.6W) 706.896.8312 7 Days 7-10. Pharmacy M-F 9-9, Sa Su 9-6. **Starbucks**, deli, bakery, salad bar.

📮 **Goin' Postal** (10.3W) 706.896.1844 Authorized FedEx, UPS, DHL & USPS shipping Center 9-6 M-F & 10-2 on Sa.⟨goinpostalhiawassee.com⟩

84.8 DEEP GAP, USFS 71
105.5 ★ ROCK GAP

Standing Indian Campground (1.5W) 828.369.0442, 828.524.6441 Campsites $16, open Apr 1 - Nov 30. Camp store (closes Oct 31) has small selection of foods.
Macon County Transit (See entry pg. 18)

109.2 WINDING STAIR GAP, US 64

Beverly Carini 850.572.7352 Amicalola - Davenport Gap. Not avail Su 9-12.
Chuck Allen 828.371.6460 hometownshuttle@gmail.com Springer Mountain to Fontana, call or text.
City Taxi 828.369.5042 Rides up to 6p, later by appt.
Jim Granato 828.342.1573 Range: ATL - Davenport Gap. Speaks Italian/German/Spanish.
Larry's Taxi Service 828.421.4987 Shuttles anywhere.
Mike Newton 828.371.8275 Amicalola Falls & Springer Mtn, to Big Creek & Standing Bear, & all points along the Southern A.T.
Roadrunner Driving Services 706.201.7719 where2@mac.com Long distance shuttles covering Atlanta to Damascus-plus!
Zen Shuttles 828.332.0228 Range: ATL - GA/NC/TN/VA

» ***Franklin, NC 28734*** *(11.4E), (Services cont'd on pg. 18...)*

$ Prices are subject to change, particularly at hotels. Prices published in this guidebook were given in fall of 2017 & often represent a significant discount for hikers. Businesses intend to keep these prices throughout 2018, but they are not obliged to do so.

Postal workers are present before & after the window closes at most post offices, and may retrieve a package for you. Doing so is a courtesy not an obligation. Do not impose on them unnecessarily.

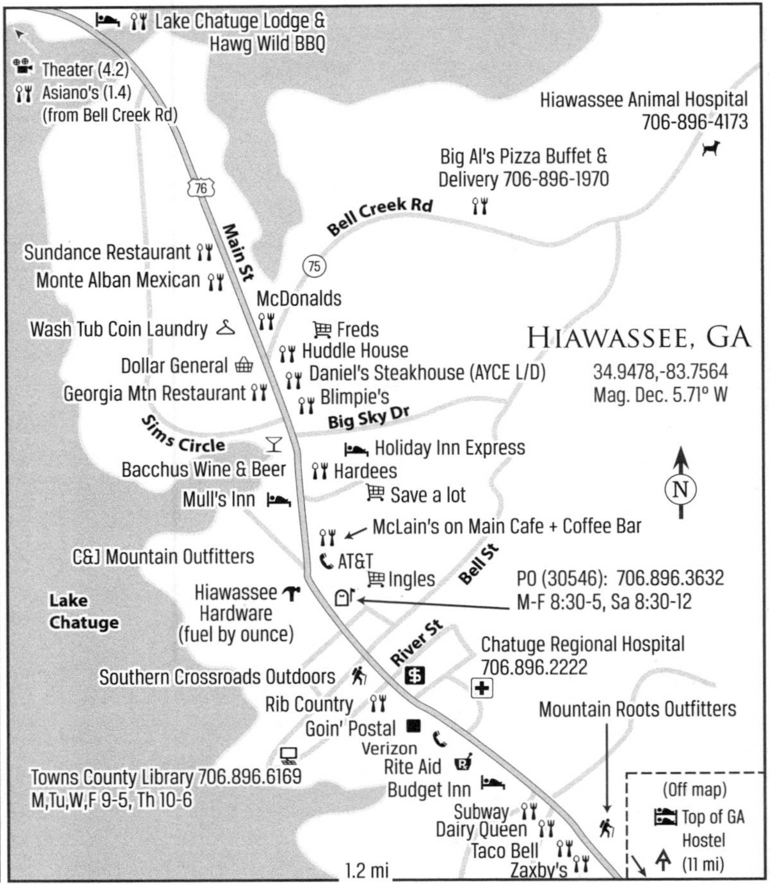
Lake Chatuge Lodge &
Hawg Wild BBQ
Theater (4.2)
Asiano's (1.4)
(from Bell Creek Rd)
Hiawassee Animal Hospital
706-896-4173
Big Al's Pizza Buffet &
Delivery 706-896-1970
Bell Creek Rd
76
75
Main St
Sundance Restaurant
Monte Alban Mexican
McDonalds
Wash Tub Coin Laundry
Freds
Huddle House
HIAWASSEE, GA
Dollar General
Daniel's Steakhouse (AYCE L/D)
34.9478,-83.7564
Mag. Dec. 5.71° W
Georgia Mtn Restaurant
Blimpie's
Big Sky Dr
Sims Circle
Holiday Inn Express
Bacchus Wine & Beer
Hardees
N
Save a lot
Mull's Inn
McLain's on Main Cafe + Coffee Bar
C&J Mountain Outfitters
AT&T
Ingles
Bell St
PO (30546): 706.896.3632
M-F 8:30-5, Sa 8:30-12
Lake
Chatuge
Hiawassee
Hardware
(fuel by ounce)
River St
Chatuge Regional Hospital
706.896.2222
Southern Crossroads Outdoors
Rib Country
Mountain Roots Outfitters
Goin' Postal
Verizon
Rite Aid
Towns County Library 706.896.6169
M,Tu,W,F 9-5, Th 10-6
Budget Inn
(Off map)
Top of GA
Hostel
(11 mi)
Subway
Dairy Queen
Taco Bell
Zaxby's
1.2 mi

2111.0	79.9	Sassafras Gap		4300
2110.7	80.2	Piped Spring . . . . ◑		4513
2110.1	**80.8**	**Muskrat Creek Shelter**. . . . . ☽◑☁⊏(6)		4562
		22.8◀15.4◀7.3◀▶4.9▶12.5▶21.2		
2109.3	81.6	Whiteoak Stamp, old roadbed, Chunky Gal Trail to west, blue blazed. . . . . . ◑☁		4620
		water trail A.T. east, blue blazed camp trail A.T. west signed with register box.		
2108.2	82.7	Wateroak Gap		4490
2107.9	83.0	Spring . . . . ◑		4568
2106.7	84.2	Spring . . . . ◑		4548
2106.1	84.8	Deep Gap, USFS 71, Kimsey Creek Trail. . . . . 35.0396,-83.5525 🅿 ◑ ☁ (pg. 15)		4341
		Signed campsite with register box on KC Trail & blue blazed water trail		
2105.7	85.2	Spring to west . . . . ◑		4516
2105.2	**85.7**	**Standing Indian Shelter**, creek 70 yards downhill . . . . ☽◑☁⊏(8)		4742
		20.3◀12.2◀4.9◀▶7.6▶16.3▶19.7		
2104.9	86.0	Spring . . . . ◑		4815
2103.7	87.2	Standing Indian Mountain, summit (0.1E). . . . . 📷		5435
		Campsites on side trail to summit. Lower Ridge Trail to west.		
2101.8	89.1	Spring. . . . . ◑		4944
2100.8	90.1	Beech Gap Tenting area with water. . . . . ◑☁		4460
2099.7	91.2	Stream. . . . . ◑		4404
2099.1	91.8	Coleman Gap		4221
2098.1	92.8	Timber Ridge Trail to west		4639
2097.6	**93.3**	**Carter Gap Shelter** . . . . ☽◑☁⊏		4528
		19.8◀12.5◀7.6◀▶8.7▶12.1▶20.1 Spring south of shelter, 100 yards downhill.		
2097.0	93.9	Stream. . . . . ◌		4738
2096.5	94.4	Spring . . . . ◑		4921

⚠ **PATH (Protecting the Appalachian Trail Hiking Experience):**
The NHC is working to increase camping capacity at shelters & established campsites between Bly Gap & Wesser, NC in order to decrease the number of single tent sites located within sight of the trail. There are signed locations (No Camping/Revegetation Area) with recommended alternative camping locations. Please use the register boxes at campsites to help gather visitor use info.

2093.9	97.0	Betty Creek Gap, Several tent sites west on blue blazed Betty Creek Trail.		4300
		◑☁ Campsite with register box		
2093.1	97.8	Mooney Gap, USFS 83, Ball Creek Rd, stream 0.1 north.		4498
2091.7	99.2	USFS 67, To bypass Albert Mt, take road 0.2W to parking area, ...		4843
		then take side trail 0.2 from parking area back to AT north of summit		
2091.4	99.5	Albert Mountain, fire tower. . . . . 📷 ♨		5250

| 2091.2 | 99.7 | Albert Mountain bypass, west 0.2 to parking on USFS 67 . . . . 🅿 | 5052 |
| 2090.8 | 100.1 | Site of former Big Spring Shelter. Land reclamation underway, no camping . . . . | 4978 |

> ⚠ White blazes on the north side of trees are identical to the blazes on the south side. Make sure you are headed in the right direction, especially when sleepily leaving shelters in the morning.

2088.9	102.0	**Long Branch Shelter** (0.1W)(2012) seven tent pads . . . . ♦ ☽ 🝆 ⊏ (16)	4479
		21.2◄16.3◄8.7◄►3.4►11.4►18.2	
2088.1	102.8	Glassmine Gap, Long Branch Trail 2.0W to USFS 67	4185

> A "kick-over" double blaze indicates that you should watch for a turn in the direction of the upper blaze (a right turn in this image).

2085.5	105.4	**Rock Gap Shelter** (1965), four tent pads. . . . . ☽ ♦ 🝆 ⊏ (8)	3772
		19.7◄12.1◄3.4◄►8.0►14.8►19.6	
2085.4	105.5	Rock Gap, 0.7E to Wasalik Poplar and water. . . . . 35.094,-83.5226 🅿 (pg. 15)	3732
2084.8	106.1	Wallace Gap, W. Old Murphy Rd, stream to north . . . . ♦	3738

2081.7	109.2	Winding Stair Gap, US 64. . . . . 35.1196,-83.548 🅿 ♦ (pg. 15)	3690
		piped spring east of steps, **Franklin, NC** (10.0E)	
2081.5	109.4	Forest Service road, waterfall . . . . ♦	3727
2081.4	109.5	Stream, No camping here, camp at Moore Creek campsite . . . . ♦	3812
2081.1	109.8	Logging road	4026
2080.9	110.0	Moore Creek Campsite to west, signed & blazed . . . . 🝆 ♦	4011
		Water & level area for 8 tents with register box.	
2080.6	110.3	Swinging Lick Gap	4100
2079.7	111.2	Panther Gap.	4480

2077.5	113.4	**Siler Bald Shelter** (0.5E steep), south end of shelter loop trail . . . ☽ ♦ 🝆 ⊏ (8)	4769
		20.1◄11.4◄8.0◄►6.8►11.6►17.4	
2077.1	113.8	Siler Bald, summit (0.2W), shelter (0.3E), north end of shelter loop trail . . . . 📷	5001
2076.3	114.6	Piped spring . . . . ♦	4481
2076.0	114.9	Footbridge, stream . . . . ♦	4374
2075.9	115.0	Wayah Crest Picnic Area (0.1W) . . . . 35.154,-83.5807 🅿	4258
2075.8	115.1	Wayah Gap, Wayah Rd . . . . (pg. 18)	4180
2075.4	115.5	AT skirts USFS 69	4352
2075.0	115.9	USFS 69, meadow	4480
2074.6	116.3	Wilson Lick Trail, 0.2W to historic site	4630
2074.1	116.8	USFS 69, piped spring to east . . . . ♦	4993
2073.7	117.2	Bartram Trail to west	5236
2073.5	117.4	0.1E to Wine Spring Rd, meadow, campsites 0.1E, water on west side of AT . ♦ 🝆	5290

| 2072.0 | 118.9 | USFS 69 . . . . | 5188 |
| 2071.8 | 119.1 | Paved footpath to latrines and parking . . . . .35.179,-83.5622 🅿 🚻 ♿ | 5298 |

» *Franklin, NC 28734* (11.4E), (...services cont'd from pg. 15)

Visitor Center (Chamber of Commerce) (13.1E) 828.524.3161 cindy@franklin-chamber.com 98 Hyatt Rd. M-F 9a-5p-year-round, Sa 9a-5p (May-Oct). List of hiker svcs & shuttles.(visitfranklinnc.com)

Microtel Inn & Suites (10.8E) 828.349.9000 Prices vary, c. b'fast, $25/pet. Mail: 81 Allman Dr, Franklin, NC 28734.

Baltimore Jack's Place Hostel (11.5E) 828.524.2064 Bunks $20 1st night/$15 after. Pvt rooms $55EAP. Owner Ron Haven shuttles Mar-Apr at 9a & 11a to Rock/Wallace/Winding Stair Gaps. Guests free ret to trail. WiFi, shower w/o stay $5. Coin laundry. Print Smokies permit for free. **Three Eagles Outfitter** on site. Mail: #7 Derby St, Franklin, NC 28734.

Budget Inn (11.5E) 828.524.4403 Hiker rate: $40S, $50D + tax, pet friendly, coin laundry, WiFi, Mail: 433 E Palmer St, Franklin, NC 28734.

Gooder Grove AT Hostel (11.9E) 828.332.0228 One block from Main St. amenities. Bunks $21, pvt room $43, $5 EAP, tent/hammock $13PP. Free thru shuttle from Rock Gap/Winding Stair Gap. Shuttling, section hike parking. Laundry-$6, shower w/out stay-$5. Local guide. Pet friendly. Boarding. Mail: 130 Hayes Circle, Franklin, NC 28734.(goodergrove.com)

Sapphire Inn (13E) 828.524.4406 $49.95 S/D/K, $59.95 2Q (up to 4PP). Pet fee $15. Mail: 761 East Main St, Bus 441, Franklin, NC 28734.<sapphireinnfranklin.com>

Comfort Inn (13.1E) 828.369.9200 10% Thru-hiker disc, b'fast, laundry. Call in adv for pet-friendly room. Mail: 313 Cunningham Rd, Franklin, NC 28734.

Outdoor 76 (10E) 828.349.7676 Open M-Sa 10-7. Specialty, lightweight, AT gear, clothing & comprehensive footwear. PEDORTHIC trained footwear experts, specializing in foot problems. Free summit bandana & 10% off for thru-hikers. Shipping svcs, fuel/oz, shakedowns, WIFI, & free hugs. Sign AT banner. Mail: 35 E Main St, Franklin, NC 28734.(outdoor76.com)

Three Eagles Outfitters (10.6E) 828.524.9061 (Main store) Two locations in Franklin: Main store: 78 Siler Rd & Downtown: 7 Derby St. Call # for both locations. Full-svc outfitter, 24 Yrs experience on the AT. On site staff footwear specialists. Full-svc outfitter, canister & fuel/oz, UL gear, rainwear, clothing & footwear. 10% A.T. thru-hiker discount. FREE Class of 2018 AT tee & free beer w/qualifying purchase. Shuttle list avail. Will hold/ship pkgs. Free WiFi. Will shuttle to main store w/notice from town locations. Siler Rd has coffee & espresso bar.

Rock House Lodge (10E) 828.349.7676 Taproom/restaurant inside Outdoor 76, M-Sa 10-9. 18 Craft beers on draft, wine, food, darts, indoor shuffleboard, community instruments, big screen TV. Live music. Weekly food specials.

Lazy Hiker Brewing Co. (11.2E) 828.349.2337 Food truck, pet-friendly patio, live music F-Sa. Free WiFi. At hiker banner. M-Th 12-9p; Fr-Sa12-11p; Sun 12-8p.

1st Baptist Church (11.4E) 828.369.9559 Free b'fast daily Mar 14-Apr 14

The Rathskeller Coffee Haus & Pub (11.4E) 828.369.6799 Beer, wine & coffee shop. Baked goods & sandwiches. Tu-Th 8a-7p, Fr-Sa 8a-11p. Live music on wkends.

Currahee Brewing (13.9E) 828.634.0078 Free access to WiFi, books, printers & charging outlets. Food Truck on site. Maildrop avail. Pet & family friendly. M-Th: 12-9, F-Sa: 12-10p, Su: 2-8p.

Lenzo Animal Hospital (11.6E) 828.369.2635 M-F 8:30-5, Sa 8:30-12. Emergency clinic 828.452.1478.

Franklin Health & Fitness (14.1E) 828.369.5608 50% Off hiker disc for guest pass & 10% off massage. Guest pass hikers have full access to wellness facility incl indoor heated saltwater swimming pool, whirlpool, locker rooms + all classes (incl Yoga).

Macon County Transit (15.1E) 828.349.2222 Scheduled shuttles M-F from Feb 26-May 25, (other dates call). Stops: Winding Stair Gap 9:30, 12:30, & 3:30; Rock Gap 9:45, 12:45, & 3:45. $3PP/ride. Multiple p/u locations in town at 9, 12 & 3.

115.1		WAYAH GAP, WAYAH RD
123.8	★	BURNINGTOWN GAP, WAYAH RD
128.6		TELLICO GAP NC 1365, OTTER CREEK RD

Nantahala Mtn Lodge (4.3W) 828.321.2340 (after 7p 828.321.9949) aquone.cabins@gmail.com. Run by 2010 thru-hiker, "Wiggy". Prices incl b'fast. Bunks (w/bedding) $35PP. Pvt room-2 twin beds $75. Pvt room & BR w/king bed $85. Shuttle to/from Wayah Gap, Tellico Gap, & Burningtown Gap $5PP ea way. 3-Course evening meal avail $12.50. Laundry $5PP. Cash only under $50. Slackpacking options Rock Gap to Fontana w/reservations. Parking for section hikers $4/day. No pets. Guest mail: 63 Britannia Dr, Aquone, NC 28781.(northcarolinalogcabin.rentals/at.html)

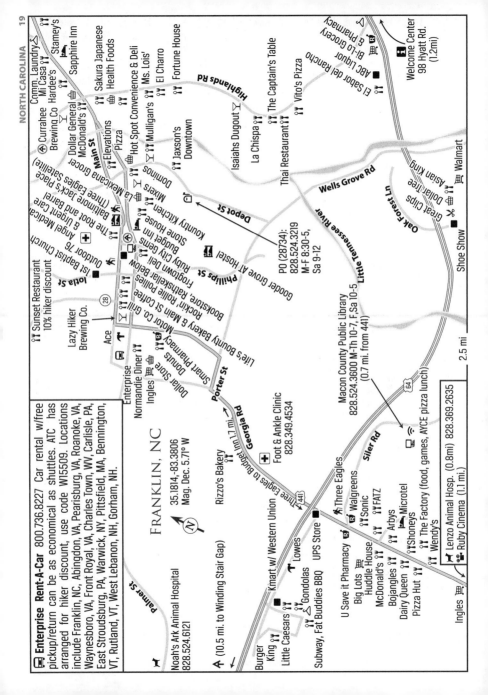

FRANKLIN, NC

35.1814, -83.3806
Mag. Dec. 5.71° W

Enterprise Rent-A-Car 800.736.8227 Car rental w/free pickup/return can be as economical as shuttles. ATC has arranged for hiker discount, use code W15509. Locations include Franklin, NC, Abingdon, VA, Pearisburg, VA, Roanoke, VA, Waynesboro, VA, Front Royal, VA, Charles Town, WV, Carlisle, PA, East Stroudsburg, PA, Warwick, NY, Pittsfield, MA, Bennington, VT, Rutland, VT, West Lebanon, NH, Gorham, NH.

Noah's Ark Animal Hospital
828.524.6121

↑ (10.5 mi. to Winding Stair Gap)

Palmer St.

Welcome Center
98 Hyatt Rd.
(1.2mi)

Comm. Laundry
Mi Casa
Stamey's
Hardee's
Sapphire Inn

Currahee
Brewing Co
Dollar General
McDonald's
Elevations Pizza

Sakura Japanese
Health Foods
Ms. Lois'
El Charro
Fortune House

Hot Spot Convenience & Deli
Mulligan's
Jaxson's
Downtown

Highlands Rd

El Sabor del Rancho
ABC Liquor
Bi-Lo grocery
B Pharmacy

Vito's Pizza
The Captain's Table
Isaiahs Dugout
La Chispa
Thai Restaurant

Main St
Mixers
Dominos
La Mexicana Grocer

The Root and Barrel
Baltimore Jack's place
(Three Eagles Satellite)

Angel Medical
& Urgent care

Outdoor 76
1st Baptist Church

Iotla St.

Depot St

Wells Grove Rd

Oak Forest Ln
Little Tennessee River

Great Clips
Dollar Tree
Asian King
Walmart

Shoe Show

2.5 mi

Sunset Restaurant
10% hiker discount

Lazy Hiker
Brewing Co.

Ace

(28)

Budget Inn
Stone House
Kountry Kitchen

Motor Co. Grill
Rockin' Rollie Pollies
Bookstore, Rathskeller, below
Frogtown Deli
Ruby Gems
City Gems

Phillips St

PO (28734):
828.524.3219
M-F 8:30-5,
Sa 9-12

Gooder Grove AT Hostel

Life's Bounty Bakery & Main St Coffee

Enterprise
Normandie Diner
Ingles

Dollar Store
Donuts
Smart Pharmacy

Porter St

Three Eagles to Budget Inn 1.7 mi

Georgia Rd

Rizzo's Bakery

Foot & Ankle Clinic
828.349.4534

Macon County Public Library
828.524.3600 M-Th 10-7, F,Sa 10-5
(0.7 mi. from 441)

Siler Rd

The Factory (food, games, AYCE pizza lunch)

64

441

Kmart w/ Western Union
Lowes
Gondolas
UPS Store

Burger
King
Little Caesars
Subway, Fat Buddies BBQ

U Save it Pharmacy
Big Lots
Huddle House
McDonald's
Bojangles
Dairy Queen
Pizza Hut

Three Eagles
Walgreens
Sonic
FATZ
Arbys
Microtel
Shoneys
Wendy's

Lenzo Animal Hosp. (0.8mi) 828.369.2635
Ruby Cinema (1.1 mi.)

Ingles

2071.6	119.3	Wayah Bald, stone tower and paved footpath . . . . 📷 🏛	5342
2071.0	119.9	⚠ NoBos: AT to left, Bartram Trail to east, campsite, spring to west of trail . 💧 ⛺	4887
2070.7	120.2	**Wayah Bald Shelter**, east to shelter, west 0.2 to water . . . . 🌙 💧 ⛺ ⊏ (8)	4712
		18.2◄14.8◄6.8◄►4.8►10.6►15.5 10 tent sites.	
2069.4	121.5	Licklog Gap, signed tent sites with register box along . . . . ⛺ 💧 (0.5W)	4440
		blue blaze water trail just out of site of the A.T.	
2068.0	122.9	Intersection with old roadbed and side trails, AT turns to east	4515
2067.4	123.5	Stream. . . . . 💧	4323
2067.1	123.8	Burningtown Gap, NC 1397 . . . . 35.2223,-83.5622 🅿 (pg. 18)	4236
2066.7	124.2	Spring . . . . 💧	4511
2065.9	125.0	**Cold Spring Shelter** (Built by CCC in 1930's) . . . . 🌙 💧 ⛺ ⊏ (6)	4926
		19.6◄11.6◄4.8◄►5.8►10.7►18.6 Trail to 10 tentsites on ridge 100 yds N on AT.	
2065.2	125.7	Copper Ridge Bald, views . . . . 📷	5080
2064.0	126.9	Side trail 0.1E to Rocky Bald, views . . . . 📷	5030
2063.8	127.1	Big Branch Campsite, signed . . . . 💧 ⛺	4978
		four tent sites with register box, spring	
2062.3	128.6	Tellico Gap, NC 1365, Otter Creek Rd . . . . 35.268,-83.5726 🅿 (pg. 18)	3850
2060.9	130.0	Wesser Bald, east 40 yards to observation tower, panoramic views . . . . . 📷 🏛	4627
2060.2	130.7	Spring-fed stone cistern on blue-blazed trail (0.1E) . . . . 💧	4208
2060.1	130.8	**Wesser Bald Shelter** (0.1W) . . . . 🌙 ⛺ ⊏ (8)	4092
		17.4◄10.6◄5.8◄►4.9►12.8►21.9 Spring 0.1S on AT (at switchback).	
		Cables. Just north of shelter trail, Wesser Creek Trail to east.	
2058.3	132.6	The Jumpoff, views . . . . 📷	3940
2056.7	134.2	Weak spring. . . . . 💧	3008
2055.2	135.7	**A. Rufus Morgan Shelter** . . . . 🌙 💧 ⛺ ⊏ (6)	2184
		15.5◄10.7◄4.9◄►7.9►17►23.1 Shelter in view to east, stream west of AT.	
2054.7	136.2	Multiple streams and footbridges . . . . 💧	1997
2054.2	136.7	US 19 & 74, **Nantahala Outdoor Center** . . . . 35.3312,-83.5922 🅿 (pg. 24)	1732
2054.1	136.8	Side trail to bunkhouse.	1771
2052.6	138.3	Wright Gap, dirt road	2403
2051.7	139.2	Grassy Gap, Grassy Gap Trail to west . . . . 💧	2979

| 2051.4 | **139.5** | Wade Sutton Memorial . . . . | ♦ | 3012 |

| 2050.1 | **140.8** | Spring . . . . | ♦ | 3575 |
| 2049.5 | **141.4** | The Jump-up, views to Nantahala Gorge . . . . | 📷 | 3814 |

| 2048.2 | **142.7** | Swim Bald . . . . | | 4710 |

2047.3 **143.6 Sassafras Gap Shelter** (0.1W) (2002) . . . . ☽ ♦ ◖ ⊏ (14) 4391
18.6◄12.8◄7.9◄►9.1►15.2►21.9 Reliable spring front-right of shelter.

| 2046.1 | **144.8** | Cheoah Bald . . . . | 📷 | 5062 |
| 2045.9 | **145.0** | Bartram Trail to west . . . . | | 4911 |

> Rocks that glitter are embedded with mica. North
> Carolina leads the nation in production of the mineral.

| 2043.6 | **147.3** | Locust Cove Gap, water to west . . . . | ♦ ◖ | 3642 |

| 2042.5 | **148.4** | Simp Gap . . . . | | 3558 |

2040.6 **150.3** Stecoah Gap, NC 143, ... 35.3582,-83.7179 🅿 🛆 ♦ (pg. 24) 3165
Sweetwater Cr Rd (paved). Hostel, B&B. Blue-blaze west 200 ft on NC 143, then left
250 ft on abandoned road to water.
| 2039.6 | **151.3** | Sweetwater Gap, start of "Jacob's Ladder" . . . . | | 3270 |
| 2039.0 | **151.9** | Cliff, west 20 yards to view. . . . . | 📷 | 3868 |

2038.2 **152.7 Brown Fork Gap Shelter** . . . . ☽ ♦ ⊏ (6) 3813
21.9◄17◄9.1◄►6.1►12.8►24.6 Reliable spring to right of shelter.
| 2038.0 | **152.9** | Brown Fork Gap . . . . | ♦ | 3600 |
| 2037.5 | **153.4** | Brushnell Knob . . . . | | 3928 |

| 2036.1 | **154.8** | Hogback Gap . . . . | 🛆 | 3500 |

| 2035.3 | **155.6** | Cody Gap, water 0.2W . . . . | ♦ ◖ | 3620 |

| 2033.3 | **157.6** | Yellow Creek Gap, stream . . . . | ♦ | 3255 |
| 2032.9 | **158.0** | County Rd 1242, Yellow Creek Rd. . . . . 35.4105,-83.7657 🅿 (pg. 25) | | 2954 |

2032.1 **158.8 Cable Gap Shelter** . . . . ☽ ♦ ◖ ⊏ (6) 2878
23.1◄15.2◄6.1◄►6.7►18.5►21.6 Stream in front of shelter.

SoBo NoBo 1000 3000 5000

2030.7	**160.2**	Black Gum Gap		3403
2029.3	**161.6**	Walker Gap		3450
2029.0	**161.9**	Footbridge, stream	♦	3266
2027.3	**163.6**	Spring	♦	2287
2026.6	**164.3**	NC 28 (paved). . . . . .35.4414,-83.7968 **P** (pg. 25)		1756
		Fontana 28 AT Crossing, Fontana Dam, NC (2.0W)		
2025.4	**165.5**	**Fontana Dam Shelter** "Fontana Hilton" (0.1E) . . . . 🚻 🚽 🚿 ♦ ⌐ (20)		1853
		21.9◄12.8◄6.7◄▸11.8▸14.9▸17.8		
2025.0	**165.9**	**Fontana Dam Visitor Center**. . . . . 35.452,-83.8013 **P** **i** (pg. 28)		1700
2023.8	**167.1**	Great Smoky Mountains National Park southern boundary . . . . (pg. 28)		1862
		NoBo reenter woods, SoBo join road. Benton MacKaye Trail northbound		
		diverges from the AT and follows road to east. The BMT reconnects with		
		the AT at Davenport Gap in approximately 100 miles (BMT miles).		
2021.8	**169.1**	Boulder jumble, throne-shaped rock . . . . 📷		3314
2021.5	**169.4**	Stream. . . . . ◇		3487
2020.3	**170.6**	Shuckstack, fire tower 0.1E. . . . . 📷 🔭		3889
2019.9	**171.0**	Sassafras Gap		3667
2019.0	**171.9**	Birch Spring Gap . . . . ◇ ⛺		3736
		Campsite west 100 yards down slope, tent pads, cables, spring unreliable.		
2017.0	**173.9**	Side trail 3.1W to Gregory Bald		4443
2016.8	**174.1**	Doe Knob, NoBo follow NC/TN border; SoBo enter NC.		4520
2016.4	**174.5**	Mud Gap.		4327
2015.3	**175.6**	Ekaneetlee Gap . . . . ♦		3842
2013.6	**177.3**	**Mollies Ridge Shelter**, spring . . . . ◇ ⌐ (12)		4585
		24.6◄18.5◄11.8◄▸3.1▸6▸12.1		
2013.1	**177.8**	Devils Tater Patch.		4775
2012.0	**178.9**	Little Abrams Gap		4120
2011.6	**179.3**	Big Abrams Gap.		4115

2010.5   **180.4**   **Russell Field Shelter**, spring 0.1W . . . . ◊ ⊏ (14)   4347
                  21.6◄14.9◄3.1◄►2.9►9►14.7

2009.0   **181.9**   Stream. . . . . ♦   4749

┌───┐
✽   Sarvis Tree – Also called "serviceberry." Blooms with plentiful petite white-petaled flowers.
└───┘

2007.6   **183.3**   **Spence Field Shelter** (0.2E) on Eagle Creek Trail. . . . . ☽ ◊ ⊏ (12)   4914
                  17.8◄56◄2.9◄►6.1►11.8►13.5 100 yards north, Bote Mountain Trail to west.
2007.2   **183.7**   Jenkins Ridge trail to east   4948
2006.5   **184.4**   Rocky Top, views . . . . 📷   5440
2005.9   **185.0**   Thunderhead Mountain.   5527

2005.2   **185.7**   Water to west . . . . ♦   4965

2003.3   **187.6**   Starkey Gap   4552

2002.5   **188.4**   Sugar Tree Gap   4435

2001.5   **189.4**   **Derrick Knob Shelter**. . . . . ♦ ⊏ (12)   4884
                  12.1◄9◄6.1◄►5.7►7.4►13   Reliable spring near shelter. Cables.
2001.2   **189.7**   Sams Gap, water 100 yards west, on left side of Greenbrier Ridge Trail. . . . . ♦   4771

1999.2   **191.7**   Cold Spring Knob   5204
1999.0   **191.9**   Miry Ridge Trail to west.   4944
1998.8   **192.1**   Buckeye Gap   4817

1995.8   **195.1**   **Silers Bald Shelter**, spring 75 yds right of shelter . . . . ♦ ⊏ (12)   5452
                  14.7◄11.8◄5.7◄►1.7►7.3►15.3
1995.6   **195.3**   Silers Bald, survey mark on boulder, AT turns to east . . . . 📷   5607
1995.4   **195.5**   Welch Ridge Trail to east   5442

1994.1   **196.8**   **Double Spring Gap Shelter** 13.5◄7.4◄1.7◄►5.6►13.6►21 . . . . . ☽ ◊ ⊏ (12)   5509
                  Best water 15 yards from crest on NC side. Water is also 35 yards down TN side.
1993.5   **197.4**   Goshen Prong Trail to west.   5775

�"⊛🏕🛉⚑⊞♿🍴🅿🛏🚿△🛗📶🚲⊠ **Nantahala Outdoor Center** 888.905.7238 media@noc.com Complex w/ lodging, food, gear & whitewater rafting. Non-guest coinop showers Apr-Oct. In-season office hrs 8-5. Reservations recommended, even for hostel. Walk-ins w/out reservation, check-in at General Store or **River's End Restaurant.** CC ok. Campus wide WiFi. Events at NOC: **Southern Ruck** Jan 12-15,

🏕⊠**Base Camp Bunkhouse** $39.99/2, $79.99/4, $109.99/6, $139.99/8 incl shower, common area, & kitchen. Pets $10.

🍴⊠**River's End Restaurant** (B/L/D); **Big Wesser BBQ** opens mid-Apr.

⊠**Wesser General Store** Open Mar-Oct.(noc.com)

Outdoor Elements Festival Apr 13-14: Movie Night Friday, thruhiker dinner Sat live music, fun & giveaways. Gear reps for support & repairs. Extended restaurant & store hrs. Lodging avail onsite.

🚲🛒⊠△ **NOC Outfitters** Full line of gear, trail food, fuel/ oz. Gear shakedowns. Open daily, extended hrs in summer. Can print Smokies permits. Ask about shuttles. Thru-hikers 10% off 1 full price item. Mail dated & marked "Hold for AT Hiker": 13077 Hwy 19W, Bryson City, NC 28713.

🚐🏕🛒🛗⊠ **Jude Julius** 828.736.0086 Hiawassee, GA to Newfound Gap.

🏕🛒🍴🛗⇨⊠ **Nantahala General Store & Lodge** 828.488.4559 nantahalageneral@gmail.com Greystone House (Airbnb): $200/ night. Topton, NC. Shuttle avail, 4 BR, 4 BA, furnished, WiFi, DirecTV, washer/dryer, grill. Camping Cabins (up to 4) w/mini kitchen $69.95. Nov-May: $49.95, 3 BR cabins (up to 8) $129. Free p/u & ret for guests.

🛏🚐🛗⇨⊠ **Nantahala Cabins** (3E) 828.488.1622 rentals@ nantahalacabins.com 8 Cabins, 1-8 People. Call for thru hiker rate. Hot tubs, kitchen/bath, A/C, heat, linens provided, some w/laundry. Shuttles avail, prices vary.(nantahalacabins.com)

» **West of 19 & 74**

🏕🛗⊠ **Nantahala Log Cabin Lodge** (1.5W) 706.589.6438 cindyjanemax@gmail. com

150.3   STECOAH GAP, NC 143

🏕🛗⇨⊠ **Appalachian Inn** (1.1E) 828.735.1792 info@appalachianinn.com Luxurious log cabin, great view $135-150D. Incl p/u & ret from Stecoah Gap, full country b'fast. Add'l charge for L/D. Some rooms have jacuzzi tubs. Cash/check/ CC.(appalachianinn.com)

🏕🛉🍴△🛗⇨⊠ **Cabin in the Woods** (2.7E) Donna 828.735.1930 or Phil 828.735.3368 Hiker lodging $20PP incl ride to/from Stecoah Gap, shower, bathroom. Pvt cabins avail but are often booked (reserve early), $15 resupply trip to Robbinsville. For-fee shuttles ranging from Amicalola to Hot Springs or to Knoxville/ Asheville bus stations & airports. Family style b'fast $6, dinner $10, laundry $3/load. No CC. No Maildrops.(thecabininthewoods.com)

🏕🛉🍴△🛗⇨⊠**Stecoah Wolfcreek Hostel** (3.2E) 828.735.0768 lonnie479@gmail. com Open Jan-Dec. $25PP. Free p/u & ret to Stecoah Gap. Washer/dryer, full beds, TV, kitchen. Local diner nearby. Resupply shuttle after 5p wkdays.

» **Robbinsville, NC** (7.1W from Stecoah Gap)

🛏⇨⊠ **Microtel** (7.2W) 828.479.6772 Call for rates. Pet fee $50.

🛏⇨ **San Ran Motel** (7.2W) 828.479.3256 Call for rates. Fridge, coffee, m'wave. hiker friendly. No smoking/pets.

🛏△🛗⇨⊠ **Sweetgum Suites** (10.5W) 828.735.1300 2BR/IBA w/laundry, hot tub, full kitchen, living room, cable, & Wi-Fi

🛏△🛗⊠ **The Owl's Perch** (18.5W) 828.479.9791 Open Mar-Dec. Hiker rate $70S, $100D incl p/u & ret from Stecoah Gap w/quick stop at Ingles, simple b'fast. Seperate "bunkhouse" w/Queen bed, full bath, linens, kitchenette, grill & b'fast. Fee for dinner if requested. W/D avail. No pets. CC or cash ok.(grahamcountytravel.com/ the-owls-perch/)

🛏🍴△🛗⇨⊠ **Buffalo Creek B&B** (18.7W) 828.479.3892 robmason@rocketmail.com Hiker rate (no drive-ins) $65S, $55D, $45PP for 3. Incl brew. Open Apr-Oct, call for avail other months. Print Smokies permit here. Guest only mail: 4989 W Buffalo Rd, Robbinsville, NC 28771.(buffalocreekbedandbreakfast. com)

ROBBINSVILLE, NC

35.3241,-83.8025
Mag. Dec. 5.73° W

📶 Library 828.479.8796
Sun-M closed, Tue 11a-8p,
W, Th, F 9a-6p, Sa 9a-1p
Moose Branch Rd

Knight St

N Maine St

Ford St

0.7 mi

Wendy's

PO (2877):
828.479.3397
M-F 9-4:30

San Ran

El Pacifico

Family Dollar
Southern Gals
McDonalds

ACE

Subway

123

Sweetwater Rd

8 mi.

Dollar
General

Walgreens   Ingles 828.479.6748
7-10, 7 days

Microtel

Pop & Nana's, The Scoop

Wash Board

158.0   YELLOW CREEK RD

The Hike Inn (3.1E) hikeinn@graham.main.nc.us A hiker-only service run by Jeff & Nancy Hoch since 1993. By reservation only. All long distance hikers should call pre-hike so they can better accommodate you. Open yr-round for accommodations & transportation. Call, e-mail, or visit website for more info, reservations & directions.〈thehikeinn.com〉

» West of Yellow Creek Rd

Yellow Mtn Rental (1W) 828.735.1300 3BR/2BA mobile home for up to 5, $75/night. Laundry, hot tub, living room, satellite, & free WiFi

Creekside Paradise B&B (2.2W)
828.346.1076 postandwilson@gmail.com Cynthia/Jeff, Room: $60PP, $45PP if 2+per room. Camping $10. Stay incl p/u & ret from Yellow Creek Gap, laundry, hot tub, & free slackpack. B'fast & resupply trip to town incl w/room rental or $10 for campers. Dinner $15PP. P/U & ret from Stecoah Gap/Fontana $5, NOC $15. Pets welcome. Mail: 259 Upper Cove Rd, Robbinsville, NC, 2877l.

164.3   NC 28, FONTANA 28 AT CROSSING, 🚻 Bathrooms,
vending machines, GSMNP maps ($1), house phone to call for shuttle. Snacks & canned meats avail. from bait store on dock 0.1E.

Fontana Shuttle 828.498.2211 $3PP ea way between A.T. Crossing (Marina), Visitor Center at Fontana Dam, AT "Hilton" Shelter & Font. Village. 8:30-6 Daily, Mar 1- May 15. On call after May 15.

Steve Claxton 828.736.7501, 828.479.9608 steve@steveclaxton.com Licensed shuttle range Springer-Hot Springs & 3 area airports. Slackpacking. 2016 Thru hiker.

» Fontana Village, NC 28733 (2.2W from NC 28)For all facilities contact: 800.849.2258 or 828.498.2211
(services cont'd on pg. 28...)

Great Smoky Mountains NP 〈nps.gov/grsm〉
Backcountry Info: 865.436.1297
Reservations: 865.436.1231 **A permit is required & there is a backcountry fee**-$4PP/night up to $20PP for up to 7 nights/8 days. An on-line system allows you to pay & print a permit up to 30 days in advance. Hikers who meet the definition of an Appalachian Trail thru-hiker (those who begin & end their hike at least 50 miles outside the park and only travel on the A.T. in the park) are eligible for a $20 thru-hiker permit (valid for 38 days from the date issued for an up to 8 day hike through the Park) 〈smokiespermits.nps.gov〉

Shelters - The only near-trail campsite is Birch Spring, otherwise hikers must stay in shelters. Reservations req'd for section hikers. If shelter is full, thru-hikers must give up bunk space & tent in vicinity of shelter. Hikers must use bear cables to secure food food storage cables provided at all backcountry campsites. Occasionally shelters are closed when bear activity becomes problematic. Check website for closures.

Bear activity has been reported at various shelters in the park. Hikers must use the

No pets!- Dogs are not permitted in the park!! Below are kenneling options, vaccination records often required:

Loving Care Kennels 865.453.2028, 3779 Tinker Hollow Rd, Pigeon Forge, TN 37863. Pickup your dog at Fontana Dam and return him/her to Davenport Gap. $375 for one dog, $525 for two. Will deliver maildrops upon pickup/return. Call at least 2 days in advance (preferably from NOC if NoBo). 〈lovingcarekennels.com〉

Barks & Recreation 865.325.8245 Does not offer rides, but you can d/o p/u from 2159 East Pkwy Gatlinburg, TN. M-Sa 7-8, Su 10-6. 〈barksandrecgatlinburg.com〉

Standing Bear Farm (see pg. 34) 〈fb.com/standingbearfarm〉

1991.6	199.3	Mt Buckley	6603
1991.6	199.3	Trail 0.5E to Clingman's parking area ⚠ NoBo: AT is left fork of this intersection	6553
1991.3	199.6	Clingmans Tower Path, paved path between tower and parking area	6643
1991.2	199.7	Clingmans Dome, tower to east 🔘 ক̃(pg. 28)	6658
1990.8	200.1	Mt Love	6446
1989.7	201.2	Collins Gap	5737
1988.9	202.0	Mt Collins	6187
1988.5	202.4	Sugarland Mtn Trail, **Mt Collins Shelter** (0.5W) ☽♦⊏(12)	5958
		13◄7.3◄5.6◄►8►15.4►20.6 Cables. Small spring 0.1 beyond shelter.	
1988.2	202.7	Fork Mountain Trail east to Clingmans Dome Rd ♦	5889
1987.3	203.6	Spring ♦	5629
1985.5	205.4	Road Prong Trail, AT skirts Clingmans Dome Rd. 35.6094,-83.4467 🅿	5273
1985.1	205.8	Mingus Ridge, two wild hog containment bridges	5436
1983.6	207.3	Newfound Gap, US 441 35.6112,-83.4257 🅿 ♟ ⬛ 🔘 (pg. 28)	5045
		Large parking area, restrooms. No potable water. **Gatlinburg, TN** (15.0W)	
1981.8	209.1	Sweat Heifer Creek Trail to east	5834
1980.8	210.1	0.2W to Mt Kephart, 0.6W to Jumpoff (views), Blvd Trail 5.5W to Mt LeConte 🔘	6035
1980.5	210.4	**Icewater Spring Shelter** to east. 🔘☽♦⊏(12)	5935
		15.3◄13.6◄8◄►7.4►12.6►20.3 Spring 75 yards north on AT.	
1979.6	211.3	South end of Charlies Bunion Loop Trail (0.1W) 🔘	5521
1979.5	211.4	North end of Charlies Bunion Loop Trail 🔘	5468
1979.3	211.6	Unmarked side trail 0.1W to original Charlies Bunion. 🔘	5419
1979.1	211.8	Dry Sluice Gap Trail to east. 🔘	5399
1978.5	212.4	The Sawteeth 🔘	5396
1978.2	212.7	Porters Gap	5365
1975.4	215.5	View 🔘	5743
1974.4	216.5	Bradleys View 🔘	5481
1973.1	217.8	**Pecks Corner Shelter** (0.5E) on Hughes Ridge Trail ☽ ◊ ⊏(12)	5556
		21◄15.4◄7.4◄►5.2►12.9►20 Spring just south of shelter side trail.	
1972.2	218.7	Eagle Rocks, view. 🔘	5842

SoBo NoBo   1000   3000   5000

| 1971.4 | **219.5** Copper Gap . . . . | | 5515 |

1971.4 **219.5** Copper Gap 5515

1970.7 **220.2** Mt Sequoyah, AT skirts summit 5945

1968.7 **222.2** East ridge of Mt Chapman 6215

1967.9 **223.0** **Tri-Corner Knob Shelter** 20.6◄12.6◄5.2◄►7.7►14.8►25.3 . . . . ☾ ◖ ⊏ (12) 5895
1967.8 **223.1** Balsam Trail to east. 5963

1966.5 **224.4** Guyot Spring, trail skirts Mt Guyot . . . . ◖ 6302
1966.0 **224.9** Spring . . . . ◖ 6223

1965.0 **225.9** Deer Creek Gap . . . . 📷 6054

1964.3 **226.6** Yellow Creek Gap 5900
1964.2 **226.7** Plane wreckage. 5875
1964.1 **226.8** Snake Den Ridge Trail, 5.3W to Cosby Campground 5790

1961.8 **229.1** Camel Gap, Camel Gap Trail to east 4671

1960.2 **230.7** **Cosby Knob Shelter**, 100 yards east . . . . ☾ ◖ ⊏ (12) 4788
          20.3◄12.9◄7.7◄►7.1►17.6►25.9
1959.4 **231.5** Low Gap, 2.5W to Cosby Campground. 4240

1957.3 **233.6** Mt Cammerer Trail, 0.6W to summit, lookout tower. . . . . 📷 ♖ 4948
1957.0 **233.9** Spring . . . . ◖ 4689

1955.1 **235.8** Lower Mt Cammerer Trail, Cosby Campground (7.8W) 3467

1954.1 **236.8** Chestnut Branch Trail, 2.1E to . . . . .35.7593,-83.1069 🅿 (2.0E) 2874
          parking at Big Creek Ranger Station and north end of BMT.
1953.9 **237.0** Spring . . . . ◖ 2822

1953.1 **237.8** **Davenport Gap Shelter**, spring to left of shelter . . . . ◖ ⊏ (12) 2592
          20◄14.8◄7.1◄►10.5►18.8►23.6
1952.2 **238.7** TN 32, NC 284, Davenport Gap, cross road where pavement ends . . . . **(pg. 34)** 1975
          Great Smoky Mountains National Park northern boundary

SOBO NOBO   1000   3000   5000

» *Fontana Village, NC 28733* (2.2W from NC 28) (..services cont'd from pg. 25)

🅿🛏♻🍴🛒⚕💲⛽✉ **Fontana Lodge** (2.2W) 800.849.2258, 828.498.2211 info@ fontanavillage.com Thru-hiker rate (ask) $79 (up to 4). No pets. Price higher on high-demand nights. Cabins $79/BR, pets welcome. Computer & printer in lobby can be used for Smokies permit. Mail ($5 non-guest fee): Fontana Village Resort, ATTN: [Hiker Name], 300 Woods Rd, Fontana Dam, NC 28733⟨fontanavillage.com⟩

🛒 **General Store** (2.2W) 800.849.2258, 828.498.2211 Grocery store, frz-dried food, Coleman/ alcohol/oz, canister fuel during thru hiker season, small selection of gear items. Open Mar 10 - Thanksgiving.

🅿🛏♻🍴🛒⚕💲⛽ **Fontana Village Pit Stop** (2.2W) 800.849.2258, 828.498.2211 Hot dogs, sausage dogs, personal size pizza, nachos, snacks, soda & tobacco products. Stocks hiker food & fuel when General Store is closed. Open daily 9-5, later in summer.⟨fontanavillage.com⟩

🍴 **Mountainview Bistro, Wildwood Grill** (2.2W) 800.849.2258, 828.498.2211 Bistro open yr-round B/L/D, Grill Apr-Oct.

△ **Laundromat** (2.2W) 7 Days, yr-round. Detergent at General Store if front desk closed.

165.9 FONTANA DAM VISITOR CENTER

🅿♻⚕ **Fontana Dam Visitor Center** (0.2W) 828.498.2234 Soda machine outside (may or may not work), ice cream sold inside when open (9a-6p daily May-Oct), free showers.

199.7

CLINGMANS DOME, 35.5572,-83.4939 🅿🚻🏛♿ *Highest point on the AT. Parking lot 0.5E on a paved walkway. No sinks in restrooms. Gift shop near parking area sells water 10a-6p Apr 1-Nov 30 but often sells out. It's 7 mi from the parking area to Newfound Gap on Clingmans Dome Rd; Rd is closed to cars Dec 1 - Apr 1.*

207.3 ★ NEWFOUND GAP, US 441(.ıll AT&T WEAK)

🅿 **A Walk in the Woods** 865.436.8283 Guides, Vesna & Erik Plakanis. Resupply & shuttling (hikers & dogs). Range: Springer to Damascus (company based in Gatlinburg). Special thru-hiker rates.

🅿 **Cherokee Cabs** 828.269.8621 Short & long distance shuttles 24/7 covering all trailheads in the Smokies & nearby cities. Call for rates. ⟨cherokeecabs.com⟩

» *Gatlinburg, TN 37738* (15W)

🅿♻💲✉ **Johnson's Inn** (13.8W) 800.842.1930 20% 0ff for thru-hikers. Family-owned establishment & hiker friendly.⟨johnsonsinn.com⟩

Days Inn (14.7W) 865.436.5811

🅿♻💲✉ **Motel 6** (14.8W) 865.436.7813 Reasonable rates. Pool. Pets under 25 lbs free, 26-50 lbs $10, 50+lbs $20. Trolley stops at the front door. CC ok. Mail: 309 Ownby St, Gatlinburg, TN 37738.

🅿♻ **Microtel Gatlinburg** (15.1W) 865.436.0107 $44.95/up, c. b'fast, pets $10. Maildrop w/reservation: 211 Historic Nature Trail, Gatlinburg, TN 37738.

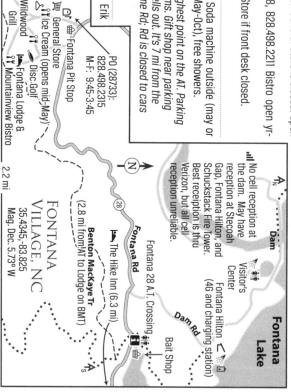

NORTH CAROLINA / TENNESSEE

» **Cherokee, NC 28719** *(20.7E)*, ☎828.497.3891, M-F 9-4:30
Large town, many services.
🚆 **Cherokee Transit** (17.5E) 866.388.6071
» **Cherokee, NC (services cont'd on pg. 34....)**

Roaring Fork Rd

1A

East Pkwy

Whole Earth Grocer

321

Baskins Creek Bypass

Cross Roads Inn & Suites

321 441

3

Gatlinburg Visitors Center (1.8mi from 321)

Cherokee Transit

No Way Jose's Cantina

5

GSM Pkwy

6

Subway

Day Hiker

Johnson's Inn

Ben & Jerry's

Cherokee Orchard Rd

The Best Italian (2)

Pizza Hut

Econo Lodge at Conv Center (2)

Sugarlands Distilling

Dunkin Donuts

Reagan Dr

Loco Burro

McDonald's

Microtel

Subway

Historic Nature Tr

Walgreens

Five Guys

Flapjacks

The Best Italian (1)

Mellow Mushroom

Starbucks

8

Quality Inn

Fridays

Smoky Mtn Brewery

River Rd

Leconte

441

Park Grill Steakhouse

Econo Lodge on the River (1)

NOC Great Outpost

Bennett's BBQ (Br, Lun, & Din)

Texas Roadhouse

Days Inn

10

Ski Mtn Rd

Travel Lodge

Grand Prix

Old Dad's General Store

Newfound Gap 15mi.

Cici's Pizza

Motel 6

GATLINBURG, TN

35.7239, -83.4939
Mag. Dec. 6.01° W

N

Mass Transit Center for the Gatlinburg Trolley (near Aquarium). Stops marked by numbered squares. 50 cents per ride in-town (have exact change). Routes on 30-min loop. Stops west of the transit center (6-10) including NOC & hotels are on "green" route. Stops east (3, 1A, 2A, 3A) including Food City & PO are on "blue" route.

Services off map, distances from 1A

0.4 mi. to:	🍴	Alamo Steakhouse
1.0 mi. to:	✚	First Medical 865.436.7267
1.6 mi. to:	✉	PO (37738): 865.436.3229 M-F 9-5, Sa 9-11
1.6 mi. to:	🏪	Food City
2.1 mi. to:	🧺	Super Suds Coin (24 hr)
4.2 mi. to:	📖	Library 865.436.5588 MWF 10-5, Tu,Th 10-8, Sa 10-1

1.5 mi

Gatlinburg is a tourist mecca with dozens of restaurants & motels. Many more business-es are omitted than are shown on the map.

🛏🏕 **Crossroad Inn & Suites** (15.6W) 865.436.5121
🏕✉ **NOC Great Outpost** (14.6W) 865.277.8209 Open 7 days 10-9, (Jan-May 10-6). Full line of gear, white gas/denatured/oz. Free showers & pack storage. Mail: 1138 Parkway, Gatlinburg, TN 37738.
🏕 **The Day Hiker** (15.3W) 865.430.0970 Yr-round 7 days. Basic hiking supplies w/ shoes & fuel (no food). Hrs vary by season. (thedayhiker.com)
✚ **Echota Family Care** (19.4W) 865.567.1909 echota.family.care@gmail.com M-F & on call 24 hrs w/no add'l charge. On the Trolley Route/daytime.
■ **Gatlinburg Mobile Massage** (26.7W) 865.250.0676 Special thru-hiker rate $70/hr.(gatlinburgmobilemassage.com)

1951.1	239.8	Stateline Branch, multiple crossings	♦	1698
1950.6	240.3	Pigeon River Bridge.		1372
1950.3	240.6	I-40 underpass		1435
1950.1	240.8	Stream.	♦	1568
1949.5	241.4	Green Corner Rd (gravel) hostel to west.	♦ (pg. 34)	1761
1947.4	243.5	Painter Branch, cross branch to campsites. Blue-blazed trail east across Painter Creek to campsite and spring.	♦ ◪	2845
1947.1	243.8	Stream.	♦	3084
1946.5	244.4	Spanish Oak Gap, trail joins old roadbed		3465
1945.1	245.8	Snowbird Mountain, grassy bald, side trail 50 yards to FAA tower on summit.	📷 ⩜	4263
1944.3	246.6	Wildcat Spring uphill from trail	♦	4083
1943.6	247.3	Turkey Gap		3630
1942.8	248.1	Spring	♦	3022
1942.6	248.3	Deep Gap, **Groundhog Creek Shelter** (0.2E)	☽♦⊿ (6)	2897

25.3◄17.6◄10.5◄►8.3►13.1►23.0 Stone shelter, reliable spring to left. Cables.

1940.8	250.1	Spring downhill, east 30 yards	♦	3566
1940.3	250.6	Rube Rock Trail to Hawks Roost		3872
1939.7	251.2	Brown Gap, USFS 148A	♦	3500

"Max Patch" is a homophone that replaced the original name "Mack's Patch". The summit was cleared for cattle and is maintained as a bald.

1937.2	253.7	Cherry Creek Trail, water 0.3E	♦	4338
1936.9	254.0	SR 1182, Max Patch Rd, stream to north 35.7963,-82.9627 P♦		4254
1936.6	254.3	Dirt road, west to parking, east to Buckeye Ridge P		4376
1936.2	254.7	Max Patch Summit (no fires)⚠ NoBos turn right at north end of bald 📷		4629
1935.7	255.2	Stream.	♦	4375
1935.2	255.7	Roadbed, Buckeye Ridge Trail to east		4209
1934.6	256.3	Stream.	♦	4119
1934.4	256.5	Water to east (signed)	♦	4025
1934.3	256.6	**Roaring Fork Shelter**, water 0.1S or 0.4N, 7 tent pads, cables. ☽♦⊿⊏ (10)		4025

25.9◄18.8◄8.3◄►4.8►14.7►28.9

1933.9	257.0	Footbridge, stream	♦	3957
1933.2	257.7	Footbridge		3740
1932.8	258.1	Stream (many in area)	♦	3623
1932.1	258.8	Two streams about 0.1 mile apart	♦	3453

SoBo   NoBo

1931.3	**259.6**	Footbridge		3534
1931.0	**259.9**	Footbridge, stream	♦	3492
1930.8	**260.1**	Lemon Gap, NC 1182, TN 107		3550
1930.1	**260.8**	Stream.	♦	3955
1929.6	**261.3**	Walnut Mountain, grassy clearing.		4299
1929.5	**261.4**	**Walnut Mountain Shelter** 23.6◄13.1◄4.8◄►9.9►24.1►32.7. . . . . ☽♦◖⌁ (6)		4252

Walnut Mt tr. to west. Cables. Water 0.1 behind, campsite in field beyond water.

1928.8	**262.1**	Kale Gap, campsite 125 yards north on AT.		3725
1928.1	**262.8**	Catpen Gap, 0.1 east to campsite atop small knoll	◖	4126
1927.7	**263.2**	Streams	♦	4297
1927.4	**263.5**	Unnamed gap.		4451
1927.1	**263.8**	Bluff Mountain		4686
1926.4	**264.5**	Spring 50 yards west.	♦	4195
1925.8	**265.1**	Old roadbed, spring.	♦	3921
1925.5	**265.4**	Big Rock Spring located in ravine	♦	3730
1924.9	**266.0**	Dirt road		3407
1924.3	**266.6**	Brook with cascades	♦	2978
1923.9	**267.0**	Old Rd		2710
1923.0	**267.9**	Garenflo Gap, Shut-In Trail to west . . . . .35.8534,-82.8759 🅿		2500
1922.3	**268.6**	Taylor Hollow Gap, two footbridges, one over a stream	♦	2639

1919.6	**271.3**	**Deer Park Mountain Shelter** (0.2E) water at gap west of AT. . . . . ☽♦◖⌁(5)		2319
		23.0◄14.7◄9.9◄►14.2►22.8►30.1 Cables. Gragg Gap 0.1 north on AT.		
1918.8	**272.1**	Deer Park Mountain.		2571

1916.4	**274.5**	NC 209 + US 25/70, **Hot Springs, NC** . . . . 35.8895,-82.8323 🅿 **(pg. 34)**		1326
1916.0	**274.9**	French Broad River, US 25/70 bridge		1339
		⚠ NoBo turn east through gap in guardrail immediately after crossing river.		
1915.1	**275.8**	Lovers Leap Rock, several rock outcroppings, Silver Mine Trail to west . . . . 📷 ♦		1686

1913.1	**277.8**	Pump Gap, trail crossing		2130
1912.7	**278.2**	Springs	♦	2299
1912.2	**278.7**	North intersection with Pump Gap Loop Trail	◖	2410

1911.6	279.3	Pond with boxed spring	♦	2467
1911.3	279.6	⚠ NoBo: AT 0.3W on dirt road. Cross Mill Ridge to gravel road.		2604
		(double-blazed oak tree). Go 0.1W on gravel road and reenter woods to east.		
1910.8	280.1	Stream.	♦	2429
1910.5	280.4	Tanyard Gap, US 25/70 overpass . . . . 35.91,-82.791 🅿		2270
1909.1	281.8	Piped spring	♦	3039
1908.6	282.3	Roundtop Ridge Trail west 3.5 miles to Hot Springs (former path of AT)	♦	3194
1908.1	282.8	Side trail 0.1W to campsite, Rich Mountain Lookout Tower, ... 📷 🎋 ♦ 🏕		3506
		piped spring north on AT.		
1907.6	283.3	Spring	♦	3195
1907.2	283.7	Hurricane Gap, northmost of two gravel road crossings		2945
1906.9	284.0	Grave stone		2990
1905.4	285.5	**Spring Mountain Shelter** 28.9◄24.1◄14.2◄►8.6►15.9►22.6 . . . 🌙♦🏕⛺ (5)		3536
		Water 75 yards down blue-blazed trail on east side of AT. Cables.		
1903.6	287.3	Deep Gap, Little Paint Creek Trail, west 200 yards to spring	♦	2892
1902.2	288.7	Spring in ravine 30 yards west	♦	2735
1901.6	289.3	NC 208, TN 70, Allen Gap, Paint Creek 0.2W.	◊	2218
1900.6	290.3	AT skirts gravel road		2348
1900.1	290.8	Log Cabin Road, hostel to west. . . . . **(pg. 35)**		2376
		Private home in view to east, please do not trespass.		
1896.8	294.1	**Little Laurel Shelter** 32.7◄22.8◄8.6◄►7.3►14.0►22.8 . . . . . . 🌙♦🏕⛺ (5)		3652
		Boxed spring 100 yards down blue-blazed trail behind shelter. Campsites west		
		side of AT, south of shelter. Cables.		
1895.0	295.9	Pounding Mill Trail to east. 0.2W to Camp Creek Bald Lookout Tower. . . . . 🎋		4750
		Tower is beyond first cluster of buildings and catwalk is locked (no view)		
1894.2	296.7	Jones Meadow, spring 100 yards south	♦	4460
1893.2	297.7	Trail west to Jones Meadow, 30 yards east to Whiterock Cliff..		4480
1893.0	297.9	0.1W to view from Blackstack Cliffs . . . . 📷		4501
1892.8	298.1	Bearwallow Gap, Jerry Miller Trail to east, Firescald bypass to west reconnects . .		4421
		with AT 1.5 miles north. AT between bypass points is rocky and strenuous.		

1892.1	298.8	Big Firescald Knob . . . . 📷	4566
1891.2	299.7	Firescald bypass to west, reconnects with AT 1.5 miles south.	4208
1890.5	300.4	Round Knob Trail to west	4284
1889.7	301.2	Fork Ridge Trail to east	4254
1889.5	301.4	Chestnut Log Gap, **Jerry Cabin Shelter** . . . . ☾ ♦ ⊏ (6)	4146

30.1◄15.9◄7.3◄►6.7►15.5►25.6 Water opposite shelter. Cables.

1888.7	302.2	Bald Ridge	4535
1888.3	302.6	Sarvis Cove Trail to west	4565
1887.9	303.0	Howard C. Bassett Memorial, old roadbed before and after	4705
1887.6	303.3	Big Butt Mountain, summit to west, short bypass trail.	4815
1887.2	303.7	Blue-blazed trail to west	4670
1885.8	305.1	Shelton Gravesite to east	4441

> ⚠ AT northbound from Flint Gap to Rice Gap is compass south.

1884.3	306.6	Cross stream . . . . ◊	3959
1883.5	307.4	Flint Gap.	3438
1882.8	308.1	**Flint Mountain Shelter**, water on AT 50 yards north of shelter. . . . . . ☾ ♦ ⊏ (8)	3555

Bear cables. 22.6◄14.0◄6.7◄►8.8►18.9►29.5

1882.7	308.2	Spring . . . . ◊	3553
1881.8	309.1	Spring . . . . ◊	3353
1881.4	309.5	AT + roadbed south end	3250
1881.3	309.6	Spring . . . . ◊	3244
1880.7	310.2	AT + roadbed north end.	3293
1880.3	310.6	Devil Fork Gap, NC 212 . . . . 36.0105,-82.6086 🅿	3096
1879.8	311.1	Rector Laurel Rd, spring north on AT. . . . . . . 36.0065,-82.607 🅿 ♦	2928
1879.4	311.5	Stream. . . . . ♦	3206
1879.1	311.8	Cascade. ♦	3386
1878.9	312.0	Stream. . . . . ♦	3576
1878.3	312.6	Sugarloaf Gap.	4016
1876.9	314.0	Lick Rock	4522
1876.2	314.7	Big Flat, campsite to east . . . . ◭	4265
1875.2	315.7	Rice Gap, dirt road	3800
1874.0	316.9	**Hogback Ridge Shelter** (0.1E) . . . . ☾ ♦ ⊏ (6)	4324

22.8◄15.5◄8.8◄►10.1►20.7►31.2 Spring 0.2 mile beyond shelter. Cables.

| 1873.4 | 317.5 | High Rock, view 70 yards west on blue-blazed trail . . . . 📷 | 4460 |

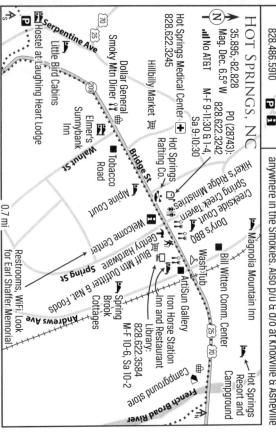

Davenport Gap
828.486.5910

Big Creek Ranger Station (1.3E) 🅿️ 🛈

HOT SPRINGS, NC
35.895, -82.828
Mag. Dec. 6.5° W
📶 No AT&T

🅿️ Serpentine Ave

Hostel at Laughing Heart Lodge

Little Bird Cabins

Smoky Mtn Diner
Dollar General

Hot Springs Medical Center ✚
828.622.3245

PO (28743):
828.622.3242
M-F 9-11:30 & 1-4,
Sa 9-10:30

Elmer's Sunnybank Inn

Hillbilly Market

Hiker's Ridge Ministries

Hot Springs Rafting Co.

Spring Creek Tavern
Creekside Court

Dory's BBQ

Tobacco Road

Bluff Mtn Outfitter & Nat. Foods
Gentry Hardware

Welcome Center

ArtiSun Gallery

Iron Horse Station Inn and Restaurant

Magnolia Mountain Inn

Bill Witten Comm. Center

Library:
828.622.3584
M-F 10-6, Sa 10-2

WashTub

Spring Brook Cottages

Hot Springs Resort and Campground

Campground store

Walnut St. · Bridge St. · Alpine Court · Andrews Ave · Spring St

French Broad River

0.7 mi

Restrooms, WiFi! Look for Earl Shaffer Memorial

» Cherokee, NC 28719 (...services cont'd from pg. 29)

🏨📶 Qualla Motel & Cabins (17.4E) 828.497.5161 Hiker rates, free laundry, WiFi, across street from grocery/pharmacy. Pets ok.⟨quallacabinsandmotel.com⟩

Microtel Inn & Suites (20.7E) 828.497.7800 $65, higher on wkends, incl b'fast. Coin laundry, pool. Adjacent supermarket, fast-food, shoe store. Mail: (Fed Ex/UPS only) 674 Casino Tr, Cherokee, NC 28719.

238.7   DAVENPORT GAP, NC 234, GREAT SMOKY MTN NP

Highlands Shuttle Service 423.625.0739, 865.322.2752 mdron@bellsouth.net Ron McGaha shuttles from Winding Stair Gap, NC to Damascus, VA & anywhere in between. Side trips anywhere in the Smokies. Also p/u & d/o at Knoxville & Asheville airports & bus stations. Can do resupply & maildrops. Experienced AT hiker having hiked all the A.T. in his svc area & all 900 mi of Smokies trls. Member ATC & 900 miler club. Adv notice if possible.⟨highlandsshut tleservice.com⟩

🏕️ Big Creek Campground (2.1E) 865.436.1297, 865.436.1231 $14/Site No showers or electricity. Open early Apr - late Oct. Rates/dates may change, may require reservations in 2018 - call. Chestnut Branch Trail (2.0mi) connects campground to AT 0.1S of Davenport Gap Shelter. From ranger station on CBT, compass north 0.3 mi to Country Store, compass south 0.6 mi to campsites.

Big Creek Country Store (1.5E) 828.476.4492 thebigcreekcountrystore@gmail.com   Hiker-friendly resupply. Showers in 2018. Call for hrs.⟨fb.com/ bigcreekcountrystore⟩

241.4   GREEN CORNER RD

Standing Bear Farm (0.2W) 423.487.0014, 423.608.0149 Yr-round, hosted by Maria. Bunk $20, Tenting $15PP & up, Cabin-$25PP, Treehouse $30PP/$50-2. Reasonably priced resupply, beer, cook-yourself meals. All stove fuels. Daypacks for slackpackers. Shuttles anywhere. Kennel service & dog shuttle for hike through Smokies, $260. Directions (see map); Cross I-40, stay on AT up rock stairs. 1.0 to gravel rd, turn trail west (compass north) 200 yds to white farmhouse on right. Parking $5/car/day. CC ok. Mail: 4255 Green Corner Rd, Hartford, TN 37753. ⟨fb.com/standingbearfarm⟩

274.5   NC 209, US 25/70

» Hot Springs, NC 28743, 11.5% tax added to all Hot Springs lodging prices.

Welcome Ctr 828.622.9932 WiFi accessible after hrs.

Alpine Court Motel 828.206.3444 Check at Tobaccoo Rd next door. Tax-incl prices; $57S, $67D, $10EAP. Cabin $100/PN. Bunkroom $25PP Charges +fee if CC.

Elmers Sunnybank Inn & Hostel 828.622.7206 Located across from Dollar General, at 26 Walnut St. Traditional thru-hikers $25PP semi-pvt & pvt room, incl linens, towel & shower. Gourmet organic vegetarian meals avail. No cells/smoking/CC. Staffed by former thru-hikers, the Inn has hosted A.T. hikers since 1948,& offers an extensive library & well-equipped music room. WFS possible. Mail: PO Box 233, Hot Springs, NC 28743.(sunnybankretreatassociation.org)

ArtiSun Gallery & Cafe 828.539.0030 Ice Cream, coffee, wine, baked goods, artwork gallery, & shops open daily.(fb.com/artisungallery)

Iron Horse Station 866.402.9377 Hiker rate $65D. Restaurant, tavern & coffee shop. Serves L/D, & offers some vegetarian options. Live music Tu, We, Fr, Sa, Su. (theironhorsestation.com)

Creekside Court 828.206.5473 Hiker rate (must ask), pets allowed.(lodginghotspringsnc.com)

Spring Creek Tavern 828.622.0187 info@thespringcreektavern. com M-Th 11-10, Fr-Sa 11-11. Su 11-9. 50 Varieties of beer, special AT burger, outdoor deck, live music Fr-Sa nights. 3 Rooms for rent, book online.(thespringcreektavern.com)

Little Bird Cabins (0.06W) 828.206.1487 On Serpentine Ave before NC 209, US25/70. Cabin sleeps 6, incl kitchenette. Reserv by phone or online. Pet fee $15. CC ok. Open yr-round. Price $85-$115/ night.(littlebirdcabinrentals.com)

Hostel at Laughing Heart Lodge (0.14W) 828.206.8487 US25/70$20PP bunks, $25 semi-pvt, $35 single pvt, $45D pvt (one full-size bed). Open yr-round. All rooms include am coffee, shower & towel, movies, hiker kitchen, WiFi. Pets $5 in limited rooms. Tenting w/ shower $10S $15D (one tent). Shower only $5. Laundry $5 incl soap. Quiet time 10p-7a. Lodge rooms $100 include c. b'fast, call/text 828.622.0165 to reserve. Mail: 289 NW Hwy 25/70, Hot Springs, NC 28743.

Hot Springs Resort & Spa (0.19W) 828.622.7676 Tenting $30+ up to 4. Camping cabins (no TV, no linens, common bath/showers) tax-incl prices; $55.88/5, $73.76/8. Pets $10. Motel-style room (linens, TV, some w/mineral water bath) $120-$300. Mineral water spa $25S before 6p; 3-person rate $40 before 6p, $45 after 6p. Camp store carries snacks & supplies; Massage therapy avail. CC ok.(nchotsprings.com)

Mountain Magnolia Inn (0.2W) 800.914.9306 Hiker rates $75S $95D when rooms avail incl AYCE b'fast. Dinner Th-M.(mountainmagnoliainn.com)

Bluff Mountain Outfitters 828.622.7162 Daily 8-6, S-Th 9-5, Fr-Sa 9-6. Full svc outfitter, fuel/oz. Complete resupply, natural foods grocery & hiker foods. WiFi. ATM & scale inside. Shuttles Franklin-Damascus & area airports & bus stations. SoBo hikers can print GSMNP permits. Ships UPS pkgs. Mail: (USPS) PO Box 114 Hot Springs, NC 28743 or (FedEx/UPS) 152 Bridge St.(bluffmountain.com)

Dory's Restaurant 828.622.9400 7 days 11a-8p.

Smoky Mountain Diner 828.622.7571 M-Sa 6a-8p; Su 7a-2p. Hiker special 12 oz burger.

Hot Springs Library 828.622.3584 Hikers Welcome! M-F 10a-6p, Sa 10a-2p.(madisoncountylibrary.net)

Hiker's Ridge Ministries 828.691.0503 godswayeen@gmail.com M-Sa 9-3, Mar 14 - May 15. Place to relax, coffee, drinks, snacks & restroom.

■ **Glenda Dolbeare** (0.14W) 603.204.7893 Licensed Massage Therapist. Will come to Laughing Heart for massage svcs.

290.8   LOG CABIN ROAD. (dirt/gravel road)

Hemlock Hollow Inn (0.7W) 423.787.1736 hemlockhollowinn@gmail.com Open Feb 15-Jun 30 & Sep 15-Nov 15. Off season avail w/reservation, call for avail. Go west on Log Cabin Dr, follow blue blazes on telephone poles & signs. Call ahead for free p/u. Bunkroom $25PP w/linens, $20 w/out. Cabin for couples w/linens $60. All rooms heated. Tent site $12PP. Pets $5. All stays incl shower, free ret ride to trail. Non-guest shower & towel $5. Long term resupply, some gear, cold drinks, foods, fruit, fuels. Shuttles avail. slackpacking welcomed. Parking/WiFi free for guests, fee for non-guest. PayPal ok. Mail (ETA mandatory): 645 Chandler Circle, Greeneville, TN 37743.(hemlockhollowinn.com)

1871.6	319.3	Sams Gap, US 23, I-26 . . . . 35.9529,-82.5606 🅿 (pg. 38)	3724
1869.8	321.1	Meadow	4436
1869.3	321.6	Street Gap, gravel road	4100
1869.1	321.8	Powerline	4183
1867.9	323.0	Low Gap, campsite downhill to west with piped spring . . . . ♦ ◭	4300
1867.1	323.8	Spring . . . . ♦	4670
1866.7	324.2	Powerline	4842
1865.6	325.3	Blue-blazed trail 100 yards west to water; bypass trail to east . . . . . . ♦	5059
1865.5	325.4	Spring . . . . ♦	5210
1865.3	325.6	Yellow-blazed trail to west	5365
1865.1	325.8	Big Bald, survey marker	5516
1864.5	326.4	Big Stamp, treeless saddle on ridge, bypass trail to east . . . . ♦	5379
1864.2	326.7	Dirt road	5262
1863.9	327.0	**Bald Mountain Shelter** (0.1W) . . . . ☾ ♦ ∠ (10)	5064
		25.6◄18.9◄10.1◄►10.6►21.1►33.9 Spring on side trail to shelter. Cables.	
1863.7	327.2	Piped Spring (0.2W) on blue blazed trail . . . . ♦	4982
1862.5	328.4	Little Bald (tree covered)	5220
1861.4	329.5	Spring . . . . ♦	4406
1860.4	330.5	Whistling Gap, campsite . . . . ◊ ◭	3889
1859.8	331.1	Trail 0.1E to High Rocks	4241
1858.7	332.2	Stream, two footbridges . . . . ♦	3570
1858.2	332.7	Spivey Gap, US 19W, stream south of gap. 36.0319,-82.4202 🅿 (0.5W) (pg. 38) ♦	3200
1857.8	333.1	Ogelsby Branch, cross twice on footbridge . . . . ♦	3555
1856.9	334.0	Stream. ♦	3820
1856.7	334.2	Devils Creek Gap, dirt road	3754
1854.5	336.4	Stream. ♦	2984
1854.4	336.5	Stream. ♦	2963
1853.6	337.3	Stream. ♦	3036
1853.3	337.6	**No Business Knob Shelter** Reliable water on AT 0.3S of shelter. . . . ◊ ◭ ∠ (6)	3181
		29.5◄20.7◄10.6◄►10.5►23.3►32.4	
		Reliable water on AT 0.3S of shelter.	

| 1850.9 | **340.0** | Temple Hill Gap, Temple Hill Trail . . . . . | | 2850 |

1848.8 **342.1** Views to Erwin . . . . 📷 2694

1847.1 **343.8** River Rd, Unaka Springs Rd, ...36.1042,-82.4467 🅿 (pg. 38) 1662
         Erwin, TN (3.8W). AT to east, crossing Nolichucky River on bridge
1846.8 **344.1** Railroad tracks 1707

1845.8 **345.1** Side trail East to Nolichucky Gorge Campground before footbridge . . . ♦ (pg. 42) 1744
         Trail not signed
1845.4 **345.5** Footbridge, stream . . . . ♦ 1797
1845.0 **345.9** Footbridge, stream . . . . ♦ 1883
1844.6 **346.3** Stream . . . . ♦ 1992
1844.3 **346.6** Footbridge 2088
1844.1 **346.8** Footbridge . . . . ♦ 2184

1842.8 **348.1** **Curley Maple Gap Shelter**, water south of shelter . . . . ⌐ ◊ 🔥 ⊏ (14) 3039
         31.2◄21.1◄10.5◄►12.8►21.9►31.9
1842.3 **348.6** Spring . . . . ◊ 3193
1841.7 **349.2** Stream . . . . ◊ 3272
1841.5 **349.4** Stream . . . . ◊ 3308

1838.7 **352.2** Indian Grave Gap, TN 395 . . . . .36.1096,-82.3616 🅿 ♦ (pg. 42) 3350
         Water 0.1E outside of curve in road.
1838.2 **352.7** Survey marker (USFS 381-28) 3696
1838.0 **352.9** Powerline 3740
1837.6 **353.3** USFS 230, Red Fork Rd (gravel) 3770

1835.3 **355.6** Beauty Spot Gap, clearing . . . . 36.1163,-82.3372 🅿 4321
         Parking to west, trail parallel to USFS 230 from here north to Deep Gap.
1834.8 **356.1** Piped spring & campsites 100 yards west across USFS 230 . . . . ♦ 🔥 4141
1834.4 **356.5** AT skirts Red Fork Rd 4564

1833.3 **357.6** Unaka Mountain, dense spruce forest 5180

MAP AT-4 ▸ AT-5 | TENNESSEE

ERWIN, TN (SOUTH)
36.1475,-82.4139
Mag. Dec. 6.82° W

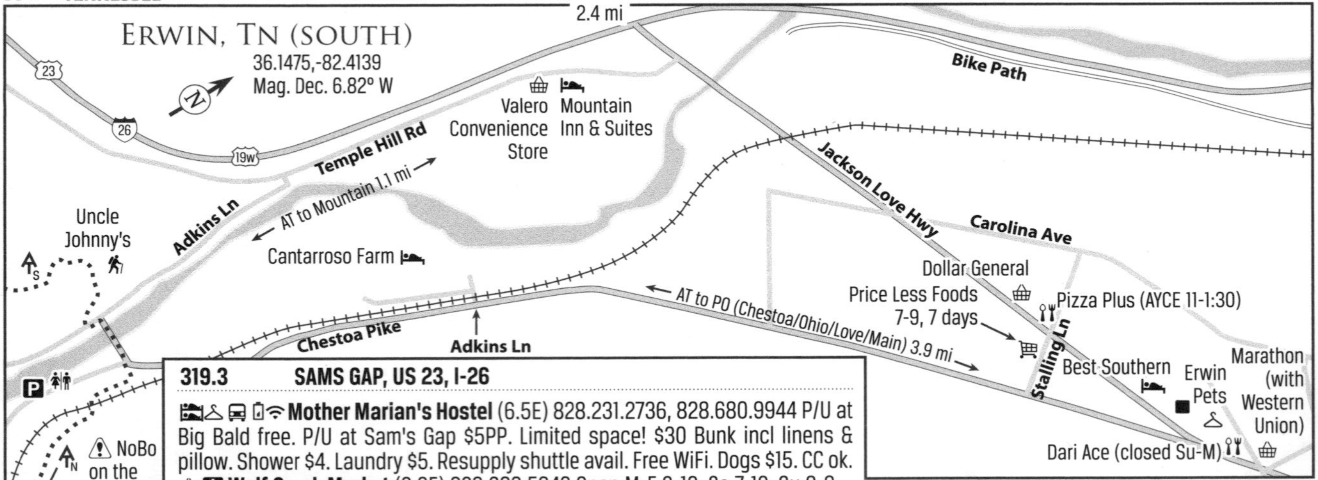

N↓ 2.4 mi

(23) (26) (19W)

Bike Path

Adkins Ln

Cantaroso Farm ⛺

Chestoa Pike

Temple Hill Rd

← AT to Mountain 1.1 mi →

Adkins Ln

⛽ Valero
⛒ Mountain Convenience Store

⛒ Mountain Inn & Suites

← AT to PO (Chestoa/Ohio/Love/Main) 3.9 mi →

Jackson Love HWY

⛒ Dollar General
⛒ Price Less Foods 7-9, 7 days

Carolina Ave

Stalling Ln

Best Southern ⛒
⛒ Pizza Plus (AYCE 11-1:30)

Dari Ace (closed Su-M)

Marathon (with Western Union) ⛒
Erwin ⛒ Pets ⛺

Map legend box (top):

🅿 on the A.T.

⚠ NoBo the A.T. will actually show compass South here.

Jones Branch

USA Raft
Mountain
River Guide
Nolichucky
Gorge
Campground

319.3　SAMS GAP, US 23, I-26

🏠🛏🚿🍴📶 **Mother Marian's Hostel** (6.5E) 828.231.2736, 828.680.9944 P/U at Big Bald free. P/U at Sam's Gap $5PP. Limited space! $30 Bunk incl linens & pillow. Shower $4. Laundry $5. Resupply shuttle avail. Free WiFi. Dogs $15. CC ok.

⛒ 🛒 **Wolf Creek Market** (3.3E) 828.689.5943 Open M-F 6-10, Sa 7-10, Su 8-9.

🍴 **Little Creek Cafe** (2.8E) 828.689.2307 M-Th 6-2, F 6-8, Sa 7-2. Clsd Su.

332.7　SPIVEY GAP, US 19W

🏠🛏🚿🍴⛺📶🛒✉ **Nature's Inn Hostel & Cabins** (2.8W) 828.216.1611 Open 3/1 thru 11/15. Call for free shuttle from Sams Gap, Street Gap & Devil's Fork. Hostel main house pvt rms: $44-$55, incl linens & towel. 4 Creekside cabins: each sleep 3, $22PP. Bunkhouse: $20PP sleeps 5. Hammock: $15PP. Tent: $10PP. Pvt hilltop cabin: $85PP: full kitchen, living rm, & bath. "Sleeping Porch": $30PP. Shower $5, linens $5, laundry $6 (incl soap). Resupply store (trail supplies, fuel). Socialized pets free (on site-on lead). 3 Outdoor Kennels w/doghouses (free). Shuttles/slackpacking (fee-based). Mail free w/reservation: 4872 Old Asheville Hwy, Flag Pond, TN 37657.⟨naturesinnhostel.com⟩

343.8　RIVER RD, UNAKA SPRINGS RD

✉ **HikerShuttles.com** 423.330.7416, 910.409.2609 hikershuttles@gmail.com Owners Tom (10-K) & Marie (J-Walker) Bradford. Erwin based, licensed & insured.

All area trailheads, bus stations, airports, outfitters, etc.⟨hikersshuttles.com⟩

✉ **Shuttles by Sarge** 423.735.8278 shuttlesbysarge@gmail.com Goes anywhere.⟨shuttlesbysarge.com⟩

🏠🛏🚿⛺🅿🐕🍴📶✉ **Uncle Johnny's Nolichucky Hostel and Outfitters** 423.735.0548 Open yr-round only 60 ft from the trail.3 Free town shuttles/day for all guests. Tenting $15PP.⟨riverside-hammocking $17.50, incl showers w/towel & soap (non-guest $5). Smart TV, WIFI, grills. Large 50 x 16' covered hammock area w/individual lighting, electrical outlets & a 15' picnic table for $17.50PP. Hostel, $22PP. Full linens $5. Fridge/m'wave/computer. Cabins w/AC & heat - reg/$25-$35PP, large Condo/Cabin-$65-$105PN. Laundry

ERWIN, TN (NORTH)

2.4 mi

N

Map labels:

Bike Path

19W / 23 / 26

Main St

Corner Grill

Jackson Love

Ottio Ave

Carolina Ave

Levelin St

Mohawk Dr

Love St

Opekiska St

Chasing Vapors

Hawg-N-Dawg

Visitor Center

Clinchfield Drug

Ace

Unicoi County Library
423.743.6533
M-F 10-6, Sa 11-3

P.O. (37650):
423.743.9422
M-F 8:30-4:45,
Sa 10-12

Steel Rails Coffee

Taco Bell

BoJangles

Pal's Hamburgers

McDonalds
Shell Station
Huddle House

Super 8

Walgreens

Happy Hour Liq

Elm Ave

PO to Pizza Hut 1.2 mi

CVS

Maple Ave

Food Lion w/ Western Union

Family Dollar
China Kitchen

El Corita

Barber

24 Hr Celebrity Laundry

Little Caesars

3Y KFC

Hardees/
Red Burrito

Pizza Hut

Azteca Mexican

Rock's (closed Su)

Dollar Store
Rite Aid

Subway

395

Unicoi Animal Hospital 423.743.9172
(2 mi from edge of map on Main St)

Walmart Plaza with liquor store. Also Verizon.
Restaurants: Los Jalepenos & Primo Italian
(3 mi from edge of map, I-26 exit 34)

Johnson City, TN (all major services) 15mi
Mahoneys 423.282.5413
Overmountain Outdoors
423.218.6864

Urgent Care of Erwin ✚ ✚ Unicoi County Hospital 423.743.3141
423.330.6177 ✚ ✚

(multiple machines) $5. Dog friendly for socialized pets. Shuttles/slackpacking (fee). Parking $2-$3/day. Bike, kayak, tube, rafting trips. No charge maildrops: 151 River Rd, Erwin TN 37650. ⟨unclejohnnys.net⟩

▲⊛⚲⊡P ▤⚑⌂≈🛏⚟ **Cantarroso Farm & Apiary** (0.9W) 423.833.7514 cantarrosofarm@gmail.com Nine acre farm & apiary on the Nolichucky River overlooking class three rapids. Clean & quiet setting w/personal svc. Free beverage & candy bar at p/u. Two cabins: $30PP (2-7) or $45/$65 pvt, Free WiFi, heat/AC, coffee/tea, full size beds, linens, shower, toilet, toiletries, towel, refrigerator, m'wave, toaster oven, cooking gear, grill & fire pit. Stay incl free p/u & ret to Chestoa trail head, & use of fishing gear for trout & small mouth bass fishing. Add'l charge for laundry, town shuttles, bikes, slackpacking options. No pets. Open yr-round. Mail: 777 Bailey Ln, Erwin TN 37650. ⟨cantarrosofarm.com⟩

▲⚲≋⊡⊠ **Mountain Inn & Suites** (1.2W) 423.743.4100 Hiker rate $79.99S, $10EAP incl hot b'fast buffet. No pets. Coin laundry. Hot tub (Apr-Oct) & swimming pool (Mem Day-Labor Day). Guest mail: 2002 Temple Hill Rd, Erwin TN 37650.

» Erwin, TN 37650 (3.9W) ⟨Hostel & Cantarroso Farm near trail⟩

▲⎈≈⊡⊠ **Best Southern** (2.1W) 423.743.6438 Call for rates.

▲⚲⊡⚑≈⊡⊠ **Super 8** (4.1W) 423.743.0200 $59.99D, $10EAP, max 4, incl b'fast, coin-laundry. No pets. Guest Mail: 1101 N Buffalo St, Erwin TN 37650.

⊟⊟ **Primo's Italian Restaurant** (7.6W) 423.735.1100 Su-Th 11a-9:30p, F-Sa 11a- 10p (near Walmart) BYOB.

■ **Baker's Shoe Repair** (3.8W) 423.743.5421 Also repairs jackets & pack.

| 1831.1 | **359.8** | Low Gap, campsite, weak stream 0.1W . . . . ⬧ | 3900 |

1830.2 **360.7** Footbridge, stream . . . . ⬥ 4129
1830.0 **360.9 Cherry Gap Shelter** 33.9◄23.3◄12.8◄►9.1►19.1►24.5 . . . . ⬥ ⟋ (6) 3963
Spring 120 yards on blue-blazed trail behind shelter to the left.
1829.6 **361.3** Unmarked trail crossing 3906

1828.6 **362.3** Little Bald Knob, trail skirts summit 4367
1828.4 **362.5** Stream. . . . . ⬧ 4291

1826.9 **364.0** Iron Mountain Gap, TN 107, NC 226 . . . . 36.1433,-82.2332 🅿 (pg. 42) 3723

1825.6 **365.3** Campsite, piped spring 0.1W from signpost near north end of clearing. . . . ⬥ ☁ 4015

1824.5 **366.4** Rock pillar. 4429

1822.8 **368.1** Greasy Creek Gap, campsite at gap, water 0.2W,. . . . . (pg. 42) 4034
Greasy Creek Hostel 0.6E
1822.0 **368.9** Campsite, weak spring 0.1W . . . . ⬧ ☁ 4118

1820.9 **370.0 Clyde Smith Shelter** (1976) (0.1W). . . . . ⬥ ☁ ⟋ (10) 4487
32.4◄21.9◄9.1◄►10►15.4►17.2 Water 0.1 left of shelter, tent sites behind.

1819.7 **371.2** Little Rock Knob, views to west, south of summit . . . . 📷 4918
1819.4 **371.5** Stream. . . . . ⬥ 4764
Here north to Roan parking, NoBo trail bearing is compass south.
1818.6 **372.3** Stream. . . . . ⬥ 4373

1817.5 **373.4** Hughes Gap, TN 1330, Hughes Gap Rd. . . . . 36.1368,-82.141 🅿 4040
1817.1 **373.8** Water 50 yards east . . . . ⬥ 4234

✹ Golden ragwort - Small flower with yellow center and small floppy petals. "Field flower" that can create a sea of yellow.

1814.5 **376.4** Ash Gap, campsite at gap, water 0.1E . . . . ⬧ ☁ 5350

1812.1	**378.8**	Toll House Gap, saddle between Roan . . . . 36.104,-82.1331 🅿 ⛺🚹♦	6190
		High Bluff & Knob, 0.1E to parking, picnic area, open Mem day - Oct 1.	
1811.9	**379.0**	Chimney (remnant)	6132
1810.9	**380.0**	**Roan High Knob Shelter** (0.1E) . . . . ♦ ⬛ ⊏ (15)	6186
		31.9◄19.1◄10◄►5.4►7.2►23.6 Piped spring, highest shelter on AT.	
1809.9	**381.0**	⚠ NoBo: watch for AT turning west off of the wide treadway	5784
1809.1	**381.8**	Several footbridges, streams . . . . ♦	5508
1809.0	**381.9**	Carvers Gap, TN 143, NC 261 . . . . 36.1068,-82.1106 🅿 ⤵	5512
		Access road to summit (1.9mi) open approx. Mem Day - Oct 1	
1808.3	**382.6**	Round Bald, 30 yards east to summit, views . . . . 📷	5827
1807.6	**383.3**	Jane Bald, big rock slab, views back to Roan Mtn . . . . 📷	5808
1807.0	**383.9**	Side trail 0.5E to Grassy Ridge Bald and views, AT to west. . . . . 📷 ♦	5899
1806.8	**384.1**	Springs . . . . ♦	5860
1806.1	**384.8**	Campsite to west . . . . ⬛	5391
1805.5	**385.4**	**Stan Murray Shelter** . . . . △ ⊏ (6)	5059
		24.5◄15.4◄5.4◄►1.8►18.2►27.8	
		Spring on blue-blazed trail opposite shelter.	
1803.7	**387.2**	**Overmountain Shelter** (0.3E) Yellow Mountain Gap . . . . 📷 ⤵♦⬛⊏(20)	4662
		17.2◄7.2◄1.8◄►16.4►26►34.2 Converted barn. Water on way to shelter.	
1802.5	**388.4**	Two intersections with old roadbed	5189
1802.2	**388.7**	Side trail 0.1E to Big Yellow Mountain	5260
1801.8	**389.1**	Little Hump Mountain, clearing . . . . 📷 ⬛	5459
1801.6	**389.3**	Piped spring, campsites to north and south . . . . ♦ ⬛	5147
1801.5	**389.4**	Bradley Gap, spring east 100 yards . . . . ⬛	4950
1800.0	**390.9**	Fence	5406
1799.1	**391.8**	Hump Mountain, Stan Murray plaque, NoBo have several false summits . . . 📷	5587
1798.4	**392.5**	Fence	5230
1797.7	**393.2**	Spring . . . . ♦	4941
1797.4	**393.5**	Spring . . . . ♦	4829
1796.8	**394.1**	Doll Flats, **NC-TN** border . . . . ♦ ⬛	4600
1796.7	**394.2**	Stone steps, view. . . . . 📷	4293
1796.7	**394.2**	Spring west of trail, massive stone wall. . . . . ♦	4102
1796.3	**394.6**	Stream. . . . . ♦	3203
1796.2	**394.7**	Wilder Mine Group campsite, piped spring 150 yds north on A.T. . . . ⬛ ♦	3092
1796.2	**394.7**	Apple House Tentsite . . . . ⬛ (1)	3037
1796.1	**394.8**	US 19E **Elk Park, NC (2.4E) Roan Mtn, TN** (3.5W) . . . . (pg. 42)	2895
1795.9	**395.0**	Bear Branch Rd, streams north of road . . . . 36.1794,-82.0128 🅿 ♦	2900
1795.1	**395.8**	AT + Jeep Path, south end, stream . . . . ♦	3188
1794.7	**396.2**	AT + Jeep Path, north end	3441
1793.7	**397.2**	Open ridge with views to east and west . . . . 📷	3758
1793.2	**397.7**	Isaacs Cemetery	3581
1792.8	**398.1**	Buck Mountain Rd, water at church 0.1E . . . . ♦	3487

345.1

🏕 ⛺ 🚿 **Nolichucky Gorge Campground** (0.09E) 423.743.8876 Tent or bunkroom (when avail) $11.50up, incl shower. Cabin $80/up. Well-behaved leashed pets ok. Small camp store. CC ok.⟨nolichucky.com⟩

352.2

SIDE TRAIL TO:

🏕 ⛺ △ ⛺ 🚿 **Poplar Creek Farmstay** (5.5E) 828.688.1653 2BR Creekside Apt. Rental (sleeps 6), starting at $99. 2 Night min. $25 cleaning. Dogs under 40lbs; $25, over 40 lbs: $40. Laundry $2. Cable TV, WiFi, full kitchen, food items for sale on site. Pets welcome. 10 Min from Indian Grave Gap in Poplar, NC.

364.0

INDIAN GRAVE GAP

🏕 **Rock Creek Recreation Area (USFS)** (3W) 423.638.4109 Tent site $12, Open May-Nov.

》 *Buladean, NC* (4.1E)

368.1

GREASY CREEK GAP

🏕🏠🛏🍴🥤△⛺🅿🚿🖥📮 **Greasy Creek Friendly** (0.6E) 828.688.9948 All lodging prices incl tax: $15PP bunkhouse, $20PP/up indoor beds, $7.50PP tenting incl shower. Shower w/out stay $3. Pets ok outside. Pup Shed $15PP (2 beds)pets ok. Open yr-round (call ahead Dec-Feb). Sabbath observed(sundown Fr to sundown Sa). Limited kitchen privileges. 6p Takeout/dinner run from Mtn Grill. Store of goods for multi-day resupply incl snacks, meals, veg. options. Coleman/alcohol/oz. Shuttles Hot Springs to Damascus. Parking $2/night. Free long distance calls w/ in US. CC ok. Directions: take Old Woods Rd trail east, follow curve to the left, then take the 1st right (should be going downhill all the way). Hostel is 1st house to the right. Mail: 1827 Greasy Creek Rd, Bakersville, NC 28705.⟨GreasyCreekFriendly.com⟩

394.8

US 19E

🏕🏠⛺🍴🛏🍴🅿🅿📮 **The Station at 19E** (0.7E) 575.694.0734 Yr-round, $30pp flat rate (pvt rooms avail) incl bunk, shower, laundry & fresh linens. Craft beer & food avail on site. Full outfitter/resupply. Shuttles & slackpack options. Secure parking $10/day or $2/day w/shuttle. Mail: 9367 Hwy 19E, Roan Mountain, TN 37687. Maildrop free w/stay $5 non-stay.⟨thestationat19e.com⟩

🏕🏠🍴△🅿🚿 **Mountain Harbour B&B/Hiker Hostel** (0.3W) 866.772.9494 Hostel over barn overlooking creek $25PP, semiprivate king bed $55D, treehouse $75D, incl linens, shower, towel, full kitchen, wood burning stove, video library. Tenting w/shower $10, non-guest shower w/towel $5, laundry w/soap $5. B'fast $12 when avail. B&B rooms $125-165 incl b'fast, separate shower & fireplace,

---

ROAN MOUNTAIN, TN

36.1773,-82 (trailhead)
Mag. Dec. 7.05° W

← AT to PO 3.7

PO (37687):
423.772.3014
M-F 8-12 & 1-4,
Sa.7:30-9:30

Roan Mtn Disc Golf

Roan Mt Community Park

Puerto Nuevo Mexican

Cloudland Market

Roan Mtn Pharmacy

Carter Community Bank

Highlander BBQ

Bob's Dairyland

Subway

143

Redi Mart

Smoky Mtn Bakers

Cloudland DR

3.8 mi

Good Samaritan Thrift Store

Shell Creek General Store

Dollar Store

Buck Mtn Rd

Roan Mtn Animal Hospital 423.772.4124

Highland Clinic of Chiropractic

Frank & Marty's Pizza

19E

Buck's Cuts Barber Shop

Roan Mtn B&B

A/C, refrigerator, cable TV/DVD. Food trailer (seasonal) & General Store on-site, open also to non-guests, sells fuel canisters & full resupply. Slackpack/long distance shuttles by arrangement. Secured parking $10/day or $2/day w/shuttle. Open yr-round. Mail: (non-guests $5) 9151 Hwy 19E, Roan Mountain, TN 37687. ⟨mountainharbour.net⟩

🍴 **Frank & Marty's Pizza** (2.2W) 423.772.3083 Tu,W,Sa, 4-9; Th-F, 11-9; Closed Su-M.

» **Elk Park, NC 28622** (2.2E)(see services on map)

» **Roan Mountain, TN 37687** (3.7W), Annual **Roan Mountain Hiker Festival**, Roan Mountain Community Park, May 4, 5 & 6th. Tent City $5. Farmer's Market. Live music. Vendors. Free trailhead shuttles ⟨fb.com/trailmagicshuttle⟩.

🥾🛏🚿♿️Ⓟ🛜 **Roan Mountain B&B** (4.8W) 423.772.3207 Yr-round, hiker friendly! Reservations recommended but walk-in's welcome. Hiker rate $75S, $95D Incl. b'fast. Near shopping/restaurants. Free p/u & ret-Hwy 19E. 5p Shuttle to town every day or 1 mi walk to eat/ resupply. Pets ok w/prior approval. Boot dryer! No alcohol/inside smoking. Laundry $5. Shuttles & slackpacking avail. Section hiker parking. CC ok.⟨roanmtbb.com⟩

🥾🛏♿️🛒🔌🛜✉️ **Doe River Hiker Rest** (6.4W) 575.694.0734 doeriverhikerrest@gmail.com Open yr-round. Free shuttle w/stay. $30PP (flat rate) incl pvt room, shower, laundry, fresh linens. Shuttles to town. Slackpack avail. Maildrop to The Station at 19E.

🛒 **Redi Mart** (3.3W) 423.772.3032 M-Sa 8-10, Su 9-10.

🛒 **Cloudland Market** (3.7W) 423.772.3201 M-Sa 8-7.

🍴 **Smoky Mountain Bakers** (3.1W) 423.957.1202 Tu-Sa 8-8, fresh bread, wood-fired pizza.

🍴 **Bob's Dairyland** (3.3W) 423.772.3641 6 days, 7a-7p. Clsd W.

🍴🛒 **Highlander BBQ** (3.4W) 423.895.3013 hturbyfill@hotmail.com Hiker friendly, good food, shuttle to/from trailhead & lodging for patrons. Ask about bunks & showers that are only 150 yds from the A.T.

» **Banner Elk, NC 28604** (9.9E)

🏠🛏♿️Ⓟ🛜 **Harmony Hostel** (9.9E) 828.898.6200 info@harmony-hostel.com Hiker friendly. Safe & clean w/comfortable beds. Spacious semiprivate sleeping areas, incl linen, shower & communal kitchen. No bunkbeds. Laundry $6. Walk to restaurants in Banner Elk. Free shuttle from Hwy 19E at 3p & 6p for hostel guests. Add'l shuttle services avail for fee. Supply stop at Dollar General. Free b'fast incl toast & jam, oatmeal, fruit, tea/coffee & boiled eggs (limit 2) on request. Section hiker parking. No smoking/drugs/alcohol. Not the typical hiker hostel. $45.00 + tax/ person.

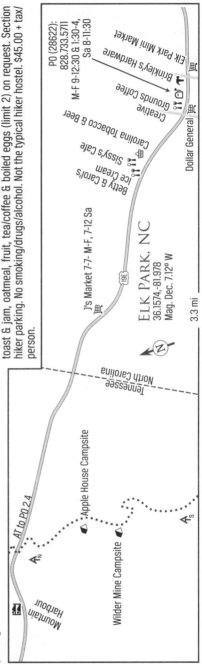

PO (28622): 828.733.5711
M-F 9-12:30 & 1:30-4,
Sa 8-11:30

Brinkley's Hardware

Elk Park Mini Market

Creative Grounds Coffee

Carolina Tobacco & Beer

Sissy's Cafe

Betty & Carol's Ice Cream

Dollar General

J's Market 7-7, M-F, 7-12 Sa

ELK PARK, NC
36.1574, -81.978
Mag. Dec. 7.12° W

19E

3.3 mi

Tennessee / North Carolina

AT to PO 2.4

Mountain Harbour

Wilder Mine Campsite

Apple House Campsite

1792.5	**398.4**	Campbell Hollow Rd, streams south of road	♦	3380
1792.2	**398.7**	Footbridge at bottom of ravine		3399
1791.8	**399.1**	Footbridge, stream	♦	3370
1790.7	**400.2**	Side trail 0.1E to Jones Falls	♦	3018
1790.0	**400.9**	Campsite, Elk River 0.1E	♦ ◮	2731
1789.6	**401.3**	Stream.	♦	2691
1788.6	**402.3**	Stream (cross twice)	♦	2838
1787.8	**403.1**	Footbridge, stream	♦	2988
1787.4	**403.5**	Mountaineer Falls to west	♦ ◮	3054
1787.3	**403.6**	**Mountaineer Shelter**, water 70 yards from shelter.	♦ ⊏ (14)	3183
		23.6◄18.2◄16.4◄►9.6►17.8►33.6		
1786.5	**404.4**	Campsite to east	♦ ◮	3229
1786.1	**404.8**	Slide Hollow Stream, footbridge	♦	3346
1785.9	**405.0**	Roadbed.		3505
1785.7	**405.2**	Walnut Mountain Rd		3604
1784.8	**406.1**	Footbridge, stream (many in area)	♦	3444
1784.0	**406.9**	Bench, view.	📷	3514
1783.4	**407.5**	Upper Laurel Fork	♦	3274
1782.7	**408.2**	Footbridge, stream	♦	3401
1782.5	**408.4**	USFS 293 (gravel), waterfall south on AT	♦	3421
1781.7	**409.2**	Spring	♦	3328
1781.5	**409.4**	Spring	♦	3329
1781.1	**409.8**	Footbridge, stream	♦	3438
1780.7	**410.2**	Hardcore Cascades.	♦	3378
1779.9	**411.0**	Stream.	♦	3595
1779.4	**411.5**	Campsite, several streams and footbridges	♦ ◮	3560
1777.8	**413.1**	Rock outcropping, views.	📷	3908
1777.7	**413.2**	**Moreland Gap Shelter**.	♦ ⊏ (6)	3815
		27.8◄26◄9.6◄►8.2►24►30.8		
		Water source long way downhill across from shelter.		
1775.5	**415.4**	Piped spring	♦	3815
1775.1	**415.8**	Forest Service road.		3778
1774.4	**416.5**	Trail skirts White Rocks Mountain		3967
1773.1	**417.8**	Trail to Coon Den Falls 0.8E downhill		3411

1772.0	**418.9**	Stream. . . . . ♦	2837
1771.6	**419.3**	Barn	2593
1771.4	**419.5**	Dennis Cove Rd, USFS 50, hostels . . . . 36.2643,-82.1231 **P** (pg. 46)	2508
1770.6	**420.3**	Footbridge . . . . ♦	2452
1770.3	**420.6**	Switchback⚠ Path straight ahead is high water bypass, reconnects at L.F. Shltr	2374
1770.1	**420.8**	Laurel Falls . . . . ♦	2105

⚠ Do not swim close to falls, there is a dangerous whirlpool

1769.5	**421.4**	**Laurel Fork Shelter** 34.2◄17.8◄8.2◄►15.8►22.6►30.2 . . . . ♦ ⊏ (8)	2161
1769.1	**421.8**	Waycaster Spring, two footbridges over Laurel Fork . . . . ♦	1992
1768.6	**422.3**	Side trail to **Hampton, TN** US 321 (1.0W). . . . . (pg. 47)	1949

Hampton is west on 321.

| 1766.0 | **424.9** | Pond Flats, campsite, spring 0.1N on AT. . . . . ⬙ ⬥ | 3689 |

1763.2	**427.7**	Campsite to east . . . . ⬥	2244
1762.9	**428.0**	NoBo: east on Shook Branch Rd . . . . 36.301660,-82.128085 (pg. 47)	2019
1762.8	**428.1**	US 321, **Hampton, TN** (2.6W) . . . . 36.3019,-82.129 **P** 🏕🚻🚮♦ (pg. 47)	1990

NoBo: turn west after crossing 321
Shook Branch Recreation Area, picnic area, sandy beach. No Camping.

| 1761.3 | **429.6** | Griffith Branch . . . . ⬙ | 2053 |
| 1760.9 | **430.0** | Location of CLOSED Watauga Lake Shelter . . . . | 2078 |

Closed 4/15/16 due to bear activity. Not known if or when it will reopen. No picnicking, lingering or overnight camping.

| 1759.7 | **431.2** | Watauga Dam, AT on road for 0.4 mi south & north of dam, sparsely blazed.. . . . | 2014 |

| 1758.4 | **432.5** | Wilbur Dam Rd . . . . 36.3288,-82.1115 **P** | 2250 |

| 1755.4 | **435.5** | Spring. . . . . ♦ | 3316 |

| 1753.7 | **437.2** | **Vandeventer Shelter**, views . . . . 📷 ♦ ⊏ (6) | 3558 |

33.6◄24◄15.8◄►6.8►14.4►22.7
Water 0.3 mile down very steep blue-blazed trail 0.1S of shelter.

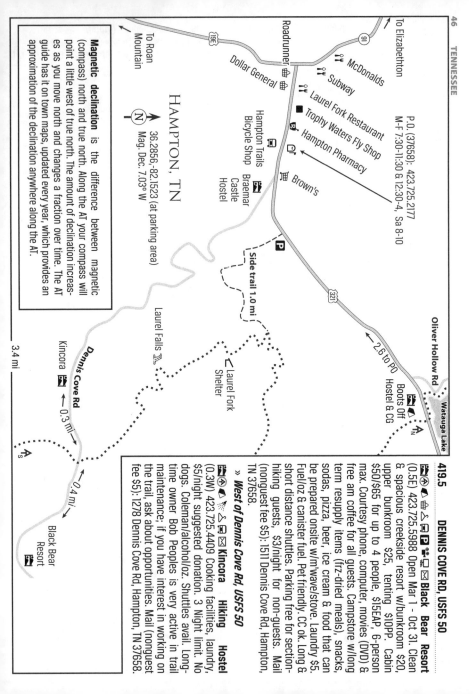

Magnetic declination is the difference between magnetic (compass) north and true north. Along the AT your compass will point a little west of true north. The amount of declination increases as you move north and changes a fraction over time. The AT guide has it on town maps, updated every year, which provides an approximation of the declination anywhere along the AT.

To Roan Mountain

To Elizabethton

HAMPTON, TN

(N) 36.2856, -82.1523 (at parking area)
Mag. Dec. 7.03° W

P.O. (37658): 423.725.2177
M-F 7:30-11:30 & 12:30-4, Sa 8-10

19E

Roadrunner
Dollar General
McDonalds
Subway
Laurel Fork Restaurant
Trophy Waters Fly Shop
Hampton Pharmacy
Brown's

Hampton Trails
Bicycle Shop

Braemar
Castle
Hostel

P

Side trail 1.0 mi

321

Oliver Hollow Rd

Watauga Lake

2.6 to PO

Boots Off
Hostel & CG

Laurel Falls

Laurel Fork
Shelter

Dennis Cove Rd

Kincora
0.3 mi
0.4 mi

Black Bear
Resort

3.4 mi

419.5 DENNIS COVE RD, USFS 50

(0.5E) 423.725.5988 **Black Bear Resort** & spacious creekside resort w/bunkroom $20, upper bunkroom $25, tenting $10PP. Clean Cabin $50/$65 for up to 4 people, $15EAP, 6-person max. Courtesy phone, computer, movies (DVD) & free am coffee for all guests. Campstore w/long term resupply items (frz-dried meals), snacks, sodas, pizza, beer, ice cream & food that can be prepared onsite w/m'wave/stove. Laundry $5. Fuel/oz & canister fuel. Pet friendly. CC ok. Long & short distance shuttles. Parking free for section-hiking guests, $3/night for non-guests. Mail (nonguest fee $5): 1511 Dennis Cove Rd, Hampton, TN 37658.

» West of Dennis Cove Rd, USFS 50

(0.3W) 423.725.4409 **Kincora Hiking Hostel** $5/night suggested donation. 3 Night limit. No dogs. Coleman/alcohol/oz. Shuttles avail. Long-time owner Bob Peoples is very active in trail maintenance; if you have interest in working on the trail, ask about opportunities. Mail (nonguest fee $5): 1278 Dennis Cove Rd, Hampton, TN 37658.

422.3 SIDE TRAIL TO HAMPTON (1.0W)

» *see Hampton, TN below*

428.0 SHOOK BRANCH RD

🅿🅑🍴⛺🏠⛽🦽♿🅟📶🅟📷 **Boots Off Hostel & Campground** (0.2W) 239.218.3904 jimgregory77@hotmail.com Bunkhouse $20 PP incl linen & lockable storage. Cabin bunks $20 PP incl linen (sleeps 4 PPL), call for pvt space options. Tent/hammock $10 PP, All incl local shuttle, shower, c. b'fast, kitchen amenities, & bon fire. Laundry $5. Kayak, canoe, SUP rentals for Watauga Lake (5 min walk). Parking for fee. Non guests: $5 shower, $5 maildrop, shuttles for fee from any crossing Erwin to Damascus. Dog friendly, call in adv. No dogs in bunkhouse.(fb.com/bootsoffhostelandcampground)

428.1 US 321

🅿🍴🚲📶📷 **Dividing Ridge Campground** (1.1W) 423.957.0821 1219 US Hwy 321. Hiker Friendly. Call for p/u! Will shuttle guest hikers to/from trail heads. Local shuttles & am coffee are incl w/stay. Open most of the yr, closed some in winter (call). Showers w/towels & wash cloths provided, bathrooms, WiFi, charging stations, & a wash tub for gear washing. Donation based.

» *Hampton, TN 37658 (2.4W)*

🚲 **Hampton Trails Bicycle Shop** (2.5W) 423.725.5000 brian@hamptontrails. com (hamptontrails.com)

🏠🛒📶 **Brown's Grocery & Braemar Castle Hostel** (2.4W) 423.725.2411, 423.725.2262 Open yr-round. Both operated by Sutton Brown; check-in at grocery to stay at the hostel for shuttles. Store open M-Sa 8-6, closed Su. Store accepts CC; hostel is cash only. Pets ok. WiFi at hostel only.

» *Elizabethton, TN (8.1W)(services 5 mi. north of Hampton)*

🏠📶📷 **Americourt** (7.4W) 423.542.4466 $60+tax, up to 4, incl c. b'fast. Pets $25. Not avail race wkends. Mail:1515 Hwy 19E, Elizabethton, TN 37643.
🛒 **Food City, Ingles, Big Lots** (8.3W)
🍴 **Little Caesars, Arbys** (6.9W)
🎬 **State Line Drive-in** (6W) 423.542.5422 Open seasonally. Shows Fr-Su.

» *Bulter, TN (9.3E)*

🛏⛺🏠📶📷 **Iron Mountain Inn** (14E) 423.768.2446 ironmountaininn@ gmail.com Yr-round. 10mi from Hampton. Call for p/u or for directions. Fee for p/u & ret. B&B room $100S/$150D, incl b'fast. Log cabin w/hot tub under the stars, $50PP, no b'fast. CC ok but w/5% fee. Free laundry. Shuttles from Watauga Lake to Damascus. Pets ok. Mail: c/o Woods, PO Box 30, Butler, TN 37640.(creeksidechalet.net)

448.6 TN 91

» *TN 91 (4.5E to Shady Valley services at next mile marker)*

🏠⛺⛽📶📷 **Switchback Creek Campground** (2.6E) 407.484.3388 Apr 1 - Oct 31. 1.8E to Sluder Rd, turn right for 0.2mi, then right on Wallace Rd. 0.6mi to 570 Wallace Rd, Shady Valley, TN 37688. Cabin for two $40, campsite $12+tax. Cash only. Showers, laundry, WiFi. Call for ride at TN91/Low Gap. Pets allowed for camping only.

455.1 LOW GAP, US 421

» *Shady Valley, TN 37688 (2.7E)*, ☎423.739.2173, M-F 8-12 Sa 8-10
🍴 **Raceway Restaurant** (2.8E) 423.739.2499 Open 7-8 all days except W 7-2 & Su 8-2.
🏪🍴 **Shady Valley Country Store & Deli** (2.8E) 423.739.2325 Open-seasonal. May 1-Oct 31: M-F, 7-8; Sa, 8-8; Su, 9-6; Closes earlier in winter. Deli serves burgers & sandwiches. Coleman fuel.

Bear Interactions & Bear Canisters

Due to increasing bear/human interactions, the Appalachian Trail Conservancy strongly recommends the Use of Bear Canisters for food storage while overnight camping along the A.T. in GA, NC, & TN.

1749.9	441.0	Campsite 0.1N, stream 100 yards east	⬧ ⛺	3857
1748.6	442.3	Turkeypen Gap		3979
1747.7	443.2	Powerline		4126
1747.1	443.8	Spring	⬧	4000
1746.9	444.0	**Iron Mountain Shelter**, spring 0.3S on AT	⛺ ⊏ (6)	4096
		30.8◄22.6◄6.8◄►7.6►15.9►35.6		
1745.6	445.3	Nick Grindstaff Monument		4090
1743.1	447.8	Footbridge, stream, bog bridges north of stream.	⬧	3554
1742.7	448.2	Roadbed.		3584
1742.3	448.6	TN 91. 36.4814,-81.9603 🅿 (pg. 47)		3508
		Shady Valley, TN (3.5E) South end of handicap-accessible trail.		
1741.5	449.4	North end of handicap-accessible trail		3615
1739.3	451.6	**Double Springs Shelter**	⬧ ⊏ (6)	4078
		30.2◄14.4◄7.6◄►8.3►28.0►34.5 Spring 80 yards left of shelter.		
		Rich Knob to south, Holston Mtn Trail to north.		
1737.7	453.2	Locust Knob.		3636
1735.8	455.1	Low Gap, US 421 . . . . 36.5386,-81.9489 🅿 ⬧ (pg. 47)		3384
		Piped spring on south side of road.		
		Shady Valley, TN (2.7E)		
1734.4	456.5	Low stone wall on east side of AT		3565
1733.9	457.0	Double Spring Gap, campsite	⛺	3539
1733.5	457.4	Weak, muddy spring east side of AT.	⬧	3638

1611.9   **579.0**   Stream (unreliable) . . . . ⬙ 2889

1611.0   **579.9**   **Jenkins Shelter**, creek 100 yards north on AT. . . . . ☽ ◆ ⬥ ⊏ (8) 2400
           39.4◄20.1◄10.7◄►13.5►23.2►37.7

> ✱   Mountain Laurel – Shrub similar to the rhododendron. Grows five to ten feet
>   high and blossoms with abundant cup-shaped white flowers.

1606.6   **584.3**   Laurel Creek, VA 615 (gravel) . . . . 37.1025,-81.2022 🅿 ◆ ⬥ 2450
           Intersection with Trail Boss Trail. Campsite just north of road.

1604.7   **586.2**   Trail Boss Trail to west 3099

1602.7   **588.2**   Views to west . . . . 📷 2996

1601.8   **589.1**   Powerline 2721

1600.3   **590.6**   AT on gravel road from here north to US 52 3088
1599.7   **591.2**   US 52 (North Scenic Hwy), **Bland, VA** (2.5E), **Bastian, VA** (3W) . . . . . (pg. 60) 2905
1599.3   **591.6**   AT crosses over I-77 on VA 612 2780
1598.9   **592.0**   VA 612 parking, Kimberling Creek, drinking discouraged . . 37.1389,-81.1266 🅿 ⬙ 2600

1597.5   **593.4**   **Helveys Mill Shelter** (0.3E) . . . . ☽ ◆ ⊏ (6) 3121
           33.6◄24.2◄13.5◄►9.7►24.2►33.7
           Water source 0.3 mile down switch-backed trail in front of shelter.

519.6 DICKEY GAP, VA 650

» *Troutdale, VA 24378* (2.6E)

🏕🚶🛁🚿 **Troutdale Church Hostel** (2.6E) 276.677.4092 Mar 15-Nov 15. Bunkhouse w/m wave, shower. Tenting also avail. Pets outside. No drugs/alcohol. Donations appreciated. Hikers welcome to service in hiker attire. Pastor Ken Riggins. N0 maildrops. 62 Sapphire Ln, Troutdale.

PO (24375): 276.677.3200
M-F 8:30-12:30 & 1:30-3:30,
Sa 8:15-10:30

Partnership Shelter →
3.2 mi: to Sugar Grove

← 6 mi. to Marion

Mt Rogers Visitor Center

7.6 mi

81 Marion ● Valero

Co. Road 650

Co. Rd 670

Co. Rd 672

Trimpi Shelter

Teas Rd

Sugar Grove Exxon

Dickey Gap

Troutdale

(25 mi. of ⬆ are shown on this map)

Troutdale Baptist Church Hostel
Co. Rd 603

PO (2437)
276.677.3221
M-F 8-12
Sa 8-11:30

🏕🚶🛁🛏🅿🍴📶🏪🚿☕ **Sufi Lodge** (3.1E) 276.677.0195 sufilodgeva@gmail.com Sufi Lodge is a unique place to stay in Troutdale, VA run by James & Suzanne who are becoming known for their good food & friendly, spiritually uplifting atmosphere. Wellness center on the property for those in need of some TLC.(sufilodge.org)

🏪 **Fox Creek General Store** (6.2E) 276.579.6033 foxcreekgeneralstore@gmail.com 4mi. south on Rt 16, M-F: 7-7, Sa, 7-6, Deli.

533.7   VA 16, PAT JENNINGS VISITOR CENTER

🅿🚶🅿 **MRNRA HQ** 276.783.5196 M-F 8-4:30, Sa-Su 9-4 yr-round. Permit req'd for overnight parking (gate locked @ 4:30p).

🚕 **Eller Taxi Service LLC** 276.759.2200 ellertaxi@yahoo.com 7a to 9p M - Sa, Closed Su. Can deliver restock items, food, etc. to The Atkins (Groseclose) or to Pat Jennings Visitors Ctr at Hwy 16. Covers SW Va. From Tri-Cities Airport to Roanoke Airport.

🏕🚶🛁🛏 **Boudicca's Legacy Hiker Hostel** (4.8W) 276.768.8753 Bunks $25PP. Pvt room $35PP w/2 beds. Laundry $4, non-guest shower $4, meals when able. No drugs. 6 mi from Partnership Shelter. Closed 2 wks in Dec & Nov.

🚌 **Marion Transit** 276.782.9300 Visitor center p/u at 8:30a, 11a, & 2p. Bus only stops if someone calls. Bus loops through Marion w/many stops. 50¢/ride.

Library
276.783.2323
M-Th 9-8, Sa 9-4

27 Lions

Wooden Pickle
Hester's B&B
Fudgery
Macado's
Wolfe's BBQ

Yummy Yummy (Japanese)

PO (24354):
276.783.505I
M-F 9-5, Sa 9:30-12

🍴 6.1 mi

16

9.1 mi

Cook's Laundry
Hardee's
City Pool
Rite Aid
Wendy's

Pizza Perfect
Taco Bell/KFC
greyhound 276.783.7114
Food City & Dollar Store
(weekdays only)
Walgreens
McDonalds
Sonic
Pizza Hut

Park Place
Drive-in
Food Lion
Arby's
Subway
Walmart, Ingles
My Puerto
Travel Inn
Econo Lodge
America's Best
Value Inn

Tractor Supply
Dollar Tree

MARION, VA
36.8345,-81.5167
Mag. Dec. 7.56° W

Smyth County
Comm. Hospital
276.378.1000

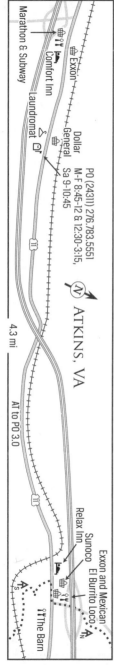

Marathon & Subway

⊕ Exxon
🏍️♿️ Comfort Inn

☕ Laundromat 🏧

🏧 Dollar
General

PO (24311) 276.783.5551
M-F 8:45-12 & 12:30-3:15,
Sa 9:10-45

Ⓝ ATKINS, VA

4.3 mi ⟶

At to PO 3.0

⊕ Exxon El Burrito Loco ⟶Ⓝ
Sunoco
Relax Inn
🏍️ 🏧
🍴 The Barn

Exxon and Mexican

» *Sugar Grove, VA 24375* (3.2E)(PO on map)

» *Marion, VA 24354* (6W) Lodging impacted by Bristol Speedway races Apr 13-15, May 18-20, & Aug. 15-18.

🛏️⊕📶🌧️⊠ **Econo Lodge** (8.5W) 276.783.6031 econolodge24354@gmail.com $54.99 - $64.99, hot b'fast, fridge, m'wave, pets ok (fee), some smoking rooms. Mail: 1420 N Main St, Marion, VA 24354.

🛏️♿📶⊠ **Travel Inn** (8.6W) 276.783.5112 $37.99S $42.99D $7EAP. On Marion Transit route. Guest Mail (non-guest $5): 1419 N Main St, Marion VA 24354.

🛏️📶 **America's Best Value Inn** (8.9W) 276.378.0481

🏃⊠ **Army Navy Store** (6.6W) 276.783.3832 Located in downtown Marion. Offers a variety of hiking supplies. Multiple fuels avail by the oz, pocket stoves, water purification accessories, Darn Tough & Injinji socks, & more. Mail: 219 E Main St, Marion, VA 24354.

🎬 **Park Place Drive-In** (8W) 276.781.2222 Walk-ins welcome. Also has mini-golf, arcade, & ice cream shop. Open seasonally.

542.3 VA 615, LINDAMOOD SCHOOL

🛏️🅿️⊠ **Rambunny & Aqua** (1E) 276.783.3754 rambunnyat@yahoo.com Shuttle referrals & other help. Parking in field w/a 3 dog alarm system, by donation.

🅿️ ■ **Settler's Museum** (0.1E) 276.686.4401 Park at farm Apr 1-Nov 15.

545.1 VA 683, US 11, I-81

🅿️⊠ **Skip & Linda** 276.783.3604 By appt, Damascus to Pearisburg.

🛏️🏃♿🅿️🌧️⊠ **Long Neck Lair** (0.4E) 276.698.2079 longnecklair@gmail.com Alpaca Farm located just off I-81 (exit 54, Groseclose) & steps away from access points to the AT. Tent site avail for $10PP/night incl shower. Room w/queen sleeper sofa, pvt bath & pvt entrance, refrigerator & m'wave, for $65/night up to 2 people. Beautiful views, hot tub, & hammocks.(longnecklair.com)

🍴⊕🅿️⊠ **The Barn Restaurant** 276.686.6222 M-Sa 7-8, Su 7-3, 16oz hiker burger, Sunday buffet 11-2, parking for section hikers $5/day, $25/wk. Mail: 7412 Lee Highway Rural Retreat, VA 24368.

» *Atkins, VA 24311* (3W), *Intersection is between Atkins & Rural Retreat in the township of Groseclose.*

🛏️🏃🅿️🌧️⊠ **Relax Inn** (0.06W) 276.783.5811 $45S $50D, $5EAP (max 4), pets $10. Parking $3/day. Call for shuttle availability. Guest mail (limit 2 boxes, non-guest $5): 7253 Lee Hwy, Rural Retreat, VA 24368.

🛏️🌧️⊠ **Comfort Inn** (3.7W) 276.783.2144 Hiker rate $79.95D $10EAP. C. b'fast. Guest mail: 5558 Lee Hwy, Atkins, VA 24311.

555.2 VA 610, OLD RICH VALLEY RD

🛏️🅿️📶🌧️🏃♿🅿️ ■ 🅿️ **Quarter Way Inn** (0.8W) 276.522.4603 tina@quarterwayinn.com Apr 1-Jun 30. 1910 Farmhouse run by 09 thru-hiker Tina (Chunky) & husband, Brett. $30PP for indoor bunkroom w/comfy mattress, pillow, shower, towel, laundry, loaner clothes, & am coffee. $45S, $75D Pvt room; or, $18PP tenting both incl the same. Gourmet b'fast $12 when 3 or more request it - incl honey & apple butter from their bees. Resupply (canister/gas/alcohol, Mountain House, pasta sides, oatmeal, etc). Pizza, pop & ice cream. Extensive VHS collection, free phone calls, and hammock chairs hanging from a Sycamore tree. Slackpacking from Marion/Partnership Shelter & Atkins often avail - call in adv. Parking $3/day. CC ok. No dogs. ID req'd.(quarterwayinn.com)

557.6 VA 42, O'LYSTERY PAVILION, (private, do not use)

🔥🏠🛏🚿⛺🏪🅿🚭📶📫 **Bear Garden Hiker Hostel** (0.05E) 248249.1951 beargardenhikerhostel@gmail.com Open yr-round. Bunkhouse sleeps up to 19: $20. Parking, c. b'fast, m'wave & fridge in bunkhouse, solar shower, privy & wringer washer w/dryer. Chapel on site. Small house -sleeps up to 6: $75

🏠🛏🚿📶📫 **Appalachian Dreamer Hiker Hostel** (2.5W) 276.682.4061 mspain7857@aol.com Call in adv from Atkins or Bland for p/u from VA 42, or walk west approximately 2.0 mi from VA 42 or VA 610 crossing to Dotson Ridge Rd. Hostel is at the top of Dotson Ridge Rd. Very poor or non existing cell phone svc at trail crossing. Working farm, no pets allowed. Dinner & b'fast provided, laundry, & WiFi. Photo ID req'd. Must sign insurance release. Under 18 must be w/parent (proof of relationship req'd). Limited resupply, shuttle to town (fee), shuttle for slackpacking when time permits. Bunk room w/6 bunks, 2 baths, & very limited tent sites w/access to basement bath. No alcohol/drugs. 2 Night max. Check website for rules. $20 Donation requested.(appalachiandreamerhikerhostel.com)

575.4 VA 623

🔥🏠🛏🚿📶📫 **Garden Mountain Hostel** (4.8W) 276.472.2150 Yr-round. Hard to find, call for shuttle. $3 One way/$5 round trip. Tenting & bunks $15-$30. Pvt rooms avail $60 (suggested donation). Kitchen use & fuel avail. Guest only mail: 1404 Banks Ridge Rd, Burkes Garden, VA 24651.

591.2 US 52, NORTH SCENIC HWY

🚐 **Bubba's Shuttles** 276.730.5869 bubbashuttleat4me@yahoo.com From Damascus to Pearisburg & Roanoke Airport. Prefer Texts.

🏠🍴 **Brushy Mountain Outpost** 276.266.0537 On the trail. Open M-F 8-6, Sa 7-2, closed Su. Deli store, sandwiches, burgers, b'fast etc. Lipton sides, tuna packs, Ramen, Jetboil fuel, denatured alcohol by the oz.

» **Bland, VA 24315** (3E to PO or Citgo, 4E to hotel & restaurants)
📫276.688.3751, M-F 8:30-11:30 & 12-4, Sa 9 -11

🔥📶📫 **Big Walker Motel** (3.7E) 276.688.3331 $66.13(1-2), $71.64(3-4), pets OK. Fridge & m'wave. Guest mail: (UPS) 70 Skyview Ln, (or USPS) PO Box 155, Bland VA 24315.

🏠🍴🏪 **Citgo, Bland Square Grill** (2.9E) 276.688.3851 Open 7 days 6:30-7 yr-round. Groceries, Canister fuel & Heet, Grill serves B/L/D.

🏪 **Grants Supermarket** (2.9E) 276.688.0314 M-Sa 8-8, Su 10-7.
🏪 **Dollar General** (3.2E) 276.688.6164 7 days 8-10.
🍴 **Subway, Dairy Queen** (3.7E)
➕ **Bland Family Clinic** (3.2E) 276.688.0500 M 10a-6p, Tu 11a-7p, W-clsd, Th 9a-5p, F 10a-2p. Must call ahead: sometimes closes early.
📚 **Bland County Library** (3E) 276.688.3737 M & F, 10a-5p; Tu-Th, 10a7p; Sa, 10a-2p. 697 Main St.

» **Bastian, VA 24314** (3W) 276.688.4631, 📫 M-F 8-12, Sa 9:15-11:15

🍴 **Pizza Plus** (3.9W) 276.688.3332 Su-Th 11a-10p, F-Sa 11a-11p.
➕ **Bland County Medical Clinic** (3.8W) 276.688.4331 M 8-6, Tu-Th 8-8, F 8-5. 12301 Grapefield Rd.
💊 **Bland Pharmacy** (3.8W) 276.688.4204 M&W-F 9a-5p, Tu 9a-8p, Sa 9a-12p, clsd Su.

Trail Etiquette

Avoid using a cell phone anywhere within the trail corridor, especially in shelters or within earshot of other hikers. Turn ringer off.

When hikers approach one another on the trail, the uphill hiker has the right-of-way, but the rule is irrelevant. If a hiker is approaching, look for an opportunity to step aside, regardless of your position. Be aware of hikers approaching from behind, and step aside so that they may pass.

Take only as much shelter space as you need to sleep. Shelter spaces cannot be reserved for friends who have yet to arrive. If you bring alcohol to a shelter or campsite, do so discreetly. Soon after dark is bedtime for most hikers.

The AT is liberating, and outlandish behavior is part of AT lore. Be considerate; boisterous and erratic behavior may be unsettling to strangers stuck in the woods with you. Conversely, hikers seeking a serene experience should be aware that AT hiking is, for many, a social experience. Be tolerant. Stay flexible; be prepared to move on rather than trying to convince others to conform to your expectations.

APPALACHIAN TRAIL
CONSERVANCY®

The ATC works with the National Park Service, 31 volunteer maintaining clubs, and multiple other partners to engage the public in conserving this essential American resource. Their website, www.AppalachianTrail.org, contains information about trail history and protection, hike planning, volunteer opportunities, and trail conditions. Please join or donate to the ATC.

Dispose of Waste Properly

▶ Pack it in; pack it out. Leave any donated items at hiker boxes in town rather than at campsites or shelters.

▶ Walk at least 100 feet (40 steps) away from shelters, water sources and campsites to dispose of urine, toothpaste, cooking water and strained dishwater, and to wash bodies, dishes or clothing. Minimize any use of soap.

▶ Use the privy only for human waste and toilet paper. Pack out disposable wipes and hygiene products.

▶ If there is no privy, walk at least 200 feet (80 steps) away from campsites, shelters, trails and water sources to bury feces in a hole 6 to 8 inches deep.

▶ Bury or carry out toilet paper.

Camping & Campfire Regulations

Camping & Campfire regulations along the A.T. change frequently. Many are addressed in The A.T. Guide. Please visit www.appalachiantrail. org/camping for comprehensive listing to familiarize yourself with camping and campfire regulations for the entire A.T.

ATC Voluntary Thru-hiker Registration

ATC's Voluntary Thru-hiker Registration helps prospective thru-hikers to choose start dates that best avoid the impacts of overcrowding. Section hikers, even though you will not register, make use of the information to avoid peak dates. ⟨http://appalachiantrail.org/home/explore-the-trail/thru-hiking⟩

Bear Interactions & Bear Canisters

Due to increasing bear/human interactions, the Appalachian Trail Conservancy strongly recommends the use of bear canisters for food storage while overnight camping along the A.T. in GA, NC, & TN. Recommended canisters: http://sierrawild.gov/bears/food-storage

Solid, non-pliable "bear canisters" are required if you camp in GA each year between Jarrard Gap & Neel Gap from March 1 to June 1.

Within the Great Smoky Mtn NP all food must be hung from cables; even food within bear canisters.

Baxter State Park Permit Requirements

Stop at Monson Visitor Center (pg. 220) to preregister for their Baxter State Park permit and get important information you'll need to know about the 100mile wilderness.

Minimize Campfire Impacts

▶ Use stoves for cooking – if you need a fire, build one only where it's legal and in an existing fire ring. Leave hatchets and saws at home – collect dead and downed wood that you can break by hand. Burn all wood to ash.

▶ Do not try to burn trash, including foil, plastic, glass, cans, tea bags, food, or anything with food on it. These items do not burn thoroughly. They create noxious fumes, attract wildlife like skunks and bears, and make the area unsightly.

▶ Where campfires are permitted, leave the fire ring clean by removing others' trash and scattering unused wood, cold coals, and ashes 200 feet away from camp after the fire is cold and completely out.

ApalachianTrail.org

1590.9	600.0	VA 611 (gravel)	37.1453,-81.0094 🅿	2820
1590.6	600.3	Stream, unreliable	◊	2679
1589.5	601.4	Brushy Mountain		3101
1587.8	603.1	**Jenny Knob Shelter** (0.1E),	) ♦ ⊏ (6)	2668
		spring 0.1 on blue blaze left of shelter 33.9◄23.2◄9.7◄►14.5►24.0►40.1		
1587.1	603.8	Stream	♦	2328
1586.8	604.1	Stream, campsite	♦ ⌂	2264
1586.6	604.3	Lickskillet Hollow, VA 608, footbridge	37.1569,-80.9614 🅿 ♦ (pg. 64)	2200
1585.4	605.5	Powerline		2771

❋ Rhododendron – 10-15 foot tall shrubs with broad waxy leaves. Grows in thick stands that the AT sometimes tunnels through. Flowers grow in large bouquets of ruffled pink.

SoBo NoBo 1000 3000 5000

1581.4	609.5	Kimberling Creek, suspension bridge, drinking discouraged	◊	2025
1581.3	609.6	VA 606, parking to east	37.1757,-80.9083 🅿 (pg. 64)	2041
		Trent's Grocery (0.5W)		
1579.5	611.4	Dismal Falls Trail, 0.3W to waterfall, camping on side trail.	♦ ⌂	2343
		Road on other side of falls sometimes brings visitors by car.		
1579.2	611.7	Stream, campsite	♦ ⌂	2273
1577.8	613.1	Footbridge		2365
1577.6	613.3	Footbridge, stream	♦	2390
1577.3	613.6	Two streams	♦	2453
1576.7	614.2	Woods road		2585
1576.2	614.7	Streams, footbridge	♦	2528
1575.8	615.1	Footbridge, stream (2)	♦	2453
1575.6	615.3	Dismal Creek, gravel road, campsite, footbridge to north	♦ ⌂	2447
1575.4	615.5	Ribble Trail 3.0W connects with AT near Big Horse Gap		2452
1574.8	616.1	Center of one-mile stretch with at least 6 stream crossings by footbridge.		2477
1574.1	616.8	Clearing, side trail to west	♦	2513
1573.9	617.0	Footbridge, stream (2)	♦	2516
1573.5	617.4	Dirt road		2580

1573.3	617.6	**Wapiti Shelter** (0.1E) 37.7◄24.2◄14.5◄►9.5►25.6►38.2 . . . . ☽♦⊏ (5)	2603
1573.1	617.8	Stream. . . . . ♦	2651
1572.7	618.2	Stream. . . . . ♦	2802
1572.0	618.9	Spring . . . . ♦	3342
1570.7	620.2	View . . . . 🔟	3896
1568.4	622.5	Side trail 0.1E to radio tower, views from ledge in front of tower . . . . 🔟	4027
1567.8	623.1	Ribble Trail west, wide grassy path, reconnects with AT south of Wapiti Shelter . .	3800
1567.7	623.2	Big Horse Gap, USFS 103⚠ Sometimes confused with Sugar Run Gap, ...	3749
		which is 1.5N. There is a short sign south of road, west of AT	
1566.5	624.4	Woods road	3485
1566.1	624.8	Sugar Run Gap, Sugar Run Rd (gravel), bear left at fork for hostel . . . . **(pg. 64)**	3395
		(small sign on tree), hostel on right. Woods Hole Hostel (0.5E)	
1564.7	626.2	View, 30 yards east. . . . . 🔟	3910
1563.9	627.0	Side trail to forest service road	3557
1563.8	627.1	**Docs Knob Shelter**, reliable spring to left of shelter . . . . ☽♦⊏ (8)	3541
		33.7◄24.0◄9.5◄►16.1►28.7►32.6	
1562.6	628.3	Spring . . . . ♦	3399
1560.8	630.1	Spring . . . . ♦	3150
1560.1	630.8	Powerline, view . . . . 🔟	3431
1558.0	632.9	View . . . . 🔟	3693
1557.9	633.0	Campsite and water (0.2W) from AT on Blue Blazed Trail. . . . . 🔟	3693
1557.4	633.5	Angels Rest 0.1W to view. . . . . 🔟	3550
1556.2	634.7	Roadbed.	2595
1555.5	635.4	Cross Ave (paved), VA 634, **Pearisburg, VA** (0.7E)	2010
1555.4	635.5	Stream with small cascade . . . . ♦	1929
1554.4	636.5	Narrows Rd Parking Area, **Narrows, VA** (3.6W) . . . . .37.3341,-80.7553 🅿 (pg. 65)	1603

604.3

Lickskillet Hollow, VA 608

🚶⚷🏠🚲➪✉ **Lickskillet Hostel** (0.8E) 276.779.5447 Church at corner of VA 608/42. Hostel owner is Mongo. Donations accepted. WiFi, laundry, & slackpacking. Daily shuttle to Bland. Not a party place. Guest Mail: 35 Price Ridge Rd, Bland, VA 24315.

609.6

VA 606

🚶⚷🏠➪✉ **Larry Richardson** 540.921.4724 Range: Bland to Pearisburg.

🚶⚷🏠➪✉ **Zero Days Inn** (5.1E) 239.285.4583 Call Jeremy for p/u from VA 606 / 608 / 611/ 615 & Hwy 52 (small fee). Bunks $25, Pvt room $35. Hiker suite w/TV & laundry $45. Slackpacking avail, full kitchen, grill, limited resupply incl fuels. WiFi/satellite TV. Laundry $4. Alcohol ok.

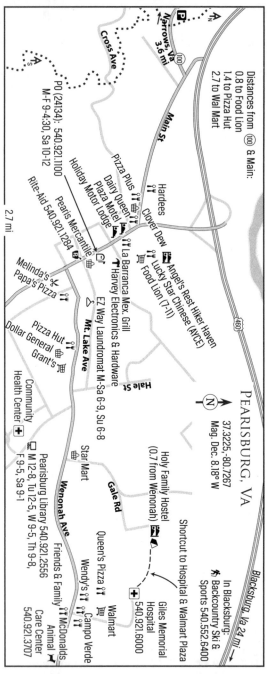

Distances from (100) & Main:
0.8 to Food Lion
1.4 to Pizza Hut
2.7 to Wal Mart

P0 (24134): 540.921.1100
M-F 9-4:30, Sa 10-12

2.7 mi

PEARISBURG, VA
37.3225, -80.7267
Mag. Dec. 8.18° W

In Blacksburg:
🎿 Backcountry Ski & Sports 540.552.6400

Blacksburg, Va 24 mi →

Narrows, Va 3.6 mi

Cross Ave

Main St

Pizza Plus 🍴
Hardees 🍴
Dairy Queen 🍴
Plaza Motel 🛏
Holiday Motor Lodge 🛏
Clover Dew 🍴
Pearis Mercantile
Rite-Aid 540.921.1284

Melinda's 🍴
Papa's Pizza 🍴
La Barranca Mex. Grill 🍴
Harvey Electronics & Hardware
Angel's Rest Hiker Haven 🛏
Lucky Star Chinese (AYCE) 🍴
Food Lion (7-11)
EZ Way Laundromat M-Sa 6-9, Su 6-8
Mt. Lake Ave

Holy Family Hostel (0.7 from Wenonah) 🛏

Shortcut to Hospital & Walmart Plaza

Giles Memorial Hospital 540.921.6000

Pizza Hut 🍴
Dollar General
Grant's
Hale St

Community Health Center ✚

Pearisburg Library 540.921.2556
M 12-8, Tu 12-5, W 9-5, Th 9-8, F 9-5, Sa 9-1

Star Mart

Gale Rd

Queen's Pizza 🍴

Wenonah Ave

Friends & Family 🍴
Care Center
Animal
540.921.3707

Campo Verde 🍴
Walmart
Wendy's 🍴
McDonalds 🍴

🚶⚷🏠🚲➪✉ **Dismal Falls Retreat** (1W) 276.928.0450 rentmygetaway@yahoo.com Cabin rental, call for rates/reservations. Turn Rt on Dismal Creek Rd, just W of Trent's Grocery. 0.5M from VA606. Kitchen, pool table, limited shuttle. (rentmygetaway.com)

🚶🏠🍴🛒➪✉ **Trent's Grocery** (0.5W) 276.928.1349 50th yr in business. Yr-round, M-Sa, 7-8. Sun, 8-8. ATM, deli w/pizza, hamburgers, hot dogs & more. Camping $6 (hammocking avail), shower $3, laundry $3. Coleman/alcohol/oz & canister fuel. CC ok. Soda machines outside. Shuttles (276.613.443]). Mail: 900 Wilderness Rd, Bland, VA 24315. (fb.com/TrentsGrocery)

624.8

Sugar Run Gap, Sugar Run Rd (gravel)

🚶⚷🏠🍴🛏➪✉ **Woods Hole Hostel & B&B** (0.4E) 540.921.3444 Isolated 1880's chestnut-log cabin discovered by Roy & Tillie Wood in 1940. One of the oldest hostels on trail - opened in 1986. Granddaughter, Neville & Michael, continue legacy w/emphasis on organic gardening, yoga(free), & massage therapy. Heated bunkhouse $20. Camping

NARROWS, VA

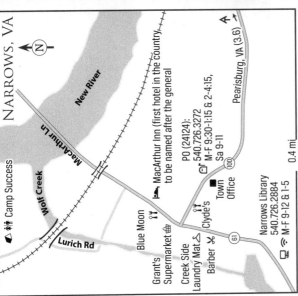

N

New River

MacArthur Ln

Wolf Creek

Camp Success

Lurich Rd

🛏 MacArthur Inn (first hotel in the country, to be named after the general

PO (24124):
📞 540.726.3272
M-F 9:30-1:15 & 2-4:15,
Sa 9-11

100

Pearisburg, VA (3.6)

0.4 mi

Blue Moon

Grant's Supermarket 🏛

Creek Side Laundry Mat
Barber

Clyde's

Town Office

61

Narrows Library
540.726.2884
M-F 9-12 & 1-5

(non-guest) $8. On site restaurant serves b'fast Th- Su, Dinner Th 5p-8p. Mtn Music 1am 6:30-9p. Mail: 117 MacArthur Ln, Narrows, VA 24124.

⛺ Camp Success (4.7W) 540.726.2423 Camping $5 tent/ night, no showers. Check-in at Town Office 540.726.3020 M-F, 9-5. Call ahead for after-hrs arrivals or print permit from website for dropbox.⟨townofnarrows.org⟩

🛒 Grants Supermarket (3.7W) 540.726.2303 M-Sa 8-9, Sun 9-8.

🍺 Right Turn Clyde Brewing Co. (3.6W) 540.921.7283 Th-Fr 6-10; Sa 3-10.

$12PP. Pets ok. Indoor rooms: $30PP. Shared/$60. Pvt (500miles+). $90 Reg rate. Farm fresh b'fast, $10. Laundry, fuel/fuel canisters, shuttles/slackpack. Closed Wed. Call to inquire. Guest Mail: 3696 Sugar Run Rd, Pearisburg, VA 24134. ⟨woodsholehostel.com⟩

636.5 NARROWS RD PARKING AREA

🚗 Don Raines 540.921.7433 ratface20724@aol.com Anytime/place. Slackpacking avail

🚗 Tom Hoffman 540.921.1184 gopullman@aol.com Mid-range shuttles centered in Pearisburg. Can be flexible.

» *Pearisburg, VA 24134 (1E on US 100)*

🏨 Holiday Motor Lodge (1.1E) 540.921.1552 Yr-round lodge. Hostel open May 1-Sep 15. Prices incl tax: $20 bunkroom w/TV, pets free. Rooms $50. $10 Pet fee. Pool. Mail: 401 N Main St, Pearisburg, VA 24134.

🏨 Plaza Motel (1.1E) 540.921.2591 $44S $55D incl tax, no pets, CC ok. Mail: 415 N. Main St, Pearisburg, VA 24134.

🏨 Angel's Rest Hiker Haven (1.5E) 540.787.4076 Open yr-round. Bunks $25, pvt rooms $35-$55, tent/hammock $12PP. Cabin tents w/air mattress avail for groups. Laundry $4 (non-guest laundry & shower $5). WiFi, Cable, Roku, & DVD. Pets $5. Military Disc. Reduced rate for Acupuncture, tattoo, & massage. Cash/CC ok. WFS when avail. Mail: 204 Douglas Ln, Pearisburg, VA 24134.⟨angelsresthikershaven.com⟩

🏨 Holy Family Hostel (2.8E) 540.626.3337 Volunteer caretaker, Patrick Muldoon. Please do NOT call for a ride. Check-in directions posted. Suggested donation $10PP, 2 night max. Open Mar-Nov; otherwise call. Hot shower, fridge, & grill. Keep hostel clean & noise down (church in residential area). Well behaved pets. No drugs/alcohol.

🛒 Pearis Mercantile (1.3E) 540.921.2260 M-Sa 10a-5:30p Hiker friendly, trail foods, packs, tents, gear, fuel/oz, tyvek, etc...

➕ Community Health Center (1.9E) 540.921.3502 M-F 8-4:30 Quick, low-cost healthcare, hikers welcome.

🔧 Harvey Electronics & Hardware (1.2E) 540.921.1456 M-F 9-5, Sa 10-4. Cell phones & supplies, canister fuel, alcohol/oz, tent repair kits.

» *Narrows, VA 24124 (3.6W on VA 100)*

🏨 MacArthur Inn (3.7W) 540.726.7510: Allen Neely. Hiker rooms $45 (sleeps 4), other rooms avail. Call for ride from Pearisburg area trailheads $5 round trip. Longer shuttles & slackpacking by arrangement. Free long distance phone, cable TV & WiFi, & use of kitchen. In center of town, all svcs in walking distance. Shower

| 1553.8 | **637.1** | US 460, Senator Shumate Bridge, New River, Circle under north end of bridge. . . | 1589 |
| 1552.8 | **638.1** | Landfill Rd (dirt), don't drink from stream . . . . | 1587 |

> ❋ Fire Pink - Scarlet-colored flower with five snake-tongued petals.

1550.3	**640.6**	Cross Clendennin Rd (VA 641), follow Pocahontas Rd for 0.1mi	2190
1549.5	**641.4**	Powerline	2637
1549.3	**641.6**	Dirt road, Stream . . . . ♦	2685
1548.3	**642.6**	Piped spring (can go dry in late summer). . . . . ◊	3157
1547.7	**643.2**	**Rice Field Shelter** (0.1E) 40.1◄25.6◄16.1◄►12.6►16.5►25.3 . . . . ☽ ⊏ (7)	3375
		Stiles south & north. Unreliable water to left behind shelter 0.3 mile down hill.	
1547.1	**643.8**	Cell tower	3368
1546.6	**644.3**	Powerline, view . . . . ▣	3435
1546.1	**644.8**	Campsite west, water to east . . . . ♦ ⛺	3300

SoBo   NoBo   1000   3000   5000

1542.6	**648.3**	Symms Gap, campsite to west. . . . . ⛺	3320
1541.6	**649.3**	Groundhog Trail to west	3421
1540.8	**650.1**	Campsite . . . . ⛺	3388
1540.0	**650.9**	Dickenson Gap	3300
1537.6	**653.3**	Allegheny Trail to west	3726
1535.7	**655.2**	Streams . . . . ◊	2964
1535.1	**655.8**	**Pine Swamp Branch Shelter** 38.2◄28.7◄12.6◄►3.9►12.7►18.5 . . . ☽♦ ⊏ (8)	2532
		TEMPORARILY CLOSED in 2017 (overhead hazzards)	
1534.8	**656.1**	Stony Creek Valley, 0.1E to parking on VA 635. . . . . 37.4191,-80.6046 🅿	2381
1534.3	**656.6**	Stream. . . . . ♦	2400

1533.7	**657.2**	Footbridge, stream	⬥ 2435
1532.7	**658.2**	Bridge over Stony Creek, VA 635, don't drink water from creek	2450
1531.7	**659.2**	Gravel road	3121
1531.4	**659.5**	Spring 100 yards east	⬥ 3362
1531.2	**659.7**	**Bailey Gap Shelter** 32.6◄16.5◄3.9◄►8.8►14.6►21.0 . . . . . ☽⬥⊏ (6)	3510
		Water 0.2S on AT, then east down blue-blazed trail.	
1530.2	**660.7**	Spring	⬥ 3721
1528.6	**662.3**	Spring	△ 3760
1527.5	**663.4**	VA 613 (gravel), Mountain Lake Rd	3950
1527.3	**663.6**	Wind Rock, view, campsite. . . . . 📷 ◭	4100
1526.5	**664.4**	Woods road	4054
1524.9	**666.0**	Lone Pine Peak	4026
1524.4	**666.5**	War Branch Trail to east	3507
1524.0	**666.9**	Spring	⬥ 3267
1522.4	**668.5**	**War Spur Shelter**, spring north on AT . . . . ☽⬥⊏ (6)	2361
		25.3◄12.7◄8.8◄►5.8►12.2►18.2	
1521.6	**669.3**	VA 632, cross Johns Creek on footbridge	⬥ 2080
1521.5	**669.4**	Footbridge, stream, campsite	⬥◭ 2058
1520.5	**670.4**	Spring	⬥ 2627
1519.6	**671.3**	Rocky Gap, VA 601 (gravel)	3264
1519.0	**671.9**	Johns Creek Mountain Trail to west	3782
1517.8	**673.1**	Kelly Knob, view. 📷	3730
1516.6	**674.3**	**Laurel Creek Shelter** 18.5◄14.6◄5.8◄►6.4►12.4►22.5 . . . . ☽⬥⊏ (6)	2798
		Water 60 yards north of shelter junction and west of AT.	
1516.4	**674.5**	Stream.	⬥ 2753
1516.0	**674.9**	Piney Ridge	2614
1514.5	**676.4**	Pasture, several fence stiles	2227
1514.1	**676.8**	Footbridge, Sinking Creek, VA 42, **Newport, VA** (8.0E) . . . . (pg. 72)	2097
		"Trail east" is compass west (NoBo right, SoBo left to town).	

1513.3	677.6	VA 630 (paved), chimney, and footbridge close together . . . . ♦	2145
1512.9	678.0	Keffer Oak, largest oak tree on AT in south, over 18′ around, over 300 yrs old . . .	2322
		Dover Oak along AT in NY is slightly larger.	
1512.5	678.4	Powerline	2526
1511.1	679.8	Powerline	3223
1510.4	680.5	Bruisers Knob	3417
1510.2	680.7	**Sarver Hollow Shelter** (0.4E) (2002) . . . . ☽ ♦ ⊏ (6)	3402
		21.0◀12.2◀6.4◀▶6.0▶16.1▶29.7	
1508.3	682.6	View . . . . 📷	3381
1508.0	682.9	View . . . . 📷	3354
1506.9	684.0	North end of ridge crest on Sinking Creek Mountain, ...	3368
		Eastern Continental Divide West is old route of AT leading 2.5 miles to Old Hall Rd.	
1505.3	685.6	Stream. . . . . ◊	2703
1504.2	686.7	**Niday Shelter**, water on opposite side of AT . . . . ⌐ ☽ ♦ ◖ ⊏ (6)	1988
		18.2◀12.4◀6.0◀▶10.1▶23.7▶24.7	
1502.8	688.1	VA 621, Craig Creek Rd . . . . 37.3793,-80.25 🅿	1547
1502.3	688.6	Many footbridges crossing Craig Creek and feeder streams. . . . . ♦	1583
		within a mile north of road.	
1499.8	691.1	Bench at southern crest of Brush Mountain	2988
1499.1	691.8	Audie Murphy Monument.	3100
		Murphy was most decorated American soldier of World War II.	
		Monument on blue-blazed trail to west.	
1495.3	695.6	Footbridge, Trout Creek , VA 620 (gravel) . . . . ♦	1548
1494.9	696.0	Powerline	1749
1494.1	696.8	**Pickle Branch Shelter** (0.3E) . . . . ☽ ♦ ◖ ⊏ (6)	1951
		22.5◀16.1◀10.1◀▶13.6▶14.6▶17.0 Tenting along trail to shelter.	
		Water on steep trail 0.2 mile downhill from shelter.	

| 1493.1 | **697.8** View . . . . 📷 | 2392 |

1490.2	**700.7** View . . . . 📷	2963
1489.9	**701.0** Cove Mountain . . . . 📷	3020
	Trail 0.1E to Dragons Tooth (stone monolith), views.	

1489.1	**701.8** Lost Spectacles Gap	2520
1488.7	**702.2** Rawies Rest, view . . . . 📷	2482
1488.5	**702.4** View . . . . 📷	2307

| 1487.8 | **703.1** Scout Trail west to Dragons Tooth Parking . . . . 🅿 | 2039 |
| 1487.4 | **703.5** VA 624, Newport Rd . . . . **(pg. 72)** | 1810 |

| 1486.6 | **704.3** Footbridge taken out by flood. Must ford stream or rock hop . . . . | 1816 |

1486.1	**704.8** Fence stile	1842
1485.8	**705.1** VA 785, Blacksburg Rd	1790
1485.5	**705.4** Footbridge, Catawba Creek, fence stile, treat water . . . . ⬥	1770

> ⚠ The AT is mostly on National Park Service Land from Newport Rd to Mtn Pass Rd (roughly from Catawba through Troutville). Camping permitted only in designated locations (at the shelters, Lamberts Meadow Campsite and the Pig Farm Campsite).

1481.5	**709.4** VA 311, **Catawba, VA** (1.0W) . . . . 37.3801,-80.0898 🅿 **(pg. 72)**	1990
	2 porta potties in parking lot	
1480.9	**710.0** Footbridge	2030
1480.5	**710.4** **Johns Spring Shelter** (2003) 29.7◀23.7◀13.6◀▶1.0▶3.4▶9.4 . . 🌙 ⬥ 🍂 ⌐ (6)	1957
	Unreliable spring 25 yrds left front of shelter.	
1480.1	**710.8** Footbridge	2110
1479.5	**711.4** **Catawba Mountain Shelter** (1984) Camping to north . . . . . . 🌙 ⬥ 🍂 ⌐ (6)	2203
	24.7◀14.6◀1.0◀▶2.4▶8.4▶22.8	
	Blue-blaze to water 100 yards from front of shelter.	

1477.8	**713.1** McAfee Knob; excellent views, no camping . . . . 📷	3197
1477.3	**713.6** Powerline	2781
1477.2	**713.7** Water to east, Pig Farm campsite, same water source as shelter . . . . ⬥ 🍂	2682
1477.1	**713.8** **Campbell Shelter** (1989), water 150 yards to left of shelter . . . . . 🌙⬥ 🍂 ⌐ (6)	2636
	17.0◀3.4◀2.4◀▶6.0▶20.4▶26.6	

| 1474.0 | **716.9** Brickeys Gap, Lamberts Meadow Trail to east . . . . | 2194 |

1472.2	**718.7**	Tinker Cliffs, 0.5 mile cliff walk, views back to McAfee Knob. . . . . 📷	3000
1471.7	**719.2**	Scorched Earth Gap, Andy Layne Trail to west	2600
1471.1	**719.8**	**Lamberts Meadow Shelter** 9.4◄8.4◄6.0◄►14.4►20.6►27.9 . . . ☽◊◑⊏(6)	2126
1470.8	**720.1**	Lamberts Meadow Campsite, Sawmill Run . . . . ◊◑	2000
		Footbridge, stream. North of footbridge an east trail rejoins AT at Brickeys Gap.	
1468.6	**722.3**	Blue-blazed trail west to view . . . . 📷	2217
1466.7	**724.2**	Angels Gap	1692
1466.4	**724.5**	Powerline	1840
1465.7	**725.2**	Hay Rock, view . . . . 📷	1955
1464.5	**726.4**	Powerline, view . . . . 📷	1920
1463.7	**727.2**	Powerline	1959
1462.9	**728.0**	Powerline	1386
1462.3	**728.6**	Powerline, railroad tracks, bridge	1165
1461.7	**729.2**	US 220, **Daleville, VA**. . . . . (pg. 72)	1253
1460.5	**730.4**	I-81, trail passes under on VA 779	1400
1460.2	**730.7**	US 11, RR tracks, **Troutville, VA** (0.8W). . . . . . . 37.4045,-79.8895 🅿 (pg. 72)	1300
1459.9	**731.0**	Fence stile	1497
1459.7	**731.2**	VA 652, Mountain Pass Rd	1450
1459.4	**731.5**	Fence	1521
1456.7	**734.2**	**Fullhardt Knob Shelter** (0.1E) . . . . ☽◊◑⊏(6)	2632
		22.8◄20.4◄14.4◄►6.2►13.5►20.0 Water source can run dry if no recent rainfall. Treat water from cistern.	

1453.9	**737.0**	Salt Pond Rd, USFS 191	2248
1453.1	**737.8**	Curry Creek, Curry Creek Trail to west . . . . ♦	1572
1452.3	**738.6**	Stream. . . . . ♦	1670
1451.0	**739.9**	Wilson Creek, Colliers Pit historical marker to north . . . . ♦	1549
1450.5	**740.4**	**Wilson Creek Shelter** 26.6◄20.6◄6.2◄►7.3►13.8►20.8 . . . . . ☽♦◖⊂ (6)	1854
		Reliable stream 0.3 mile downhill in front of shelter.	
1450.0	**740.9**	Spring . . . . ♦	2000
1448.1	**742.8**	Blackhorse Gap, dirt road, Blue Ridge Parkway (BRP) mile 97.7 to east	2404
1447.4	**743.5**	BRP 97.0, Taylors Mountain Overlook . . . . ▣	2350
1445.6	**745.3**	BRP 95.3, Harveys Knob Overlook . . . . ⟴ ⎕ ▣	2527
1443.9	**747.0**	Hammond Hollow Trail to west	2327
1443.2	**747.7**	**Bobblets Gap Shelter** (0.2W) 27.9◄13.5◄7.3◄►6.5►13.5►18.4 . . . . ☽♦⊂ (6)	2086
		If spring to left of shelter dry, look farther downstream.	
1442.4	**748.5**	BRP 92.5, Peaks of Otter Overlook . . . . ▣	2341
1441.8	**749.1**	BRP 91.8, Mills Gap Overlook . . . . ⎕ ▣	2450
1440.1	**750.8**	Bearwallow Gap, footbridge, stream, VA 43, 0.2E to BRP 90.9 . . . . . . ◊ **(pg. 76)**	2228
		Buchanan, VA (5.0W)	
1438.5	**752.4**	Cove Mountain	2720
1438.1	**752.8**	Little Cove Mountain Trail to east	2517
1436.7	**754.2**	**Cove Mountain Shelter** 20.0◄13.8◄6.5◄►7.0►11.9►17.2 . . . . . . ☽◖⊂ (6)	1942
1436.5	**754.4**	View . . . . ▣	1970
1435.0	**755.9**	Buchanan Trail	1790

676.8   VA 42, SINKING CREEK, "Trail E" here is compass W

Sublett Place (1.6W) 540.544.3099 Home & cottage for rent, prices seasonal. Ask for hiker rate.⟨thesublettplace.com⟩

Joe's Trees (1.6W) 540.544.7303 Limited summer/fall hrs (call ahead). 7 Days Nov 18-Dec 17. Closed Dec 18 thru Apr. Drinks, jerky, cheese, jams.⟨joestrees.com⟩

» **Newport, VA 24128 (8E)**
☎540.544.7415, M-F 8:15-11:30 & 12:30-3:15, Sa 9-11
Grocery store & PO near intersection of 42 & 460.

Super Val-U (7.6E) 540.544.7702 Su-Th 5:30-10, F-Sa cls 10:30

703.5   VA 624, NEWPORT RD

Four Pines Hostel (0.4E) 540.309.8615 bifmitch@gmail.com Owner, Joe Mitchell. Yr-round hostel is a 3-bay garage w/shower. Please leave donation. Laundry $3 wash/$3 dry. Pet friendly. Shuttles to/from The Homeplace Restaurant (Th-Su) & to Catawba Grocery. Longer shuttles for fee. Mail: 6164 Newport Rd, Catawba VA 24070.

Catawba Grocery (0.4W) 540.384.8050 West 0.3 mile to VA 311 & then left 0.1 mile to store, 7 days/wk 6a-10p, Grill M-F 5a-8p, Sa Su 6a-8:30p, serves b'fast, pizza, burgers, ice cream.

709.4   VA 311

» **Catawba, VA 24070 (1W)**
☎540.384.6011, M-F 9-12, 1-4, Sa 8-10:30

Homeplace Restaurant (1.3W) 540.384.7252 Th-F 4-8, Sa 3-8, Su 11-6, Popular AYCE family-style meals including drink & tax; $15 (two meats) $16 (three meats), $9 (kids 3-11).

729.2   US 220

» **Daleville, VA 24083** (2.4W) West of the A.T.

Outdoor Trails (0.3W) 540.992.5850 Full svc outfitter. White gas & denatured alcohol/oz. Computer for internet use, shuttle service. Open M-F 9-8, Sat 9-6 during hiking season (Apr 25-Jul 2); open M-F 10-8, Sat 10-6 the rest of the year. Mail (commercial pkgs $2): Botetourt Commons, 28 Kingston Dr, Daleville, VA 24083.

Kroger Grocery Store and Pharmacy (0.4W) 540.992.4920 24hr, pharmacy M-F 9-9, Sa 9-7, Su 10-6.

» **Daleville, VA 24083** East of the A.T.

Three Li'l Pigs BBQ (0.3W) 540.966.0165 Open yr-round, extended summer hrs M-Th 11a-9p, Sa 11a-10:30p, Su 11a-9p. Hiker friendly, hand-chopped BBQ ribs & wings, large selection of beer, some locally-brewed. Thru-hikers get free banana pudding dessert (w/meal purchase) Mid-Apr - Jun 1.

Super 8 (0.1E) 540.992.3000 $59.36 + tax, c. b'fast, pool, CC ok, no pets.

Howard Johnson Express (0.2E) 540.992.1234 $49.95 Hiker rate, c. b'fast, game room & pool. Pets $10. Guest mail: 437 Roanoke Rd, Daleville, VA 24083.

Comfort Inn (0.8E) 540.992.5600 Hiker rate $55D+$10EAP, c. b'fast, pets $25

Motel 6 (0.8E) 540.992.6700 $40.99D + $6EAP, pets ok (no fee).

Holiday Inn Express (0.9E) 540.966.4444 Seasonal - Ask for Hiker rate, no pets. Mail: 3200 Lee Hwy, Troutville, VA 24175.

Quality Inn (0.9E) 540.992.5335 Hikers $62D/up + tax, full hot b'fast, pets $15.

Red Roof Inn (0.9E) 540.992.5055

Gander Mountain (4.8E) 8195 Gander Way. Will re-open spring 2018. New ownership.

» **Roanoke, VA (11.3E)** A large city w/airport approx 11.3 mi from the A.T.

Duck 'n Hut Hikers Hostel (18.3E) 540.819.2164 ducknhuthikershostel@gmail.com Donation based hostel. Open yr-round. Shuttle range: Mouth of Wise, VA - Tyro, VA. Dogs welcome! $1/mi + gas for long distance p/u.

Walkabout Outfitter (9.5E) 540.777.0990 valleyview@walkaboutoutfitter.com M-Sa 10-8, Su 12-6 & (10.3E) 540.777.2727 roanoke@walkaboutoutfitter.com M-Sa 10-5:50, Su 10-4.⟨walkaboutoutfitter.com⟩

Sportsman's Warehouse (10E) 540.366.9700 3550 Ferncliff Ave NW. Full svc outfitter w/full line of gear incl fuel, frz dried foods, boots, clothes & trekking poles.

730.7   US 11

Homer Witcher 540.266.4849 Trail maintainer & 2002 thru hiker.

» **Troutville, VA 24175** (0.8W) **Troutville Trail Days** Jun 1-3, 2018 at Town Park. Free hiker dinner, gear repair, live music, food, vendors, & 5k race.
(services cont'd on pg. 76...)

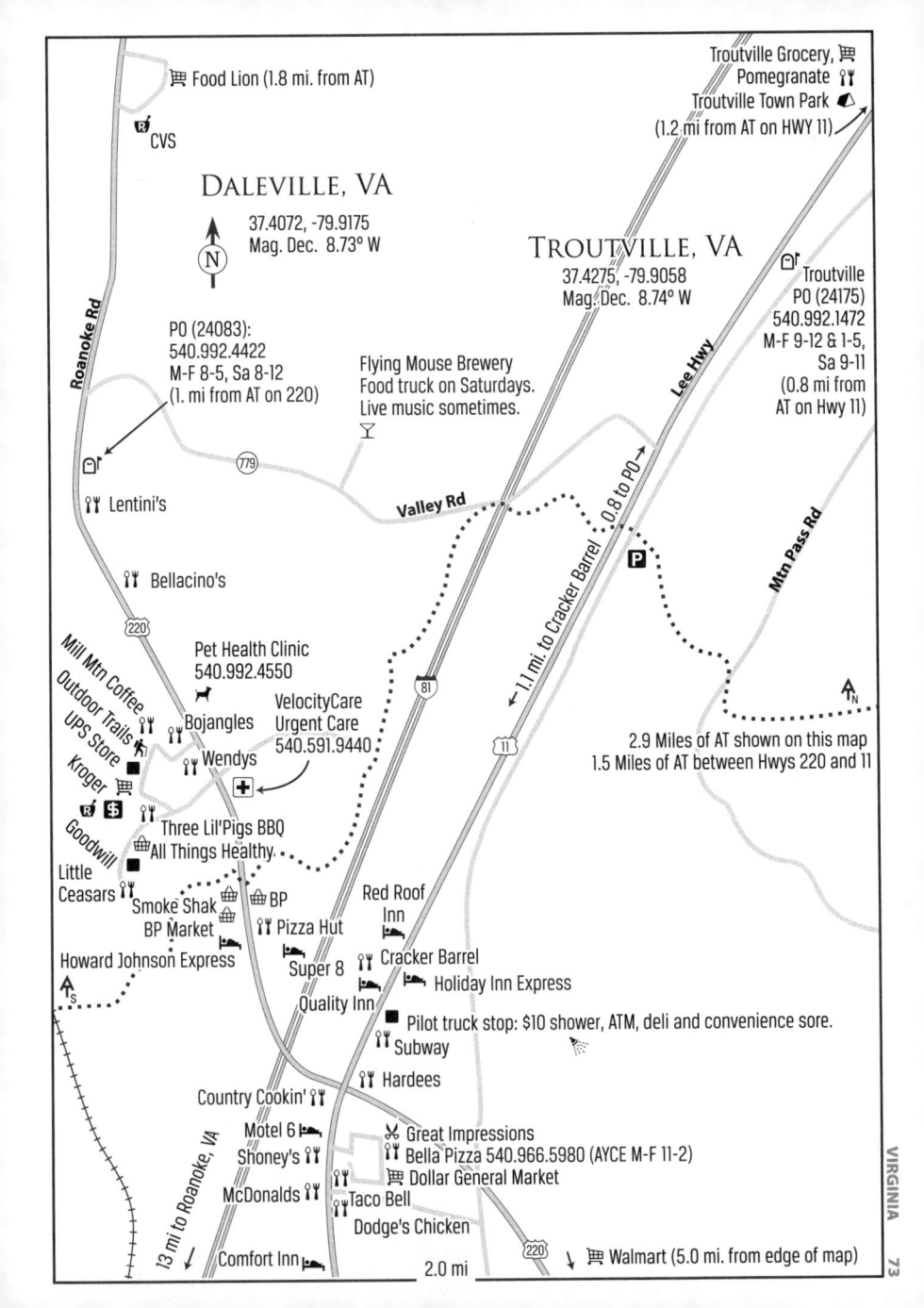

1433.5　757.4　Cross Jennings Creek on VA 614 bridge . . . . .37.5291,-79.6225 **P** ♦ (pg. 76)　951
　　　　　　　Swimming hole, campsites. **Buchanan, VA** (5.0W)
　　　　　　　⚠ Bearing of NoBo AT in this area is more south than north.

1431.9　759.0　Fork Mountain. . . . .　2042

1430.7　760.2　Stream south of powerline. . . . . ♦　1239
1430.4　760.5　Stream. . . . . ♦　1271
1430.0　760.9　Stream. . . . . ♦　1192
1429.7　761.2　**Bryant Ridge Shelter.** . . . .) ♦ ⊏ (20)　1277
　　　　　　　20.8◀13.5◀7.0◀▶4.9▶10.2▶22.6　Stream on trail to shelter.
　　　　　　　Blue-blazed trail 0.1N of shelter leads 0.5E to VA 714.

1426.6　764.3　Campsite, 0.1W to spring (signed). . . . . △ ◭　2937

1425.4　765.5　Floyd Mountain . . . .　3560
1424.8　766.1　**Cornelius Creek Shelter** (0.1E). . . . .) ♦ ◭ ⊏ (6)　3114
　　　　　　　18.4◀11.9◀4.9◀▶5.3▶17.7▶21.6 Water on trail to shelter. Privy behind shelter.
1424.5　766.4　Stream. . . . . ♦　3027
1423.9　767.0　Black Rock Overlook, view 200' west . . . . 📷　3450
1423.6　767.3　Footbridge, stream . . . . ♦　3306
1423.3　767.6　Intersection with Cornelius Creek Trail . . . .　3224

1422.2　768.7　Apple Orchard Falls Trail 1.1W to 200' waterfall, 0.1E to Sunset Field, ...　3351
　　　　　　　USFS 812 (Parkers Gap Rd) 0.1N on AT.

1420.7　770.2　Apple Orchard Mountain, Federal Aviation Admin (FAA) tower, views . . . . . . 📷　4225
1420.4　770.5　The Guillotine. . . . .　4005

1419.8　771.1　BRP 76.3. . . . .　3900
1419.5　771.4　**Thunder Hill Shelter** 17.2◀10.2◀5.3◀▶12.4▶16.3▶25.1. . . . . .) △ ◭ ⊏ (6)　3917
　　　　　　　Poor water source, tentsites north of shelter

1418.5　772.4　Hunting Creek Trail, BRP 74.9. . . . .　3594
1418.1　772.8　0.1E to BRP 74.7 Thunder Ridge Overlook . . . . 📷 🗑　3501

1416.3　774.6　Harrison Ground Spring . . . . ♦ ◭　3307

1415.7　775.2　Spring . . . . ♦　2908

1414.8　776.1　Petites Gap, gravel road, BRP 71.0 to east. . . . .　2369

| 1413.6 | **777.3** | Highcock Knob, ... | 3064 |

| 1412.6 | **778.3** | Marble Spring, campsite, spring 100 yards west . . . . ◗ ⬢ | 2349 |
| 1412.1 | **778.8** | Sulphur Spring Trail south crossing . . . . | 2456 |

> .ıll (NoBo) Poor cell reception at US 501, consider calling ahead if you need ride.

1410.3	**780.6**	Gunter Ridge Trail, Hickory Stand	2650
1409.8	**781.1**	Sulphur Spring Trail north crossing	2588
1409.0	**781.9**	Big Cove Branch, stream . . . . ◗	1890

1407.1	**783.8**	**Matts Creek Shelter**, Matts Creek Trail 2.5E to US 501 . . . . ◗ ◗ ⊏ (6)	848
		Ford knee deep Matts Creek to get to shelter 22.6◀17.7◀12.4◀▶3.9▶12.7▶22.2	
1406.3	**784.6**	AT parallels James River from here north for 1.0 mile, no camping	695

1405.1	**785.8**	James River footbridge, longest foot-use-only bridge on AT	678
1404.9	**786.0**	US 501, VA 130, **Big Island VA** (5.6E), **Glasgow VA** (5.9W) . . . . . . ▣ (pg. 77)	680
1404.7	**786.2**	Lower Rocky Row Run Bridge, stream . . . . ◗	679
1403.8	**787.1**	VA 812, USFS 36 (gravel) . . . . 37.6048, -79.3883 ▣	801
1403.4	**787.5**	Stream. . . . . ◗	919
1403.2	**787.7**	**Johns Hollow Shelter** . . . . ◗ ◗ ⬢ ⊏ (6)	1021
		23.9◀18.3◀3.9◀▶8.8▶18.3▶23.9 Springs to left and right of shelter.	

| 1401.2 | **789.7** | Little Rocky Row Trail to west, view just north on AT . . . . 📷 | 2416 |

| 1400.1 | **790.8** | Big Rocky Row, view . . . . 📷 | 2992 |

| 1398.6 | **792.3** | Saddle Gap, Saddle Gap Trail. . . . . | 2600 |

| 1397.5 | **793.4** | Saltlog Gap, Saltlog Gap Trail . . . . ◗ (0.5W) | 2573 |

| 1396.0 | **794.9** | Bluff Mountain, Ottie Cline Powell monument, views . . . . 📷 | 3372 |

1394.9	**796.0**	Punchbowl Mountain.	2850
1394.4	**796.5**	**Punchbowl Shelter** (0.2W), spring front left of shelter . . . . . ◗ ◗ ⬢ ⊏ (6)	2487
		25.1◀12.7◀8.8◀▶9.5▶15.1▶25.3	

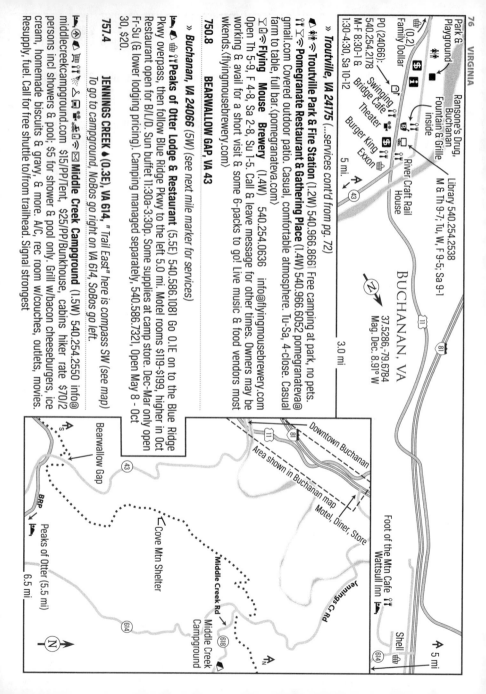

» **Troutville, VA 24175** (...services cont'd from pg. 72)

△ ⛺ ⛲ ⊛ **Troutville Park & Fire Station** (1.2W) 540.966.8661 Free camping at park, no pets.

⛲ ¶ ⚥ ⊛ **Pomegranate Restaurant & Gathering Place** (1.4W) 540.966.6052 pomegranateva@gmail.com Covered outdoor patio, Casual, comfortable atmosphere. Tu-Sa, 4-close. Casual farm to table, full bar.(pomegranateva.com)

⊠ ⬛ ⊛ **Flying Mouse Brewery** (1.4W) 540.254.0636 info@flyingmousebrewery.com Open Th 5-9, F 4-8, Sa 2-8, Su 1-5. Call & leave message for other times. Owners may be working & avail for a short visit & some 6-packs to go! Live music & food vendors most wkends.(flyingmousebrewery.com)

750.8   BEARWALLOW GAP, VA 43

» **Buchanan, VA 24066** (5W) (see next mile marker for services)

To go to campground, NoBos go right on VA 614, SoBos go left.

🏍 △ ⛺ ¶ ⚥ **Peaks of Otter Lodge & Restaurant** (5.5E) 540.586.1081 Go 0.1E on to the Blue Ridge Pkwy overpass, then follow Blue Ridge Pkwy to the left 5.0 mi. Motel rooms $119-$199, higher in Oct Restaurant open for B/L/D. Sun buffet 11:30a-3:30p. Some supplies at camp store. Dec-Mar only open Fr-Su (& lower lodging pricing). Camping managed separately, 540.586.7321, Open May 8 - Oct 30, $20.

757.4   JENNINGS CREEK ♦ (0.3E), VA 614. *"Trail East" here is compass SW (see map)*

🏍 🄰 🍴 🛒 ⛺ △ ⛲ 🚿 ⬛ ⊛ **Middle Creek Campground** (1.5W) 540.254.2550 info@middlecreekcampground.com $15/PP/Tent, $25/PP/Bunkhouse, cabins hiker rate $70/2 persons incl showers & pool; $5 for shower & pool only. Grill w/bacon cheeseburgers, ice cream, homemade biscuits & gravy, & more. A/C, rec room w/couches, outlets, movies. Resupply, fuel. Call for free shuttle to/from trailhead. Signal strongest

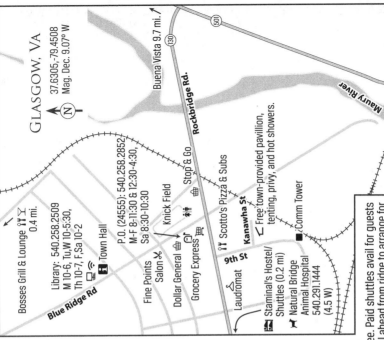

GLASGOW, VA

37.6305,-79.4508
Mag. Dec. 9.07° W

N

Blue Ridge Rd

Bosses Grill & Lounge ⛺🍴🏕
0.4 mi.

Library: 540.258.2509
M 10-6, Tu,W 10-5:30,
Th 10-7, F,Sa 10-2
🛏📶 🏛 Town Hall

Rockbridge Rd.

Buena Vista 9.7 mi.

↑ 5 mi.

Maury River

P.O. (24555): 540.258.2852
M-F 8-11:30 & 12:30-4:30,
Sa 8:30-10:30

Knick Field

Fine Points
Salon ✂

Stop & Go

Dollar General ⛪

🍴 Scotto's Pizza & Subs

Grocery Express 🏪 🚻

9th St

Kanawha St

Laundromat 🏧

Stanimal's Hostel/
Shuttles (0.2 mi)

✈ Natural Bridge
Animal Hospital
540.291.1444
(4.5 W)

Comm Tower

⌐ Free town-provided pavillion,
tenting, privy, and hot showers.

0.9 mi

---

near NoBo parking area. Night regist avail. If you'd rather walk, go trail east on 614 for 0.2 mi, then left 1 mile on 618. Guest Mail: 1164 Middle Creek Rd, Buchanan, VA 24066.(middlecreekcampground.com)

» *Buchanan, VA 24066 (5W on VA 614)/(I-81 exit 168)*

🛏⛺🍴♿📶 **Wattstull Inn** (4.8W) 540.254.1551 Hiker rates starting $65+tax. Pets $15. C. b'fast, pool. Ask about shuttles. 🍴**Foot of the Mtn Cafe** on-site, serving L/D.

786.0   US 501, VA 130

🚐 **Ken Wallace** 434.609.2704 Range: Buchanan- Waynesboro.

🚐 **Stanimal's Shuttle Service** 540.290.4002 Covers all of VA.

🚐 **Gary Serra** 757.681.2254 garydhiker@gmail.com Gary has completed the AT twice in sections & is familiar w/all trail heads. P/U at Glasgow & Buena Vista trail heads. Roanoke, Lynchburg & Charlottesville airports, & Amtrak station. Long distance ok incl Washington DC or further. Sells fuel canisters.

» *Big Island, VA 24526 (5.6E), ⛪434.299.5072, M-F 8:15-12, 1-4, Sa 8-10*

⛪🍴✉ **H&H Food Market** (4.9E) 434.299.5153 7 days 5:30-9, B/L/D served 6:30-8, Mail: 11619 Lee Jackson Hwy, Big Island, VA 24526.

✚ **Big Island Family Medical Center** (5.5E) 434.299.5951 M-Tu & Th-F 8:30-5. Clsd Sa-Su.

» *Glasgow, VA 24555 (5.9W)*

🏛 **Town Hall** (6.3W) 540.258.2246 Maintains shelter & Knick Field restrooms. 🛏⛺🍴♿🚿🧺🏧📶🍳🚐 **Stanimal's 328 Hostel & Shuttle Service** (6.5W) 540.480.8325 adamStanley06@gmail.com Free guest p/u & ret from 501 James River trailhead, WiFi, free laundry services, shower, clean linens & bunks w/mattresses. Property is ultra clean & features 55" flat screen w/ Netflix. Pizza, drinks & ice cream + snacks avail for purchase at reasonable prices. Caretaker provides b'fast for $6 & dinner for $10. Full house avail to hikers + kitchen privileges. $30/night plus pvt room options avail for add'l fee. Paid shuttles avail for guests & non-guests at lowest rates. No cell service at 501 trailhead. Guests can call ahead from ridge to arrange for p/u at 501. Owned & operated by Adam Stanley "STANIMAL" AT '04 PCT '10. (stanimals328.com)

» *Glasgow, VA (services cont'd on pg. 80...)*

1394.0	796.9	BRP 51.7 Punchbowl Mtn Overlook, water north of road. 37.6738,-79.3347 🅿 🚮 ♦	2170
		⚠ SoBo hikers must go right & uphill a few yards to find AT on other side.	
1393.7	797.2	VA 607, Robinson Gap Rd (gravel), **Buena Vista, VA** (6.0W) . . 37.6761,-79.332 🅿	2100

> ▁▍ (SoBo) Poor cell reception at US 501, consider calling ahead if you need ride.

1391.8	799.1	Rice Mountain	2166
1391.2	799.7	Spring . . . . ♦	1669
1390.8	800.1	Dirt road	1306
1389.9	801.0	Reservoir Rd (gravel), Pedlar River Bridge. . . . . . . 37.6705,-79.2845 🅿 ♦ ⌂ campsite 0.2S of road.	952
1388.2	802.7	Spring . . . . ♦	1164
1387.4	803.5	Stream. . . . . ♦	1116
1386.9	804.0	Swapping Camp Rd (gravel)	1286
1386.6	804.3	Stream. . . . . ♦	1344
1384.9	806.0	**Brown Mountain Creek Shelter** . . . . ☽ ♦ ⌂ ⊏ (6)	1358
		22.2◄18.3◄9.5◄►5.6►15.8►22.4 Swimming hole. Camping opposite side of creek. In dry conditions, get water from Brown Mountain Creek south of shelter.	
1383.1	807.8	US 60, Long Mountain Wayside . . . . .37.7234,-79.2506 🅿 (pg. 80) **Buena Vista, VA** (9.3W)	2065
1382.2	808.7	USFS 507 (dirt)	2650
1380.3	810.6	Bald Knob, not actually bald	4059
1379.3	811.6	Hotel Trail, **Cow Camp Gap Shelter** (0.6E). . . . . ☽ ♦ ⊏ (8)	3468
		23.9◄15.1◄5.6◄►10.2►16.8►24.4 Water source on blue-blazed trail left of shelter before small stream crossing.	
1378.1	812.8	Cole Mountain, views. . . . . 📷	4022
1376.8	814.1	Hog Camp Gap, USFS 48 (gravel), grassy meadow,. . . . . ♦ ⌂ many campsites. Signed spring just north of road crossing and 0.3 east.	3503
1375.9	815.0	Tar Jacket Ridge, view . . . . 📷	3847
1374.6	816.3	Salt Log Gap, USFS 63, two gravel road crossings	3257

SoBo   NoBo

1373.4	**817.5**	USFS 246	3556
1372.9	**818.0**	Greasy Spring Rd, Lovington Spring Trail to west	3600
1371.0	**819.9**	Piney River north fork . . . . ♦ ⌂	3492
1369.8	**821.1**	Elk Pond Branch . . . . ♦ ⌂	3724
1369.1	**821.8**	**Seeley-Woodworth Shelter** . . . . ☽ ♦ ⌞ (8)	3811

25.3◄15.8◄10.2◄►6.6►14.2►20.4 Piped spring 0.1 mile downhill to right.

1368.9	**822.0**	Stream. . . . . ♦	3751
1368.0	**822.9**	Rock Spring, west 100 yards to campsite and spring . . . . ♦ ⌂	3516
1366.8	**824.1**	Spy Rock Rd (formerly Fish Hatchery Rd, unpaved) . . . . **(pg. 81)**	3454
1366.4	**824.5**	Campsite, Spy Rock 0.1E, rock outcrop requiring scramble, view . . . . . . 📷 ⌂	3799
1364.2	**826.7**	Cash Hollow Rd	3280
1363.4	**827.5**	VA 826 (dirt road not easily passable).	3350
1362.5	**828.4**	**The Priest Shelter** (0.1E) 22.4◄16.8◄6.6◄►7.6►13.8►29.6 . . . . . . ☽ ♦ ⌞ (8)	3901
1362.0	**828.9**	The Priest, views on AT south of summit . . . . 📷	4063
1360.4	**830.5**	View . . . . 📷	2936
1358.9	**832.0**	Cripple Creek . . . . ♦	1837
1357.7	**833.2**	VA 56, Tye River suspension bridge . . . . 37.8384,-79.0231 🅿	970
1356.5	**834.4**	Roadbed.	1693
1356.0	**834.9**	Mau-Har Trail to west, rejoins AT to the south at Maupin Field Shelter	2033
1355.1	**835.8**	Stream. . . . . ♦	1754
1354.9	**836.0**	**Harpers Creek Shelter** . . . . ☽ ♦ ⌂ ⌞ (6)	1874

24.4◄14.2◄7.6◄►6.2►22.0►34.7 Harpers Creek in front of shelter. Privy uphill.

Map

← Lexington, VA 6 mi.

Food Lion, Dollar General and CVS 0.9 mi.

(N)

10th

BUENA VISTA, VA
37.7341,-79.3537
Mag. Dec. 9.16° W

♦ Glen Maury Park
🛏🍴 Holy Cow Ice Cream (0.6mi from 501, via 10th)

Domino's (dine-in seating) 540.261.1111

Edgewater Animal Hospital

Amish Cupboard

Don Tequilas

Ice Slice

T-N-T's

Hardware

Original Italian Pizza

JJ's Meat Shak

Lewis Grocery

Buena Vista Coin Laundry

PO (24416): 540.261.8959 M-F 8:30-4:30

Canton Chinese Restaurant

Mecicap Pharmacy 540.261.2896

Library 540.261.2715
M & W-F 10-5:30
Tu 10-7 Sat 10-1

Magnolia Ave

Exxon
Burger King
Budget Inn
Subway

Family Dollar

Hardees

Sheltman's Grocery

501

15th

20th

21st

29th St

9.3 mi. →

Visitor Center
Buena Vista Motel

Kenny's Burgers
Nick's Italian
1am Rock Island Grille
Todd's BBQ

12th

Text

» *Glasgow, VA* (...services cont'd from pg. 77)

🛒 **Glasgow Grocery Express** (6.1W) 540.258.1818 M-Sa 6-11:30p, Su 8-1130p, Coleman/alcohol/oz, canisters/heet.

🍴🍺 **Bosses Grill & Lounge** (7W) 540.258.3076 L/D, pool table.

✈ **Natural Bridge Animal Hospital** (10.8W) 540.291.1444 M-F 8a-6p, Sa 10a-2p.

807.8   US 60, LONG MOUNTAIN WAYSIDE

🚖 **E's-y Rider Cab Company** 540.461.2467 24x7. Covers all VA.(esyridercab.com)

🚖 **Ken Hawkins** 540.817.9640 roberthawkins5403@comcast.net

🚐 **Three Springs Shuttles** 434.922.7069 nancy@rinkenberger.us Local & long distance shuttles.

» *Buena Vista, VA 24416* (9.3W)

🏕🚻🅿 **Regional Visitor Center** (8.9W) 540.261.8004 Multi-day parking-must check in during business hrs 9a-5p.

🛏 **Buena Vista Motel** (9.1W) 540.261.2138 $44-$79 Rooms have fridge & m'wave, free local calls.

🛏 **Budget Inn** (10W) 540.261.2156 $59.95/up. Pets $10 & must use smoking room. Close to Subway, Burger King, ice cream & grocery.

🏕 **Glen Maury Park Campground** (12.6W) 540.261.8004 AT hiker special $5 tentsite. Sometimes WFS. Free shower, even w/out stay, South end of town across river. Maury River Fiddlers Convention mid-Jun.

🛒 **Lewis Grocery** (10.6W) 540.261-6826 M-F 9-9, Sa 9a-8:30p, Su 12p-8:30p, short order grill w/excellent burgers & salads.

🛒 **Food Lion** (11.3W) 540.261.7672 7 days, 7-10.

🛒🍴 **Amish Cupboard** (10.2W) Deli, ice cream, jerky, candy & dried foods. M-F, 10-7 (deli 10-6); Sa, 10-5:30.⟨theamishcupboard.com⟩

✈ **Edgewater Animal Hospital** (10.4W) 540.261.4114 M-F 8-6, Sa 8-12.

✈ **Maury Express** 800.964.5707 M-F 8-6, Sa 10-4. Area bus makes hourly loop though BV & connects w/ Lexington loop bus. 50¢ (exact change req'd). ⟨radartransit.org/ridership-information/maury-express/⟩

» *Lexington, VA 24450 (17.2W)*

🛏⚠🖥✉ **Brierley Hill B&B** (18.2W) 540.464.8421 relax@brierleyhill.com Open yr-round. Mid week, "Zero Day Thru Hiker Special." $99PP double occupancy. Incl shuttle svc to/from US 60 trailhead, b'fast, free use of laundry, & Wi-Fi. Mail: 985 Borden Rd, Lexington, VA 24450.

🥾🚲🖥 **Walkabout Outfitter** (24.3W) 540.464.4453 lexington@walkaboutoutfitter.com M-W 10-5:30, Th-Sa 10-7, Su 12-5 Full svc outfitter owned by Tina & Kirk Miller (Flying Monkey '99). Fuel canisters, bags, packs, shoes, socks, clothes. ⟨walkaboutoutfitter.com⟩

824.1 SPY ROCK RD

» *Montebello, VA 24464 (2.4W to post office, general store. Go downhill on gravel road 1.1W to parking area on Fish Hatchery Rd. Watch for right turn 0.5 from AT, and watch for blue blazes. Follow F.H. Road (turn right at intersection) 0.9mi. to Crabtree Falls Hwy (VA 56). Go left on VA 56 0.4 miles to post office.)* ☎540.377.9218, M-F 10-2, Sa 10-1

📧 **Earl Arnold** 540.377.2119 earlarnold@aol.com Range: James Rvr to Rockfish Gap.

🛏⚠⛺ **Montebello Camping & General Store** (2.4W) 540.377.2650 Store open yr-round. Summer hrs: Su-Th 8a-6p, F-Sa 8a-8p. Camping & laundry Apr 1 - Oct 31. Thru-hiker rate on tentsite $15 (1 person), $22.50 (2), $30 (3+).

833.2 VA 56, TYE RIVER

🛏🖥 **Blue Heron Cottage** (0.6E) 540.421.8534, 845.797.1778 maf4rr@virginia. edu $100 Su-Th, $125 F-Sa. Queen+couch sleeps 3 on Tye Rvr, Shuttle to town $20.

842.2 MAUPIN FIELD SHELTER

🛏⚠🏠🍴🛒🖥 **Royal Oaks Cabins** (1.7W) 540.943.7625 royaloaksresort@gmail. com Cabin (hiker rate) $50D M-Th, $70D F-Su, Tenting $20 up to 2. Cabin & tenting incl WiFi & shower. From Maupin Field (first paved rd). Turn left on BRP for 0.5mi to Love Rd (814). Turn right for 100 ft to Royal Oaks. Shuttle for cabin guests from Reeds Gap. Country Store open yr-round M-Sa, 10-6; Su, 12-4; snacks, sodas, canned food & deli on-site.

843.9 REEDS GAP, RTE 664, *5.0E to pub, 2.8W (S on BRP) to Royal Oaks (listed previously)*

🛏⚠🖥🍴🍺 **Devils Backbone Brewpub** (5.5E) 434.361.1001 On Rte 664 at intersection w/Patrick Henry Hwy (151). 7 Days 7a-9p, till 10p F-Su. Serves B/L/D. Hikers welcome to camp onsite for free. P/U rarely avail, but morning ret ride often provided. ⟨dbbrewingcompany.com⟩

△ Water Sources

Be aware of trail conditions before heading out, and tune in to advice from outfitters and other hikers. The trail gets rerouted, springs dry up, streams alter their course. Be prepared to deal with changes, particularly late in the season. Never carry just enough water to reach the next spring.

American Hiking Society

Founded in 1976, American Hiking Society is the only national organization dedicated to promoting and protecting America's hiking trails, their surrounding natural areas and the hiking experience.

To learn more about American Hiking Society and our programs such as National Trails Day, National Trails Fund, and Volunteer Vacations, visit AmericanHiking.org or call (800) 972-8608.

1353.4	837.5	View . . . . 📷	2781
1353.0	837.9	Chimney Rock, view . . . . 📷	3164
1351.6	839.3	Three Ridges Mountain.	3937
1350.8	840.1	Hanging Rock Overlook, view . . . . 📷	3479
1348.7	842.2	**Maupin Field Shelter**. 🌙 ◊ ☁ ⌐ (6) **(pg. 81)**	2739

20.4◄13.8◄6.2◄►15.8►28.5►41.5 Piped spring behind shelter.
Privy to right of shelter on unmarked path. Mau-Har Trail northern intersection.
Jeep road leads 1.4mi to BRP.

| 1347.0 | 843.9 | Reeds Gap, VA 664, BRP 13.6 in view to west . . . . .37.9016,-78.9853 🅿 **(pg. 81)** | 2650 |
| 1346.5 | 844.4 | Three Ridges Overlook, BRP 13.1 . . . . 37.907,-78.9795 🅿 ⛨ | 2700 |

⚠ Staying in or within 100 yards of any single AT shelter south of Waynesboro is limited to 3 nights in a 30-day period. This also applies to Davis Farm and Davis Path Campsites.

1344.3	846.6	Stream. . . . . ♦	2607
1343.5	847.4	Rock Point Overlook, view to west . . . . 📷	2791
1342.7	848.2	Cedar Cliffs, view . . . . 📷	2800
1342.2	848.7	Dripping Rock, BRP 9.6, spring . . . . 37.9411,-78.9369 🅿 ♦	2950
1341.9	849.0	Laurel Springs Gap, spring. . . . . ♦	2847
1341.0	849.9	Side trail 0.3W to Humpback picnic area	3215
1340.2	850.7	Campsite, view . . . . 📷 ☁	3538
1339.4	851.5	Humpback Mountain	3634
1338.4	852.5	Trail 0.2W to view at The Rocks . . . . 📷	3261
1336.7	854.2	Spring . . . . ♦	2504
1335.7	855.2	Spring . . . . ♦	2322
1335.6	855.3	Side trail 0.2W to Humpback Gap, BRP 6.0	2324
1334.7	856.2	Glass Hollow Overlook, view to east . . . . 📷	2257

| 1334.3 | 856.6 | Side trail 1.3W to Humpback Visitor Center . . . . . . 37.9692,-78.8974 🅿 ℹ ♦ | 2277 |
| 1334.2 | 856.7 | Albright Loop Trail to west . . . . | 2213 |

| 1332.9 | 858.0 | **Paul C. Wolfe Shelter** 29.6◄22.0◄15.8◄►12.7►25.7►38.9 . . . . . ☽♦⊏(10) | 1574 |
| | | Mill Creek 50 yards in front of shelter. Waterfall with pool 100 yards. | |

| 1332.1 | 858.8 | Small cemetery . . . . | 1855 |

| 1331.4 | 859.5 | Cabin ruins, chimney . . . . | 2062 |
| 1331.1 | 859.8 | Spring . . . . ♦ | 2041 |

| 1329.8 | 861.1 | Stream. . . . . ♦ | 1880 |

| 1328.9 | 862.0 | Stream. . . . . ♦ | 1715 |

1327.9	863.0	US 250 + Blue Ridge Pkwy . . . . 38.0311,-78.8591 🅿 ℹ ∦ ☎ (pg. 86)	1917
		Rockfish Gap, **Waynesboro, VA** (3.7W), I-64 overpass, south end of Skyline Dr.	
1326.9	864.0	Shenandoah National Park (SNP) . . . . (pg. 88)	2220
		Entrance station and self-registration for overnight permits.	

| 1324.2 | 866.7 | Skyline 102.1, McCormick Gap . . . . | 2451 |

| 1322.9 | 868.0 | Bears Den Mountain, communication towers, tractor seats . . . . | 2885 |

| 1322.4 | 868.5 | Skyline 99.5, Beagle Gap . . . . 38.0729,-78.7935 🅿 | 2550 |

| 1321.6 | 869.3 | Little Calf Mountain . . . . 📷 | 2917 |

| 1320.9 | 870.0 | Calf Mountain . . . . | 2990 |

1320.2	870.7	**Calf Mountain Shelter** (0.3W) . . . . ☽♦(0.2W)⦿⊏(6)	2668
		34.7◄28.5◄12.7◄►13.0►26.2►34.4 Spring on way to shelter. Bear pole.	
1319.7	871.2	Powerline	2293
1319.6	871.3	Spring . . . . ♦	2285
1319.2	871.7	Gravel road 0.1W to Skyline 96.9, Jarman Gap	2248

| 1319.0 | 871.9 | Spring, just south of woods road . . . . ♦ | 2140 |

| 1317.4 | 873.5 | Skyline 95.3, Sawmill Run Overlook . . . . 📷 | 2200 |
| 1316.0 | 874.9 | Turk Mountain Trail to west. . . . . | 2657 |

| 1315.8 | 875.1 | Skyline 94.1, Turk Gap. . . . . 38.129,-78.7849 🅿 | 2600 |

| 1313.8 | 877.1 | Skyline 92.4 . . . . | | 3007 |
| 1313.5 | 877.4 | Wildcat Ridge Trail east to Skyline 92.1 . . . . | 38.1484,-78.7746 🅿 | 2923 |

| 1310.8 | 880.1 | Skyline 90.0, spur trail to east leads to Riprap parking area. . . . . 🅿 | 2753 |
| 1310.4 | 880.5 | Riprap Trail branches to west . . . . | 2980 |

| 1309.7 | 881.2 | Skyline 88.9. . . . . | 2619 |

❀ Turks Cap Lily – Petals of this down-facing large flower curl back to form a bun shape (Turk's cap). Common color is flame orange and yellow, speckled with brown dots.

1307.9	883.0	Skyline 87.4, Black Rock Gap, Paine Run Trail	38.2066,-78.7496 🅿	2321
1307.7	883.2	Skyline 87.2		2391
1307.2	883.7	**Blackrock Hut** (0.2E) 41.5◄25.7◄13.0◄►13.2►21.4►33.8 . . . . . ☽ ♦ ◖ ⊏ (6)	2749
1306.8	884.1	Trayfoot Mountain Trail to west	3085
1306.7	884.2	Blackrock, views from summit, which is skirted by the AT . . . . 📷	3104
1306.1	884.8	Blackrock parking area.	38.2222,-78.7332 🅿	2925
1305.6	885.3	Skyline 84.3.		2800
1305.5	885.4	Jones Run parking	38.2301,-78.7263 🅿	2804
1304.9	886.0	Two trails west to Dundo Campground. Picnic area south, primitive campsites north (for group use w/fee) . . . . ♦ ⛟ 🕴	2768
1304.2	886.7	Skyline 82.9, Browns Gap	38.2404,-78.7109 🅿	2600
1303.6	887.3	Big Run Loop Trail to west	2834
1303.3	887.6	Skyline 82.2.	2781
1302.8	888.1	West to Doyles River Parking Overlook, Skyline 81.9 . . .	38.2468,-78.6948 🅿 📷	2872

| 1302.0 | 888.9 | Doyles River Traill, west to Skyline 81.1, ... | 38.2542,-78.683 🅿 ♦ | 2866 |
| | | east to Doyles River Cabin (locked), 0.3E to spring, 1.2E to falls | |

1301.2	889.7	Trail to Loft Mtn amphitheater	3174
1301.1	889.8	Trail to **Loft Mtn Campground** (go here if camping) . . . . ♦ ◖ (pg. 89)	3277
1300.5	890.4	Trail to **Loft Mtn Campground** . . . . ♦ ◖ (pg. 89)	3290
1300.1	890.8	Powerline	3233
1299.9	891.0	Trail to **Loft Mtn Store** (in view to west). . . . . (pg. 89)	3155

| 1298.7 | 892.2 | Frazier Discovery Trail 0.3W to Loft Mtn Wayside . . . . | 3303 |
| 1298.6 | 892.3 | Frazier Discovery Trail to west . . . . | 3298 |

| 1297.7 | 893.2 | Trail to 0.5W to Loft Mtn Wayside (flatter than FDT), Ivy Creek spring 0.1W . . . ♦ | 2965 |

| 1297.1 | 893.8 | Cross Ivy Creek . . . . ♦ | 2569 |

| 1296.4 | 894.5 | View to west . . . . 📷 | 2946 |

| 1295.6 | 895.3 | West to Skyline 77.5, Ivy Creek Overlook. . . . . 🅿 📷 | 2889 |

| 1294.0 | 896.9 | **Pinefield Hut** (0.1E), Skyline Dr (0.1W) Problem bear in 2017. . . . . ☽ ◊ 🌢 ⊏ (6) | 2463 |

1294.0 **896.9** **Pinefield Hut** (0.1E), Skyline Dr (0.1W) Problem bear in 2017. . . . . ☽ ◊ 🌢 ⊏ (6) 2463
38.9◄26.2◄13.2◄▶8.2▶20.6▶32.1 Spring on trail to shelter and 50 yards
behind. Both unreliable. Campsites uphill, beyond shelter.

1293.8 **897.1** Skyline 75.2, Pinefield Gap. . . . . 38.2902,-78.6419 🅿 2590
1293.0 **897.9** Weaver Mountain 2894

1291.9 **899.0** Skyline 73.2, Simmons Gap . . . . ◊ 2250
Simmons Gap ranger station on paved road 0.2E from where AT crosses Skyline.
Water avail at pump outside buildings.

1289.1 **901.8** View east to Powell Gap Hollow . . . . 📷 2619

1288.6 **902.3** Skyline 69.9, Powell Gap 2294

1287.0 **903.9** Skyline 68.6, Smith Roach Gap 2600

1285.8 **905.1** **Hightop Hut** (0.1W), reliable spring 0.1 from shelter . . . . ☽◊ 🌢 ◖(8)⊏ (6) 3175
34.4◄21.4◄8.2◄▶12.4▶23.9▶34.8

1285.3 **905.6** Spring east of AT . . . . ◊ 3515
1285.1 **905.8** View to west from flank of Hightop Mtn . . . . 📷 3531

1283.7 **907.2** Skyline 66.7 (Hightop Mtn Parking Area) . . . . 38.3449,-78.5531 🅿 2650

1282.7 **908.2** Stream. . . . . ◊ 2510
1282.4 **908.5** Skyline 65.5, Swift Run Gap, **Elkton, VA** (6.4W) . . . . ◊ ℄ (pg. 89) 2367
Bridge over US 33, access road north of bridge 0.1W to phone,
water (treat), SNP self-registration

1280.8 **910.1** Saddleback Mtn Trail to east. 3017

1279.8 **911.1** Trail 0.3E to spring, no camping . . . . ◊⊘ 2958
1279.3 **911.6** South River Picnic Area 0.1W. . . . . 38.3817,-78.5192 🅿 (0.1W)♀♂◊ 2894
Falls Trail to east.
1278.9 **912.0** South River Fire Road. 2882

1277.3 **913.6** Baldface Mountain 3607

1276.1 **914.8** Spring, Pocosin Cabin (locked), Parking on Skyline. . . . . 38.4136,-78.4897 🅿 ◊ 3150
1276.0 **914.9** Trail west to parking on Skyline . . . . 🅿 ◊ 3158

863.0 ROCKFISH GAP, US 250 + BLUE RIDGE PKWY

🅷 🅐 🅿 ⓢ **Rockfish Gap Visitor Center** 540.943.5187 Open most days 9-5. Info on town svcs & trail angels. Many lodging facilities offer free p/u & ret from here. Long-term parking ok. Leave contact info & ret date.

⊠ **DuBose Egleston** 540.487.6388 "Yellow Truck" shuttles Roanoke to Harpers Ferry (fee).

⊠ **Stanimal's 328 Shuttle Service,** avail 24/7 & covers all of VA & north to DC. Owned by Adam Stanley AT '04, PCT '10. ⟨fb.com/ stanimalshostel⟩⟨stanimals328.com⟩

🏕 🕍 ⚐ ⊠ **Galleywinter Farm** (5E) 434.244.2663 gail@leadingforth.com Campsites, rustic barn, & rooms in farm house. Can sleep up to 8 not incl camping. 4 Pvt BR in house. Yoga/ massage avail, laundry svc, meals on request for extra fee.

Inn at Afton (7.2E) 540.942.5201 Hiker rate $45+tax, pets allowed. Some restaurants deliver here.

🏕 ⚐ ⓢ ⊠ **Colony House Motel** (0.7W) 540.942.4156 $42-60+tax, pets $10, some snacks sold onsite, rooms have m'wave & fridge. Ask about tenting onsite. Mail: 494 Three Notched Mtn Hwy, Waynesboro, VA 22980.

🕍 **King's Gourmet Popcorn** (0.1W) 434.882.2078 7 days, M-Th 9a-7p, F 9a-8p, Sa-Su 8a-8p. Hot dogs, sodas, coffee, pork rinds, kettle corn, & gourmet popcorn. CC OK.

» **Waynesboro, VA 22980** (4.5W on I-64) *Hiker Fest* On Jun 9, gather at Heritage on Main at 11a for food and a movie. Camping area has pavilion, grill & solar charger; shower at nearby YMCA.

🅷 🏕 ⚐ ⊠ **Grace Hiker Hostel** (4.5W) 804.814.6841 endAtend@aol.com Supervised Lutheran Church hostel open May 21-Jun 17, clsd Su nights. 2 Night limit! Please do not call the church office. Check-in 5-8p, check-out 9a; hikers staying over may leave packs. Cots in air-conditioned Fellowship Hall, showers, WiFi, big-screen TV & DVD, hiker lounge w/kitchenette, snacks, & b'fast foods. 20 Hiker max. No pets, smoking, drugs, alcohol, firearms, or foul language. Donations gratefully accepted. Congregation cooks free dinner Th nights followed by optional vespers service.

⚐ 🛁 **YMCA** (4.5W) 540.942.5107 Free camping & showers. Use of YMCA facilities $10. Check-in at front desk, need photo ID.

🅷 ⚐ ⓢ ⊠ **Belle Hearth B&B** (5.2W) 540.943.1910 info@bellehearth.com $105D, (seasonal higher), incl b'fast, pool, p/u & ret. No smoking/alcohol/pets. Guest only mail 320 S Wayne Ave, Waynesboro, VA 22980. ⟨bellehearth.com⟩

🅷 ⚐ ⊠ **Quality Inn** (6.5W) 540.942.1171 Hiker rates $65.99S $70.99D +$10EAP (max 2) + tax. Sa/Su higher. Pets $10. Incl c. b'fast.

🅷 🏕 🕍 ⚐ ⓢ ⊠ **Stanimal's 328 Hostel** (6.9W) 540.290.4002 adamstanley06@gmail.com $30 Hostel incl p/u & ret to trail, mattress w/clean linens, shower w/towel, soap, loaner clothes, & laundry incl. Pvt rooms avail + full kitchen privileges. Computer, WiFi & DVDs on site. Snacks, pizza, sandwiches, drinks, & ice cream for sale. Discounted slackpacking for multi-night guests. Large property located downtown near grocery, restaurants, & fast food.

🅧 ⚐ 🛒 ⊠ **Rockfish Gap Outfitters** (3W) 540.943.1461 M-Sa 10a-6p, Su 12p-5p. Full svc outfitter, Coleman/ alcohol/oz, other fuels, shuttle info. Frz-dried foods. Located between town & trail; ask your ride to stop on the way. No aqua blaze. ⟨rockfishgapoutfitters.com⟩

🕍 **Ming Garden** (5.6W) 540.942.8800 AYCE.

🕍 **Weasie's Kitchen** (6W) 540.942.8800 Sa 6a-2p, Su 7a-2p.

🕍 **Heritage on Main** (6.2W) 540.946.6166 Hiker-friendly sports bar, beer, burgers, salads. M-Th 11a-12a, F-Sa 11-1a. Live music W&Sa, trivia Th.

🔧 **Ace Hardware** (5.7W) 540.949.8229 Canister & Coleman fuel. Alcohol/oz.

Waynesboro 3.7 mi. →
Colony House Motel 0.5
ROCKFISH GAP
King's Gourmet Popcorn
Visitor Center 🅷🅿
Inn at Afton
Skyline Drive
Blue Ridge Pkwy
SNP Entrance Station
64 · 250
N

WAYNESBORO, VA

38.0692, 78.8895
Mag. Dec. 9.52° W

N

Weasie's Kitchen
BZ Laundromat
Mi Rancho
250

3.7 mi
0.8 mi Rockfish Gap Outfitters
0.5 mi Basic City Beer Co

South River

South River Greenway (0.9 mi)

Hiker-camping with hammock posts and solar powered charger. Permit required from trail angel, YMCA, or info center

Constitution Park
Healthy Habit
The French Press
Stella, Bella & Lucy Heritage on Main
Green Leaf Grill
Graham's Shoe Services (also repairs gear) 540.943.7463
Tourism Info Center
Jakes
Sam's Hot Dogs
PO (22980): 540.942.7320 M-F 9-5, Sa pickup (only, back door) 8-12
Ming Garden AYCE L/D 540.943.3172
Kroger (24hrs) 540.942.6746, M-F 9-9, Sa 9-5,
Library 540.942.6746
YMCA Showers
Arch Ave
Market Ave
12th St
Belle Hearth B&B
Grace Lutheran
Wayne Ave
1.5 mi

Broad St
Clio's
Ace
Quality Inn
Main St
11th St
Federal St
Walnut Ave
Maple Ave
14th St
Royal Mart

Walmart Neighborhood Mkt.
Animal Hospital 540.943.3081
Tailgate Grill
Farmhaus on Main
New York Flying Pizza
Kline's dairy bar
CVS
Dollar General
Papa Johns
Family Dollar
Little Caesar's
Pizza Hut
Laundry Land
Hardees
Poplar Ave
Stanimal's Hostel
Magnolia Ave
Scotto's
Cookout
Subway
Arby's
Rite Aid
McDonalds
Burger King
Gavid's
250
340

0.9 from 340:
Budget Inn: 540.942.9551
Royal Inn: 540.949.8253

West 2.1 mi to interstate 64 interchange where there is:

Martin's, Wal-Mart, Target, and a dense cluster of restaurants and motels including:

Chick-fil-A, Cracker Barrel, McAlisters, Outback, Wendy's, Silk Roads, KFC, Ruby Tuesdays, Buffalo Wild Wings, Applebees, Panera Bread

Best Western: 540.942.1100
Comfort Inn: 540.932.3060
Days Inn: 540.943.1101
Super 8: 540.943.3888
HI Express: 540.932.7170

Augusta Health Urgent Care
8a-7p everyday 540.245.7940

Zeus 8 Digital Movie Theater

Shenandoah National Park (SNP)

540.999.3500 | www.nps.gov/shen | Emergency line: 800.732.0911

Shenandoah National Park (SNP) requires possession of a valid SNP backcountry permit for overnight hikes within the park. You may obtain backcountry permits from self-registration sites at the south and north entrance of the AT into SNP, at park entrance stations and visitor centers, or by mail (see contact information above). There is also a required Park entry fee of $10 per individual, and this can be paid at any entrance station, visitor center, or front country campground.

Concrete 4"x4" signposts are used to mark intersections. Information is stamped into an aluminum band at the top of the post.

What is known as a "shelter" on most of the AT is called a "hut" in Shenandoah, and three-sided day-use-only structures are called "shelters." When overnighting in the park, please use the huts or designated campsites, which are usually near the huts.

Backcountry stay is limited to 14 consecutive nights; two at any one location. If you cannot tent in a designated campsite, follow LNT principles of dispersed camping. Tenting at a new location is limited to one night and must be:

▸ 20 yards from the trail (preferably out of view).
▸ One quarter mile from any park facility (roads, campgrounds, lodges, visitor centers, and picnic areas).
▸ 10 yards from any water source.
▸ 50 yards from other camping parties, building ruins, or "no camping" signs.
▸ Not within designated "no camping" locations.

Groups are limited to 10. Campfires are only permitted at NPS-constructed outdoor fireplaces at the huts. Pets must be leashed at all times.

Lodges and campgrounds are typically full on weekends. A small number of unreserved walk-in tentsites are avail. on a first-come, first-served basis at all campgrounds except Lewis Mtn.

Delaware North Companies Parks & Resorts 877.247.9261 Operates the Skyland Resort, Big Meadows Lodge and Lewis Mountain Cabins, gift shops & camp stores and restaurants within Shenandoah National Park; many readily accessible from the trail. (goshenandoah.com)

The Park Service Operates campgrounds. Call 877.444.6777 or visit (recreation.gov) to reserve campsites. All campsites accommodate 2 tents and up to 6 persons. All except Mathews Arm have coin operated laundry and showers. Many facilities are closed November-May and all are closed December-March.

🖶 **Yellow Cab of the Shenandoah** 540.692.9200 serves all of SNP (24/7). Pet friendly, accepts CC.

If You Plan to be a 2000-Miler

The ATC recognizes hikers who have completed the trail, all at once or in sections, with a "2000-miler" certificate. Your name will be printed in the Spring issue of ATC's member magazine, **AT Journeys**, and listed on ATC's website. The honor system application states that conditional bypasses and reroutes are acceptable and that "issues of sequence, direction, length of time or whether one carries a pack are not considered." The number "2,000" is used out of tradition, and does not imply that hiking less than the full mileage qualifies. Feel free to set your own agenda on the AT, but if 2000-miler recognition is important to you keep in mind that the application will ask if you "have made an honest effort to walk the entire Trail."

889.8, 890.4 ★ LOFT MOUNTAIN CAMPGROUND
891.0 LOFT MOUNTAIN WAYSIDE

🏕🚗🍴⚕△ **Loft Mountain Campground** 434.823.4675 Campsites $15. AT skirts the campground, & several short side trails lead to campsites & the camp store(8a-7p). Showers, laundry & snacks avail at camp store. No mail drops. Open early-May to late-Oct.

🍴 **Loft Mountain Wayside** 434.823.4515 1.1 Mi from camp store, serves B/L/D, short-order menu. Open early Apr - mid Nov, daily 9-7.

908.5 US 33, SWIFT RUN GAP, US 33 is also known as
Spotswood Trail. The AT crosses over US 33 on the Skyline Drive. North of the bridge, take access road to the west to reach US 33.

🏕△🍴🛏✉ **Country View Motel** (2.9W) 540.298.0025 countryviewlodging@gmail.com Room $75/1Q, $92/2Q. No charge for laundry, but you must have detergent. $10 round trip shuttle from Swift Run Gap only. Mail for guests: 19974 Spotswood Trail, Elkton, VA 22827⟨countryviewlodging.com⟩

🏕⚕△🏕**Swift Run Camping** (4W) 540.298.8086, 540.713.8292 $20 Hiker campsite, open yr-round. Pool, & snack bar seasonal.

🍴🍴**Blueridge Country Store & Deli** (4.5W) 540.298.9826 M-F 5a-8p, Sa 6a-8p, Su 8a-7p.

» *Elkton, VA 22827* (6.5W), ☎540.298.7772, M-F 8:30-4:30, Sa 9-11

🏦 **Food Lion** (8.2W) 540.298.9455
🏦 **Rite Aid** (8.2W) 540.298.2234 M-Sa 8a-8p, Su 10a-8p.
🍴🍴 **Pizza Hut, Subway, Dairy Queen, McD's** (6.4W)

» *Harrisonburg, VA 22801* (23.6W)
☎540.574.6074, Mo-Fr: 9a - 4p, Sa: 10a - 1p, Su: Closed

🏕△✉ **Walkabout Outfitter** (23.6W) 540.434.9900 harrisonburg@ walkaboutoutfitter.com ⟨walkaboutoutfitter.com⟩

916.7, 916.8 LEWIS MOUNTAIN CAMPGROUND

🏕🚗🍴⚕△ **Lewis Mountain Campground & Cabins** 540.999.2255, 877.247.9261 Campsites $17, small bunkhouse, cabin rates seasonal. Open mid-Mar - late Nov. Camp store open same dates, Su-Th 9-6, F-Sa 9-7. Reservations 877.247.9261.

LOFT MOUNTAIN CAMPGROUND

Skyline Drive

Wayside 🍴🍴
Frazier Discovery Trail
Approx. 4.4 miles of A.T. shown on map
Campstore
Trails to campground
2.0 mi
Doyles River Cabin
Trail to ampitheater
P.

SWIFT RUN GAP

Skyline Drive
SNP self-registration
0.3 between roads
Spotswood Trail
Elkton, VA 6.5 mi
Motels 2.9 mi

1274.2	916.7	West to **Lewis Mtn Campground & Cabins** . . . . 38.4372,-78.479 📄 ♦ (pg. 89)	3443
1274.1	916.8	West to **Lewis Mtn Campground** . . . . 38.4372,-78.479 📄 ♦ (pg. 89)	3393
1273.4	917.5	**Bearfence Mountain Hut** . . . . 📄 🌙 ◊ 🔺(6) ⊂ (6)	3198
		(0.2E; 0.1 on gravel rd, 0.1 on side trail) 33.8◄20.6◄12.4◄►11.5►22.4►26.8	
1272.7	918.2	Bearfence Mountain Loop Trail, two intersections 0.2 mile apart, views 0.1E . . . 📷	3548
1272.2	918.7	Skyline 56.4, Bearfence Mtn Trail, parking 0.1W . . . . 38.4524,-78.4669 📄	3390
1270.8	920.1	Skyline 55.1, Bootens Gap . . . . 38.4675,-78.4573 📄	3243
1270.3	920.6	Laurel Prong Trail to east	3536
1269.9	921.0	Hazeltop	3812
1268.0	922.9	Skyline 52.8, Milam Gap, parking to east . . . . 38.4988,-78.4457 📄	3300
1267.4	923.5	Spring, No camping in Big Meadows clearing within sight of Skyline Dr . . . . ♦	3270
1266.9	924.0	Tanners Ridge Rd (gravel), cemetery	3318
1266.3	924.6	Lewis Spring & Road, Lewis Falls 0.5W . . . . 38.4524,-78.4669 📄 ♦ (pg. 92)	3330
		Gravel road 0.2E to Skyline, then left 0.2 to **Big Meadows Wayside**	
1265.8	925.1	Rock outcropping, view . . . . 📷	3637
1265.4	925.5	Trail to **Big Meadows Lodge**, Lewis Falls 0.5W . . . . (pg. 92)	3558
1265.0	925.9	Trail east to **Big Meadows Campground** . . . . (pg. 92)	3546
1264.8	926.1	David Spring 20 yards west . . . . ♦	3490
1264.6	926.3	Stream . . . . ♦	3369
1263.8	927.1	Fishers Gap, Skyline 49.3 to east, maintenance road	3050
1263.6	927.3	Franklin Cliffs, view . . . . 📷	3035
1262.5	928.4	Trail to Spitler Knoll parking, 4 cars . . . . 38.5482,-78.4138 📄	3250
1261.9	929.0	**Rock Spring Hut** (0.2W) . . . . 🌙 ♦ 🔺(9) ⊂ (8)	3509
		32.1◄23.9◄11.5◄►10.9►15.3►28.4 Locked cabin in front.	
1261.6	929.3	Trail east to Hawksbill Mountain, no camping anywhere above 3600'	3619
1260.6	930.3	Hawksbill Gap, parking to east . . . . 38.5629,-78.3825 📄	3361
1260.1	930.8	Stream, trail to Crescent Rock Overlook, parking to east . . . . 📄 📷 ♦	3429
1259.3	931.6	Spring . . . . ♦	3323
1258.4	932.5	Spring . . . . ♦	3436
1258.1	932.8	Skyland stables, service road . . . . 38.5867,-78.3834 📄	3550
1257.5	933.4	Trail to **Skyland Resort & Restaurant** (0.1W) . . . . 📄 (pg. 92)	3760
1257.4	933.5	Skyland service road north . . . . 38.5926,-78.376 📄	3699
1256.9	934.0	Trail to Stony Man Summit (0.2W) Highest point on the AT in SNP	3837
1256.3	934.6	Little Stony Man Cliffs, overlook to west . . . . 📷	3582
1256.1	934.8	Passamaquoddy Trail	3428
1255.8	935.1	Spur trail to parking . . . . 38.6059,-78.3664 📄	3254
1255.4	935.5	Stony Man Overlook . . . . 38.6123,-78.3625 📄 📷	3093
1255.0	935.9	Nicholson Hollow Trail	3109
1254.8	936.1	Crusher Ridge Trail	3173

| 1254.2 | **936.7** | Corbin Cabin Trail . . . . | 3122 |
| 1253.8 | **937.1** | Powerline . . . . | 3304 |

1253.1	**937.8**	Pinnacles Picnic Area & Parking, restrooms, water from faucet . . . . . 🅿 🚻🌲⚓💧	3410
1252.9	**938.0**	East to Skyline 36.4, side trail to Jewell Hollow Overlook. . . . . 📷	3359
1252.6	**938.3**	Leading Ridge Trail to west.	3379

| 1252.0 | **938.9** | The Pinnacle . . . . 📷 | 3730 |

1251.0	**939.9**	**Byrds Nest #3 Hut**, spring 0.4E on service road . . . . 💧🌙🔥⌐ (8)	3266
		34.8◄22.4◄10.9◄►4.4►17.5►28.0	
1250.6	**940.3**	View . . . . 📷	3343
1250.3	**940.6**	Meadows Spring Trail to east . . . . 💧(0.3E)	3354
1249.7	**941.2**	Overlook, Mary's Rock to west . . . . 📷	3423

| 1248.8 | **942.1** | Spring . . . . 💧 | 2853 |

1248.0	**942.9**	Trail to Panorama RR parking, powerline . . . . 38.6605,-78.3221 🅿 🚻🌲💧	2340
1247.8	**943.1**	US 211, Thornton Gap, **Luray, VA** (9W) . . . . **(pg. 92)**	2239
1247.7	**943.2**	Skyline 31.2	2327

1246.6	**944.3**	**Pass Mountain Hut** (1939) (0.2E) . . . . 🌙💧🔥⌐ (8)	2789
		26.8◄15.3◄4.4◄►13.1►23.6►31.7 2 bear poles, 2 privies, and 8 tent sites. Piped	
		spring 15 yards behind shelter.	
1245.8	**945.1**	Pass Mountain	3052

| 1244.7 | **946.2** | Beahms Gap Overlook, parking to east . . . . 🅿 📷 | 2490 |
| 1244.3 | **946.6** | Spring to west . . . . 💧 | 2436 |

| 1243.4 | **947.5** | Neighbor Mtn Trail, Byrds Nest #4 day use picnic area. . . . . 💧(0.5E) | 2675 |

1239.7	**951.2**	Stream, Jeremys Run Trail . . . . 💧	2238
1239.2	**951.7**	**Elkwallow Wayside** (and Gap) 0.1E on side trail or on Skyline 23.9 . . . . 🚻⚓🍴	2480
		Grill B/L/D, limited groceries, vending outside, 9-7 Early April-Early Oct.	
		Frost-free pump at picnic area south of wayside.	
1238.5	**952.4**	Range View Cabin (locked) 0.1E . . . . 💧(0.1E)	2969
1237.7	**953.2**	Skyline 21.9, Rattlesnake Point Overlook . . . . 📷	3083
1237.1	**953.8**	Tuscarora Trail to **Mathews Arm Campground** (0.7W) . . . . 🔥	3400
		Primitive campground open May-Oct; no services. Tent sites $14.	
1236.7	**954.2**	Skyline 21.1, Hogback parking . . . . 🅿	3350
1236.4	**954.5**	Skyline 20.8, Hogback Overlook . . . . 📷	3350

| 1235.2 | **955.7** | Skyline 19.7, Little Hogback parking 50 yards east . . . . 🅿 | 3019 |
| 1235.1 | **955.8** | Little Hogback Mountain, view. . . . . 📷 | 3050 |

924.6
925.5

LEWIS SPRING RD, *(see map for easiest access)*
★ BIG MEADOWS LODGE

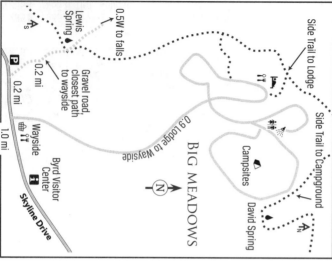

△⚑♨️⛽🍴⛺ **Big Meadows Lodge** 540.999.2221 Open early May - mid Nov. Lodge rooms, cabins, & suites. Reservations req'd. Some pet-friendly rooms. B:7:30-10a, L:12-2p, D:5:30-9p. Fuel/oz at gas station. Open mid Mar thru mid Nov.

🏠♨️🍴⛽ **Big Meadows Wayside** 540.999.2221 (lodge) B/L/D. Room M-F 4p-11p, Sa-Su 2p-11p.

BIG MEADOWS

N

Side Trail to Lodge

Side Trail to Campground

Campsites

David Spring

0.9 Lodge to Wayside

Lewis Spring

0.5W to falls

Gravel road, closest path to wayside

0.2 mi

P 0.2 mi

Wayside 🏠🍴

Byrd Visitor Center ℹ️

1.0 mi

Skyline Drive

A_S

A_N

925.9 BIG MEADOWS CAMPGROUND

△👣⚡🔥 **Big Meadows Campground** 540.999.3231 $20/tent site, 6 persons/site, self-register after hrs. Coin laundry & showers. Open mid-Mar thru mid-Nov check dates.

933.4 SIDE TRAIL TO SKYLAND

🏠♨️🍴⛽ **Skyland Resort & Restaurant** 540.999.2212 Open late Mar-late Nov, check dates. Rates seasonal, reservations req'd. Dining room hrs B: 7:30-10:30, L: 12-2:30, D: 5:30-9. Nightly entertainment. Tap Room 2-11. Snack foods & sodas sold at gift shop & vending machines.

943.1 US 211, THORNTON GAP

🏠👣♨️ **Brookside Cabins & Restaurant** (4.7W) 540.743.5698 $85-$200 cabins open yr-round, range in size (2-6 persons). A few have kitchen & hot tub, no TV or phone. Restaurant AYCE F-M, Buffet 4p-8p 7days in summer, closed Dec-Mar.

🏠♨️🍴🛒🏕️ **Days Inn - At Shenandoah National Park** (7.4W) 540.743.4521 luraydaysinn@gmail.com $89.95-$149.95D, $10EAP, cont. B, pets under 50 lbs $15, pool.⟨daysinn-luray.com⟩

🏠👣♨️🛒🏕️ **Yogi Bear's Jellystone Park** (5.3W) 540.743.4002 Cabins $121-$594 hold 4-15. Summer wkend 3 night min/4 on holiday wkend (rates may change). Tent sites $66-$112, 2 night min. Open late Mar to late Nov. Pets at tentsites & some cabins. All stays incl free water slide, paddle boat, mini golf. Mem to Labor Day snack shop serving hamburgers, hot dogs, pizza. Coin laundry, camp store, pool. Showers for guests only.

🏠♨️🍴🛒🏕️ **Open Arms Hostel** (7.7W) 540.244.5652 openarmsluray@gmail.com Call/text for avail. Open yr-round, w/in a mile of town. 8 twin beds $30PP, camping $15PP w/shower & kitchen privileges. B'fast/soda/snacks for sale on site. Laundry $5/load. Free guest p/u & d/o at Thornton Gap. Free Guest Mail: 1260 E Main St, Luray, VA 22835 ($2 for non-guest) Pet friendly. Cats on site.⟨openarmsluray.com⟩

🏠♨️🍴 **Cardinal Inn** (8.2W) 888.648.4633 Hiker summer rate: Su-Th $75, F-Sa $110. No pets.

» **Luray, VA 22835** (9.4W)*Farmer's Market held on Saturdays May-Sep, 9a-1p.*

ℹ️ **Visitor Center** (9.3W) 540.743.3915 Daily 9-5. 5 Mi north of town on Shenandoah River.

🏠 **Woodruff House B&B** (9.6W) 540.244.7588

🏠👣♨️🍴 **Mimslyn Inn** (9.7W) 540.743.5105 $169/up. Speakeasy on site M-Th 3p-10p: Fr-Sa 3p-11p, Su 2p-10p. Dinner 4-11p, full bar, W-Th,F entertainment.⟨mimslyinn.com⟩

🏠♨️🍴🛒 **Best Western** (9.8W) 540.743.6511 Call for rates, pet fee $20.

◉🌲⌂☒ Budget Inn (9.8W) 540.743.5176 $69.95D/up, $79.95D/up wkends +$10EAP. Pets $10. Mail (non-guests pay $10): 320 W Main St, Luray, VA 22835.

◉🌲 South Court Inn B&B (9.8W) 540.843.0980 stay@southcourtinn.com Discounted rate for hikers $100S/D when rooms avail, incl big b'fast. No pets, no smoking outside only. Wir sprechen Deutsch.

◉🌲☒ Luray Caverns Motels (10.6W) 540.743.6551, 888.941.4531 East & West buildings, std room Su-Th $79D; F-Sa $110D, +$8EAP. 20% Discount coupon on food at Luray Caverns. No pets. Mail w/reservation: 831 W Main St, Luray, VA 22835.

◉🌲 Rock Tavern River Kamp (14.6W) 540.843.4232 vahorselady@ rocketmail.com Tent sites for up to 4ppl ea $45+tax (showers incl). Yurts from $110.00/night + tax for up to 4ppl. Waterfront property.⟨massanuttensprings.com⟩

🔥⌂🌲☒ Appalachian Outdoors Adventures (9.2W) 540.743.7400 aoaluray@gmail.com Full svc outfitter, Coleman/alcohol/oz, canisters, Dr. Bonner's/oz, frz-dried foods. M-Th 10-6, F-Sa 10-8, Su 1-5. Mail: 2 West Main St, Luray, VA 22835.

✂ Main Street Barber Shop (9.4W) 540.244.2815 Hiker friendly walk in haircuts for men & women $7.50 incl beard trim. M-F 9a-5p, Sa 9a-1p, clsd W & Su.

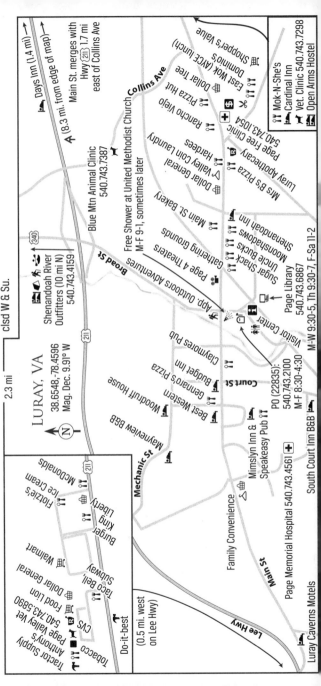

← Days Inn (1.4 mi) →

↑ (8.3 mi. from edge of map)

Main St. merges with Hwy (211) 1.7 mi east of Collins Ave

Collins Ave

East Wok (AYCE lunch)
Domino's
Shopper's Value
Dollar Tree
Pizza Hut
Rancho Viejo
Page Free Clinic 540.743.1054
Luray Apothecary
Mrs B's Pizza
Valley Coin Laundry
Hardees
Dollar General
Main St. Bakery
Sugar Shack
Uncle Bucks
Gathering grounds
Moonshadows
Shenandoah Inn

| Mok-N-She's |
| Cardinal Inn |
| Vet. Clinic 540.743.7298 |
| Open Arms Hostel |

Blue Mtn Animal Clinic 540.743.7387

Free Shower at United Methodist Church M-F 9-1, sometimes later

App. Outdoors Adventures

Broad St

Page 4 Theaters

Shenandoah River Outfitters (10 mi N) 540.743.4159

(340)

(211)

2.3 mi

LURAY, VA
38.6548,-78.4596
Mag. Dec. 9.91° W

N↑

Page Library 540.743.8867 M-W 9:30-5, Th 9:30-7, F-Sa 11-2

Visitor Center

Court St

Claymores Pub
Budget Inn
Gennaro's Pizza
Best Western
Woodruff House
Mayview B&B

PO (22835): 540.743.2100 M-F 8:30-4:30

Mimslyn Inn & Speakeasy Pub

South Court Inn B&B

Page Memorial Hospital 540.743.4561

Mechanic St

Family Convenience

Main St

Lee Hwy

Luray Caverns Motels

(0.5 mi. west on Lee Hwy)

Flotzie's Ice Cream
McDonalds
Burger King
Liberty
Subway
Taco bell
Dollar General
Food Lion
Walmart
CVS
Do-it-best
Tractor Supply
Anthony's
Page Valley Vet 540.743.5890
Tobacco

1234.6	**956.3**	Skyline 18.8		2795
1233.5	**957.4**	**Gravel Springs Hut** (0.2E), spring en route to shelter . . . . 🌙 ◗ ◖ ⌐ (8)		2635
		28.4◀17.5◀13.1◀▶10.5▶18.6▶24.1▶		
1233.3	**957.6**	Skyline 17.7, Gravel Springs Gap . . . . 38.7678,-78.2335 🅿		2666
1232.5	**958.4**	View west . . . . 📷		3068
1232.2	**958.7**	South Marshall Mountain		3212
1231.7	**959.2**	Skyline 15.9, parking to west. . . . . 🅿		3050
1231.0	**959.9**	North Marshall Mountain, view . . . . 📷		3368
1230.0	**960.9**	Hogwallow Flat		2959
1229.5	**961.4**	Skyline 14.2, Hogwallow Gap . . . . 38.7898,-78.1887 🅿		2739
1227.8	**963.1**	Skyline 12.3, Jenkins Gap, parking to east. . . . . 38.8065,-78.1808 🅿		2339
1226.9	**964.0**	Compton Springs . . . . ◗		2700
1226.5	**964.4**	Compton Peak		2909
1225.7	**965.2**	Skyline 10.4, Compton Gap parking . . . . 38.8236,-78.1706 🅿		2434
1223.9	**967.0**	Compton Gap Tr ("VA 610/Chester Gap" post) Front Royal Hostel (0.5E) . . **(pg. 98)**		2350
1223.7	**967.2**	SNP permit self-registration station.		2334
1223.0	**967.9**	**Tom Floyd Shelter** 28.0◀23.6◀10.5◀▶8.1▶13.6▶18.1 . . . . 🌙 ◊ ◖ ⌐ (6)		1943
		bear pole, trail behind shelter and side trails north on AT lead to water.		
1222.1	**968.8**	Trail 0.4W to N. Virginia 4H Center, parking. . . . . 🅿 ⚇ **(pg. 98)**		1371
1221.5	**969.4**	VA 602, stream south of road. . . . . ◗		1083
1220.1	**970.8**	US 522, **Front Royal, VA** (3.5W) . . . . 38.878,-78.1507 🅿 **(pg. 98)**		950
1219.8	**971.1**	US 522 (east trailhead) **Mountain Home Cabbin** (0.1E) . . . . 🏠**(pg. 98)**		974
1219.3	**971.6**	Bear Hollow Creek . . . . ◗		1076
1218.2	**972.7**	Woods road		1558
1216.8	**974.1**	CCC Rd.		1800
1216.7	**974.2**	Sealock Spring, Mosby Campsite. Named after Colonel John Mosby . . . ◗ ⅄ ◖		1749
1216.0	**974.9**	Powerline		1653

SoBo   NoBo

1214.9	976.0	**Jim & Molly Denton Shelter** Porch, chairs, solar shower . . . . . ☽ ✽ � ◑ ⌐ (8)	1326
		31.7◀18.6◀8.1◀▶5.5▶10.0▶18.4 bear pole, piped spring 100 yards south.	
1213.9	977.0	Stream . . . . ◑	1048
1213.8	977.1	VA 638, powerline to south	1070
1213.1	977.8	Ridgetop clearing, bench, view . . . . 📷	1437

1211.9	979.0	VA 55 (John Marshall Hwy), Manassas Gap . . . . . 38.9092,-78.0533 🅿 (pg. 99)	800
		RR tracks to south, AT passes under I-66 on Tuckers Lane.	
1211.7	979.2	Tuckers Lane parking, Footbridge, stream . . . . 38.9113,-78.053 🅿 ◑	817

| 1210.4 | 980.5 | Stone wall . . . . | 1415 |

1209.4	981.5	**Manassas Gap Shelter** (0.1E) (1939) . . . . ☽◑◑◑ ⌐ (6)	1669
		24.1◀13.6◀5.5◀▶4.5▶12.9▶19.8 Bear Pole. Reliable spring downhill to right of	
		shelter on side trail. Blue-blazed trail south of shelter leads 0.9W to VA 638.	
1208.1	982.8	Spring . . . . ◑	1721

| 1207.4 | 983.5 | Trico Tower Trail 0.3W to comm. tower, parking on VA 638 38.9536,-78.0270 🅿 | 2080 |

> ✿ Trillium – Three-petal flower set upon three leaves. White and pink
> varieties are plentiful in the southern Appalachians.

1204.9	986.0	**Dicks Dome Shelter** (0.2E) 18.1◀10.0◀4.5◀▶8.4▶15.3▶29.5 ⌂ ☽◑◑◑ ⌐ (4)	1397
		Whiskey Hollow Creek in front of shelter (treat water). Stream on AT 75 yards	
		north of shelter side trail.	
1204.5	986.4	Powerline	1607
1203.9	987.0	Spring . . . . ◑	1753
1203.7	987.2	Signal Knob parking on VA 638 / Fire Trail Rd 0.1W . . . . . 38.9852,-77.9997 🅿	1837
1202.9	988.0	Boundary to Sky Meadows State Park	1832
1202.6	988.3	Bench, 1.7E to **Sky Meadows State Park Visitors Center** . . . . . . 🅷 🅿️ ☏◑◑	1801
		800.933.7275 Open W-Su 8-5, restrooms, soda machine, 12 sites & primitive	
		group camping, $9PP, reservation required, campers must arrive before dusk.	
1201.8	989.1	View 0.4E on Ambassador Whitehouse Trail . . . . 📷	1578

1200.2	990.7	Two footbridges, streams . . . . ◑	888
1200.1	990.8	Ashby Gap, US 50/17	945
1199.9	991.0	Trail 0.1E to parking on VA 601, Blueridge Mtn Rd . . . . 39.0157,-77.962 🅿	1080

| 1198.7 | 992.2 | Stream . . . . ◑ | 1137 |

| 1198.1 | 992.8 | Stream . . . . ◑ | 1034 |
| 1197.8 | 993.1 | Trail west to Myron Glaser Cabin (locked) . . . . | 1127 |

1197.3	993.6	Stream . . . . ◑	997
1196.9	994.0	Fishers Hill Trail to west	1093
1196.5	994.4	**Rod Hollow Shelter** (0.1W) 18.4◀12.9◀8.4◀▶6.9▶21.1▶36.7 . . . ☽◑◑◑ ⌐ (8)	891
		Piped spring left of shelter. Stream on AT south of side trail.	
1196.1	994.8	Stream, Fishers Hill Trail to west, south end of The Roller Coaster . . . . . . ◑	802
		13.5 miles of tightly packed ascents and descents.	

1194.8	996.1	Spring at Bolden Hollow		843
1193.2	997.7	Footbridge, Morgan Mill Stream, campsite	♦ ⌂	775
1192.7	998.2	VA 605, Morgan Mill Rd (gravel) . . . . 39.0721,-77.912 🅿		1047
1192.0	998.9	Stream.	♦	1010
1191.1	999.8	Buzzard Hill, AT east of summit		1251
1190.5	1000.4	Two streams	♦	804
1189.6	1001.3	**Sam Moore Shelter** (1990) 19.8◄15.3◄6.9◄►14.2►29.8►33.9 . . ♪ ♦ ⌂ ⊏ (6)		904

Springs in front of shelter and to the left. Several tent sites to left of shelter.

1189.1	1001.8	Campsite	⌂	1289
1188.3	1002.6	Spout Run Ravine, stream	♦	709
1187.1	1003.8	Footbridge, stream, campsite 60 yards north on AT	♦ ⌂	830
1186.6	1004.3	Bears Den Rocks, **Bears Den Hostel** (0.1E), view north on AT . . . . . 📷 **(pg. 99)**		1265
1186.0	1004.9	Snickers Gap, VA 7 & 679 (Pine Grove Rd) . . . . . . 39.1153,-77.8475 🅿 **(pg. 102)**		1000

If parking lot is full, vehicles parked on either shoulder will be towed

1185.2	1005.7	Stream.	♦	802
1183.8	1007.1	Stream.	♦	856
1183.5	1007.4	**VA-WV** border		1146
1183.3	1007.6	Raven Rocks, Crescent Rock 0.1E, view . . . . 📷		1252
1183.1	1007.8	Campsite	⌂	1365
1182.7	1008.2	The Roller Coaster (north end); 13.5 miles of ascents and descents	♦ ⌂	1134

Sand Spring to west, good water source, Devils Racecourse boulder field to north

1179.8	1011.1	Wilson Gap		1380
1178.6	1012.3	Two trails 0.2E to **Blackburn AT Center** . . . . 39.1877,-77.7978 🅿 **(pg. 102)**		1650
1176.9	1014.0	Laurel Springs, boardwalk	△	1449
1175.9	1015.0	Buzzard Rocks		1518
1175.4	1015.5	**David Lesser Memorial Shelter** (0.1E). . . . . ♪ ♦ ⌂ ⊏ (6)		1421

29.5◄21.1◄14.2◄►15.6►19.7►24.7 Overflow camping area below shelter.
Spring 0.2 mile downhill from shelter.

SOBO NOBO

| 1174.1 | **1016.8** | Roadbed . . . . | 1321 |

| 1172.4 | **1018.5** | Keys Gap, WV 9, markets 0.3E or W . . . . 39.2616,-77.7625 🅿 (pg. 102) | 911 |

| 1170.9 | **1020.0** | Powerline . . . . | 916 |
| 1170.2 | **1020.7** | Campsite . . . . ◔ | 1125 |

1168.5	**1022.4**	VA-WV border, Loudoun Heights, Loudoun Heights Trail to east	1117
		No camping or fires from Loudoun Heights Trial thru Potomac River	
1167.9	**1023.0**	WV 32, Chestnut Hill Rd	580

1167.0	**1023.9**	US 340, north end Shenandoah River Bridge⚠ No hitchhiking on 340 . .(pg. 102)	319
1166.7	**1024.2**	Side trail to **Appalachian Trail Conservancy** (0.2W) . . . .(pg. 102)	434
1166.3	**1024.6**	Jefferson Rock, view north to Potomac and Shenandoah Rivers . . . .📷	432
1166.1	**1024.8**	**Harpers Ferry, WV**, High Street . . . . 39.3165,-77.7558 🅿 (pg. 103)	274
1165.8	**1025.1**	Potomac River, Byron Memorial Footbridge, **WV-MD** border. North of	246
		river turn east on C&O Canal Towpath. No camping on AT section of towpath.	
1164.7	**1026.2**	Pass under Sandy Hook Bridge (US 340) . . . .(pg. 104)	248

> 🔺 MD Guidelines: camp only at designated campsites where tent
> symbols are shown). Alcohol not permitted on AT lands in MD.

1163.2	**1027.7**	C&O Canal Towpath north end, RR tracks, US 340 underpass . . . . . .(pg. 104)	246
		From Keep Tryst Rd: **Knoxville, MD (1.0E), Brunswick, MD** (2.5E)	
1162.6	**1028.3**	Weverton Rd . . . . .39.333,-77.6832 🅿	371
1161.9	**1029.0**	Trail east to Weverton Cliffs, view . . . .📷	859

1159.8	**1031.1**	**Ed Garvey Shelter** . . . . 🌙◔◑⊏(12)	1083
		36.7◄29.8◄15.6◄►4.1►9.1►16.6 Water on steep 0.4 mile trail in front of shelter.	
		2 tent sites north & south of shelter.	

| 1158.0 | **1032.9** | Brownsville Gap, roadbed . . . . | 1063 |

1156.1	**1034.8**	Gapland Rd, Gathland State Park, War Correspondents . . . 🚫🚫🚹🚾◔(pg. 105)	950
		Monument. Frost-free spigot by restrooms. No camping, No fires, no trash cans.	
1155.7	**1035.2**	**Crampton Gap Shelter** (0.3E)(1941) . . . . 🌙◔◑⊏(6)	1163
		33.9◄19.7◄4.1◄►5.0►12.5►20.7 Intermittent spring 0.1S on AT.	
		NoBo: consider bringing water from Gathland	

967.0 COMPTON GAP TRAIL, (post label "VA 610/Chester Gap")

🏠 **Mobile Mike's** 540.539.0509 Shuttles & more (Mike Evans).

🏠🍴🏧📶💲☎✉ **Front Royal Terrapin Station Hostel** (0.7E) 540.539.0509 gratefulgg@hotmail.com At the last NoBo concrete post in SNP, the A.T. turns left. NoBos go straight, follow Compton Gap Trail 0.5 mi to paved rd. Hostel is 1st home on left on paved rd. Enter in back through marked gate. Owned by Mike Evans. Open Apr 30-Jul 1, 2018. Hikers only, picture ID req'd. Bunk only $25, shower w/soap & shampoo $3, laundry $3. One night hiker special $30 incl bunk, shower, laundry, pizza & soda, $50 Two-night special also incl slackpack & 2nd night but not 2nd dinner. All visits incl free town shuttle for a fee. WiFi, charging stations, TV, library, music, room to chill. Reservations recommended. No dogs. Mail for overnight guests: 304 Chester Gap Rd, Chester Gap, VA 22623.

968.8 SIDE TRAIL TO (W)

🏕🏠🍴🚿💲 **Northern VA 4H Center** (0.4W) 540.635.7171 Swimming pool Mem-Labor Day, shower $1, concession stand. Free parking up to 30 days, register on-line or check in at office. Donations graciously accepted.⟨nova4h.com/appalachian-trail⟩

970.8, 971.1 US 522 (REMOUNT ROAD)

🏠 **Front Royal Trolly** 540.635.8007 Trolly p/u - 7 days - 2x daily at Rt 522 & AT crossing, May 15-Jul 15 8:55a & 2:20p. 50¢ PP. D/0 anywhere on Trolly route. Drivers may leave early. Please arrive 10 min prior.

🏠🛏☎📶✉ **Sharon's Shuttle** 703.615.5612 Waynesboro, PA to Vernal.

🏠🛏🍴☎ **Mountain Home Cabbin** (0.07E) 540.692.6198 mountainhomeat@gmail.com Renovated "Cabbin" at historic home of Lisa & Scott "Possible" AT12 Jenkins. SoBos: Go straight to Rte 522 (Gate 7 sign) & turn left. NoBos: At US 522 trailhead, cross rd, continue on AT for 0.3 mi parallel to 522. When trail turns left/north from 522, go right to Gate 7 sign by rd. Both: From "Gate 7" sign on 522, go east 120 yards. Mountain Home is first driveway on left w/long stone wall east of AT. Cabbin is first small red brick building. Open yr-round, call/email ahead suggested, drop-ins ok. 4S, 2D beds. $30PP incl bed, fresh linens, shower, hiker clothes, hiker box, b'fast, some cell, & town shuttle for dinner & resupply. Laundry $5. Pizza, locally-inspired food.⟨...⟩

cookies, & water. Faucet on SW corner of Cabbin. Max 1 dog/night for $5. Parking $3/day for non-guests. Mail: 3471 Remount Rd, Front Royal, VA 22630.

🏠🛏🍴📶💲☎✉ **Quality Inn** (0.13E) 540.635.3161 Ask for hiker rate, $10EAP (up to 4) incl c. b'fast. Pets $15. Pool. If you need ride back to AT in the morning, let them know at check-in. Guest laundry. **Thai Restaurant** on site. Mail: 10 Commerce Ave, Front Royal, VA 22630.

» Front Royal, VA 22630 (4W)

🏠 🅿🛏🍴🏧📶✉ **Front Royal/Warren County Visitors Center** (3.8W) 540.635.5788 tourism@frontroyalva.com 7 Days, 9-5p. Hiker goodie bags, hiker box, pack storage, cold drinks, & AT. Maps for sale. Trolly from trailhead to town runs in Spring 2x/day. Questions? Outfitter, laundry, lodging, hostel, shopping, movies, showers all w/in 2 blocks.⟨discoverfrontroyal.com⟩

🏠🛏📶 **Parkside Inn** (3.6W) 540.631.1153 Clean, hiker friendly w/mini fridge & m'wave. Trail p/u & ret when avail.

🏠🛏📶 **Super 8** (3.6W) 540.636.4888 10% Hiker discount, pets $10.

🏠🛏📶 **Royal Inn** (3.7W) 540.636.6168 $50/up, pets $10.

🏠🛏📶 **Woodward House B&B** (3.7W) 540.635.7010 Hiker rate $110D+tax w/b'fast, p/u & ret to trail. Open yr-round, CC ok.

🏠🛏💲 **Budget Inn** (4.9W) 540.635.2196

🥾🛏🏠📶 **Mountain Trails** (4W) 540-749-2470 Full svc outdoor store w/ supplies, equipment repair & advice. City operated laundry, microbrewery next door. Mail: 120 E Main St, Front Royal, VA 22630 (2 wk hold).⟨mountain-trails.com⟩

🥾📶 **Front Royal Outdoors** (6.4W) 540.635.5440 Aquablaze options ranging from Port Republic to Snickers Gap; make arrangements from Waynesboro. Will store gear while you're on the river. Avail Mar 15-Jun 30 (thru Oct 31 for SoBos). Please learn the rules for camping on the river.

🛒 **Rural King** (3.4W) 540.631.1740 New farm-supply type store next to Martin's Grocery. 5 Outlets outside to recharge mobile devices. Hiker foods, canister fuel.

🍴🍺📶 **Front Royal Brewing Co.** (3.9W) 540.631.0773 Front Royal Brewing Co. W-M 11-10. Along Trolly route, 122 E Main St, next to Mountain Trails. Charge phones, use lockers, laundry, shower, & WiFi at no charge. L/D daily, brunch on Su. Live Music on wkends. Come enjoy artisan-brewed beer & locally-inspired food.⟨frontroyalbrewing.com⟩

at the hostel door. Upper lodge, kitchen, camp store & office open 5-9p daily. Check-out 9a. Slackpacking & shuttles may be avail during summer. Parking $3/day. Hosts the **Northern Ruck** Jan 26-28, 2018. No drugs/alcohol anywhere on property. Pets welcome, but not allowed inside. Mail (p/u during office hrs): 18393 Blue Ridge Mountain Rd, Bluemont, VA 20135. (bearsdencenter.org)

979.0   VA 55, MANASSAS GAP

» **Linden, VA 22642** (1.2W)

☎ 540.636.9936, M-F 8-12 & 1-5, Sa 8-12. Pkgs only held 15 days.

🏠 **Monterey Convenience Store** (1.2W) 540.636.6791 M-F 5a-9p, Sa 7a-9p, Su 8a-9p.

🏠 **The Giving Tree** (1.2W) 540.686.6261 M-Sa 10-7; Su 10-5, Arbor Day-Christmas Eve. Local produce, ice cream, meat, dairy & more.

🍴 **Apple House Restaurant** (2.6W) 540.636.6329 Tu-Su 7-8, M 7-5 yr-round. Hiker specials, supplies & rides sometimes avail.

1004.3   BEARS DEN ROCKS

🏠 **Bears Den Hostel** (0.1E) 540.554.8708 A castle-like stone lodge, ATC owned, & PATC operated. Bunk $20PP, tenting $12PP incl full house privileges. Hiker Special: Bunk, laundry(5p-9p), pizza, soda & pint of Ben & Jerry's ice cream $30PP. All stays incl shower & self-serve pancake b'fast. CC ok. Hiker room w/TV, shower, internet & sodas accessible all day by entering a mileage code

---

FRONT ROYAL, VA

38.9108, -78.1847
Mag. Dec. 10.13° W

N ↓

Distances from Quality Inn:
0.6 to Post Office
0.7 to Martin's
0.7 to CVS 1.1 to Library
1.5 to Pizza Hut

Map labels:

- Library 540.635.3153 — M-Th 10-8, F-Sa 10-5
- Criser Rd / 340
- Joe's Steakhouse
- Castigli's (3.1 mi) ↑
- 0.9 mi
- Rural King
- Better Thymes
- Laundry
- Fox's Pizza Den
- China Jade
- Parkside Inn
- Super 8
- Royal Inn Motel
- Italian Kitchen
- Goodwill
- CVS
- Family Dollar
- Hong Kong
- Shop n Save
- Big Lots
- KFC
- Barber
- Martin's
- Tobacco
- Front Royal Diner
- Mom's Country Kitchen
- Rite Aid
- Dollar General
- **South St**
- Lester & Mowery's
- Burger King / Mojo's Grill
- McDonald's
- **Blue Ridge Ave**
- Spelunker's Ice Cream
- Woodward House B&B
- Happy Creek Ice Cream
- Pave Mint
- **Valley Health Quick Care** 540.636.0455 M-F 8-6, Sat 9-5.
- C&C Frozen Coffee
- Handi Market with Dunkin Donuts
- Thunwa Thai
- Wynn's Restaurant
- Daily Grind
- Theater
- Laundry
- Happy Creek Eatery
- Anthony's Pizza
- Laundry
- Royal Oak Animal Clinic 540.636.2000
- Quality Inn
- **Stonewall Dr**
- L Dee's Pizza Hut
- Visitor's Center
- Main St Mill & Pub
- From Royal Pancake House
- Soul Mtn Restaurant
- Down Home Bakery
- Mountain Trails Outfitter
- Mountain Trails Brewing Co
- Blue Wing Frog
- **Chester St**
- **3rd St**
- PO (22630): 540.635.8482 7983 M-F 8:30-5, Sa 8:30-1
- Coin Laundry
- Subway
- 7-11
- Papa John's
- Taco Bell
- True Value Hardware
- **4th St**
- **5th St**
- **6th St**
- **8th St**
- Warren Memorial Hospital 540.636.0300
- Shenandoah Ave
- Virginia Ave
- Wendy's
- Rancho Nuevo
- Jalisco Mexican
- Arby's
- Budget Inn
- Pizza Hut
- Melting Pot, pizza beer, wings
- 340 / 522

1153.1 **1037.8** Spring 0.5E, trail to Bear Spring Cabin (locked). . . . . ♦ 1437

1152.5 **1038.4** White Rock Cliff, view. . . . .🔳 1579
1152.3 **1038.6** Lambs Knoll 50 yards west to tower, view . . . .🔳 1733

1151.2 **1039.7** Lambs Knoll tower road (paved). 1347

1150.7 **1040.2** **Rocky Run Shelters** (0.2W) 24.7◄9.1◄5.0◄►7.5►15.7►20.6 . ☽♦◖⌒ (6)(16) 982
Left fork on side trail to better water source & old shelter. Right to new shelter.

1149.7 **1041.2** Fox Gap, Reno Monument Rd (paved), **South Mountain Creamery** (2E). 1068

1148.9 **1042.0** **Dahlgren Backpack Campground** . . . .🚹🚻⚲☂♦◖ 980
Large tenting area, picnic tables, restrooms; no fee. Note proximity to road.
1148.6 **1042.3** Turners Gap, US Alt 40, restaurant 0.1W, ... 39.4840,-77.6198 🅿 (pg. 105) 1080
Boonsboro, MD (2.5W)

1147.3 **1043.6** Monument Rd. 1256
1147.0 **1043.9** Washington Monument State Park, picnic tables, 39.4977,-77.6208 🅿 ⊕🚹☂♦ 1358
parking near entry, restrooms adjacent to visitor center.
1146.7 **1044.2** Washington Monument (0.1W). . . . .🔳 ▲ 1550

1146.4 **1044.5** Powerline 1311
1144.6 **1046.3** Boonsboro Mountain Rd, residential area. 1297
1144.3 **1046.6** Bartman Hill Trail 0.6W to Greenbrier SP . . . .(pg. 108) 1394
1143.9 **1047.0** I-70 footbridge, US 40, ... 39.5353,-77.6035 🅿 (pg. 108) 1239
Parking north end of footbridge 0.1E. Also cross Boonsboro Mtn Rd south of hwy.
1143.2 **1047.7** **Pine Knob Shelter** (0.1W) (1939), south end of loop trail. . . . . . . ☽♦◖⌒ (5) 1378
16.6◄12.5◄7.5◄►8.2►13.1►22.7 Piped spring next to shelter.

1141.6 **1049.3** Annapolis Rocks to west, campsite . . . .🔳 ⊛ ☽♦(0.2W)◖ (13) 1756
Caretaker on site. Tentsites near outstanding overlook. No fires.

1140.6 **1050.3** Black Rock Cliffs to west. 1779
1140.2 **1050.7** Black Rock Creek . . . . ◊ 1597
1140.0 **1050.9** **Pogo Memorial Campsite** . . . . ☽♦◖ 1500
Campsite east of AT, spring 100 yards west. Thurston Griggs Trail to west.

✿ Poison Ivy – Vine that can grow as ground cover or that can cling to trees or other brush. Stems redden toward the end and terminate with 3 pointed-oval leaves.

1135.2	1055.7	Wolfsville Rd, MD 17, **Smithsburg, MD** (1.5W) . . . .(pg. 108)	1340
1135.0	1055.9	**Ensign Cowall Shelter** (1999) 20.7◄15.7◄8.2◄►4.9►14.5►16.9 . . .) ◊ ◖ ⊏ (8)	1384
		Boxed spring, somewhat stagnant, south between shelter & road.	
1134.8	1056.1	Powerline	1500
1133.7	1057.2	Foxville Rd, MD 77, **Smithsburg, MD** (1.7W)	1590
1132.5	1058.4	Spring . . . . ◊	1325
1132.3	1058.6	Powerline	1345
1131.9	1059.0	Warner Gap Hollow, stream, Warner Gap Rd (gravel, AT to west). . . . . ◊	1150
1131.2	1059.7	Little Antietam Creek . . . . ◊	1075
1131.1	1059.8	Raven Rock Rd, MD 491.	1062
1130.8	1060.1	Raven Rock Cliff, view 100 yards east . . . . 📷	1288
1130.1	1060.8	**Raven Rock Shelter** (0.1W) (2010), Ritchie Rd (0.6E). . . . .) ◊ ◖ ⊏ (16)	1647
		20.6◄13.1◄4.9◄►9.6►12.0►13.2 Two story shelter.	
		Water on opposite side of AT (0.3E) on steep side trail.	
1128.3	1062.6	Ends of High Rock Loop Trail 0.2 apart . . . . 39.6948,-77.5232 🅿 📷	1795
		0.1E from either end to view and parking. Parking gated from dusk till 8am.	
		1.7 from parking area to Pen Mar Park via Pen Mar Rd.	
1125.5	1065.4	Pen Mar County Park . . . . 39.7164,-77.5072 🅿 📷 (pg. 108)	1321
		Cascade, MD (1.4E); **Waynesboro, PA** (2.1W to Walmart, downtown 4.5)	
1125.2	1065.7	**MD-PA** border, RR tracks, Mason-Dixon Line	1250
1125.1	1065.8	Pen Mar Rd	1240
1124.6	1066.3	Falls Creek, footbridge, campsite . . . . ◊ ◖	1068
1124.1	1066.8	Buena Vista Rd . . . . ◊	1290
1122.9	1068.0	Old PA 16.	1278
1122.6	1068.3	Footbridge, stream, PA 16 . . . . 39.7414,-77.5072 🅿 (pg. 110)	1200
		Blue Ridge Summit, PA (1.2E)	
1122.4	1068.5	Mentzer Gap Rd, NoBo: turn west	1250
1122.0	1068.9	Rattlesnake Run Rd (gravel)	1378
1120.5	1070.4	**Deer Lick Shelters** 22.7◄14.5◄9.6◄►2.4►3.6►10.2 . . . . .) ◊ ◖ ⊏ (2x5)	1406
		Spring 10 yards north on AT or (0.2E) on blue-blazed trail.	
1120.2	1070.7	Pipeline clearing	1489
1119.6	1071.3	Dirt road	1378
1118.3	1072.6	Orange-blazed Chickadee Snowmobile Trail	909
1118.1	1072.8	**Antietam Shelter** (1940) . . . .) ◊ ◖ ⊏ (6)	889
		16.9◄12.0◄2.4◄►1.2►7.8►13.4 Better to get water from Old Forge Park 0.1N	
1118.0	1072.9	Old Forge Picnic Area, Old Forge Rd . . . . 39.8005,-77.4793 🅿 🏛 🚻 ◊	898
1116.9	1074.0	**Tumbling Run Shelters** . . . .) ◊ ◖ ⊏ (2x4)	1082
		13.2◄3.6◄1.2◄►6.6►12.2►19.6 Piped water 75 yards right of shelter.	
1115.6	1075.3	Chimney Rocks, view to east. . . . . 📷	1900

1004.9 **SNICKERS GAP, VA 7 & 679 (PINE GROVE RD),** A.T. crosses VA 7 at Pine Grove Rd. Take P.G. Rd to restaurants. Take VA 7 0.8E, then right on route 734 for P.O.

🅿 🚲 🚿 ⓘ **Mountain Trails** (19.4W) 540-667-0030 Full svc specialty outdoor store w/ complete supplies, equipment repair & advice.(mountain-trails.com)

🏤 ⓘ 🍴 ⌂ 🛒 **The Village Market** (1.1W) 540.955.8742 thevillagemkt@gmail.com Open 11a-8p Mo-Sa. Hiker friendly. Pizza, sandwiches & more. Fuel by oz. Limited shuttle to/or delivery from store to trail, Bear's Den or Blackburn Trail W-F eve, all day Sa.

ⓘ 🍴 🛒 **Horseshoe Curve Restaurant** (0.3W) 540.554.8291 Tu-W 5-11; Th-Sa 12-11, Su 12-9. Live bands F & Sa. Good pub food.

ⓘ 🍴 🛒 ➾ **Pine Grove Restaurant** (0.9W) M-Sa, 7-8; Su, 7-2. Hikers welcome, all day b'fast.

» *Bluemont, VA 20135* (1.7E) ☏540.554.4537, M-F 10-1 & 2-5, Sa 8:30-12

1012.3 **SIDE TRAILS, BOTH (0.2E) TO:**

🅿 🚲 🚿 ⌂ 🛏 **Blackburn AT Center** (0.2E) 540.338.9028 PATC caretaker on-site yr-round. Bunks in small cabin w/wood-burning stove. On porch of main building: logbook, donation box, pay phone, & electrical outlets to charge devices. Solar shower on lower lawn, water from hose.

1018.5 **KEYS GAP, WV 9**

🏕 **Rhonda Adams** 304.596.1911 Former thru-hiker w/first hand knowledge of trail & local towns. Range: SNP Big Meadows & PenMar, to Mason-Dixon Line. Prefers text.

🏕 🅿 🚿 ⌂ 🛏 🛒 🚲 **Bear Feet Retreat Hostel** (0.1E) 703.220.0196 patsyhikermama@aol.com Beautiful post & beam home - $25/night/person ground level; beds - 1 single, 2 double, 2 double floor mattresses, one lg couch; access to full basement living space w/kitchenette, full bath, cable tv, ping pong table, games; simple b'fast food provided; shower w/o stay $5; laundry $5/load (wardrobe for borrow); ride to stores/restaurant $10 RT, except Sweet Springs Store & Torlones Restaurant $5. Can also access the hostel via side trail located 2 mi N of Lesser Bald Shelter. Where trail bends sharply trail W, there is a short trail to BFRH is on the E side of the trail.

🏕 🅿 🚲 🚿 ⌂ 🛒 ➾ **Stoney Brook Organic Farm & Hostel** (5.4E) 540.668.9067, 540.668.7123 (Matt or Nathan) Run by a Twelve Tribes spiritual community. WFS, meals, shower, laundry avail. P/U & ret from Bears Den, Blackburn Trail Ctr, Keys Gap, & Harpers Ferry. Mail: 37091 Charles Town Pike, Hillsboro, VA 20132.

🏪 ⓘ 🍴 💲 🛒 **Sweet Springs Country Store** (0.3E) 540.668.7200 M-Sa 4a-11p, Su 7a-11p. Good selection of hiker foods. Stove fuel. Mail: 34357 Charles Town Pike, Purcellville, VA 20132.

🏤 ⓘ 🍴 **Mini-Mart & Torlone's Pizza** (0.4W) 304.725 0916 Veer left at intersection.

1023.9 **US 340, SHENANDOAH RIVER BRIDGE,** *NoBos stay on the A.T. for better access to Harpers Ferry.*

🅿 🚿 ➾ 🛒 **Econo Lodge** (0.1W) 304.535.6391 $109-139 (peak midsummer-check rates), 10% hiker discount, hot b'fast bar, no pets.

🅿 🚲 🚿 ⌂ ➾ 🛒 **Clarion Inn Harpers Ferry** (1.3W) 304.535.6302 Call for rates. Used to be the Quality Inn. Newly remodeled rooms. Whitehorse Tavern onsite. 10% Hiker discount.

🅿 🚲 🚿 🛏 🛒 🚿 ➾ **Harpers Ferry KOA** (1.3W) 304.535.6895 harpersferrykoa.com 7 Days. 7a-10p/ summer, 9a-5p/winter, Camping $45/up, cabins $95/up, both prices for 2 persons, $8EAP. Coin laundry on-site, shower only $5. Cafe has limited hrs.(harpersferrykoa.com)

» *Charles Town, WV 25414* (6.8W) All major services.

🏪 🛒 **Walmart** (5.1W) 304.728.2720 w/Grocery 24hrs, pharmacy M-F 9-9, Sa 9-7, Su 10-6.

➕ **Jefferson Urgent Care** (5.1W) 304.728.8533 M-F 8-8, Sa-Su 8-5.

🐾 **Jefferson Animal Hospital** (6.8W) 304.725.0428

» *Frederick, MD 21701* (20E) All major services.

1024.2 **SIDE TRAIL TO ATC HQ (0.2W)**

🏠 🏢 ➾ 🛒 **ATC HQ** (0.3W) 304.535.6331 Open yr-round daily 9-5. Closed Thanksgiving, Christmas & New Year's. If thru-hiking or hiking the entire trail in sections, have your photo taken for the album; a postcard version of this photo may be purchased (1st one free for ATC members). Hiker lounge, register, scale, cold & hot drinks inside, along w/hats, shirts, maps, all ATC publications. Coleman/alcohol/oz for donation. Info board on

HARPERS FERRY, WV

N 39.325,-77.739
Mag. Dec. 10.5° W

1024.8 **HIGH STREET**

H P Harpers Ferry National Historical Park (0.03E) 304.535.6029 $10/Vehicle entrance fee, park up to 2 wks (must register). Free shuttle bus to lower town (starts 9a). Gates open 8a-dusk.
front porch. Mail: (USPS) PO Box 807 or (FedEx/UPS) 799 Washington St, Harpers Ferry, WV 25425.
HostelHiker.com 202.670.6323 Thorton Gap-Pen-Mar Park. To/fr DC, Dulles/Baltimore Airports.
Mark "Strings" Cusic 304.433.0028 mdcusic@frontier.com Rockfish Gap to Duncannon.

» Harpers Ferry, WV (services cont'd pg. 104...)

» Harpers Ferry, WV 25425 (more services on map)

Potomac River

Railroad Station
Amtrak: Chicago ◇ DC
MARC: Martinsburg ◇ DC

Potomac St

"Lower Town" (see inset)

Jefferson Rock

From ATC to AT 0.6

ATC

Side Trail to ATC HQ

Mena's Italian (closed Mon)

Fillmore St

Shenandoah St

P

Frederick, MD 21 mi
Washington, DC 68 mi

340

The Barn

Canal House

Washington St

Anvil

Teahorse Hostel

Polk St

Bolivar-HF Library
304.535.2301
M,Tu,F,Sa 10-5:30
W,Th 10-8

Country Cafe
304.535.2327

7-11

KOA:
Camp Store
304.535.6885

Guide Shack Cafe

A Step In Time Bakery

PO (25425) 304.535.2479:
M-F 8-4, Sa 9-12

Union St

$

Econo Lodge

340

Shoreline Rd

Charles Town (all major services) 6.7 from AT
Clarion Inn Harpers Ferry (1.3W)

Harper's Ferry National Historic Park-parking and shuttle

H P

Inset – Lower Town:

Scoops Ice Cream
General Store &
Outfitter at HF
Coffee Mill

Lower Town

Cannonball Deli

Confectionaries

Coach House Grill & Bar

Potomac St

Hannah's BBQ

Town's Inn & Sundry Store

High St

Church St

Chestnut Hill Rd

1.8 mi

Origin of town names:
Harpers Ferry - Potomac ferry service operated by Robert Harper.
Charles Town - Founded by Charles Washington, brother of George.
Frederick, MD - Frederick Calvert, 6th Baron Baltimore.

» *Harpers Ferry, WV (...services cont'd from pg. 103)*

(...services cont'd from pg. 103)

🐾⚅🖥♨️Ⓒ📶🍴$🛏🚿📖🛒 **The Town's Inn** (0.07W) 304.932.0677 karantownsend@gmail.com Pvt room $110-$160 up to 4 persons. One pet room. Hostel $35PP, Laundry $5, shuttles $1/mile, no maildrops, Visa/MC OK. Dining 6a-10p daily yr-round. Shop stocked for hiker resupply.<TheTownsInn.com>

🐾Ⓒ🖥♨️🛒📶🛏✉ **Teahorse Hostel & Resupply** (1.1W) 304.535.6848 teahorsewv@yahoo.com 0.5W of ATC. $35/Bunk. Clean accommodations incl waffle b'fast. Laundry $6. No pets/ alcohol/smoking. Walk-ins welcome! Open daily 1p-9p. Broad resupply incl many hiker favorites.(teahorsehostel.com)

🛏 **HI Harpers Ferry Hostel** (1.8W) (See info at Sandy Hook Bridge, US 340)

🐾Ⓒ🖥♨️📖🛒 **The Outfitter at Harpers Ferry** (0.08W) 888.535.2087 outfitter1996@yahoo.com Full svc outfitter w/good selection of shoes & trail food. Shuttle referrals. Open daily 10-6, mid-Mar - Dec. Seasonal hrs otherwise.<theoutfitteratharpersferry.com>

🐾Ⓒ📶🛒 **Two Rivers Treads** (7.7W) 304.885.8843 trtreads@gmail.com 15% off for thru-hikers. Specialize in minimal footwear & foot health. Carries footwear, socks, sandals/camp shoes. Also has a lot of injury prevention tools/information.<tworiverstreads.com>

🍴Ⓒ📶♨️ **Guide Shack Cafe** (0.8W) 304.995.6022 Veteran owned. M-Fr 6:30a-6:30p,Sa-Su 7a-7p. Locally roasted coffee, espresso, teas, sandwiches, soup, chili, baked goods, granola & ice cream. Gear up, climb the bouldering wall & strategize your next adventure.

🚍 **Amtrak** (0.1W) 800.872.7245 "Capitol Limited" daily HF to Washington DC Union Station 11:31a-1:05p (depart-arrive), DC to HF 4:05-5:16p, $13-$25 each way. Book early for low price.(amtrak.com)

🚍 **EPTA** 304.263.0876 Route to Charles Town (Walmart) $2.50 ea way. M-F: 9:05a, 10:42a, 12:03p, 1:24p, 3p, 4:45p, & 7:45p.

🚍 **Maryland Rail Commuter Service (MARC)** (0.1W) 410.539.5000 "Brunswick Line" M-F to Washington DC Union Station departs 5:25a, 5:50a & 6:50a, returns 4:25, 5:40 & 6:20p. $12 each way.

Harpers Ferry, WV
0.6 mi. on A.T.

Knights Inn

🐾📶♨️Ⓒ🖥🍴⚅🛒 **Knights Inn** (0.4W) 301.660.3580 $59.99/K-2, $69.99/D-2, $89.99/ D-3, $99.99/D-4, incl fridge, m'wave, c. b'fast 6-9. Hiker laundry $5, ADA defined service animals are welcome at this hotel. Restaurant across st.

🐾Ⓒ🖥♨️📶🛒✉ **HI Harpers Ferry Hostel** (0.9W) 301.834.7652 harpersferry@hiusa.org ID req'd for stay. Discounted thru hiker rate $22.40 incl tax, shower, internet & WiFi, linens, A/C & heat, daily complimentary make-your-own b'fast & dinners F & Sa. There is often free food avail in the hiker cupboard as well! Laundry $4. Tent camping $10PP incl outside showers, WiFi, phone charging on back porch. Fire pits & grill. Inside Hostel access fee for campers $5PP incl comp b'fast, cooking facility & inside showers. Service dogs OK inside, otherwise dogs on leash allowed only if camping. Basic supplies & snacks avail for purchase. Netflix movies avail. Non-guest parking $10/day. Check-in 4-10p, check-out 11a. Open Apr 13-Nov 11 for individuals, yr-round for groups. Mail: 19923 Sandy Hook Rd, Knoxville, MD 21758.(hiusa.org)

🚍🍴$ **Crown Hillside Station** (0.4W) 301.969.5013 Conv. store w/pizza, wings, & more. M-Sa 6a-9p, Su 8a-8p.

🍴$ **Guide House Grill** (0.5W) 301.655.3663 (guidehousegrill.com)

1026.2   SANDY HOOK BRIDGE, US 340

1027.7   US 340, KEEP TRYST RD

» *Brunswick, MD 21716* (2.5E), ✉(5E), 📠301.834.9944, M-F 8-4:30, Sa 9-12

🍴🛒 **Wing'n Pizza Shack** (3.8E) 301.834.5555 Delivers to HF Hostel.

1034.8   GAPLAND RD, GATHLAND SP

🏠♨️⛺♦️🏪📶📧 **The Treehouse Camp at Maple Tree** (0.5W) 301.432.5585 $30 Tentsite for up to 3 persons, $10EAP. Cottages w/wood stoves, good drinking water. Campstore has candy bars, sodas, batteries & m'wavable food. Open Yr-round. On Townsend Rd which is to the west as you exit the park.(thetreehousecamp.com)

■ **Locust Valley Bible Church** (1.7W) 240.469.1584 Rides to/fr church svcs, lunch prov when poss. P/U from H.F. High St to Monument Rd, give as much notice as possible, 1-2 days appreciated.

1042.3   TURNERS GAP, US ALT 40

🍴🍺📶 **Old South Mountain Inn** (0.07W) 301.432.6155 Tu-F 5-close, Sa 4-close, Su brunch 10:30-1:30, dinner 2-close. Men, no sleeveless shirts. Please shower 1st. Dining reserv preferred. Patio dining avail.

» *Boonsboro, MD 21713* (2.5W)

🥾🔦🏕️🛏️ **Barbara Hicks** (2.5W) 703-297-5571 Guest room w/ twin fold out couch & full bath. Reasonable rates. P/U & ret to trail (2.6 mi away). Walk to restaurants, corner store, laundry, m'wave, hot pot, light b'fast items in room. Shared use of kitchen & living room. Camping in back yard also avail.

🏠 **Cronise Market Place** (2W) 301.432.7377 M-F 9-7, Sa 9-6, Su 12-6

⛪🍴 **Crawfords** (2.5W) 301.432.2903 M-F 7a-5p, Sa 7a-3p

🍴 **Mountainside Deli & Ice Cream** (1.9W) 301.432.6700 M-Sa 10a-7p, Su 11a-5p. CC ok.

🍴 **Vesta Pizzeria** (2.4W) 301.432.6166 For p/u or delivery. Open at 11a, 7 days/wk. Delivery after 4p wkdays, all day wkends.

🍴📶 **Turn the Page Book Store** (2.5W) 301.432.4588 Full coffee svc, refreshments, books, gifts.(ttpbooks.com)

🧺 **Marcy's Laundry Center** (2.6W) 301.491.5849 M-Su 5:30a-10p.

» *Middletown, MD 21769* (5.1E)

■ **Caring Hands Chiropractic** (7.7E) 240.344.0066 Chiropractic & therapeutic massage. Call/text ahead for appt. Try for beginning of zero days for max benefit. She is also a hiker & may be able to come to you or give ride from/to trail.

↖ N

𝐑 N

4.3 mi of AT shown on this map

↖ N

BOONSBORO, MD

Boonsboro Mtn Rd

Washington Monument

Washington Monument SP

Monument Rd

Main St

AT to Market 1.9, to PO 2.4 →

← AT

40A

𝐑 S

Old South Mountain Inn 🍴🍺

Dahlgren Backpacker Campground 🅿️

Rohrersville Rd

67

Cronise Veterinary 301.416.2656

Cronise Market ⛪

Boonsboro Veterinary Hospital 301.432.1832

Library (0.5 from Main St) 301.432.5723
M-Th 10:30-7,
Fri 10:30-6,
Sa 10:15-2

PO (21713):
301.432.6861
M-F 9-1 & 2-5
Sa 9-12
(2.8 mi from AT)

Vesta Pizza 🍴🍺

Creamery 🍴🍴

Crawfords 🍴🍴

Turn the Page 🍴

Marcy's Laundry 🧺

Pete's Barber Shop ✂️

Subway 🍴

Stone Werks Coffee & Sweets

Dan's Taphouse 🍺🍴

Mountainside Deli 🍴

3.0 mi

1114.7	**1076.2**	Pipeline clearing		1916
1113.6	**1077.3**	Powerline		2027
1112.9	**1078.0**	Snowy Mountain Rd		1703
1112.3	**1078.6**	Swamp Rd, **South Mountain, PA 17261** (1.0E). . . . . (pg. 110)		1560
1111.9	**1079.0**	PA 233, **South Mountain, PA 17261** (1.2E). . . . . (pg. 110)		1605

⚠ Many springs in PA run dry in June, July & August.

1110.3	**1080.6**	**Rocky Mountain Shelters** (0.2E)(1989) . . . . ☽ ◐ ⬧ ⌐ (2x4)	1662
		10.2◀7.8◀6.6◀▶5.6▶13.0▶19.2	
		Piped spring 0.5 mile on trail to road, then right 75 yards.	

1107.3	**1083.6**	US 30, **Fayetteville, PA** (3.2W) . . . . 39.9059,-77.4786 🅿 (0.6E)(pg. 110)	960
		Overnight parking SW corner of US 30 & Pine Grove Rd, check-in at park HQ.	
1106.9	**1084.0**	Side trail to **Caledonia State Park**, pool area. . . . . (pg. 110)	934
1106.1	**1084.8**	Locust Gap Rd, Valley Trail to west.	1334

1104.7	**1086.2**	**Quarry Gap Shelters** (1935) 13.4◀12.2◀5.6◀▶7.4▶13.6▶24.5 . ☽ ◐ ⬧ ⌐ (2x4)	1471
1104.4	**1086.5**	Footbridge, stream . . . . ◐	1542
1104.0	**1086.9**	Hosack Run Trail to east	1819
1103.2	**1087.7**	5-way gravel road intersection	1984
1102.4	**1088.5**	Powerline	1867
1102.0	**1088.9**	Woods road	1986

1100.7	**1090.2**	Middle Ridge Road	2070
1100.1	**1090.8**	3 Points (intersecting gravel roads), campsite to north	1961
1099.7	**1091.2**	PATC Milesburn Cabin (locked), spring 100 yards west . . . . ◐	1681
1099.4	**1091.5**	Ridge Rd (gravel), campsite north of road . . . . ⬧	1907
1098.6	**1092.3**	Rocky Knob Trail (orange-blazed)	1902
1098.0	**1092.9**	Powerline, campsite to north . . . . ⬧	1913
1097.3	**1093.6**	**Birch Run Shelter** (2003) stream 75 yards north on AT . . . . . . ☽ ◐ ⬧ ⌐ (8)	1800
		19.6◀13.0◀7.4◀▶6.2▶17.1▶25.2	
1097.2	**1093.7**	Footbridge, stream . . . . ◐	1783
1096.0	**1094.9**	Shippensburg Rd . . . . 39.9972,-77.405 🅿	2040

1094.9	1096.0	Dead Woman's Hollow Road (gravel), **AT Midpoint**	1954
		The A.T. north of Dead Woman's Hollow Road may be temporarily rerouted for short durations. Hikers should observe signage & follow any reroutes as directed.	
1094.1	1096.8	Side trail to Michener Cabin (locked) . . . . ⚭(0.3E)	1850
1093.5	1097.4	Woods road	1849
1092.2	1098.7	Woodrow Rd (gravel), campsite 0.1N . . . . ⛺	1779
1091.7	1099.2	Stream. . . . . ⚭	1538
1091.2	1099.7	Sunset Rocks Trail to east, rejoins AT to north . . . . ⚭	1318
1091.1	1099.8	**Toms Run Shelter** (1936) . . . .))⚭⛺⊏(4)	1302
		19.2◄13.6◄6.2◄►10.9►19.0►37.2 Water behind shelter	
1090.9	1100.0	Stream. . . . . ⚭	1272
1089.9	1101.0	Michaux Rd	1330
1089.0	1101.9	Toms Run, footbridge, stream. Sunset Rocks Trail to east. . . . . ⚭	1020
1087.8	1103.1	PA 233 (paved), NoBo on road 0.1W, veer right on road into park	899
1087.5	1103.4	**Pine Grove Furnace SP, AT Museum** . . . . 40.0317,-77.3054 🅿 (pg. 111)	872
1087.0	1103.9	Fuller Lake, free showers, snack bar 11-7 daily Mem-Labor Day . . . . . . ⏐🍴⤬🚿	841

> 🚫 No camping within one mile of PGF SP; camping within the park only at designated (paid) campsites. No overnight sleeping in pavilions.

1085.1	1105.8	Campsite . . . . ⛺	1251
1084.9	1106.0	Pole Steeple Trail to west	1300
1083.9	1107.0	Campsite . . . . ⛺	1370
1081.7	1109.2	Roadbed.	1049
1081.4	1109.5	Trail to **Mountain Creek Campground** (0.7W) steep . . . . (pg. 111)	1015
1080.3	1110.6	Spring 50 yards west on marked trail . . . . ⚭	725
1080.2	1110.7	**James Fry (Tagg Run) Shelter** (0.2E), campsite west of AT . . . .))⚭⛺⊏(9)	699
		24.5◄17.1◄10.9◄►8.1►26.3►33.6 Spring uphill from shelter; water 0.2E farther.	
1079.8	1111.1	Pine Grove Rd (paved)	664
1079.6	1111.3	Stream. . . . . ⚭	639
1079.2	1111.7	⚠ Cross RR tracks; sharp east turn for NoBo, west for SoBo . . . . ⚭	633
1079.0	1111.9	PA 34, Hunters Run Rd, **Store & Deli** (0.2E) . . 40.0777,-77.1945 🅿 (0.1E) (pg. 111)	625
1077.0	1113.9	PA 94, **Mt Holly Springs, PA** (2.5W) . . . . (pg. 111)	880
1076.7	1114.2	Sheet Iron Roof Rd, campground 0.4W . . . . 40.093,-77.1641 🅿 (pg. 111)	773
1076.3	1114.6	Footbridge, stream, campsite . . . . ⚭⛺	687
1076.0	1114.9	Footbridge, stream . . . . ⚭	671
1075.6	1115.3	Old Town Rd (gravel)	736

SoBo

NoBo

1046.6 ★ BARTMAN HILL TRAIL (0.6W) TO GREENBRIAR SP
1047.0 I-70, US 40, From US 40, it is 0.4W to entrance of Greenbriar State Park, and an additional 0.7 to the visitor center, where the Bartman Trail enters the park. It's better to use the Bartman Trail.

» 🏕🏊 **Greenbrier State Park** (0.6W) 301.791.4767 Open 8a to Sunset. Camping first Fri of Apr to last full wkend in Oct. Entrance $5M-F, $7 Sa-Su, MD residents lower. Prices listed as MD resident/nonresident. Tent sites w/showers $26-30, higher wkends/holidays. Pets allowed at Dog Wood. Lunch concession stand, lake swimming, & paddle boat rentals avail Mem Day-Labor Day.

1055.7 WOLFSVILLE RD, MD 17, ♦ (0.3W) If shelter water source is dry, you may get water from ranger's house. Go 0.1E (compass south) to a gravel road on left, then 0.2 on gravel road to first house on left.

» *Smithsburg, MD 21783* (1.5W)
☐ 301.824.2828, M-F 8:30-1 & 2-4:30, Sa 8:30-12
⊕ **Dollar General Store** (1.7W) 301.824.6940 Daily 7-10.
🛒 **Food Lion** (2.5W) 301.824.7011 Daily 7-11.
¡Ψ **Smithsburg Market** (1.9W) 301.824.2171 M-Sa 8-9, Su 10-9.
¡Ψ **Dixie Diner** (2W) 301.824.5224 Tu-F 7-8, Sa-Su 7-2, clsd M.
¡Ψ **Vince's New York Pizza** (2W) 301.824.3939 M-F 11a-10.30p, Sa- Su 11a-11:30a. Delivery avail daily.(vincespizza.net)
¡Ψ **Subway** (2.5W) 301.824.3826 24 hrs 7 days.
¡Ψ **China 88** (2.6W) 301.824.7300 M-Th 11-10, F-Sa 11-10.30, Su 12-10.
¡Ψ **Rocky's Pizza** (3.3W) 301.824.3939 M-F 11a-10.30p, Su 11a-10p.
➕ **Meritus Medical Center** (8.5W) 301.824.2066 M-Sa 10:30a-10:30p, Su 11a-10p. 301.790.8000 ER open 24/7 in Hagerstown.
✚ **Rite Aid** (2.6W) 301.824.2211 Store 8a-9p, pharmacy 9a-9p.
🐾 **Smithsburg Veterinary Clinic** (1.7W) 301.416.0888 M-F 8-12/1:30-7, Sa 8-12, Appts Recommended.
🧺 **Laundry** (2W)
📖 **Library** (2.5W) 301.824.7722 M,W,Th 10-30a-7p, Tu 12:30-9p, F 10:30-6, Sa 10:15a-2p, Su clsd.

⏚ **Ace Hardware** (2.7W) 301.733.7940 M&Th 7a-6p, Tu,W, F 7a-5p, Sa 7a-3p, Closed Sun.

1065.4 PEN MAR COUNTY PARK. Open 1st Su in May - last Su in Oct. Vending & water; no camping. Restrooms locked when park closed. Bobby D's & other pizza places deliver. Pen Mar Rd passes in front of park, east of A.T. Call 240-313-2700 M-F, 7a-4p for Pen Mar parking passes which are recommended for overnight parking. Rouzerville PO is nearest to the A.T. If intending to walk to town, do so from A.T./Pen Mar intersection 0.3N of park & from PA 16. See map & svcs for options, directions from the park & from PA 16.

🛒 **Dennis Sewell** 301.241.3376 P/U from Harpers Ferry to Pine Grove Furnace SP. Will p/u Baltimore Airport. Dogs OK.
🚐 **Nina Murphy Shuttle Service** 703.946.9404 ninashuttles@yahoo.com Waynesboro, VA to Waynesboro, PA, Dulles & Reagan National AP & SNP.

» *Cascade, MD 21719* (1.4E on Pen Mar/High Rock Rd)
🛒 **Sanders Market** (2.2E) 301.241.3612 M,W-F, 8:30a-9p, Tu,Sa 8:30a-8p.
¡Ψ **Mountain Grill** (3.9E) 828.688.9061 Cash only, M-Sa 11-8. Clsd Su.
🏠 **Fort Ritchie Community Center** (1.5E) 301.241.5085 bbrowning@thefrcc.org M-Th 6-9, Fr 6-6, Sa 9-5, Su 10-4.(thefrcc.org)

» *Rouzerville, PA 17250* (2W)
¡Ψ **Bobby D's Pizza** (2W) 717.762.0388
➕ **Waynesboro Walk-in Clinic** (2.5W) M-F 8-5.
🐾 **Wayne Heights Animal Hospital** (3.2W) 717.765.9636

» *Waynesboro, PA 17214* (4.6W) *Mason-Dixon Appalachian Trail Outdoor Festival* Sa, Jun 16, 2018 at Red Run Park, 12143 Buchanan Trail E, 10-4

🏨 **Cobblestone Hotel** (2.5W) 717.762.0034 Hiker discount. $80/up +tax, incl hot b'fast, pool, hot tub.
🏨 **Burgundy Lane B&B** (5.3W) 717.762.8112 $90-1100 w/full b'fast, free laundry & shuttle to trailhead or town stop. Longer shuttles for fee. Mail: 128 W Main St, Waynesboro, PA 17268.
🏨 **Days Inn** (5.8W) $59S, $69D, $55EAP. C. b'fast, $10 pet fee, laundry next door.
➕ **Waynesboro Hospital** (4.5W) 717.765.4000 501 E Main St.

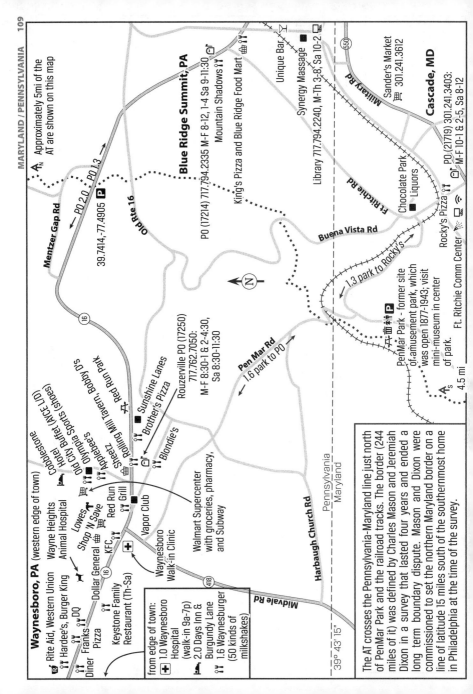

Waynesboro, PA (western edge of town)

🅿 Rite Aid, Western Union
🍴 Hardee's, Burger King
🍴 Diner 🍴🍺 DQ
🍕 Franks Pizza

Cobblestone
Hotel Buffet (AYCE L/D)
Old City Sports (shoes)
🍴🍺 Olympia's 🍴🍺 Bobby D's
🍴🍺 Applebee's 🚭 Red Run Park
🍴🍺 Rolling Mill Tavern
Sheetz 🍴🍺 Grill
Wayne Heights Animal Hospital
📚 Lowes 🏧 Shop 'N Save
🍴🍺 Red Run
🍴🍺 KFC 🍴🍺
Vapor Club
Dollar General

🅿 P0 2.0 ← P0 1.3 →
🅿 P0 2.0
39.7414,-77.4905

Mentzer Gap Rd

⚓N Approximately 5mi of the AT are shown on this map

16

Old Rte 16

🅿 Brother's Pizza
Sunshine Lanes
Rouzerville P0 (17250) 717.762.7050: M-F 8:30-1 & 2-4:30, Sa 8:30-11:30
🍴🍺 Blondie's

Keystone Family Restaurant (Th-Sa)

from edge of town:
✚ 1.0 Waynesboro Hospital (walk-in 9a-7p)
🛏 2.0 Days Inn & Burgundy Lane
🍴🍺 1.6 Waynesburger (50 kinds of milkshakes)

Waynesboro Walk-in Clinic
✚

Walmart Supercenter with groceries, pharmacy, and Subway

16

418

Midvale Rd

Harbaugh Church Rd

Pennsylvania
Maryland

39° 43' 15"

N

Pen Mar Rd
1.6 park to P0

Blue Ridge Summit, PA

P0 (17214) 717.794.2335 M-F 8-12, 1-4 Sa 9-11:30 🕐
Mountain Shadows 🍴🍺

550

Library 717.794.2240, M-Th 3-8, Sa 10-2

King's Pizza and Blue Ridge Food Mart

Unique Bar

Synergy Massage

Ft Ritchie Rd

Military Rd

Sander's Market 🏧 301.241.3612

Cascade, MD

Chocolate Park Liquors

P0 (21719) 301.241.3403: M-F 10-1 & 2-5, Sa 8-12

🍴🍺 Rocky's Pizza

Ft. Ritchie Comm Center

Buena Vista Rd

1.3 park to Rocky's

PenMar Park - former site of amusement park, which was open 1877-1943; visit mini-museum in center of park.

🅿

⚓S

4.5 mi

The AT crosses the Pennsylvania-Maryland line just north of PenMar Park and the railroad tracks. The border (244 miles of it) was defined by Charles Mason and Jeremiah Dixon in a survey that lasted four years and ended a long term boundary dispute. Mason and Dixon were commissioned to set the northern Maryland border on a line of latitude 15 miles south of the southernmost home in Philadelphia at the time of the survey.

SOUTH MOUNTAIN, PA

1.2 mi

1.3 to P0

233

233

Swamp Rd

Biesecker Gap Rd

1.0 to P0

South Mountain Rd

South Mountain Tavern

1083.6   US 30

⌂ **Freeman's Shuttle Service** 717.491.2460, 717.360.1481 Front Royal to DWG. Slackpacking Pen Mar to Duncannon.

⛺ 🚿 △ 🛏 🅿 ⌂☒ **Trail of Hope Hostel** (1.3E) 717.360.1481, 717.491.2460 slfreeman1942@gmail.com $22 Bunk, $12 camping. Coin laundry & use of kitchen. Resupply incl white gas/denatured/oz & canisters. Mail: 7798 Lincoln Way E, Fayetteville, PA 17222.

🛏 🍴 △ 🚿 ☒ **Scottish Inn & Suites** (2.6W) 717.352.2144 $59S, $69D, $10EAP, $15 pets. $5PP for p/u or ret to trail. $10 for ride to Walmart. Coin laundry. Guest Mail: 5651 Lincoln Way East, Fayetteville, PA 17222.

🏪 ⛽ 🚿 ♨ 🛒 **Timbers Restaurant & Ice Cream Parlor** (0.6W) 717.401.0605 Charging station, snacks, fuels, hiker/pet friendly. Mail: 8228 Lincoln Way, Fayetteville PA 17222

🏪 🍴 🛒 🚲 ⛽ **Rutters Convenience Store** (1.6W) 717.401.0626 24/7 w/WiFi & deli.

🍴 **Flamingo Restaurant** (2.6W) 717.352.8755 Excellent large b'fast.

» **Fayetteville, PA 17222 (3.2W)** (see map)

1084.0   SIDE TRAIL TO CALEDONIA STATE PARK

⌂ **Gary Grant Shuttles** 717.706.2578 Can shuttle individuals & groups ranging from Caledonia SP to Duncannon, to local resupply (Walmart), Greyhound & Amtrak stations. Slackpacking, fuel or-hand.

⛺ 🍴 🅿 **≈Caledonia SP** (3.9E) 717.352.2161 Open late Mar - mid Dec. Pool & snack bar open daily Mem-Labor Day, 11a-7p, weather permitting. Campsites avg $30, ($4.50 sr disc). Pets $2. $4 Shower. $6 Pool (incl shower). Check-in at office for long term parking. Free local-call phone outside office.(fb.com/Caledonia-State-Park-218708124975068)

1063.3   PA 16

» **Blue Ridge Summit, PA 17214** (1.2E)

🏪 **Dollar General** (2.8E) 717.296.1575 7 days, 8a-10p.

🍴 🍺 **Unique Bar and Grill** (2.9E) 717.794.2565 Live music.

🛏 🍴 ♨ ♿ 🚿 **Synergy Massage & Wellness Center** (1.9E) 877.372.6617 massage@synergymassage.com Will p/u & ret to trail. Free showers, hot tub & pool. Massage by appt as low as $30.(synergymassage.com)

PO (17261): 717.749.5833 ☒
M-F 12-4, Sa 8:30-11:30
South Mountain Tavern

1078.6   ★   SWAMP RD, DIRT ROAD
1079.0   PA 233

⌂ 🍴 🍺 🚿 **South Mountain Tavern** (1E or 1.2E) 717.749.3845 Free tenting/showers for patrons, open M-Sa 9a-2a, Su noon.

» **South Mountain, PA 17261** (1E or 1.2E)

PO (17261): 717.749.5833 ☒
M-F 12-4, Sa 8:30-11:30
South Mountain Tavern

FAYETTEVILLE, PA

🏪 Walmart with
💊 pharmacy &
🍴 Subway
(7mi from AT)

7.0 mi

Family Dollar

Richey Rd

Rutter's 🍴

Maria & Sal's Pizzeria 🍴

Mt Alto Rd

Rite Aid 💊

Scottish Inn

🍴 Flamingo Restaurant

Squeaky Clean

PO (17222): 717.352.2022
M-F 8-4:30; Sa 8:30-12
(3.8 mi from AT)

Dollar General

Rutter's

Trail of Hope Hostel

Timbers Restaurant
& Ice Cream Parlor

Caledonia
SP 🍴

Long Term
P AT parking 🍴
Yianni's Tavern
(1.4 from AT)

Pine Grove Rd →
233

PINE GROVE FURNACE SP

Fuller Lake & Beach

Pine Grove Rd

Park Office 🏠

Pine Grove General Store 🏛

Ironmasters Mansion Hostel 🛏

Bendersville Ln

Furnace 🏛 👫

P 👫

0.7 mi

233

1103.4   PINE GROVE FURNACE STATE PARK, *(see map)*

🏠 ⊛🔲 ⛺ **A.T. Museum** 717.486.8126 Hikers welcome to charge devices & relax in our ALDHA hiker lounge. Artifacts & photos of past hikers, signs from Springer & Katahdin. Sells halfway patch & bandana. Open Mar 24-Apr 29 wkends only 12-4; May 6-Jul 15 daily 9-4; Jul 16-Aug 19 daily 12-4; Aug 22- Oct 28 W-Sun 12-4 **Hiker Festival** May 6. **Fall Festival** Oct 20-21.

🛏⊛👜☕🔲✉ **Ironmasters Mansion Hostel** 717.486.4108 ironmasterspinegrove@gmail.com $25PP w/o meal, $35PP w/meal (dinner & b'fast). 5p check-in, 9a check-out. Open Apr 1-Oct 31. Clsd Tues & sometimes for special events. Call/email for reservations. Laundry $3. Mail: 1212 Pine Grove Rd, Gardners, PA 17324.

⛺👫P ⛺**Pine Grove Furnace State Park** 717.486.7174 Campsites (for up to 5) open late Mar - early Dec, $24/up wkdays, $26/up wkends, ($2 more for non-PA residents - SR/ADA $4.50 discount). Dogs allowed some sites. Restrooms throughout park. Register w/park office for parking overnight; cars can be left for up to 2 wks in lot compass south of Museum (interior of park). Beach/swimming area at Fuller Lake & Laurel Lake.
🏛 👫👚🍴💲 **Pine Grove General Store** 717.486.4920 Open daily 8a-7p mid May - Labor Day; wkends only mid Apr - mid May & Labor Day - Oct. Cold drinks, selection of hiking food, canister fuel, fuel/oz, socks, toiletries. Short order grill. Soda machine outside. **Home of half gallon challenge.**

The AT is on **State Game Lands** in PA from north of Peters Mtn Shelter to Wind Gap, with the exception of small patches of land, mostly near major road crossings. Watch for posted regulations. Primitive one-night camping is allowed:

▶ Only by hikers starting & ending at different locations.
▶ Within 200 ft of the AT, &

500 ft from water sources, trailheads, road crossings, & parking areas.

▶ Only small campfires are allowed, & only when wildfire danger is less than "high."

(Allentown, Bake Oven Knob, Darlington, Cove Mtn, & Rausch Gap Shelters are on State Game Lands)

1109.5   SIDE TRAIL (0.7W) TO CAMPGROUND

🔱⛺👫⛺ **Mountain Creek Campground** (0.7W) camp@mtncreekcg.com Open Apr-late Oct, cabins $55+ tax, tentsites $28. Either holds 2 adults/4 children. Camp store has sodas & ice cream, short-order grill on wkends.

1111.9   PA 34, HUNTERS RUN RD

🏛 👫💲 **Green Mtn Store** (0.3E) 717.486.4558 M-F 7a-8p, Sa 8-8, Su 9-6. Good selection of hiker foods, prepared foods, ice cream, canister fuel, heet.

1113.9   PA 94

» **Mt. Holly Springs, PA 17065** (2.5W), 🏛💲717.486.3468 M-F 8-1 & 2-4:30, Sa 9-12. 5mi farther to 81 interchange w/Walmart, movies, coin-op at Carlisle Commons.

🏠👫☕🔲 **Holly Inn, Restaurant and Tavern** (2W) 717.486.3823 $50S, $55D $5EAP, free ride to/from AT, $5 round trip from Pine Grove Furnace SP. Fri live music, Sa karaoke, Sun open mic, Restaurant, open daily, laundry nearby.
🏛 **Sheetz, Dollar General, Family Dollar** (2.1W)
👫🍴 **J & K Hi Hat Restaurant** (2.6W) 717.323.0473   M-W 6a-2p, Th-F 6a-8p, Sa-Su 7a-2p B/L/D.
🍴 **Subway, Sicilia Pizza** (2.6W)
⚕ **Holly Pharmacy** (2.2W) 717.486.5321 M-F 8:30a-7p, Sa 8:30a-3p, clsd Su.

1114.2   SHEET IRON ROOF RD

🔱⛺👫⛺ **Deer Run Campground** (0.4W) 717.486.8168 Tent w/shower $10, cabin $75+tax.

1075.0	1115.9	Rock maze		1186
1074.6	1116.3	Rock maze		1097
1074.2	1116.7	Whiskey Spring Rd, reliable water from spring	♦	830

> 🚫 No camping & 🚫 No Campfires in Cumberland Valley between
> Alec Kennedy & Darlington Shelters, except at backpackers campsite south of Boiling Springs.

1072.2	1118.7	Little Dogwood Run, campsite, orange-blazed trail 1.7E to BSA campground.	♦ ⌂	870
1072.1	1118.8	**Alec Kennedy Shelter** (0.2E), spring behind shelter is unreliable . . . . ⤴ ◊ ⌐ (7)		950
		25.2◄19.0◄8.1◄▶18.2▶25.5▶33.8		
1071.2	1119.7	Center Point Knob, original AT midpoint, White Rocks Trail 0.4E to view. . . . . 📷		1060
1069.8	1121.1	Cornfield, south end		562
1069.3	1121.6	Leidigh Dr		553
1068.6	1122.3	Backpacker's Campsite (nearby railroad tracks can be noisy)	⤴ ⌂	514
1068.4	1122.5	Bucher Hill Rd, get permit from ATC office to park overnight. 40.1478,-77.1241	🅿 ⤴	501
1068.2	1122.7	PA 174, First Street, ATC Mid-Atlantic Regional Office . . . . (pg. 116)		500
		Boiling Springs, PA		
1066.7	1124.2	Stone wall.		627
1066.1	1124.8	PA 74, York Rd. . . . . 40.1731,-77.1211 🅿		573
1065.1	1125.8	Lisburn Rd.		547
1064.6	1126.3	Byers Rd.		556
1064.5	1126.4	Footbridge, stream	♦	505
1064.1	1126.8	Trindle Rd, PA 641, kiosk . . . . 40.195,-77.1083 🅿 (pg. 117)		540
1062.9	1128.0	Ridge Rd, Biddle Rd. . . . .(pg. 117)		471
1062.4	1128.5	Old Stone House Rd, footbridge, stream	♦	474
1061.7	1129.2	Appalachian Dr		525
1061.4	1129.5	PA Turnpike (I-76) overpass		498
1060.8	1130.1	Railroad tracks		478
1060.2	1130.7	US 11, **Carlisle, PA** (0.5W). . . . .(pg. 117)		490
1059.3	1131.6	Pass over I-81 on Bernheisel Rd		485
1058.7	1132.2	Fence stile (two)		465
1057.9	1133.0	Conodoguinet Creek, footbridge alongside road . . . 40.2598,-77.1037 🅿 ⤔ ⤴ ♦		389
		Scott Farm Trail ATC Crew HQ Open May-Oct, picnic table, no camping.		
		The AT u-turns, passes under bridge, and heads north.		
1056.8	1134.1	Sherwood Drive, parking to east. . . . . .40.274,-77.0995 🅿 ♦		397
		Many footbridges, streams north and south of this road.		
1055.9	1135.0	PA 944 tunnel		480

1055.0	**1135.9**	Piped spring where AT crosses overgrown dirt road	♦	718
		NoBo planning stay at Darlington Shelter consider getting water here.		
1054.3	**1136.6**	View	📷	1102
1054.0	**1136.9**	Darlington Trail, Tuscarora Trail		1246
1053.9	**1137.0**	**Darlington Shelter** (0.1E) 37.2◄26.3◄18.2◄►7.3►15.6►22.3 . . . . . ☽ ♦ ⊏ (5)		1221
		(2005) Unreliable water on blue-blazed trail in front of shelter. Taj Mahal privy.		
1052.3	**1138.6**	Gravel road		725
1052.0	**1138.9**	Millers Gap Rd (paved)		684
1051.7	**1139.2**	PA 850 . . . . .40.3218,-77.0781 🅿		673
1050.2	**1140.7**	Service road		761
1050.0	**1140.9**	Footbridge, stream	♦	852
1049.2	**1141.7**	Pipeline, trail very rocky from here north to PA 274	📷	1319
1047.5	**1143.4**	Blue-blazed trail 0.4W to service road		1259
1046.6	**1144.3**	**Cove Mountain Shelter** (0.2E)(2000) . . . . ☽ ♦ ⊏ (8)		1274
		33.6◄25.5◄7.3◄►8.3►15.0►33.0 Spring 0.1 mile on steep side trail.		

SoBo   NoBo

1044.6	**1146.3**	Hawk Rock, view	📷	1052
1043.9	**1147.0**	⚠ Old trail to west, AT turns east (uphill for NoBo)		516
1043.5	**1147.4**	Inn Rd, trail very rocky from here south to pipeline.		380
1043.0	**1147.9**	PA 274, pass under US 11/15		385
1042.6	**1148.3**	**Duncannon, PA**, High St + Broadway . . . .(pg. 120)		393
1041.5	**1149.4**	Juniata River, bridge		366
1040.8	**1150.1**	Susquehanna River . . . . 40.396,-77.0085 🅿		376
		North end of Clarks Ferry Bridge, US 22/322, railroad tracks		
1039.9	**1151.0**	View	📷	654
1038.5	**1152.4**	Susquehanna Trail to west	♦	1188
1038.3	**1152.6**	**Clarks Ferry Shelter** (0.1E)(1993) . . . . ☽ ♦ ◭ ⊏ (8)		1212
		33.8◄15.6◄8.3◄►6.7►24.7►38.1 Piped spring just beyond shelter.		
1038.0	**1152.9**	Powerline	📷	1323

⚠ Nov. 15 - Dec15 (except Sundays): On state gamelands (much of the A.T. between Susquehanna River & Delaware Water Gap) everyone is required to wear at least 250 square inches of fluorescent orange material on the head, chest & back combined, or a fluorescent orange hat, and must be visible for 360°.

1035.4	**1155.5**	Powerline	1219
1034.5	**1156.4**	PA 225 . . . . 40.4119,-76.9299 🅿	1251
1033.9	**1157.0**	Powerline	1281
1032.5	**1158.4**	Table Rock, view . . . . 📷	1340
1031.6	**1159.3**	**Peters Mtn Shelter** (1994) 22.3◄15.0◄6.7◄►18.0►31.4►35.5 . . . . ☽ ◊ ⛺ (16)	1174
		Weak spring 0.3 mile steeply downhill from shelter (300 rock steps).	
1030.6	**1160.3**	Victoria Trail.⚠ See State Game Lands guidelines (**pg. 111**)	1195
1030.0	**1160.9**	Whitetail Trail	1314
1028.9	**1162.0**	Kinter View . . . . 📷	1320
1027.5	**1163.4**	Shikellimy Trail 0.9E to parking area . . . . 40.4377,-76.8198 🅿	1158
1026.5	**1164.4**	Campsite . . . . ⌂	1356
1025.2	**1165.7**	Spring 100 yards east on side trail . . . . ♦	700
1024.9	**1166.0**	PA 325, Clarks Creek north of road . . . . 40.4515,-76.7762 🅿 ♦	550
1024.6	**1166.3**	Spring . . . . ♦	606
1024.5	**1166.4**	Henry Knauber Trail to east	678
1023.2	**1167.7**	Spring . . . . ♦	1251
1021.6	**1169.3**	Horse-Shoe Trail to east	1650
1020.9	**1170.0**	Rattling Run . . . . ♦	1520
1018.3	**1172.6**	Yellow Springs Trail	1365
1018.2	**1172.7**	Clearing with trail register, camping . . . . ⌂	1450
		Yellow Springs Village Site, old coal mining settlement (0.7W).	
1017.3	**1173.6**	Spring . . . . ♦	1395
1016.1	**1174.8**	Sand Spring Trail west to "The General"	1361
1015.9	**1175.0**	Cold Spring Trail to east	1400

1013.7 1177.2 Spring, campsite . . . . ♦ ⛺ 1080
1013.6 1177.3 **Rausch Gap Shelter** (0.3E) 33.0◄24.7◄18.0◄►13.4►17.5►32.6 . . ☽♦⛺⊏(6) 1063
1013.1 1177.8 AT on gravel road for 0.2 mile, bridge over Rausch Creek . . . . ♦ 904
1012.8 1178.1 Cemetery to west 860
1012.6 1178.3 Stony Creek, footbridge . . . . ♦ 827

1011.5 1179.4 Second Mountain 1362

1009.8 1181.1 Field 650
1009.5 1181.4 Cross two roads: Greenpoint School Rd, then PA 443 575

1008.9 1182.0 Pass under PA 72 and cross PA 443 . . . . 40.4821,-76.5506 🅿♦ 483
Stream, campsite south of PA 72

1007.5 1183.4 Swatara Gap, PA 72, **Lickdale, PA** (2.1E) . . . .(pg. 120) 480
1007.1 1183.8 I-81, AT passes underneath 450
1006.8 1184.1 Gravel road 615

1002.9 1188.0 Abandoned powerline overlook, view . . . . 📷 1386

1000.2 1190.7 **William Penn Shelter** (0.1E)(1993). . . . . ☽♦⛺⊏(16) 1409
38.1◄31.4◄13.4◄►4.1►19.2►33.9
Water and tent sites 0.1W on blue-blazed trail.

998.1 1192.8 PA 645, Waggoners Gap Rd . . . . .40.5066,-76.3768 🅿 (pg. 120) 1219
Pine Grove, PA (3.4W)

996.9 1194.0 Fisher Lookout, view . . . . 📷 1310
996.2 1194.7 Kimmel Lookout, view. . . . . 📷 1362
996.1 1194.8 PA 501, **501 Shelter** (0.1W)(1975). . . . . 40.5125,-76.3444 🅿☽⚡♦⛺(pg. 124) 1444
35.5◄17.5◄4.1◄►15.1►29.8►38.9 **Pine Grove, PA** (4.2W), **Bethel, PA**

SoBo NoBo 1000 3000 5000

1122.7 PA 174

» **Boiling Springs, PA 17007**
♪☾ Free campsite & privy, see bottom right corner of map.
RR tracks pass near campsite.

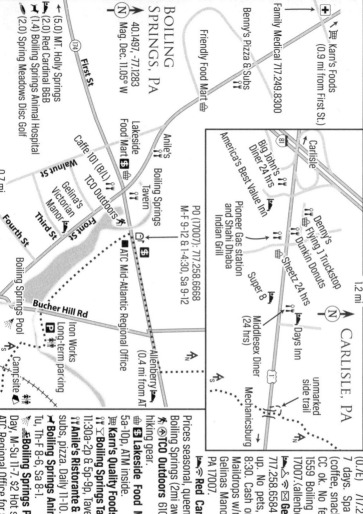

[hospital] 🍴🛒 Karn's Foods (0.9 mi from First St.)

Family Medical 717.249.8300

Benny's Pizza & Subs

Friendly Food Mart

(N) **BOILING SPRINGS, PA**
40.1497, -77.1283
Mag. Dec. 11.05° W

(74) First St

↑ (5.0) Mt. Holly Springs
(2.0) Red Cardinal B&B
(1.4) Boiling Springs Animal Hospital
(2.0) Spring Meadows Disc Golf

0.7 mi

Carlisle
(81)
Big John's Diner 24 hrs
America's Best Value Inn
Anile's
Lakeside Food Mart
Caffe 101 (B/L)
Walnut St
TCO Outdoors
Boiling Springs Tavern
Gelina's Victorian Manor
Fourth St
Third St
Front St
PO (17007): 717.258.6668 M-F 9-12 & 1-4:30, Sa 9-12
ATC Mid-Atlantic Regional Office
Bucher Hill Rd
Iron Works Long-term parking
Allenberry (0.4 mi from ATC)
Boiling Springs Pool
Campsite

1.2 mi

(N) **CARLISLE, PA**
Pioneer Gas station and Shahi Dhaba Indian Grill
Denny's
Flying J Truckstop
Dunkin Donuts
Sheetz 24 hrs
Super 8
Days Inn
Middlesex Diner (24 hrs)
unmarked side trail
Mechanicsburg
11

H ⊕✆ **ATC Mid-Atlantic Regional Office** 717.258.5771 Open wkdays 8-5. Spigot on south side of building, may be off in winter. Staff & bulletin board provides info on trail conditions. Small shop w/maps. Fuel/oz for donation.
🚌 **Mike's Shuttle Svc** 717.497.6022 Goes anywhere.

🛏⊕✆$ 🚿⊠ **Allenberry Resort** (0.7E) 717.258.3211 Restaurant/Bar open 7 days. Spa on property. Store open daily (coffee, snacks & toiletries). Pool (in season). CC ok. No fee for mail. Please call in adv: 1559 Boiling Springs Rd, Boiling Springs, PA 17007. ⟨allenberry.com⟩.

🛏⊕$⊠ **Gelinas Victorian Manor** (0.2W) 717.258.6584 Room w/shared bath $99D/up. No pets, no packs inside. B'fast at 8:30. Cash only. Laundry for guests $6/load. Maildrops w/reservation: MUST say "in care of Gelinas Manor", 219 Front St, Boiling Springs, PA 17007.

🚌🛏⊠ **Red Cardinal B&B** (2.5W) 717.245.0823 Prices seasonal, queen BR incl full b'fast, p/u & ret from Boiling Springs (2mi away). No pets/smoking.

🥾⊕$ **TCO Outdoors** 610.678.1899 Canister fuel & some hiking gear.
⊕$ **Lakeside Food Mart** (0.1W) 717.241.6163 7 days 5a-10p. ATM inside.
🛒 **Karn's Quality Foods** (1W) 717.258.1458 Daily 7a-10p.
⊕♈ **Boiling Springs Tavern** (1W) 717.258.1458 Daily 7a-10p. 11:30a-2p & 5p-9p, Tavern 11a-9p.
♈ **Anile's Ristorante & Pizzeria** (0.2W) 717.258.3614 M-F L/D subs, pizza. Daily 11-10.
🐾 **Boiling Springs Animal Hospital** (0.2W) 717.258.5070 L/D (1.5W) 717.258.4121 Mem Day-Labor Day, M-Su 11-7, Tu, Th-F 8-6, Sa 8-1.
🚿 **Boiling Springs Pool** 717.258.4121 Mem Day-Labor Day, M-Su 11-7, $2 Hot shower. If you want to swim, visit ATC Regional Office for $3 off the $12 admission.

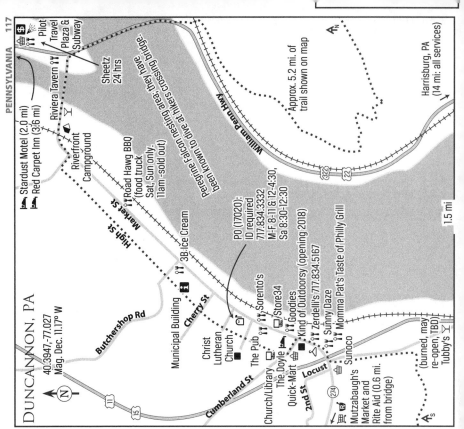

1126.8   TRINDLE RD
1128.0   ★ RIDGE RD

❀⊘🅟❖🅛 🛏⛽🛆 Pheasant Field B&B (0.7W)
717.258.0717 stay@pheasantfield.com $135/up, free p/u & ret w/stay, big b'fast, laundry for fee, behaved pets ok. Call from Trindle Rd, or from Ridge Dr, go 0.25W to Hickory Town Rd, turn left on rd, B&B on right. ⟨pheasantfield.com⟩

1130.7   US 11 (CARLISLE PIKE)

» Carlisle, PA 17013 (0.5W to hotels) The A.T. passes over the hwy on a footbridge. A side trail down to the rd is at the northwest corner of the overpass. Hotels run short of rooms (and go up in price) every other wkend when there is a car show.

🛏⚊☂ Days Inn (0.4W) 717.245.2242 Hiker rate $60, c. b'fast. Pets $20.

🛏⚊☂ Americas Best Value Inn (0.9W) 717.249.7775 $49.99/up + tax, c. b'fast, $15 pet fee.

🛏⚊☂🅧 Super 8 Motel (1W) 717.249.7000 $54.99S, $59.99D, Spcl event rates higher, c. b'fast, $10 pet fee. Guest Mail:1800 Harrisburg Pike, Carlisle, PA 17013.

🥾 Appalachian Running Company (5.8W) 717.241.5674 Good selection of trail running shoes, shoe fitting,

🍴🍺⚊☂ Flying J Truckstop (0.7W) 717.243.6659 24hrs. Store, diner, pizza by the slice, showers $12 incl towel. Coin laundry.

» Mechanicsburg, PA 17050 (5E), ⊠717.697.0321. Large city with an abundance of services, most notably: ⚕CVS(3.0E), 🛒Giant Food (4.3E), 🛒Walmart (4.6E), ⚗Appalachian Brewing Co (4.9E), 🛒Wegmans (5.4E) 🛏⚊☂Park Inn (7.0E) 717.697.0321 restaurant & bars on-site.

995.6	**1195.3**	Trail to Pilger Ruh (Pilgrims Rest), spring to east, ... ♦ ◭	1450
		Applebee Campsite to west.	
993.0	**1197.9**	Round Head, Shower Steps Trail, campsite to south on AT. . . . . 📷 ◭	1500
		Side trail to view.	
991.0	**1199.9**	Overlook, view. . . . . 📷	1404
990.6	**1200.3**	⚠ NoBo: AT turns east, Boulderfield Trail to west (straight ahead).	1271
990.5	**1200.4**	Hertline Campsite and picnic table . . . . ♦ ◭ ⯇	1200
989.8	**1201.1**	Pipeline, road paralleling pipeline, cross twice, then parallel to AT	1516
987.1	**1203.8**	Fort Dietrich Snyder Monument . . . . ♦ (0.2W)	1474
986.8	**1204.1**	PA 183, Rentschler Marker on side trail 30 yards north of road . . . . . (pg. 124)	1423
986.3	**1204.6**	Game Commission road (gravel). . . . . 💧 . . . . 40.5273,-76.2148 🅿	1479
985.5	**1205.4**	Black Swatara Spring 0.3E . . . . ⬦	1567
982.9	**1208.0**	Eagles Nest Trail to east	1601
981.7	**1209.2**	Sand Spring Trail 0.2E to spring . . . . ♦	1510
981.0	**1209.9**	**Eagles Nest Shelter** (0.3W)(1988), spring on trail to shelter . . . . ☽ ♦ ◭ ⯇ (8)	1580
		32.6◄19.2◄15.1◄►14.7►23.8►31.2	
979.1	**1211.8**	Shartlesville-Cross Mtn Rd (overgrown dirt road).	1450
976.4	**1214.5**	Phillips Canyon Spring (unmarked, unreliable) . . . . ⬦	1500

| 974.4 | 1216.5 | State Game Land Rd . . . . | 1417 |

973.8 **1217.1** Pipeline clearing, AT crosses multiple times 1413

972.2 **1218.7** Schuylkill Trail 2.4E to Hamburg, parking 0.1N . . . . 40.5796,-76.0267 🅿 564

972.0 **1218.9 Port Clinton, PA**, Broad St + Penn St. . . . . **(pg. 124)** 430
971.7 **1219.2** PA 61, Blue Mtn Rd, **Hamburg, PA** (1.7E) . . . .**(pg. 124)** 490

969.2 **1221.7** Spring to west, campsite. . . . . ⬥⛺ 1184

968.0 **1222.9** Minnehaha Spring, frequently dry . . . . 💧 1361

966.6 **1224.3** Reservoir Rd, stream north on AT . . . . .40.5896,-75.9443 🅿⬥ 878
Parking 0.3E only with permission from Hamburg Borough 610.562.7821 M-F 8-5.
966.3 **1224.6 Windsor Furnace Shelter** (0.1W)(1972) . . . . 🌙⬥⛺ (8) 848
33.9◄29.8◄14.7◄►9.1►16.5►26.5 No swimming, creek south of shelter.
965.6 **1225.3** Blue-blazed trail to Blue Rocks Family Campground (1.5E). . . . .**(pg. 124)** 997

964.7 **1226.2** Pulpit Rock, 30 yards west to privy at Pulpit Rock Astronomical Park. 🚫🚫🌙📷 1582
No camping or fires.

962.9 **1228.0** Yellow-blazed trail to **Blue Rocks Family Campground** (1.5E) . . . . . .**(pg. 124)** 1594
962.5 **1228.4** The Pinnacle, 0.1E to panoramic view, no camping or fires . . . . 📷 1615

960.8 **1230.1** Furnace Creek Trail to west 1444
960.6 **1230.3** Gold Spring, no camping or fires . . . . 💧 1372
959.9 **1231.0** Blue-blazed trail 1.5W reconnects with AT near Windsor Furnace Shelter. 1402
959.6 **1231.3** Pinnacle Spur Trail to west. 1394
959.0 **1231.9** Panther Creek, dependable . . . . ⬥ 1090

958.1 **1232.8** Parking lot 0.4E on side trail . . . . .40.6255,-75.9535 🅿 832

957.2 **1233.7** Hawk Mountain Rd, **Eckville Shelter** (0.2E) . . . . . . 🌙🚿⬥⛺ (6) **(pg. 128)** 692
38.9◄23.8◄9.1◄►7.4►17.4►24.2 Enclosed bunkroom, tent platforms, flush
toilet, spigot at side of car
956.7 **1234.2** Footbridge, stream, campsite north on AT . . . . ⬥⛺ 564

1148.3   HIGH ST

» Duncannon, PA 17020

🏠🕐 **Trail Angel Mary** 717.834.4706 2 Ann St,
Duncannon, PA 17020

🏠🕐🍴🍺🧺✉ **Doyle Hotel** 717.834.6789 $25S,
$35D, $10EAP + tax, bar serves L/D. Pool table.
Coleman/alcohol/oz & canister fuel. Visa/MC/
Disc ok. Mail: 7 North Market St, Duncannon, PA
17020.

▲🏠 **Riverfront Campground** 717.834.5252 Site
& shower $5PP, check-in daylight/dark. Shuttles.
Note proximity of RR tracks. No afterhours entry.

⛪ **Presbyterian Church** 717.834.5815 Library w/
internet W 1-4, Sa 10-2.

🅿️❄️🚿🍴 **Kind of Outdoorsy**
(0.07E) 717.433.1361 paige@kindofoutdoorsy.
com located on the trail in Duncannon. Hang
with them in their hiker lounge- relax, refuel,
resupply(kindofoutdoorsy.com)

🍴🥡 **Sorrento Pizza** (0.1E) Su-Th 11a-10:30p, Fr-
Sa 11a-11p. Bar open until 2a.

🍴 **Goodies** (0.2E) 717.836.6300 B'fast 6a-11a.

🐾 **Cove Mountain Animal Hospital** (2.6E)
717.834.5534 M-W 9a-8p, F 9a-5p, open/clsd
alternate Th & Sa.

📶 **Store 34** (0.2E) 717.834.3400 M-F 12-6, Sa 10-
2. High speed internet $3/30 min, $5/hr.

» West A.T.

🏠🚐 **Stardust Motel**   (4.4W) 717.834.9883
tanaypatel@stardust.com $45S, $55D
Sometimes p/u & ret rides avail. Pets ok.

🏠🚐 **Red Carpet Inn** (6W) 717.834.3320 $50S,
$60D + tax. p/u $5 & ret $5 from Duncannon.

🛒 **Mutzabaugh's Market** (1.1W)
717.834.3121 Hiker-friendly, open
7 days 6a-10p. P/U & ret to Doyle
4p daily.

🏠🕐 ⛪✉ **Christ Lutheran**
Church (0.1W) 717.834.3140 Free
hiker dinner W in Jun & Jul 5p-7p. On Plum St/Church St 1
block west of High St.

🏪🍴 **Pilot Travel Plaza** (0.25W) 717.834.4710 Open M-Sa
$12 showers. 0.25W of AT on US 22.

🍴 **Ranch House Restaurant** (4.1W) 717.834.3356 Open 24/7
6a-9p, Su 6:30a-7p, b'fast buffet Sa-Su untill 10:30a.

🍴 **Lumberjack's Kitchen** (6.7W) 717.834.9099 Near Red Carpet
Inn L/D M-Th 10a-9p, B/L/D Fr-Su 8a-9p.

💊 **Rite Aid** (1.1W) 717.834.6303 Next door to market.

1183.4   SWATARA GAP, PA 72

» Lickdale (Jonestown), PA (2.1E)

🏠🛏📶 **Days Inn** (2.5E) 717.865.4064 C, b'fast. Pets $15,
discount, c. b'fast, laundry, indoor heated pool, No pets.

🏠🛏🐾 **Fairfield Inn & Suites** (2.7E) 717.865.4234 Hiker
discount, c. b'fast, laundry, indoor heated pool, No pets.

🏕🍴🐾 **Jonestown KOA** (2.7E) 377.865.6411 Open 7 days.
Summer 5a-9p. Tentsite $37/up. Cabin (sleeps 4) $67/up. Pets on
leash ok.

🏠🛏🐾 **Comfort Inn** (3E) 717.865.8080 Call or stop by
for rates, incl b'fast, pool. Pets $25.

🏠🚿📶 **Love's Travel Stop** (2.7E) 717.861.7390
McDonalds, Chesters, $10 showers, ATM, all open 24 hrs.

1192.8   PA 645

🚐 **Carlin's   AT   Shuttle   Service**
570.345.0474,   570.516.3447   Range:
anywhere in PA. Commercially insured.

» Pine Grove, PA 17963 (3.4W) (svcs
on map & cont'd on pg. 124...)

Historic
iron bridge

🇦s

🇦N

LICKDALE, PA
(JONESTOWN)
🧭(N)
40.451N,-76.5137
Mag. Dec. 11.48° W

Comfort Inn

Days Inn

Wendy's

Burger King

Dunkin Donuts/Blimpie

Subway

Fairfield Inn & Suites

Jonestown KOA

McDonald's/Chester's Chicken
Love's Truck Stop: convenience store,
ATM & showers

Pizza Town II

Fisher Ave

Monroe/Valley Rd

Rail Trail 2.5 mi

72

81

1.5 mi

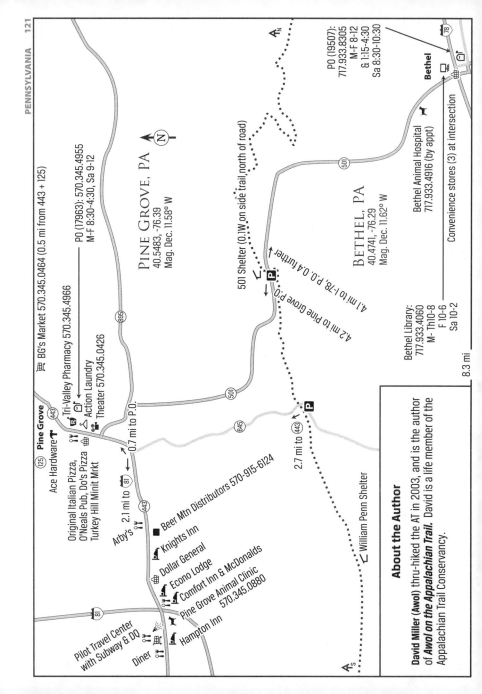

About the Author

David Miller (Awol) thru-hiked the AT in 2003, and is the author of *Awol on the Appalachian Trail.* David is a life member of the Appalachian Trail Conservancy.

955.3 **1235.6** Hawk Mtn Trail to west 1364

954.2 **1236.7** Dans Pulpit, trail register . . . . 📷 1615

953.6 **1237.3** Dans Spring 0.1E . . . . ◊ 1558

951.0 **1239.9** Tri-County Corner, ⚠ AT to west 1524

949.8 **1241.1** **Allentown Hiking Club Shelter** (1997) . . . . ☽ ◊ ◭ ⊏ (8) 1488
31.2◄16.5◄7.4◄►10.0►16.8►33.5
Unreliable spring downhill in front of shelter 0.2 mile, another 0.1 farther.
949.5 **1241.4** Springs to east; Blue 100 yards, Yellow 0.3 mi . . . . ♦ 1331

947.9 **1243.0** Fort Franklin Rd (gravel) . . . . 40.6943,-75.8419 🅿 1350

946.0 **1244.9** Trail 0.2W to restaurant (closer to AT + PA 309) 1356
945.7 **1245.2** PA 309, Blue Mountain Summit . . . . 40.7072,-75.8086 🅿 (pg. 128) 1360

943.9 **1247.0** Powerline, New Tripoli Campsite 0.2W . . . . ♦ ◭ 1431

942.8 **1248.1** Knife Edge, view . . . . 📷 1560

942.3 **1248.6** Bear Rocks, view . . . . 📷 1544

940.8 **1250.1** Bake Oven Knob Rd (gravel) . . . . 40.7446,-75.7386 🅿 1450
940.4 **1250.5** Bake Oven Knob 1560

939.8 **1251.1** **Bake Oven Knob Shelter** (1937) . . . . ◊ ◭ ⊏ (6) 1387
26.5◄17.4◄10.0◄►6.8►23.5►37.2
Trail in front leads downhill to multiple water sources, more reliable farther down.

937.4 **1253.5** Lehigh Furnace Gap, Ashfield Rd, Comm tower . . . . 40.7696,-75.6949 🅿 ♦ 1320
Piped spring 0.5E on Ashfield Road, spring is on the right side of road.

936.3 **1254.6** South Trail 0.3E to view . . . . 📷 1590

934.7	**1256.2**	North Trail (scenic route) to west, TV tower, AT is over Lehigh Valley Tunnel	1488
934.2	**1256.7**	Tower access road	1461
933.2	**1257.7**	North Trail (scenic route) to west	1065
933.0	**1257.9**	**George W. Outerbridge Shelter** (1965) Reliable piped spring 0.1N . . . . ◑ ⊄ (6)	948
		24.2◄16.8◄6.8◄▸16.7▸30.4▸61.6	
932.5	**1258.4**	Lehigh River south bank, PA 873, **Slatington, PA** (2.0E) . . . .(pg. 128)	422
932.0	**1258.9**	PA 248/145 traffic light, **Walnutport, PA** (2.0E) . . . .(pg. 128)	481
931.9	**1259.0**	Superfund Trailhead, **Palmerton, PA** (1.5W) . . . . . 40.7832,-75.6041 🅿 (pg. 128)	492
		Water 0.4W on blue-blazed trail to Palmerton.	
931.0	**1259.9**	Superfund Detour south end.	1420

> ⚠ Rocky, steep trail from Lehigh Gap. Deforested ridge due to zinc smelting from 1898-1980. Remedial activities associated with the revegetation of Blue Mountain are currently being conducted near the A.T. between Lehigh Gap & Little Gap as part of the Palmerton Zinc Pile Superfund Site. A.T. Hikers advised to stay on the A.T. & not use the road.

928.4	**1262.5**	High metallic content spring 0.1W (unmarked 40.8050,-75.5568)	1380
		emergency water source, drinking not recommended.	
928.2	**1262.7**	Superfund Detour north, powerline . . . . 📷	1368
		360 view from pile of rocks east of trail near power line tower.	
927.1	**1263.8**	Little Gap Rd, **Danielsville, PA** (1.5E) . . . . 40.8062,-75.5346 🅿 (pg. 129)	1100
926.7	**1264.2**	Tower access road (gravel) . . . . 📷	1343

923.3	**1267.6**	Dirt road, powerline.	1571
922.3	**1268.6**	Delps Trail to east, ... ◊ (0.4E) 40.8092,-75.4512 🅿 (0.7E) ◭	1580
		Campsite near trail intersection, unreliable spring 0.4E	
920.7	**1270.2**	Stempa Spring 0.6E, reliable. . . . . ◑	1559
919.8	**1271.1**	Smith Gap Rd (paved) . . . . 40.8255,-75.4143 🅿 (pg. 130)	1540
916.3	**1274.6**	**Leroy A. Smith Shelter** (0.2E)(1972) . . . . ⟩◑◭⊄ (8)	1456
		33.5◄23.5◄16.7◄▸13.7▸44.9▸51.5 Water 0.2 mile down blue-blazed trail; second source 0.2 mile farther. Piped spring 0.5 mile down service road.	

NoBo SoBo

» *Pine Grove, PA 17963 (...services cont'd from pg. 120)*

🏪🍴🏠 **Econo Lodge** (4.4W) 570.345.4099 Hiker rate when room avail incl c. b'fast. Dogs $10 allowed in smoking rooms only.

🏪🍴🏊☕🖥 **Comfort Inn** (4.6W) 570.345.8031 $70/up incl hot b'fast. Hiker friendly, pool, coin laundry. $10/Pet.

🛒 **Bergers Market** (4.7W) 570.345.3663 Open 7 days, M-F 8-9, Sa-Su 8-6.

🍴⛲🏧 **Pilot Travel Center** (4.8W) 570.345.8800 24hr, Subway, Dairy Queen & Auntie Anne's Pretzel, shower $12.

🍴 **Original Italian Pizza** (3.5W) 570.345.5432 Open Sa-Th 11-10, F 11-11. Delivers to 501 Shelter.

1194.8 PA 501

⛺🍴⚠️ **501 Shelter** (0.1W) Caretaker house nearby, solar shower, water from faucet on shower, no alcohol, no smoking in shelter, pets on leash.

» *Pine Grove, PA 17963 (3.4W) (services at PA 645 and on map)*

1204.1 PA 183

🏠🚿🍴🛏🖥📶✉️ **Rock 'n Sole Hostel** (1.6W) 570.617.6432 kragb@netzero.com Smoke/drug free family operation. A/C or heated bunkhouse. $40 Stay incl dinner & b'fast, hot outdoor shower, sink, & chemical privy. P/U & ret to 183 trail head. Resupply run to close Dollar General. Options incl laundry, mail drops (free for guests), shuttle to Cabela's, Walmart, Yuengling Brewery tour, & for slackpackers. Non-guest mail $10. Contact for scheduling & shuttle cost. (rocknsolehostel.com)

1218.9 Port Clinton, PA 19549

🛖 **Pavilion Tenting** 570.366.0489 Pavilion tenting max 2 nights. No car camping or drive-ins.

🏠🍴📶 **Union House Bed & Bath** (0.2W) 610.562.3155, after 5pm 610.562.4076 Open F & Sa. Reservations avail during wk upon request.

🏠🍴🖥✉️📶 **Port Clinton Hotel** (0.4W) 610.562.3354 Call for prices. Laundry/dining. $10 Room key deposit. Limited rooms avail. Open Tu-Su 11-9, CC ok.

🏪♿🍴 **The Peanut Shop** (0.4W) 610.562.0610 Su-M 10a-6p, Tu-F 10a-5p,

Sa 10a-8p. Soda, candy, dried fruit, trail mixes, ATM.

🍴♿ **3C's** (1W) 610.562.5925 Open daily 6a-2p.

💈 **Port Clinton Barber Shop** 484.336.8516 Corner of Rte 61 & Race St. Very Hiker Friendly! Hang out, coffee, cookies, phone charging, DIY live music - guitars & instruments, hiker boxes, shuttle info. (fb.com/portclintonbarbershop)

1219.2 PA 61, BLUE MTN RD

📶 **Rainbow Alpaca Shuttle Service** 484.560.7813 Offers slackpacking, resupply runs, emergency room visits, brewery tours, trail magic, & more.

» *Hamburg, PA 19526 (1.7E)*

🏨🍴🏊☕ **Microtel Inn** (1.7E) 610.562.4234 ✉️**Pappy T's Pub & Lounge** on site. Call/stop by for hiker rate, incl c. b'fast. Guest only mail: 50 Industrial Dr, Hamburg, PA 19526.

🏔🍴 **Cabela's** (1.9E) 610.929.7000 M-Sa 9a-9p, Su 9a-7p. Largest Cabela's store in the world w/250,000 sq ft of retail space. Hiking gear, canister fuel. P/U from trailhead if staff is avail. 🍴**Campfire Restaurant** Inside Cabela's serves Su-F 9a-5p, Sa 9a-7p.

➕ **Rite Aid** (3.5E) 610.562.9454, ➕ **CVS** 610.562.2454

➕ **Hamburg Animal Hospital** (3.4E) 610.562.5000 M-Th 9-7, F 9-5, Sa 9-11 by appointment.

♿ **Hamburg Coin Laundry** (3.3E) 610.562.4890 7 days, 6a-12a.

🚌 **Barta Bus Service** (1.9E) 610.921.0601 (Stop at Cabela's) Route w/in Hamburg $1.95/boarding.

» *Pottsville, PA 17901 (15W, compass north on PA 61)*

🍴 **Yuengling Brewery** (15W) 570.628.4890 America's oldest brewery. Tours M-F 10a-1:30p, Sa 11a-1p. Closed-toe shoes req'd.

1225.3 ★ BLUE-BLAZED TRAIL TO CAMPGROUND
1228.0 ★ YELLOW-BLAZED TRAIL TO CAMPGROUND

⛺♿🍴🚿 **Blue Rocks Family Campground** (1.5E) 610.756.6366 camp@ bluerockscampground.com Tentsite $30/up. Cabin $55/up (sleeps 2 adults, 2 children). Showers & laundry. Pets allowed in campground, but not cabins. Open yr-round w/limited days Nov-Mar. **Woody's Filling Station** open F-Su seasonally. Sells burgers, shakes, etc. Camp store (sodas, candy bars, snacks) closed Dec-Mar. CC OK. (bluerockscampground.com)

HAMBURG, PA

Many more restaurants and services further into town

Hamburg Animal Hospital
610.562.2843

Library 610.562.2843
M-F 10-5, Tu & Th 12-5

PO (19526):
610.562.7812
M-F 9-5, Sa 9-12

Franklin St

Church St

US 22

4th St

Hamburg Coin Laundry
Weis Market 6a-11p 7 days
Pharmacy 610.562.3795
M-F 9-9, Sa 8-5, Su 9-3

Blue Mtn Rd

Schuylkill River Trail (2.4 from AT to 78)

St. Lukes Urgent Care 610.628.7201

Cracker Barrel

Microtel Inn

Taco Bell

Burger King
Starbuck's
Wendy's

Lowes
McDonalds
Pizza Hut

Dunkin Donuts

Red Robin

Cigars International Restaurant

Cabela's & Campfire Restaurant

78

2.6 mi

AT to library 2.9 mi →

N

Walmart superstore with grocery & Subway

Dollar Tree
JA Buffet
Five Guys Burgers

Logan's Steakhouse

61

WaWa

PORT CLINTON, PA

40.58.-76.0267
Mag. Dec. 11.79° W

3C's Restaurant
1mi from PO

Pavillion

Race St

Port Clinton Barber Shop

Penn St

Port Clinton Hotel
Peanut Shop

PO (19549): 610.562.3787
M-F 12:30-4:30, Sa 8-11

Broad St

Port Clinton Fire Co.

Union House B&B

N

S

61

916.1	1274.8	Powerline	1489
914.4	1276.5	Pipeline	1487
912.7	1278.2	Hahns Overlook, view. . . . . 📷	1450
911.9	1279.0	Powerline	1107
911.7	1279.2	PA 33, **Wind Gap, PA** (1.0E) . . . . .40.8607,-75.2928 🅿 (pg. 130)	980
909.6	1281.3	Private road (gravel)	1591
906.0	1284.9	Campsite . . . . ⛺	1628
905.3	1285.6	Wolf Rocks bypass trail south end to west. Spring 100 yards west (treat) . . . 💧	1584
904.9	1286.0	Wolf Rocks, view . . . . 📷	1623
904.3	1286.6	Wolf Rocks bypass trail north end to west. . . . . 💧	1539
903.2	1287.7	Fox Gap, PA 191 (paved). . . . . .40.9354,-75.1969 🅿	1400
902.6	1288.3	**Kirkridge Shelter** 37.2◄30.4◄13.7◄►31.2►37.8►43.6 . . . . ☽ 💧 ⊏ (6)	1440
		Tap 0.1 mi behind shelter, off in winter.	
902.3	1288.6	Campsite, view . . . . 📷 ⛺	1490
900.7	1290.2	Totts Gap, gravel road, powerline to south	1300
900.4	1290.5	Pipeline	1382
900.1	1290.8	Roadbed.	1401
898.7	1292.2	Mt Minsi	1461
897.7	1293.2	Lookout Rock, view . . . . 📷	800
897.5	1293.4	Stream. . . . . 💧	760
896.9	1294.0	Council Rock . . . . 📷	536
896.8	1294.1	Turn east on gravel road	575
896.4	1294.5	Hiker parking lot . . . . .40.9798,-75.142 🅿	498

896.2	1294.7	PA 611, **Delaware Water Gap, PA** . . . .(pg. 134)	386
895.9	1295.0	**PA-NJ** border, I-80, Delaware River Bridge west bank	278
894.9	1296.0	Kittatinny Visitor Center . . . . 40.9720,-75.1261 🅿 ℹ️ 🏛 ⛉ ⚥ ◆	290
		NoBo: cross under I-80 and turn left.	
894.5	1296.4	Parking, V.C. is preferred for overnight parking.. . . . . . 40.9701,-75.1287 🅿 ☾	295
894.2	1296.7	Dunnfield Trail to east, reconnects with AT at Sunfish Pond (4 mi) . . . . . . ◆	445
893.0	1297.9	Holly Spring Trail . . . . ◆	950

> ⚠ New Jersey Guidelines: No campfires. Camping only at designated
> shelter areas and campsites, with some exceptions as posted.

890.9	1300.0	Backpacker Campsite, Douglas Trail to west, water south of camp . . . . . . ⛺ ◆	1326
		No fires, use bear boxes/poles, leash dogs.	
890.1	1300.8	Sunfish Pond south end, no swimming or camping. . . . .🚫 ◆	1382
889.5	1301.4	Sunfish Pond north end, rock sculptures . . . . ◆	1384
888.6	1302.3	Stream. . . . . ◆	1452
887.9	1303.0	Powerline	1565
887.8	1303.1	Kittatinny Mountain, rocky summit . . . .📷	1532
887.2	1303.7	Kaiser Trail to west	1416

SoBo NoBo 1000 3000 5000

885.4	1305.5	Camp Rd (gravel), footbridge . . . . 41.033,-75.004 🅿 ◆ (pg. 134)	1109
		Mohican Outdoor Center (0.3W)	
884.2	1306.7	Rattlesnake Swamp Trail, view. . . . .📷	1475
883.3	1307.6	Catfish Lookout Tower, picnic table below the tower . . . . ⛉ ⚥	1565
882.7	1308.2	Rattlesnake Spring on dirt road about 17 yards west of AT. . . . . ◆ ⛺	1260
882.4	1308.5	Stream. . . . . ◆	1249
882.2	1308.7	Millbrook-Blairstown Rd (paved). . . . . 41.0595,-74.9636 🅿 ⛉	1270
		Millbrook Village (1.1W) historical park with picnic area.	
881.9	1309.0	Swamp	1252
881.6	1309.3	Powerline	1384
879.5	1311.4	Campsite . . . . ⛺	1487
878.4	1312.5	Blue Mtn Lakes Rd, pump disabled, water 0.1E on road . . . . ◆	1350
		No camping in zone from 0.5 mile south of road to 3 mi. north of road.	

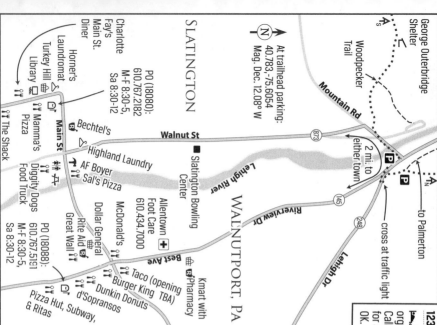

George Outerbridge
Shelter

Woodpecker
Trail

At trailhead parking:
40.783,-75.6054
Mag. Dec. 12.08° W

SLATINGTON

Charlotte
Fay's
Main St.
Diner

Horner's
Laundromat
Turkey Hill
Library

PO (18080):
610.767.2182
M-F 8:30-5,
Sa 8:30-12

Mamma's
Pizza
The Shack

Bechtel's

Highland Laundry

AF Boyer
Sal's Pizza

Main St

Slatington Bowling
Center

Walnut St

Mountain Rd

Lehigh River

2 mi. to
either town

cross at traffic light

to Palmerton

WALNUTPORT, PA

Allentown
Foot Care
610.434.7000

McDonald's
Dollar General
Rite Aid
Great Wall

Diggity Dogs
Food Truck
Pizza Hut, Subway,
& Ritas

Best Ave

Taco (opening
TBA)
Burger King
Dunkin Donuts
d'Sopransos

Kmart with
Pharmacy

PO (18088):
610.767.51E1
M-F 8:30-5,
Sa 8:30-12

Riverview Dr

Lehigh Dr

1233.7   HAWK MOUNTAIN RD. *(1.6W to Hawk Mountain Sanctuary.)*

⌂♦♦♦✉ ⊠ **Common Ground Farm & Retreat** (4.3E) 610.756.4070 50 Acre organic farm. Hiker discount $99/2-persons incl b'fast. Call about other trailheads. Slackpacking, parking for section hikers, longer shuttles for a fee. Mtn bike avail for ride to store. Laundry avail. Yr-round, no drugs/alcohol. CC OK. Mail (w/reservation): 333 New Bethel Church Rd, Kempton, PA 19529.

1245.2   PA 309

⌂♦♦♦♦✉⊠ **Blue Mountain Summit B&B** (0.1W) 570.386.2003 $95-$125D incl b'fast. Open 7 days by appt. No pets. Ok to get water at spigot at SW corner of building. Please be respectful of nonhiker guests at B&B & restaurant; OK to hang out in back. Please don't loiter in front or hang clothes to dry. Camping w/permission, no fires. Ask about shuttles. Dining Th 12-9, F 12-10, Sa 12-9; Su 12-8; Live music on Fr. 7-10, Su 5-8(Jun-Sep). CC OK. Guest Mail (call 1st): 2520 W Penn Pike, Andreas, PA 18211.⟨bluemountainsummit.com⟩

1258.4   LEHIGH RIVER, PA 873

» *Slatington, PA 18080* (2E)

⊠ **Bechtel's Pharmacy** (2.1E) Open M-F 9-8, Sa 9-2.
⊙ **Slatington Library** (2.5E) M,W: 9-7, Tu 9-3, F 9-5, Sa 8-2.

1258.9   PA 248/145

» *Walnutport, PA 18088* (2E)

⊕ **Kmart** (1.7E) 610.767.1812 Open daily 8-10, pharmacy M-F 9-9, Sa 9-5, Su 10-4. Grocery section only has dry goods (no produce).
⊠ **Rite Aid Pharmacy** (2E) 610.767.9595 M-F 9-9, Sa 9-6, Su 9-5.
Blue Ridge Veterinary Clinic (2E) 610.767.4896 Call before coming.

1259.0   SUPERFUND TRAILHEAD

⊞ **Brenda** 484.725.9396 Call for pricing. Shuttles ranging from local to bus terminals & airports.

⌂♦♦♦✉⊠ *Palmerton, PA 18071* (1.5W) *Town Ordinance: Pets must be on leash.* (6.5W) 610.377.2911 **Sunny Rest Resort** *Clothing optional* resort 2 mi outside of town, rides sometimes avail wkdays. Hotel rooms & camping. Prices higher on wkends. Restaurant (B/L/D), nightclub, 2 heated pools, pool bar, hot tub, volleyball, nature trails, 425 Sunny Rest Rd, Palmerton, PA. May-Sep. Call for current rates.

🅿 🄴 **Country Harvest** (2.1W) 610.824.3663 8a-9p, 7 days.

🍴🍺**Joe's Steaks & Subs** (1.5W) 610.826.3730 7 days L/D, deli sandwiches.

🍴🍺**Palmerton Hotel Restaurant** (1.7W) 610.826.5454 Dining Su-Th 4-10, F-Sa 11-10.

🍴🍺**Tony's Pizzeria** (1.7W) 610.826.6161 L/D, no delivery.

🄴🅶🍴⛛🏕⚕🛏🄿🛜✉ **Bert's Restaurant** (2W) 610.826.9921 Open 7 days, restaurant w/all day b'fast. Hostel: mail-drop avail w/stay. Shuttle & slackpack when avail.

1263.8   LITTLE GAP RD

🍴🍺⛛🍺**Slopeside Pub & Grill** (0.7W) 610.824.1557 0.2W & 0.5mi up driveway. Hikers welcome to water from outside spigot. Grill hrs: F-Sa 11-11, Su-Th 11-10.

⚕ **Little Gap Animal Hospital** (3.3W) 610.826.2793

» *Danielsville, PA 18038* (1.5E on Blue Mountain Dr, then left on Mountain view Dr to P0 and B&B)

🍴🍺🅿🄿🛜✉ **Filbert B&B** (2.6E) 610.428.3300 filbertbnb@ aol.com $100S, $150D +tax. Hosted by Kathy in Victorian farmhouse w/A/C. Full country b'fast incl. Free p/u at Little Gap. Fee for p/u at PA 309, Lehigh Gap, Smith Gap, or Wind Gap. Slackpacking possible DWG-Port Clinton. Parking for section hikers. Call ahead for reservations, no CC. Laundry for a fee. Italian restaurant will deliver. Guest only Mail: 3740 Filbert Dr, Danielsville, PA 18038(filbertbnb.com)

🛒 **Miller's Market** (1.6E) 610.767.6671 7 days, 8a-6p.

🍴🍺🄴 **Blue Mountain Restaurant & Ice Cream** (1.3E) 610.767.6379 Tu-F 9a-8:30p, Sa-Su 8a-9p Clsd M. B/L/D Ask about overnighting.

PALMERTON, PA

40.7996,-75.6156
Mag. Dec. 12.08°W

Ⓝ

1.0 mi

🛒🍴Palmerton Pizza
🧺 Laundromat
🏧 Convenient Mart/ATM

6th St

🍴Subway
💊Rite Aid
🍩Dunkin' Donuts⚕
🛒Family Dollar

5th St

🍴Hunan House

🄴Country Harvest
Blue Mtn Family Med
610.826.5110

📞 Verizon
✂Jan's Barber Shop
👢Carhartt/Red Wing
🍴Bert's Steakhouse

📷C&C Food Outlet
🏦BB+T
💊Shipman's Pharmacy
🍴Palmerton Restaurant
🔨Shea's Hardware

4th St

Library 610.826.3424
M, Tu 10-8, W-F 10-5, Sa 9-4

🍴Spillane's Hot Dogs &
Claude's Creamery
🍴Tony's Pizza

2nd St

Palmerton Hospital
610.826.3141 ⚕

🍴Joe's Place (Subs)
⛽Gulf Quick Stop

🍴⚕One Ten Tavern

P0 (1807):
610.826.2286
M-F 8:30-5,
Sa 8:30-12

Delaware Ave

State Rd/Red Hill Dr

Aquashicola Creek

(1.5 mi.
from P0)

Gate
path if gate locked

Lehigh River

(248)

It is not advisable to walk along PA 248, fast-moving shoulderless, SoBo intending to go to town should do so before reaching PA 248. Go west on the blue-blazed winter trail. The winter trail joins an old railroad bed and veers right uphill. Stay to the left on the railroad bed, and follow it to private parking area at the end of Red Hill Dr. (at bottom left of town map).

Cross Red Hill bridge and follow the road into town. If the bridge is gated or access is denied, hop the guardrail to PA 248, cautiously cross Aquashicola Creek on the 248 bridge, then hop the guardrail again to return to Red Hill Drive. The total distance to town is 1.5W miles on level ground.

1271.1 SMITH GAP RD (POINT PHILLIPS RD)

🚶🚲🏕🚿 **Evergreen Lake** (2.7E) East 1.7 on Smith Gap Rd, then left 1 mi on Mountain Rd. Tenting $30 (up to 2 adults, 2 children). Snack shop, laundry, free showers.

🚶🚲🏕🅿📧 **Home of John "Mechanical Man" and Linda "Crayon Lady" Stempa** (1.2W) 610.381.4606 (blue blazes on telephone poles). Eponym of the spring 0.7 mile south. Hikers welcome to water from spigot at rear of house (no need to call) & may use outside shower during daylight hrs. Pet friendly, ask about dog sitting. Please sign register. For-fee shuttles ranging from Lickdale (Swatara Gap) to Delaware Water Gap. Safe place to park your car. Only w/permission, $10 camp or stay in garage w/hot shower & towel. Ride to Kunkletown incl, & ride back to trail - call in adv. Sodas $1. Ask about stoves, fuel & maildrops.

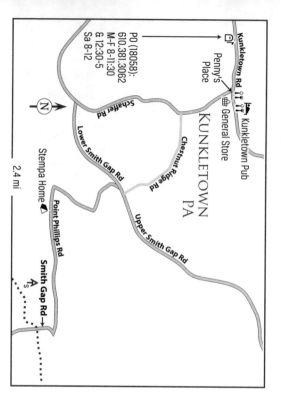

» *Kunkletown, PA 18058 (3W) (see map) West on Smith Gap Rd/Point Phillips Rd for 2 mi to stop sign, right on Upper Smith Gap Rd for 100 yds, left on Chestnut Ridge Rd for 0.9 mi to Kunkletown Rd, take a left. PO on left 0.4 mi.*

🛏🍴☕ **Kunkletown Pub** (3.4W) 610.895.4255 Room $50/up, 10% discount on L/D. Pool table. Meal delivery possible, $50 min order.

🏪 **General Store** (3.4W) 610.381.2887 Good selection of packaged foods, deli, ice cream. Summer hrs 6:30-8:30 (till 7:30 in winter).

🏠🍴 **Penny's Place** (3.4W) 7 days. Pub food & beer; good place to meet up w/helpful locals. Free pool for hikers. Sells The A.T. Guide.

1279.2 PA 33

🛏 **Creature Comforts** (3.4W) 610.381.2287 24/7 Emergency care.

» *Wind Gap, PA 18091 (1E)*

🚕 **WGM Taxi** 570.223.9289

🛏📶 **Travel Inn** (2E) 717.885.3101 $59.99D wkdays, $69.99D wkends. Room for 4 $69.99 wkdays, $79.99 wkends.

🛏📶 **Red Carpet Inn** (2.5E) 610.863.7782 Stay incl c. bfast. (cereal, juice, coffee).

🛒 **Giant Food Store** (1.9E) 610.863.8635 24hr, deli w/salad bar.

🛒 **Kmart** (2.1E) 610.863.8550 M-Sa 8a-10p, Su 8a-9p. Pharmacy M-F 10a-6p, Sa 10a-2p, Su clsd.

🍴🍺 **Beer Stein** (0.9E) 610.863.8338 M-Th3p-2a, F-Su 11a-2a. L/D wings, seafood.

🍴🍴 **Hong Kong Chinese** (1.9E) 610.863.9309 L/D buffet.

🍴🍴 **Sal's Pizza** (2.5E) Delivers.

➕ **Slate Belt Family Practice** (1.6E) 610.863.3019

➕ **Blue Valley Family Practice** (1.8E) 610.654.1000 Walk-in clinic 7 days.

💊 **CVS** (1.7E) 610.863.5341 M-F 8a-9p, Sa 9a-7p, Su 9a-5p.

🎬 **Gap Theatre** (1.1E) 610.863.3094 Mostly used for concerts.

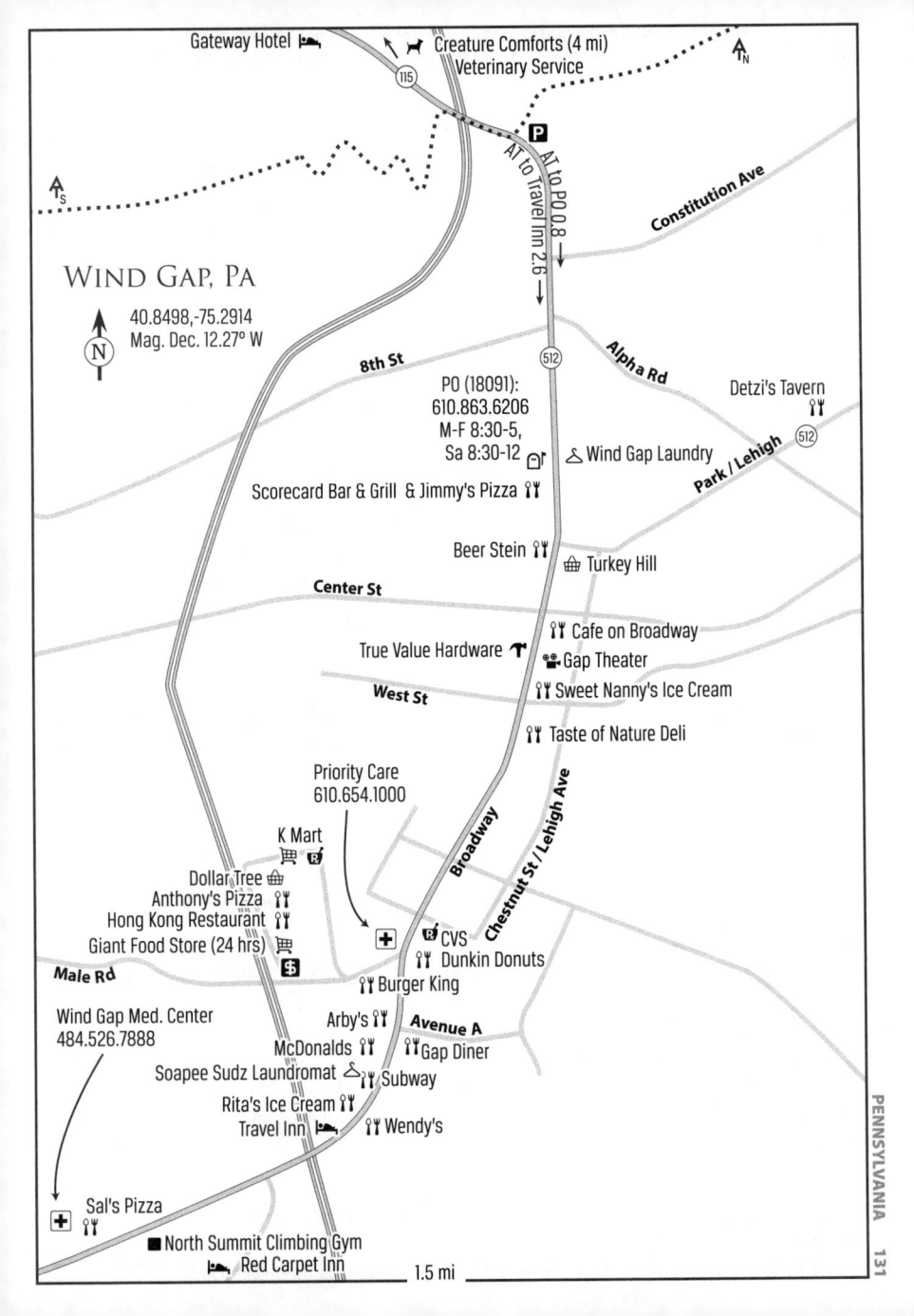

Gateway Hotel

Creature Comforts (4 mi)
Veterinary Service

115

AT to Travel Inn 2.6   AT to PO 0.8

P

Constitution Ave

WIND GAP, PA

40.8498, -75.2914
Mag. Dec. 12.27° W

N

8th St

512

Alpha Rd

Detzi's Tavern

PO (18091):
610.863.6206
M-F 8:30-5,
Sa 8:30-12

Wind Gap Laundry

Park / Lehigh

512

Scorecard Bar & Grill & Jimmy's Pizza

Beer Stein

Turkey Hill

Center St

Cafe on Broadway

True Value Hardware

Gap Theater

West St

Sweet Nanny's Ice Cream

Taste of Nature Deli

Priority Care
610.654.1000

Broadway

Chestnut St / Lehigh Ave

K Mart

Dollar Tree
Anthony's Pizza
Hong Kong Restaurant
Giant Food Store (24 hrs)

CVS
Dunkin Donuts

Male Rd

Burger King

Wind Gap Med. Center
484.526.7888

Arby's

Avenue A

McDonalds

Gap Diner

Soapee Sudz Laundromat

Subway

Rita's Ice Cream

Travel Inn

Wendy's

Sal's Pizza

North Summit Climbing Gym

Red Carpet Inn

1.5 mi

876.3 **1314.6** Side trail leads 0.5E to Crater Lake. No camping.. 1447

875.3 **1315.6** Buttermilk Falls Trail, campsites to the north . . . . ⏺ 1557

874.0 **1316.9** Campsite . . . . ⏺◊ 1293
873.6 **1317.3** Rattlesnake Mountain . . . . 📷 1492
873.3 **1317.6** Spring . . . . ◊ 1365

871.4 **1319.5** **Brink Shelter** (0.2W)(2013) 61.6◄44.9◄31.2◄►6.6►12.4►15.0. . . . . . ◊ ☽ ⌐ (8) 1229
        Bear box. Close to road. Water 100 yards to right of old shelter site.

870.2 **1320.7** Jacobs Ladder Trail. . . . . 📷 1374

868.4 **1322.5** Powerline 1260

867.8 **1323.1** US 206, Culvers Gap, **Branchville, NJ** (3.4E) . . . .(pg. 135) 935
867.5 **1323.4** Sunrise Mountain Rd (paved) . . . . 41.1797,-74.788 🅿 972

865.9 **1325.0** Culver Fire Tower (locked) . . . . 📷 ⛺ 1543

864.9 **1326.0** Stony Brook Trail 1.0W to free showers at Stony Lake 1344
864.8 **1326.1** **Gren Anderson Shelter** (0.1W). . . . . ☽ ◊ (0.1W) ⌐ (8) 1333
        51.5◄37.8◄6.6◄►5.8►8.4►13.0 Spring to left of shelter and downhill 70 yards.

863.4 **1327.5** Tinsley Trail 1446

862.4 **1328.5** Sunrise Mountain, no camping at pavilion . . . . 41.2195,-74.7182 🅿 📷 1653

861.7 **1329.2** Roadbed. 1451

860.7 **1330.2** Stream (slow outflow from pond), treatment recommended. . . . . ⏺ ◊ 1384

859.0 **1331.9** **Mashipacong Shelter** 43.6◄12.4◄5.8◄►2.6►7.2►19.6 Close to road. . ☽ ⌐ (8) 1410
        Spring (0.6N) on red-blazed Iris Trail. Sometimes water left in bear box.
858.8 **1332.1** Deckertown Turnpike . . . . 41.2523,-74.6895 🅿 1322
857.9 **1333.0** Three intersections with red-blazed trail 1418

856.4 **1334.5** **Rutherford Shelter** (0.4E) 15.0◄8.4◄2.6◄►4.6►17.0►28.5 . . . . ☽ ◊ ⏺ ⌐ (6) 1488
        Spring 100 yards before shelter on connecting trail. Slow stream. Bear box.

| 856.1 | 1334.8 | View . . . . 📷 | 1481 |

854.6 1336.3 Intersection with blue-blazed trail. 1601

853.7 1337.2 Iris Trail 0.2E to parking on NJ 23 1504
853.5 1337.4 NJ 23 . . . . 41.3026,-74.6678 🅿 ⬩ (pg. 135) 1500
    High Point State Park Headquarters, **Port Jervis, NY** (4.4W)

852.5 1338.4 Wooden tower, 0.3W to beach & concessions Mem-Labor Day 12-6 . . 📷 ♔ 🍴 🔥 1701
852.3 1338.6 Green-blazed trail 0.3W to 220' tower atop highest point in NJ . . . . . . 📷 🔥 1607
851.8 1339.1 **High Point Shelter** (0.1E) 13.0◄7.2◄4.6◄►12.4►23.9►36.0 . . . . .) ⬩ ∠ (8) 1298
    Streams on both sides of shelter. Road to privy to right of shelter. Bear box.

850.5 1340.4 Greenville Rd, County 519 (paved) 1100

849.6 1341.3 Courtwright Rd (gravel), stream on AT 0.1 south of road . . . . ⬩ 986

849.1 1341.8 Streams . . . . ⬩ 959

848.5 1342.4 Fergerson Rd (gravel), east 20 yards on road. 874

847.9 1343.0 Gemmer Rd (paved) 732
847.6 1343.3 Stream. . . . . ⬩ 702
847.2 1343.7 Two footbridges, streams . . . . ⬩ 606
846.9 1344.0 Goodrich Rd (paved) 625
846.7 1344.2 Pond. . . . . ⬩ 672

846.0 1344.9 Goldsmith Lane (gravel) 672
845.6 1345.3 Unionville Rd (paved); County Rd 651 . . . . (pg. 138) 610
845.4 1345.5 Quarry Rd 616

844.7 1346.2 Lott Rd, **Unionville, NY** (0.7W) . . . . (pg. 138) 590

> ☘ Camp only in designated sites; fires only in campsite fire rings. Hitchhiking is illegal in NY.

843.6 1347.3 NJ 284, **Unionville, NY** (0.7W), stream N of rd. . . . 41.2885,-74.5524 🅿 ⬩ (pg. 138) 437
843.2 1347.7 Lower Rd (Oil City Rd). 528
842.7 1348.2 Carnegie Rd, NoBo: follow road 0.2W 415
842.4 1348.5 State Line Rd, NoBo: follow road 0.5E 423
842.2 1348.7 Wallkill River, parking. . . . . 41.2877,-74.534 🅿 410
841.9 1349.0 AT + State Line Rd north end. NoBo: turn east into Wallkill Reserve. 405

841.1 1349.8 90 degree turn on Wallkill perimeter 387

840.7 1350.2 90 degree turn on Wallkill perimeter 399

839.9 1351.0 Liberty Corners Rd (paved). 440
839.8 1351.1 Water to west. . . . . ⬩ 516
839.4 1351.5 **Pochuck Mtn. Shelter** (0.1W) 19.6◄17.0◄12.4◄►11.5►23.6►37.9 . .) ☁ ∠ (6) 884
    Bear box. Spigot at vacant house at foot of Pochuck Mountain.

838.6 1352.3 View . . . . 📷 1111

837.8 1353.1 Pochuck Mountain . . . . 📷 1147
837.3 1353.6 Lovemma Lane (gravel). 880
837.1 1353.8 Stream. 794
836.7 1354.2 County Rd 565, **Glenwood, NJ** (1.1W), stream south of road . . . . . . ⬩ (pg. 138) 720
    SoBos planning to stay at Pochuck Mtn Shelter should get water here.

1294.7   PA 611

» *Delaware Water Gap, PA 18327*

🍴 **Kenny's Ole Dawg Shuttle** 570.534.7539 Boiling Springs, PA to the CT state line.

📧 **Pocono Cab** 570.424.2800

📧 **WGM Taxi** 570.223.9289

🏠 ♿ ⊠ **Deer Head Inn** 570.424.2000 $90/up wkdays, $120/up wkends. No pets, no TV. Restaurant & lounge open to all w/live music Th-Su. Hiker attire ok.⟨deerheadinn. com⟩

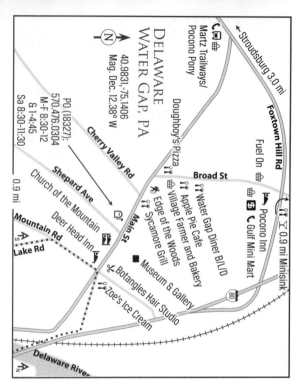

← Stroudsburg 3.0 mi

N

DELAWARE
WATER GAP, PA

40.9831,-75.1406
Mag. Dec. 12.38° W

📞📧⊞ Martz Trailways/
Pocono Pony

Doughboy's Pizza 🍴

Cherry Valley Rd

Foxtown Hill Rd

Fuel On ⊞

Shepard Ave
Church of the Mountain

Broad St

🍴 Water Gap Diner B/L/D
🍴 Apple Pie Cafe
⊞ Village Farmer and Bakery
🏠 Edge of the Woods
🍴 Sycamore Grill

📧 Pocono Inn
⊞ 💲📞 Gulf Mini Mart

Deer Head Inn
Mountain Rd
Lake Rd
Church of the Mountain

🍴 Museum & Gallery

✂ Botangles Hair Studio

🍴 Zoe's Ice Cream

80

🍴📧 0.9 mi Minisink

Main St

0.9 mi

Delaware River

N

PO (18327):
570.476.0304
M-F 8:30-12
& 1-4:45
Sa 8:30-11:30

🏠 ◉ ♿ ⊠ 🍴 **Church of the Mountain Hiker Center** (0.1W) 570.476.0345, 862.268.1120 570.992.3934, Bunkroom, showers, overflow tenting, & lean-to shelter in back. Donations encouraged. 2 Night max. No drive-ins/parking/laundry. Phone numbers of persons who can help are posted in the hostel.

🏠 🚿 **Pocono Inn** (0.5W) $65 Wkdays, $69 F & Sa + tax. No pets.

🏠 🍴 △ ♨ 🚿 **Watergap Country Club** (0.6W) 570.476.4653 $80D Su-Th, $120D F-Sa. Shower, laundry, no pets or tank-tops. Pool & Tiki-bar.

🏠 🏕 ⊠ **Edge of the Woods Outfitters** (0.3W) 570.421.6681 Full line of gear, trail food, footwear. Coleman/alcohol/oz. Shuttles from Little Gap to Bear Mtn. Open 7 days, Mem - Labor Day. Mail: (FedEx/UPS only) 110 Main St, Delaware Water Gap, PA 18327.

⊞ 🍴 **Village Farmer & Bakery** (0.4E) 7 days, 8a-8p, grill 8a-7p. Hot dog & slice of pie $2.95. B'fast sandwiches, salads, sandwiches. CC min. $1.

🍴 **Doughboy's Pizza** (0.3W) 570.421.1900 Open 7 days in summer.

📧 **Martz Trailways** (0.7W) 570.421.3040 $71 NYC roundtrip.

» *Stroudsburg, PA 18360* (3.5W) Large town w/all services, incl **Walmart** (24hrs w/pharmacy) supermarket, motels, laundry, & movie theater.

🏕 💲 **Dunkleberger's Sports Outfitter** (3.7E) 570.421.7950 M-Th 9-6, F 9-6, Su 10-5. Hiking boots, camp supplies, backpacks & clothing.⟨dunkelbergers.com⟩

📧 **Pocono Pony** 570.839.6282 Runs on 2hr-loop through Stroudsburg, $1.50/boarding.

1305.5   CAMP ROAD

🏠 ◉ 🏕 ♿ 🍴 **Knight Riders Taxi & Limo** 908.850.4450 908.362.5670 🚿 ⊠ **Mohican Outdoor Center** (0.3W) Thru-hiker rates. Bunkroom w/kitchen, water & electric $30.00PP, tenting w/bear box & privy $10PP +tax. Shower free for bunkers & tenters, or w/o stay $5. Towels & linens avail to rent. Campfires only in designated areas. Visitor Center & camp store hrs in peak season: Su-Th 8-7, F 8-9, Sa 8-8. Off season (Nov- Apr) 9-5. Water avail at lodge or at spigot near garage across the rd. Hiker box & log on site. AYCE meal service, hot b'fast, deli sandwiches, sodas, candy, & ice cream. Charging & WiFi avail. Coleman/alcohol/ oz & hiker supplies (footwear, packs, socks, poles). Operated by the AMC (memberships avail). Mail: 50 Camp Mohican Rd, Blairstown, NJ 07825.⟨outdoors.org/lodging/mohican/⟩

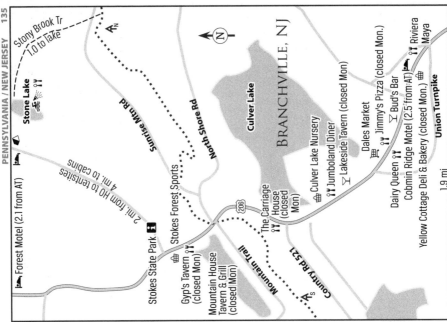

Stony Brook Tr
1.0 to Lake

Stone Lake

Forest Motel (2.1 from AT)

Sunrise Mtn Rd

2 mi. from HQ to tentsites
4 mi. to cabins

Stokes Forest Sports

Stokes State Park

North Shore Rd

206

Culver Lake

BRANCHVILLE, NJ

Culver Lake Nursery

Jumboland Diner

Lakeside Tavern (closed Mon)

Dales Market

Dairy Queen

Jimmy's Pizza (closed Mon.)

Bud's Bar

Cobmin Ridge Motel (2.5 from AT)

Riviera Maya

Yellow Cottage Deli & Bakery (closed Mon.)

Union Turnpike

1.9 mi

The Carriage House (closed Mon)

Gyp's Tavern (closed Mon)

Mountain House Tavern & Grill (closed Mon)

Mountain Trail

Country Rd 521

N

1323.1   US 206, CULVERS GAP

» West of the A.T.

Stokes SP (0.7W) 973.948.3820 Tentsites 2 mi from SP office near Rte 206; cabins 4 mi away. Rates: tentsite 1-6 persons $25/up, cabins $65/up. Rates $5 & $10 lower for NJ residents. $5 transaction fee/stay. Free showers at Stony Lake from Mem-Colum Day, accessible from 1 mi-long Stony Brook Tr.

Forest Motel (1.8W) 973.948.5456 $69S $79D + tax, pets $20, laundry $20. Free shuttle to/from trail when avail. Guest Mail: 104 Rte 206 N, Branchville, NJ 07826.

Gyp's Tavern (0.2W) 973.948.5013 Hikers welcome-inside or lakeside seating, charging outlets, economical food choices, packaged goods to go. Pet friendly. Open L/D 11a-1a Clsd Mo.<fb.com/Gyps-Tavern-23816764330>

» East of the A.T.

Dale's Market (1.7E) 973.948.3078 M-F 6-9, Sa-Su 7-9.

Jumboland Diner (1.1E) 973.948.6802 M-Sa 4a-11p, Su 5a-11p B/L/D, $2.99 b'fast, Outdoor seating avail.

» Branchville, NJ 07826 (3.4E)

Cobmin Ridge Motel (2.5E) 973.948.3459, 973.652.0780 $60/up.

1337.4   NJ 23

High Point State Park Headquarters 973.875.4800 Office open yr-round 9a-4p, Mem-Labor Day, extended hrs F 8-8, Sa 8-6. Bathrooms inside, water spigot outside. Overnight parking 0.25E. Sawmill Lake Camping Area 2.5 mi from HQ, tentsites $20 NJ resident/$25 non-resident plus $5.50 walk-in fee. Mail: 1480 State Rte 23, Sussex, NJ 07461.

Sawmill Lake Camping Area (0.25E) 2.5 Mi from HQ, tentsites $20 NJ resident/$25 non-resident plus $5.50 walk-in fee. Mail: 1480 State Rte 23, Sussex, NJ 07461.

High Point Country Inn (1.3E) $90D + tax, pets $10, no room phone. Laundry $7. Free p/u & ret to trail from NJ 23, longer shuttles for a fee. Guest Mail: 1328 NJ 23, Wantage, NJ 07461.

» Port Jervis, NY 12785 (4.4W) (services cont'd on pg. 138...)

836.0	1354.9	Roadbed.		764
835.2	1355.7	County Rd 517, **Glenwood, NJ** (1.1W) . . . . 41.2357,-74.4805 🅿 (pg. 138)		428
834.5	1356.4	Pochuck Creek suspension footbridge.		394
		Boardwalk over swamp for (0.6S) and (0.2N) of footbridge.		
833.8	1357.1	Canal Rd. . . . . 41.2266,-74.469 🅿		410
833.6	1357.3	Footbridge, Wawayanda Creek. . . . . ♦		401
832.9	1358.0	NJ 94, **Vernon, NJ** (2.4E) . . . . 41.2193,-74.4551 🅿 (pg. 139)		450

⚠ NJ: No campfires allowed. Camping is limited to shelters and official campsites

831.9	1359.0	Spring, climb up south side of mtn known as "stairway to heaven". . . . . . . ♦	973
831.5	1359.4	Pinwheels vista 0.1W, Wawayanda Mountain, side trail 0.8E to views . . . . . 📷	1340
830.6	1360.3	Footbridge, stream . . . . ♦	994
829.8	1361.1	Barrett Rd (paved), **New Milford, NY** (1.8W). . . . .(pg. 139)	1140
828.7	1362.2	Cross stream on Iron Mountain Rd . . . . ♦	1060
827.9	1363.0	**Wawayanda Shelter** (0.1W) . . . . ☽ ◑ ⊏ (6)	1194
		28.5◄23.9◄11.5◄►12.1►26.4►31.7 Water from park 0.1N and 0.2E.	
827.7	1363.2	Wawayanda State Park (0.2E) . . . . .41.1981,-74.3975 🅿 ⚲♦ ☎♦	1149
827.4	1363.5	Warwick Turnpike . . . . 41.2014,-74.3916 🅿 (pg. 140)	1140
826.9	1364.0	Footbridge, stream . . . . ♦	1107
826.0	1364.9	Long House Dr / Brady Rd . . . . 41.1955,-74.3715 🅿	1115
824.9	1366.0	Long House Creek, footbridge . . . . ♦	1085
824.1	1366.8	Ernest Walter Trail (yellow-blazed) to east	1342
823.8	1367.1	**NJ-NY** border, State Line Trail 1.0E to **Lakeside, NJ**.	1385
		0.1N on AT is Zig Zag Trail to west.	
823.4	1367.5	Prospect Rock, highest point on AT in NY. Views of Greenwood Lake to east . . 📷	1433
822.5	1368.4	Furnace Brook . . . . ♦	1157
822.2	1368.7	Ladder.	1250
820.8	1370.1	Cascade Brook . . . . ♦	1185
819.9	1371.0	Village Vista Trail, 0.8E to Greenwood Lake	1283

⚠ Despite the unimposing profile, rocks, abrupt ups & downs make this section challenging.

818.3	1372.6	Powerline	1199
817.8	1373.1	NY 17A, **Bellvale, NY** (1.6W) . . . . 41.2443,-74.2869 🅿 (pg. 140)	1180
		Greenwood Lake, NY (2.0E)	
817.2	1373.7	Pipeline clearing	1242

816.5	1374.4	Eastern Pinnacles, short bypass trail to west . . . . 🄲	1213
816.3	1374.6	Brook . . . . ♦	1045
816.1	1374.8	Cat Rocks, view . . . . 🄲	1091
815.8	1375.1	**Wildcat Shelter** (0.2W) 36.0◄23.6◄12.1◄►14.3►19.6►22.8 . . . . ☽♦🗑⌂ (8)	1070
		Spring in front of shelter.	
814.5	1376.4	Highlands Trail . . . . ♦	762
814.3	1376.6	Lakes Rd (paved), 0.1N powerline, footbridge and stream . . . . ♦	680
814.0	1376.9	Fitzgerald Falls . . . . ♦	733
812.7	1378.2	Allis Trail, Sterling Fire Tower 5.0E . . . . 🄲 🅐	1255
812.0	1378.9	Mombasha High Point . . . . 🄲	1280
810.9	1380.0	Boardwalk, pond . . . . ♦	912
810.8	1380.1	West Mombasha Rd, stream just north on AT . . . . 41.2693,-74.2146 🅿♦	933
809.9	1381.0	Buchanan Mountain	1142
809.1	1381.8	East Mombasha Rd (paved) . . . . ♦	840
808.8	1382.1	Little Dam Lake, stepping stones over creek . . . . ♦	768
807.7	1383.2	Orange Turnpike . . . . 41.2695,-74.181 🅿♦ (0.5E)	780
807.0	1383.9	Arden Mountain	1180
806.7	1384.2	Sapphire Trail	1120
806.3	1384.6	View . . . . 🄲	1040
805.9	1385.0	NY 17, **Southfields, NY** (2.1E), **Harrriman, NY** (3.7W) . . . . (pg. 141)	550
805.5	1385.4	AT on Arden Valley Rd for 0.4 mile . . . . 41.2649,-74.1544 🅿🚐 (pg. 141)	594
		Passes over NY State Thruway 87, crosses thru parking area north of bridge.	
804.2	1386.7	Island Pond Rd (gravel) 0.1E to pond . . . . ♦	1008
803.6	1387.3	Lemon Squeezer, Arden-Surebridge Trail to east	1088
803.3	1387.6	Island Pond Mountain . . . . 🄲	1298
802.9	1388.0	New York Long Path 52.0E to Manhattan	1055
802.2	1388.7	Surebridge Brook . . . . ♦	1092
801.6	1389.3	AT joins Red Dot Trail (south end)	1341
801.5	1389.4	**Fingerboard Shelter** 37.9◄26.4◄14.3◄►5.3►8.5►40.7 . . . . ♦⌂ (8)	1348
		Spring downhill to left unreliable. Water at Lake Tiorati 0.5E on Hurst Trail.	
		Problem bear in 2017.	
800.9	1390.0	Fingerboard Mountain	1322
800.4	1390.5	Arden Valley Rd (paved), Tiorati Circle (0.3E) . . . . 41.2646,-74.1544 🅿 (pg. 141)	1196
799.7	1391.2	Woods road	1027
798.3	1392.6	Footbridge, stream . . . . ♦	836
798.2	1392.7	Seven Lakes Dr	850

» **Port Jervis, NY 12785** (4.4W) (...services cont'd from pg. 135)

🏠🛏🚿🍴 **Mosey's Place** (5.7W) 845.239.3028 $30 Bunk incl laundry, & free p/u & ret to US23 High Point State Pk HQ. Free shuttles for guests to amenities. 15 Min from metro north train. Reservations req'd. Please call or text Mosey. Open Jun 1-Colum day. Hikers welcome in off season if they are home.

🏠📧 **Shop Rite Market, Price Chopper** (4.3W)

🍴 **Village Pizza** (4.2W) M-S 11a-11p, Su 11a-10p.

➕ **Bon Secours Community Hospital** (5.6W) 845.858.7000

🏠📧 **Rite Aid** (6.3W) 845.856.8342, 📧 **Medicine Shoppe** 845.856.6681

🐾 **Tri-States Veterinary Medical** (5.9W) 845.856.1914

1345.3	★	UNIONVILLE, NY
1346.2	★	LOTT RD
1347.3		NJ 284

» **Unionville, NY 10988** PO is 0.5W from any road crossing.

🏠📧👟 **Village Office** (0.4W) 845.726.3681 Tenters check-in at office or at Horler's store.

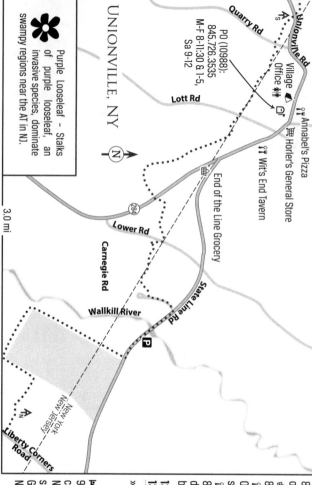

UNIONVILLE, NY

Quarry Rd

Unionville Rd

Lott Rd

PO (10988):
845.726.3535,
M-F 8-11:30 & 1-5,
Sa 9-12

Village Office

Annabel's Pizza

Horler's General Store

Wit's End Tavern

End of the Line Grocery

284

Lower Rd

Carnegie Rd

Wallkill River

State Line Rd

New York / New Jersey

Liberty Corners Road

3.0 mi

Purple Looseleaf – Stalks of purple looseleaf, an invasive species, dominate swampy regions near the AT in NJ.

🏠🍴💲 **Horler's Store** (0.4W) 845.726.3210 M-Sa 6-8, Su 7-7, short-order grill open M-Sa 6:30-2, Su 7-1.

🍴💲 **State Line Deli** (0.8W) 845.683.1566 Open 7 days, 6a-8p.

🍴 **Annabel's Pizza** (0.4W) 845.726.9992 Open 7 days, 11a-10p, burgers, pizza by slice.

🍴📺💲 **Wit's End Tavern** (0.4W) 845.726.3956 Darts, pool table. Open 7 days noon-midnight or later. Great ribs, burgers, wings.

1354.2	★	COUNTY RD 565
1355.7	★	COUNTY RD 517

» **Glenwood, NJ 07418**

🏠🚿✉ **Apple Valley Inn** (1.1W) (1.1W from either rd) ☎ 973.764.2616, M-F 7:30-5, Sa 10-2 973.764.3735 applevalleyinnbnb@gmail.com $150-$160 + tax, incl country b'fast. No pets. Shuttles to CR 517 & 565 w/ stay. Gourmet chocolate store on site. Guest only mail: PO Box 302, Glenwood, NJ 07418.

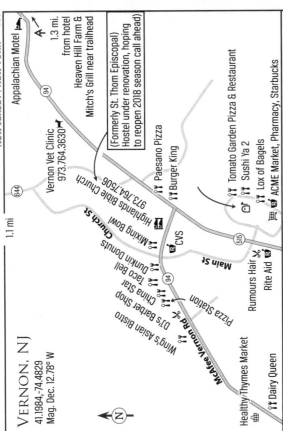

VERNON, NJ
41.1984,-74.4829
Mag. Dec. 12.78° W

Map labels:

Appalachian Motel

1.3 mi.
from hotel
Heaven Hill Farm &
Mitch's Grill near trailhead

[Formerly St. Thom Episcopal)
Hostel under renovation, hoping
to reopen 2018 season call ahead]

Vernon Vet Clinic
973.764.3630

Highlands Bible Church 973.764.7506

Paesano Pizza
Burger King

Tomato Garden Pizza & Restaurant
Sushi Ya 2
Lox of Bagels
ACME Market, Pharmacy, Starbucks

1.1 mi

Church St

Mixing Bowl
CVS

Main St

Rumours Hair
Rite Aid

Dunkin Donuts
Taco Bell
China Star
DJ's Barber Shop
pizza station
Wing's Asian Bistro

McAfee Vernon Rd

Healthy/Thymes Market

Dairy Queen

Be Prepared

Prepare for extreme weather, hazards, and emergencies
– especially the cold –
to avoid impacts from searches, rescues, and campfires.

$

Prices are Subject to Change

...particularly at hotels. Prices published in The A.T. Guide were given in fall of 2017 & often represent a significant discount for hikers. Businesses intend to keep these prices throughout 2018, but they are not obliged to do so.

🏨 🍴 ♨ 🚿 **Pochuck Valley Farms Market & Deli** (1W) 973.764.4732 Open daily M-F 6a-6p, Sa-Su 6a- 5p. B/L, produce, bakery. Water spigot & restroom.

1358.0   NJ 94

🛏 🚿 ⊠ **Rickey Farm/Rickey Ministries** (0.2E) 973.699.4950 WFS & shower or $10/day campsite/shower. This is an family farm. Please call in adv if possible.

🛏 🍴 ♨ 🚿 ⊠ **Appalachian Motel** (1.4E) 973.764.6070 $70-110D, $10EAP. Call for ride. Pets $20. Laundry $10. Guest only Mail: 367 Route 94, Vernon, NJ 07462.

🍴 ♨ **Mitch's Roadside Grill** (0.2E) 973.715.2608 "The Best" Hot dog stand. 11-4 Apr-Oct. Soda, shaded picnic tables, good spot to hitch from. May wait for hikers if call ahead.

🏪 🍴 ♨ 🛒 **Heaven Hill Farm** (0.1W) 973.764.5144 Summer hrs daily 9a-6p. Ice cream, bakery, seasonal fruit & vegetables.‹heavenhillfarm.com›

» **Vernon, NJ 07462 (2.4E)**

🏪 🛒 🍴 **Acme Market** (2.5E) M-Sa 6a-midnight, Su 6a-10p. Starbucks inside.

» **New Milford, NY** (2.7W from NJ 94
(see services at Barrett Rd)

1361.1   BARRETT RD

» **New Milford, NY 10959** (1.8W)
🍴 845.986.3557, M-F 8:30-12:30, Sa 9-11:30
(P0 1.4 W on Barret Rd, then right 0.2 on NJ 94)

■ **Sneakers to Boots** (1.5W) 845.986.0333 Open M-F 10-6, Sa 10-5, Su 11-2. Shoes by Merrell, Keen, Oboz, Salomon & others. Merino wool socks. 314 Rt 94 S.

Map labels

St. Anthony's Hospital
845.986.2276

Warwick, NY

Albert Wisner Library
845.986.1047 M-Th 9-8,
F 9-7, Sa 9-5, Su 12-4.

Warwick Laundromat

Warwick Motel

Cty Rd 1

94

Price Chopper (24 hrs)

Pin Street Bowling

Shop Rite, Rite Aid, Luca Pizza

Warwick Drive-in

Pennings Farm Market

Warwick Turnpike

New York
New Jersey

AT to Shop
Rite 2.7 mi.

Brady Rd / Longhouse Dr.

AT to motel 3.1

Orchard Grove Animal Hospital
845.986.9399

Bellvale, NY

Bellvale Market

Bellvale Farms Creamery

Prospect Rock

Village Vista Trail

Greenwood Lake, NY

17A

Greenwood Lake

Wawayanda State Park

Wawayanda Shelter

State Line Trail

5.0 mi

Guide entries

1363.5 WARWICK TURNPIKE

Pennings Farm Market (2.8W) 845.986.1059 Local produce, Pub & Grill.

Warwick Drive-In Theatre (2.5W) 845.986.4440 Walkins welcome. $11 Adults, $8 kids & seniors.

» *Warwick, NY 10990* (4.9W) 2.7 N to NY 94, 1.5 N on NY 94 to downtown w/many resaurants, PO & Library.

Meadowlark Farm B&B (9.4W) 845.651.4286 Su-Th $75D & up incl b'fast. Rates higher on F-Sa nights. Free Laundry. CC ok, pets welcome. Shuttles covering NJ & NY, $1/round-trip mile; free parking for section hikers.

△ Warwick Laundromat (4.7W) 845.987.5000

1373.1 NY 17A

Hot Dog Plus (0.2W) Open seasonally Tu-Sa 10:30-3:30.

Bellvale Farms Creamery (0.3W) 845.988.1818 Homemade ice cream, water spigot, electronic charging station. (bellvalefarms.com)

» *Bellvale, NY 10912* (1.6W)

Bellvale Market (1.7W) 845.544.7700 Options: fresh seafood, deli, gluten-free, free -range poultry. M-F 8-7, Sa 8-6; Su 8-4.

» *Greenwood Lake, NY 10925* (2E)

Night Owl Taxi 845.662.0359 Shuttles from Greenwood Lake. M-W 8-2, Th- Sa 8-4, Su 10-10.

Greenwood Lake Taxi 845.477.0314

Anton's on the Lake (2.5E) 845.477.0010 Thru-hiker rate, 2 night min. Per night: Su-Th $80S/D, F-Sa $125/up. CC ok. Rooms w/whirlpool avail. No pets/smoking. Small laundry loads only. Swimming, paddle boats & canoe. Free shuttle & slackpack w/stay. Longer shuttle for fee. Open yr-round. Guest only mail: (USPS)

PO Box 1505, (FedEx/UPS) 7 Waterstone Rd, Greenwood Lake, NY 10925.⟨antonsonthelake.com⟩

🅱️🍴💲🛜⌂✉ **Breezy Point Inn** (3.1E) 845.477.8100 $85+tax RM w/2 Dbl beds, no pets, no smoking, L/D dining daily. Closed Jan. Guest Mail: (UPS/FedEx) 620 Jersey Ave, Greenwood Lake, NY 10925.⟨breezypointinn.com⟩

» *Warwick, NY 10990 (4.5W) to downtown, see map & add'l services pg. 140*

🛏️🛜 **Warwick Motel & Suites** (4.1W) 845.986.6656 $89 (incl tax), free laundry.

1385.0   NY 17

» *Southfields, NY 10975*
(2.1E) ☎845.351.2628
M-F 10-12 & 1-5, Sa 8:30-11:30

🛏️🍴⌂ **Tuxedo Motel** (2.1E) 845.351.4747 $54.50S, $59.50D, $10EAP. No pets, no cooking. Food delivery options. Visa/MC ok. Mail: 985 Route 17 South, Southfields, NY 10975.⟨tuxedomotel.com⟩

🅿️🛒🍴🛏️🛜📶⌂✉ **Rosebud Hostel** (53.9E) 347.510.6785 rob.rosa@gmail.com $79/Night incl pvt room & b'fast. Pets welcome. No-smoking, pvt room & b'fast. Pets welcome. No-smoking. Located in Queens, NY. Mass transit avail to Manhattan. Free laundry service. CC 0k.

⛽ **Valero** (1.9E) 0.1 W of PO. 5a-11p, Sa-Su 6a 11p.

» *Harriman, NY 10926 (3.7W) Lodging, groceries, restaurants and more.*

1385.4   ARDEN VALLEY RD PARKING

🚌🅿️ **Harriman Shuttle** Leaves Tuxedo Train Station at 10:50a on wknd & holiday mornings only, w/ p/u here at 11:43 & Tiorati Circle at 11:40.

Connects to Southfields. $5/ride.⟨myharriman.com/harriman-shuttle-bus⟩

1390.5   ARDEN VALLEY RD (TIORATI CIRCLE)

🍴🏊🏕️⛲🚻 **Lake Tiorati Beach** (0.3E) 845.429.8257 9-7 daily mid Jun-mid Aug. Wkends only spring & fall. Restrooms, free showers, vending machine, swimming.

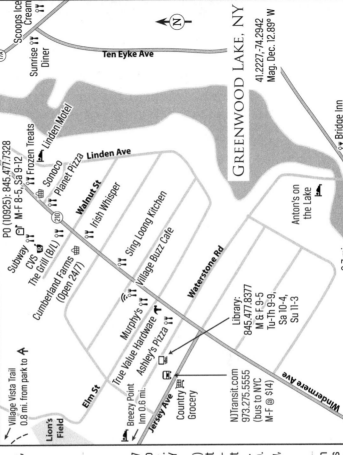

796.2 1394.7 **William Brien Memorial Shelter** 31.7◄19.6◄5.3◄►3.2►35.4►44.4. . . ◊ ∠ (8) 1075
Unreliable spring-fed well 80 yards down blue-blazed trail to right of shelter.
Yellow-blazed Menomine Trail to east.

795.3 1395.6 AT joins Red Dot Trail (north end) 914

794.9 1396.0 Black Mountain, views, can see NY City skyline . . . . 📷 1192

794.1 1396.8 Palisades Parkway, busy 4-lane divided hwy. NY City 34E. Visitor. . . . . 🚻 ♦ ☎ 680
center in median 0.4W, soda & snack machines.⚠ Watch blazes next 3mi. north.

793.8 1397.1 Beechy Bottom Brook, footbridge, parking 0.8W . . . . 🅿 ◊ 610

793.0 1397.9 **West Mountain Shelter** (0.6E) 22.8◄8.5◄3.2◄►32.2►41.2►49.0 . . . 📷 ∠ (8) 1221
Views of Hudson River & NYC.

792.3 1398.6 Views from ridge of West Mountain . . . . 📷 1137

791.2 1399.7 Seven Lakes Dr 610

790.6 1400.3 Perkins Memorial Dr 794

788.8 1402.1 Bear Mountain, Perkins Memorial Tower, ... 41.3112,-74.0072 🅿 📷 🅰 1305
Vending machines, view of NYC skyline.

788.2 1402.7 Perkins Memorial Dr (south end of 0.3 mi. roadwalk) 1001

786.9 1404.0 Bear Mountain State Park, Hessian Lake . . . . 41.313,-73.989 🅿 (pg. 144) 190

786.5 1404.4 Tunnel under US 9, Trailside Museum, bear cage is lowest point on AT . .(pg. 144) 177

786.0 1404.9 Bear Mountain Bridge, Hudson River, **Fort Montgomery, NY** (1.8W) . . . (pg. 144) 200

785.5 1405.4 NY 9D, Bear Mountain Bridge north end. 198

784.8 1406.1 Camp Smith Trail, 0.6E to Anthonys Nose, views of Hudson River . . . . 📷 727

783.8 1407.1 Hemlock Springs Campsite . . . . ◊ ⛺ 503

783.6 1407.3 Manitou Rd (gravel). . . . . 41.3296,-73.9533 🅿 460

782.6 1408.3 Osborne Loop Trail to west (blue-blazed) 774

782.2 1408.7 Curry Pond Trail to west (yellow-blazed) 857

781.2 1409.7 Osborne Loop Trail to west (blue-blazed) 862

780.7 1410.2 Carriage Connector Trail to west (yellow-blazed). 513

780.2 1410.7 US 9 + NY 403, **Peekskill, NY** (4.5E) . . . .(pg. 144) 400

779.1 1411.0 Old Highland Turnpike (paved) 461

779.6 1411.3 Franciscan Way (paved), **Graymoor Spiritual Life Center** (0.4E) . . . . .(pg. 145) 540

779.5 1411.4 Two gravel roads 466

777.7 1413.2 Blue-blazed trail 0.1W to Denning Hill . . . . 📷 900

776.9 1414.0 Old Albany Post Rd (gravel), Chapman Rd 607

775.9	1415.0	Canopus Hill.	813
775.3	1415.6	Brook .... ♦	395
775.2	1415.7	Canopus Hill Rd (paved) ....(pg. 145)	420
774.2	1416.7	South Highland Rd (paved), stream north side of road. .... ♦	570
773.4	1417.5	Stream. .... ♦	655
772.7	1418.2	Catfish Loop Trail (red-blazed)	941
771.5	1419.4	Dennytown Rd (paved), Three Lake Trail to west ...... 41.4206,-73.8689 **P** ♦	860
		Water on side of pump building, open late-Apr-Oct.	
771.3	1419.6	Catfish Loop Trail to east (red-blazed)	814
769.9	1421.0	Sunken Mine Rd (gravel), stream to north.	800
768.7	1422.2	Three Lakes Trail	986
767.8	1423.1	NY 301, Canopus Lake, **Clarence Fahnestock SP** (1.0E) ....(pg. 145)	920
767.2	1423.7	Fahnestock Trail to west	1101

⚠ NoBo: Upon reaching the park, AT turns left through playground then follows path at edge of lake.

765.8	1425.1	Green-blazed trail to lake, **Clarence Fahnestock SP** (0.2E) ..... 📷 ♦ (pg. 145)	998
		View of the lake from AT north of this intersection.	
765.0	1425.9	Stream. .... ♦	1023
763.6	1427.3	Shenandoah Mountain, view, painted 911 Memorial Flag. .... 📷	1282
763.2	1427.7	Long Hill Rd (gravel)	1018
762.7	1428.2	Powerline	1000
762.1	1428.8	Shenandoah Tenting Area 0.1W, water source contaminated (pump closed). . ◣	900
761.7	1429.2	Brook .... ♦	758
760.9	1430.0	Bridge over brook. .... ♦	355
760.8	1430.1	Hortontown Rd, ... 41.5141,-73.7918 🚮 ☽ ♦ ◣ ⌁ (6) (pg. 145)	357
		RPH Shelter (1982) 40.7◄35.4◄32.2 ◄►9.0►16.8►25.6 Treat pump water.	
760.5	1430.4	Footbridge, stream, Taconic State Pkwy underpass .... ♦	529
757.3	1433.6	Hosner Mountain Rd, footbridge, stream (do not drink, farm upstream)	500

1404.0   BEAR MOUNTAIN STATE PARK

» *Bear Mountain, NY 10911 (0.4E)*

1404.4   ⊛TRAILSIDE MUSEUM AND ZOO

🏨🛏♨🍴💲 🖥 **Bear Mountain Inn** (0.3E) 845.786.2731 $149/Up+tax, c. b'fast. Dining options: **1915, Blue Tapas Bar & Hiker Cafe** in the inn, seasonal concession lakeside.⟨visitbearmountain.com⟩

■ ⊛**Trailside Museum and Zoo** 845.786.2701 The A.T. goes through the zoo. Open 10-4:30; no charge for hiking through. No dogs. Lowest elevation on the AT (124) is within the park. If closed, or if you have a dog, use bypass (see map).

🏨 Fairbridge Inn & Suites
(3.0 from AT)

🏨 Holiday Inn Express (1.6 mi from circle)

■ Mobile Market
🍴💲 Bagel Cafe

■ Barnstormer BBQ

Bear Mtn
Bridge Motel

PO (10922):
845.446.8459
M-F 8-1 & 2:30-5,
Sa 9-12

Bear Mtn
Bridge Motel

Old Oak Inn 🍴

Richie's 🍴🍴

Foodie's Pizza

FORT
MONTGOMERY, NY

PO (10922):
845.446.8459
M-F 8-1 & 2:30-5,
Sa 9-12

(N)
41.32,-73.9915
Mag. Dec. 13.07° W

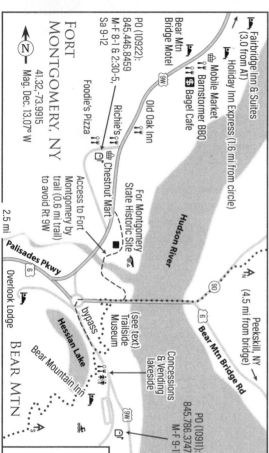

2.5 mi

Palisades Pkwy

Overlook Lodge

BEAR MTN

Hessian Lake

Bear Mountain Inn

bypass

Hudson River

(see text)
Trailside
Museum

Concessions
& Vending
lakeside

Access to Fort
Montgomery by
trail (0.6 mi trail)
to avoid Rt 9W

Fort
Montgomery
State Historic Site

Chestnut Mart

Peekskill, NY ⟶

Aₙ
(4.5 mi from bridge)

(90)

Bear Mtn Bridge Rd

(9W)

PO (10911):
845.786.3747
M-F 9-11

Aₛ

1404.9   BEAR MOUNTAIN BRIDGE

» *Fort Montgomery, NY 10922 (1.8W)*

🏨🛜 ⊠ **Overlook Lodge** (0.6W) 845.786.2731 $149/Up +tax, c. b'fast, some pet rooms.

🏨♨🛜 ⊠ **Bear Mountain Bridge Motel** (1.5W) 845.446.2472 $75D/up, hiker friendly, no pets, Visa/MC ok, trail p/u & ret way for up to 9 passengers. Buffet lunch $10, dinner $15. 1 Acre-farm. Clean, simple rooms, no TV, shared single person bathrooms in hallways. Laundry $3. Fuel/oz & some hiker foods. Parking for section hikers. Mail w/ reservation: 17 Cricketown Rd, Stony Point, NY 10980.⟨stonypointcenter.org/AT⟩

🏨 **Fairbridge Inn & Suites** (2.9W) 845.446.9400 $85D, c. b'fast. Pets $15.

» *Highland Falls, NY (3.8W)*

⊛🍴💲🛏🚿🅿🛜⊠ **Stony Point Center** (8.7E) 845.786.5674 ext. 100 reservations@ stonypointcenter.org Call 7:30a-6p or register online. Use code "ATHike" for discount: $50S wkdays, $80S wkends $10EAP up to 3. Incl. b'fast. Drug free 35 acre retreat w/farm & pottery workshop. Shuttle from rec area $10 ea way for up to 9 passengers. Buffet lunch $10, dinner $15. 1 Acre-farm. Clean, simple rooms, no TV, shared single person bathrooms in hallways. Laundry $3. Fuel/oz & some hiker foods. Parking for section hikers. Mail w/ reservation: 17 Cricketown Rd, Stony Point, NY 10980.⟨stonypointcenter.org/AT⟩

⊞ **Rite Aid** (3.7W)

🍴💲 **Dunkin' Donuts** (4W) & many other restaurants.

🏪🍴💲🚿🅿🛜 **My Town Marketplace** (3.7W) 845.446.3663 24/7, deli serves B/L/D. Water spigot on north side of building.

1410.7   US 9, NY 403

⊞ **Highland Falls Library** (4W) 845.446.3113 M, Th-F 10-5, Tu 10-7, W 10-8, Sa 10-2.

🏪🍴💲🛜📶 **Appalachian Market** 845.424.6241 At trailhead. Hiker-friendly, open 24/7, deli serves B/L/D. Water spigot on north side of building.

Fort Montgomery State Historic Site

Side trail starting from end of bridge guardrail 0.6W passes through Revolutionary War fort for which the town is named. The side trail is roughly the same length as the roadwalk but is more interesting. View the Hudson River bridge down the barrel of a cannon.

» **Peekskill, NY 10566** *(4.5E)*
☎914.737.6437
M-F 9-5, Sa 9-4. Large town.

1411.3   FRANCISCAN WAY

⚐☉❂☌Graymoor Spiritual Life Center *(0.4E)* Hikers
845.424.2111   gslc@atonementfriars.org
permitted to sleep (free) at monastery's ball field
picnic shelter Mar-Nov. Has water, privy & shower.
Follow signs & blue- blazes; stay left at both forks
in the rd.⟨graymoorcenter.org⟩

1415.7   CANOPUS HILL RD

⌂☕🍴🔲♿ **Putnam Valley Market** *(1.6E)*
845.528.8626 Directions: 0.3E on Canopus Hill Rd,
right on Canopus Hollow Rd for 0.1 mi, left on Sunset
Hill Rd for 1.2 mi. Pizza, hot food from the grill, ATM,
open M-Sa 6-9, Su 6-7.

1423.1   NY 301, CANOPUS LAKE *(IE to SP)*
1425.1   ★ SIDE TRAIL ENTRY *(0.2E to SP beach)*

⚐☕🍴🔲♿🚿 **Clarence Fahnestock State Park** 845.225.7207, 800.456.2267
Open mid Apr - mid Dec. Thru-hikers get 1 free night of camping. Concession
at beach open wkends only Mem Day - Jun; open daily Jul - Labor Day. M-Sa
9-5, Su 9-6.

1430.1   HORTONTOWN RD, RPH SHELTER *(Ralph's Peak Hiker Cabin)*

☕🍴 **Carlo's Pizza Express** 845.896.6500 Pizza delivery after 4p only.

1435.2   NY 52

⚐⌂🔲☕♿ **Mountaintop Market Deli** *(0.5E)* 845.221.0928 Open daily
5a-8p, ATM, pay phone inside, welcome to water from faucet on side of
building & electric outlets. Ask about nearby camping.
☕🍴 **Danny's Pizzeria** *(0.5E)* 845.223.5888 Pizza by the slice.

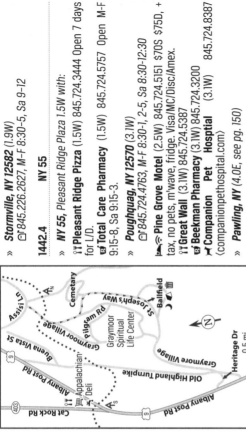

» **Stormville, NY 12582** *(1.9W)*
☎845.226.2627, M-F 8:30-5, Sa 9-12

1442.4   NY 55

» **NY 55**, *Pleasant Ridge Plaza 1.5W with:*
☕🍴 **Pleasant Ridge Pizza** (1.5W) 845.724.3444 Open 7 days
for L/D.
🔲 **Total Care Pharmacy** (1.5W) 845.724.5757 Open M-F
9:15-8, Sa 9:15-3.

» **Poughquag, NY 12570** *(3.1W)*
☎845.724.4763, M-F 8:30-1, 2-5, Sa 8:30-12:30

🛏♿ **Pine Grove Motel** (2.5W) 845.724.5151 $70S $75D, +
tax, no pets, m'wave, fridge. Visa/MC/Disc/Amex.
☕🍴 **Great Wall** (3.1W) 845.724.5387
🔲 **Beekman Pharmacy** (3.1W) 845.724.3200
🐾 **Companion Pet Hospital** (3.1W) 845.724.8387
⟨companionpethospital.com⟩

» **Pawling, NY** *(4.0E, see pg. 150)*

Town Etiquette

Ask permission before bringing a pack into a place of
business. Assume that alcohol is not permitted in hostels
& campsites until told otherwise.

Don't expect generosity, and show appreciation when
it is offered. If you are granted work-for-stay, strive to
provide service equal to the value of your stay.

Respect hotel room capacities; hotel owners should
know how many people intend to stay in a room. Try to
leave hotel rooms as clean as a car traveler would. If a
shower is available, use it.

755.7	**1435.2**	NY 52, **Stormville, NY** (1.9W) . . . . 41.541,-73.7328 🅿 (pg. 145)		800
755.1	**1435.8**	Stream, footbridge . . . . ⬦		837
754.5	**1436.4**	AT on Old Stormville Mountain Rd for 0.1 mile		971
754.3	**1436.6**	AT on Stormville Mountain Rd for 0.1 mile, crosses over I-84		950
754.1	**1436.8**	Grape Hollow Rd		955
752.8	**1438.1**	Side trail 0.6W to Indian Pass		1170
751.9	**1439.0**	Mt Egbert		1329
751.8	**1439.1**	**Morgan Stewart Shelter** . . . . ☽ ⬦ ⊏ (6)		1311
		44.4◄41.2◄9.0◄►7.8►16.6►20.6		
750.7	**1440.2**	Depot Hill Rd, parking 0.1W. . . . . 41.5715,-73.6807 🅿		1230
748.9	**1442.0**	Railroad track, Whakey Lake Stream. . . . . ⬦		684
748.8	**1442.1**	Old Route 55		699
748.5	**1442.4**	NY 55, **Poughquag, NY** (3.1W) . . . . 41.5897,-73.6592 🅿 (0.1W) (pg. 145)		720
748.2	**1442.7**	Beekman Uplands Trail to west		762
747.4	**1443.5**	Footbridge, stream (more streams in this area) . . . . ⬦		703
747.1	**1443.8**	Nuclear Lake south end, loop trail to east (yellow-blazed).		752
746.2	**1444.7**	Nuclear Lake north end, loop trail to east.		775
745.8	**1445.1**	Beekman Uplands Trail to west		875
744.9	**1446.0**	Footbridge, swampy area . . . . ⬦		1045
744.6	**1446.3**	Penny Rd		1131
744.3	**1446.6**	West Mountain . . . . 📷		1200
744.0	**1446.9**	**Telephone Pioneers Shelter** (0.1E), shelter trail crosses stream . . . . ☽ ⬦ ⊏ (6)		902
		49.0◄16.8◄7.8◄►8.8►12.8►21.2 If dry, get water from residence 0.7N.		
743.3	**1447.6**	County Rd 20, West Dover Rd, **Pawling, NY** (3.1E) . . . . ⬦ ✳ (pg. 150)		565
741.2	**1449.7**	Footbridge, stream, boardwalk from here north to RR track . . . . ⬦		463
740.9	**1450.0**	NY 22, **Appalachian Trail RR Station** . . . . . . 41.5938,-73.5871 🅿 🛒 (pg. 150)		480
		Wingdale (4W), **Pawling** (2.6E) hot dog stand often here in summer, deli 0.6E		
740.7	**1450.2**	Hurd Corners Rd, wooden water tower . . . . ⬦		480
740.0	**1450.9**	Stream to west . . . . ⬦		591
739.2	**1451.7**	Hammersly Ridge.		1060
739.0	**1451.9**	Red Trail		1006
738.5	**1452.4**	Yellow Trail to east		938
738.2	**1452.7**	Red Trail to east.		972
738.1	**1452.8**	Green trail west, Red Trail east.		986
737.2	**1453.7**	Pawling Nature Reserve to east		900

| 736.2 | **1454.7** | Stream. . . . . | ◦ | 799 |

736.2 **1454.7** Stream. . . . . ◦ 799

735.6 **1455.3** Leather Hill Rd (gravel), stream to south . . . . ◦ 750

735.2 **1455.7** **Wiley Shelter** 25.6◀16.6◀8.8◀▶4.0▶12.4▶19.7 pump 0.1N . ☽◦ (treat)☁ ⌂ (6) 701
735.0 **1455.9** Duell Hollow Rd 557
734.7 **1456.2** Footbridge, stream . . . . ◦ 437

734.0 **1456.9** **NY-CT** border, Hoyt Rd . . . . 41.6418,-73.5208 🅿 400
733.7 **1457.2** Side trail to parking, brook to north . . . . ◦ 429
733.4 **1457.5** CT 55, **Gaylordsville, CT** (2.5E). . . . . 41.6447,-73.5193 🅿 **(pg. 151)** 445
         Wingdale, NY (3.3W)

732.2 **1458.7** Ten Mile Hill, Herrick Trail to east 1000

731.2 **1459.7** **Ten Mile River Shelter** (0.1E) 20.6◀12.8◀4.0◀▶8.4▶15.7▶25.7 . . . . ☽◦☁⌂ 277
         Water (hand pump) to left. Group campsites across river and up trail to left.
731.1 **1459.8** Ten Mile River, Ned Anderson Memorial Bridge . . . . ◦☁ 260

729.9 **1461.0** Bulls Bridge Rd (paved) + Schaghticoke Rd . . . . . 41.6756,-73.5102 🅿 **(pg. 151)** 366
         AT on Schaghticoke Rd (gravel) 0.3 mile

728.7 **1462.2** **CT-NY** 1027

728.1 **1462.8** View to west from exposed slab of rock, many good sitting boulders. . . . . . 📷 1205

┌──┐
│ 🚭Campfires prohibited in CT. Camping only in designated sites. │
└──┘

726.7 **1464.2** **NY-CT**, stream to north . . . . ◦ 1223
726.4 **1464.5** Indian Rocks, view to east . . . . 📷 1249

725.7 **1465.2** Schaghticoke Mountain Campsite & privy 0.1W, stream on AT . . . . ◦☽☁ 904

724.9 **1466.0** Stream. . . . . ◦ 988

723.8 **1467.1** Thayer Brook . . . . ◦ 914

722.8 **1468.1** **Mt Algo Shelter** 21.2◀12.4◀8.4◀▶7.3▶17.3▶28.6 . . . . ☽◦☁⌂ 638
722.5 **1468.4** CT 341, Schaghticoke Rd, **Kent, CT** (0.8E) . . . .(pg. 152) 350
722.4 **1468.5** Macedonia Brook . . . . ◦ 335
721.9 **1469.0** Numeral Rock Trail to east 801

719.7 **1471.2** Skiff Mountain Rd (paved), stream to south . . . . ◦ 771

719.0 **1471.9** Calebs Peak 1124
718.7 **1472.2** St. Johns Ledges, steep stone steps down to Housatonic River . . . . 📷◦ 883

717.8 **1473.1** River Rd south end, NoBo: turn west on road for 0.8 mile 382

717.0	1473.9	Kent Rd to west		428
716.8	1474.1	River Rd north end		389
715.5	1475.4	**Stewart Hollow Brook Shelter** (0.1W). . . . . ☽ ◊ ◐ ⊏ (6)		398
		19.7◀15.7◀7.3◀▶10.0▶21.3▶28.7 Footbridge over SH Brook.		
714.9	1476.0	Stony Brook, campsite to west . . . . ◊ ◐		414
713.4	1477.5	Footbridge, stream . . . . ◊		452
713.1	1477.8	River Rd . . . . 41.8057,-73.395 🅿 ◊		460
712.9	1478.0	Dawn Hill Rd (paved)		583
712.2	1478.7	Silver Hill Campsite 0.1E, pavilion, ... ☽ ◊ ◐		926
		water from pump is a great source, 35-40 pumps needed to start water flow		
711.4	1479.5	CT 4, **Cornwall Bridge, CT** (0.9E). . . . . ◊ (pg. 153)		700
		High water bypass 0.5E on CT 4, then left on unpaved Old Sharon Rd for 0.5 mi.		
711.2	1479.7	Old Sharon Rd (gravel), Guinea Brook south of road		756
711.1	1479.8	Breadloaf Trail 0.1E, view. . . . . 📷		944
710.0	1480.9	Hatch Brook . . . . ◊		880
709.8	1481.1	Pine Knob Loop Trail 1.0E to Housatonic Meadows State Park		1005
709.1	1481.8	Another intersection with Pine Knob Loop Trail to east.		1044
708.8	1482.1	Caesar Rd, Caesar Brook Campsite, stream to north . . . . ☽ ◐ ◊		798
707.3	1483.6	Stream. . . . . ◊		879
706.7	1484.2	Carse Brook, footbridge . . . . ◊		810
706.6	1484.3	West Cornwall Rd, **West Cornwall, CT** (2.2E), **Sharon, CT** (4.7W) . . . (pg. 153)		849
706.3	1484.6	Pass through cracked boulder similar to Lemon Squeezer.		1175
705.5	1485.4	**Pine Swamp Brook Shelter** . . . . ☽ ◊ ◐ ⊏ (6)		1087
		25.7◀17.3◀10.0◀▶11.3▶18.7▶19.9		
704.6	1486.3	Mt. Easter Rd		1150
704.0	1486.9	Woods road		1291
703.8	1487.1	Woods road		1287
703.1	1487.8	Sharon Mountain Campsite 0.1W, stream nearby. . . . . ◊ ◐		1134
702.3	1488.6	Hang Glider View . . . . 📷		1103
700.2	1490.7	Belters Campsite 0.2W, view. . . . . 📷 ☽ ◊ ◐		746
699.9	1491.0	US 7, CT 112		520
699.5	1491.4	US 7, parking, bridge over Housatonic River . . . ◊ 41.9327,-73.3635 🅿 (pg. 153)		518
698.9	1492.0	Mohawk Trail 0.5E to view . . . . 📷		565
698.3	1492.6	Warren Turnpike, footbridge, stream to north . . . . ◊		535
697.5	1493.4	Water St parking. **Falls Village, CT**(0.3E) . . . . 41.9558,-73.3675 🅿 〰 (pg. 154)		559
697.2	1493.7	Iron Bridge (Amesville Bridge) over Housatonic River		533

696.8	1494.1	Housatonic River Rd, AT crosses road twice 0.2 mi. . . . . . 41.9623,-73.374 🅿 📷		626
		apart. In between are two short trails east to views of great falls.		
696.3	1494.6	Spring . . . . ♦		808
694.9	1496.0	Mt Prospect		1475
694.2	1496.7	**Limestone Spring Shelter** (0.5W), road 0.25 farther. . . . . ☾♦⚌⊏ (6)		1304
		28.6◄21.3◄11.3◄►7.4►8.6►17.0		
694.1	1496.8	Rands View (field) . . . . 📷		1250
693.6	1497.3	Giants Thumb		1293
692.8	1498.1	Stream. . . . . ♦		1038
690.5	1500.4	AT on US 44 for 0.2W		700
690.2	1500.7	AT on Cobble Rd, **Salisbury, CT** (0.5W) . . . . **(pg. 154)**		706
689.8	1501.1	Undermountain Rd (paved) **Salisbury, CT** (0.8W)41.9941,-73.42685 🅿 ☾**(pg. 154)**		720
689.6	1501.3	Stream. . . . . ♦		828
688.5	1502.4	Streams (multiple) . . . . ♦		1110
687.7	1503.2	Lions Head Trail 0.5W to Bunker Hill Rd		1496
687.5	1503.4	Lions Head, view, bypass trail to west . . . . 📷		1729
686.8	1504.1	**Riga Shelter**, spring. Tent platform behind shelter . . . . . 📷 ☾♦⚌⊏ (6)		1646
		28.7◄18.7◄7.4◄►1.2►9.6►9.7		
686.2	1504.7	Ball Brook Campsite, stream . . . . ♦⚌		1720
685.6	1505.3	**Brassie Brook Shelter**, stream 20 yards north on AT. . . . . ☾♦⚌⊏ (6)		1733
		19.9◄8.6◄1.2◄►8.4►8.5►22.8		
685.1	1505.8	Undermountain Trail 1.9E to CT 41		1834
684.9	1506.0	Bear Mountain Rd to west		1920
684.6	1506.3	Bear Mountain, rock observation tower, view. North side steep & rocky. . . 📷 ⩎		2316
684.2	1506.7	Unmarked trail 0.6W to Mt Washington Rd		1808
684.0	1506.9	Paradise Lane Trail to east, **CT-MA** border 50 yards north (not marked).		1693
683.8	1507.1	Sages Ravine Campsite to west . . . . ♦⚌		1538
683.4	1507.5	Sages Ravine, Misplaced border sign at footbridge. . . . . ♦		1491
		AT parallel to stream for 0.3 mile, swimming holes.		
682.1	1508.8	Laurel Ridge Campsite 0.1W, spring to south . . . . ☾♦⚌		1629
681.9	1509.0	Stream. . . . . ♦		1670

⚠ Massachusetts: Fires at designated sites (fireplace/ring) only. Camping permitted only at designated sites.

680.1	1510.8	Mt Race, views along ridgeline for 0.6S . . . . 📷		2365
679.0	1511.9	Race Brook Falls Trail 0.3E to campsite . . . . ☾♦⚌		1950
678.3	1512.6	Mt Everett . . . . 📷		2602
677.6	1513.3	Guilder Pond Picnic Area, Mt Everett Rd. . . . . ☾♦		2081
677.2	1513.7	**The Hemlocks Shelter** (0.1E) 17.0◄9.6◄8.4◄►0.1►14.4►19.7 . . . ☾◊⊏ (10)		1910

1447.6 COUNTY RD 20, WEST DOVER RD, *Dover*
Oak north side of road, largest oak tree on A.T. Girth 20' 4" and estimated to be over 300 years old.

🏠 **Martin and Donna** 845.505.1671, 845.546.1832 Nights & wkends only. Range :RPH Shelter to Kent, CT.

» *Pawling, NY 12564 (3.1E, see map)*

▲🏕⛴**Edward R. Murrow Memorial Park** (3.1E) Town allows hikers to camp in park near the pavilion. 1 night only. 1 Mi from the center of town. Park offers lake swimming. No pets.

♟️¶**Vinny's Deli** (3.1E) 845.855.1922 ¶**Gaudino's Pizzeria**

845.855.3200, ¶**Mama Pizza II** 845.855.9270, ¶**Great Wall** 845.855.9750.
¶¶**McGrath's Tavern** 845.855.3444 M&F 12-5p, Tu-Th 10a-8p, Sa 10a-4p, clsd Su in summer.
📻📚**Pawling Free Library** (2.9E) 845.855.3444 M&F 12-5p, Tu-Th 10a-8p, Sa 10a-4p, clsd Su in summer.

1450.0 NY 22, APPALACHIAN TRAIL RR STATION

🏠✦🏕♨️ **Native Landscapes & Garden Center** 845.855.7050 Open daily 9-5, no loitering after hrs. Owner Pete Muroski is hiker-friendly. Free outside shower, charging, use of restrooms. Drinks, snacks, frz-dried meals, & canister fuel sold at the garden center. Mail: 991 Route 22, Pawling, NY 12564.
🚲¶🏕⛴**Tony's Deli**

(0.7E) 845.855.9540 Sandwiches. Open daily 3:30a-midnight. Ask about camping.

» *Pawling, NY 12564 (2.5E)*

🚍⛴📧 **Dutchess Motor Lodge** (2.7W) 845.832.6400 89+tax. Ride for a fee when avail. A/C, free long distance, guest laundry $7, one pet room. Mail: 1512 Route 22, Wingdale, NY 12594

» *Wingdale, NY 12594 (4W)*

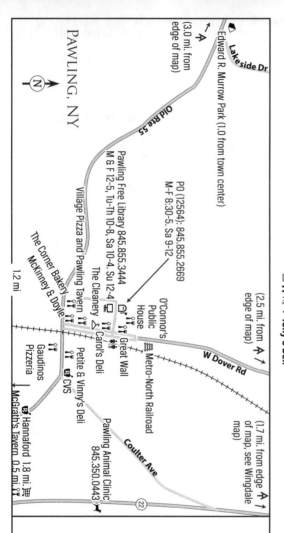

PAWLING, NY

⬆N

Edward R. Murrow Park (1.0 from town center)

(3.0 mi. from edge of map)

Lakeside Dr

Old Rte 55

Pawling Free Library 845.855.3444 M & F 12-5, Tu-Th 10-8, Sa 10-4, Su 12-4

Village Pizza and Pawling Tavern

PO (12564): 845.855.2669 M-F 8:30-5, Sa 9-12

The Corner Bakery

McKinney & Doyle

The Cleanery

O'Connor's Public House

Carol's Deli

Great Wall

Metro-North Railroad

1.2 mi

Gaudinos Pizzeria

Petite & Vinny's Deli

CVS

Hanaford 1.8 mi.

McGrath's Tavern 0.5 mi.

(2.5 mi from edge of map)

W Dover Rd

Pawling Animal Clinic 845.350.0443

Coulter Ave

(22)

(1.7 mi from edge of map, see Wingdale map)

(1.7 mi from edge of map, see Wingdale map)

🚈 **MTA Metro-North Railroad** 212.532.4900 ⟨mta.info\mnr\⟩

Stations on the AT and in Pawling & Wingdale/ Harlem Valley. Trip from AT to NYC Grand Central Station requires a transfer, costs approx. $28 one-way and takes about two hours, $44 round trip. Now takes credit/debit or cash on train. Schedule varies by season. Also connects to other cities in NY and CT.

1457.5   CT 55

» **Gaylordsville, CT 06755** *(2.5E to Rt 7, go right &
0.6 on Rt 7 to PO & diner)*

🍴 **Gaylordsville Diner** *(3E)* 860.210.1622 B/L/D.

» **Wingdale, NY 12594** *(4W) (see map.)*

1461.0

BULLS BRIDGE RD, SCHAGHTICOKE RD, 🌉 *(0.4E) To covered bridge with view of
the Housatonic cascading down the backside of a dam. The one-lane bridge was
built in 1842. Wooden bridges are covered to protect the wood deck and trusswork
from the elements.*

» *(0.2 Beyond bridge)*

🏪 💲 **Bulls Bridge Country Store** *(0.4E)* Fruit, ice cream, soda. M-W 6a-7p, Th-Sa 6a-8p, Su 6:30a-6p.
🍴 ⛺ **Bulls Bridge Inn** *(0.4E)* 860.927.1000 M-Th 5-9, F 5-9:30, Sa 12-9:30, Su 12- 9. American cuisine
(dinners $10-26), casual atmosphere, bar.

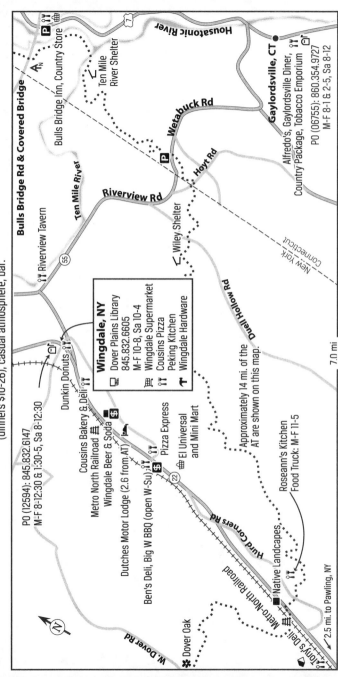

Wingdale, NY

📚	Dover Plains Library
	845.832.6605
	M-F 10-8, Sa 10-4
🏪	Wingdale Supermarket
🍴	Cousins Pizza
	Peking Kitchen
✛	Wingdale Hardware

Approximately 14 mi. of the
AT are shown on this map.

PO (12594): 845.832.6147
M-F 8-12:30 & 1:30-5, Sa 8-12:30

Cousins Bakery & Deli

Metro North Railroad

Wingdale Beer & Soda

Pizza Express

El Universal
and Mini Mart

Dutches Motor Lodge (2.6 from AT)

Ben's Deli, Big W BBQ (open W-Su)

Roseann's Kitchen
Food Truck: M-F 11-5

Native Landcapes

Metro-North Railroad

2.5 mi. to Pawling, NY

Tony's Deli

Hurd Corners Rd

Duell Hollow Rd

Dover Oak

W. Dover Rd

Dunkin Donuts

Riverview Tavern

Riverview Rd

Ten Mile River

Wiley Shelter

Bulls Bridge Rd & Covered Bridge

Wetabuck Rd

Hoyt Rd

Bulls Bridge Inn, Country Store

Ten Mile
River Shelter

Housatonic River

Gaylordsville, CT

Alfredo's, Gaylordsville Diner,
Country Package, Tobacco Emporium
PO (06755): 860.354.9727
M-F 8-1 & 2-5, Sa 8-12

New York
Connecticut

7.0 mi

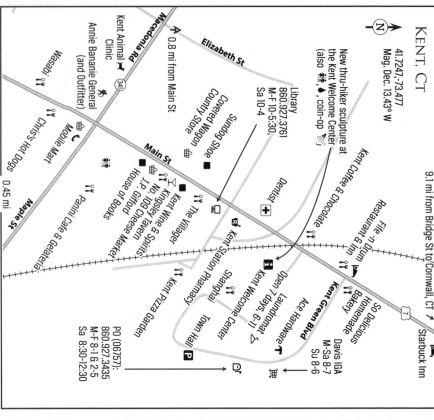

KENT, CT

(N)

41.7247,-73.477
Mag. Dec. 13.43° W

New thru-hiker sculpture at the Kent Welcome Center (also 🚻, ♿, coin-op)

Elizabeth St

Macedonia Rd
0.8 mi from Main St

(34)

Kent Animal Clinic

Annie Bananie General (and Outfitter)

Wassaic

Library
860.927.3761
M-F 10-5:30,
Sa 10-4

Covered Wagon Country Store

Sundog Shoe

Main St

Mobile Mart

Maple St   0.45 mi

Chris's Hot Dog

Panini Cafe & Gelateria

J.P. Gifford
House of Books

Kent Wine & Spirits
No. 109 Cheese Market
The Village

Dentist

Kent Coffee & Chocolate

Kent Station Pharmacy

Shanghai

Kent Welcome Center
Open 7 days, 6-11

Kent Pizza Garden

Laundromat

Town Hall

Ace Hardware

Kent Green Blvd

Fife 'n Drum Restaurant & Inn

So Delicious Homemade Bakery

Davis IGA
M-Sa 8-7
Su 8-6

PO (06757):
860.927.3435
M-F 8-1 & 2-5
Sa 8:30-12:30

9.1 mi from Bridge St to Cornwall, CT ↗

Starbuck Inn

1468.4   CT 341, SCHAGHTICOKE RD

» *Kent, CT 06757 (0.8E)(15% lodging tax)*

🅿 🍴🚻♿ ▣Kent Welcome Center (0.9E) Directly behind the RR station (now a pharmacy), restrooms, hot shower ($2 in quarters), water bottle filler, phone charging.

🛏🍴🛜▨Fife 'n Drum Inn & Restaurant (1.1E) 860.927.3509 Hiker room rates $140D+tax wkdays, $170D+tax wkends, $25EAP+tax. No pets. Front desk closed Tu, so make prior arrangements for Tu night stays. Guest Mail: (USPS) PO Box 188 or (FedEx/UPS) 53 N Main St, Kent, CT 06757.(fifendrum.com)

🛏🛜Starbuck Inn (1.3E) 860.927.1788 $207D/up + tax, incl full b'fast & afternoon tea. Sometimes discounted mid-wk, CC ok, no pets.(starbuckinn.com)

🛏🛜Cooper Creek B&B (3.7E) 860.927.4334 Hiker rate Su-Th $110D+tax. Wkend rates $145-200+tax, 2.5mi. north of town on US 7. Shuttles to/from Kent w/stay, slackpacking & longer shuttles for a fee.

🥾🖥💲🛜▨Annie Bananie General Store (0.8E) 860.927.3377 Summer hrs M-Sa 9a-10p, 10a-8p Su. Sells of gear. Inside has hot dogs, coffee, snacks, barrels of candy, chocolates. Shuttles anywhere. Mail: 5 Bridge St, Kent, CT 06757.(bcoutfitters.com)

🖥💲🛜JP Gifford (0.9E) 860.592.0200 M-Sa 7a-6p, Su 7a-5p. B'fast sandwiches, salads, bakery, coffee & supplies.

■ House of Books (0.9E) Old-fashioned book store w/ UPS services, open M-Fr 10a-5p Sa 10a-5:30p, Su 11a-5p.

■ Sundog Shoe (1E) 860.927.0009 10% Hiker discount on footwear (Salomon, Merrell, High-Tech, Keen, Cascadia), socks (Darn Tough), Dirty Girl Gaiters & footbeds (Superfeet, Power Step).

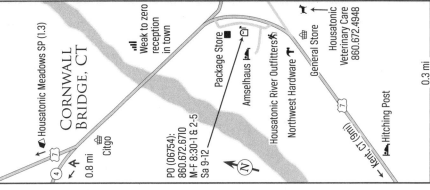

Housatonic Meadows SP (1.3)

CORNWALL BRIDGE, CT

0.8 mi

Citgo

Weak to zero reception in town

Package Store

Amselhaus

Housatonic River Outfitters

Northwest Hardware

PO (06754);
860.672.6710
M-F 8:30-1 & 2-5
Sa 9-12

General Store

Housatonic Veterinary Care
860.672.4948

Kent, CT (9mi)

Hitching Post

0.3 mi

1479.5   CT 4

» *Cornwall Bridge, CT 06754 (0.9E)*

⊨⚲⚑♨🍴 **The Amselhaus** (1.1E) 860.248.3155 robin@theamselhaus.com $85S, $100D, $50EAP. 3 BR apartment incl laundry, sat. TV, local & long-distance phone. Rides avail. Located behind carpet store, check-in at gray house next door to apartments. Mail: C/O Robin Vogel, 7 River Rd S, Cornwall Bridge, CT 06754.

⊨⚲🛏♨🍴 **Hitching Post Motel** (1.2E) 860.672.6219 $85/Up wkdays, $95/up wkends. Pets $10, laundry $5, shuttles $2/mi Guest mail: 45 Kent Rd, Cornwall Bridge, CT 06754.

⊨🏕⚑ **Housatonic Meadows State Park** (2.1E) 860.672.6772 Camping & Cabins 1.3 mi N of town on US7. Campsite $17 for CT residents, $27 (non-res), $3 walk-in fee for first night. Cabins $50 CT residents, $60 (non-res) w/2 night min. No hammocks. Usually open mid May - Oct. May close as early as Labor day. Reg at main cabin by gate. No alcohol.

⊨🛏♨ **Cornwall Inn** (3.2E) 860.672.6884 Su-Th starting at $129D tax, incl c. b'fast. Wkends 10% hiker discount. 2.2 Mi S on US 7. P/U & ret to trailhead. Other shuttles for a fee. Seasonal pool/hot tub. Pet fee. Mail w/ reserv.⟨cornwallinn.com⟩

🥾⚑ **Housatonic River Outfitters** (1E) 860.672.1010 hflyshop@aol.com Some hiker gear, Aquamira.

⊨👣⚑🛒 **Cornwall Country Market** (1E) 860.619.8199 M-F 6a-5p, Sa-Su 7-5. Hiker friendly, hot meals, b'fast, groceries, charging stations.

🍷⚑ **Cornwall Package Store** (0.9E) 860.672.6645 M-Sa 10-7, Fri 10-8, Su 11-3. Beer/Wine store. Water spigot outside. Stop to sign their register.

1484.3   WEST CORNWALL RD

» *West Cornwall, CT 06796 (2.2E)*
   ☎860.672.6791, M-F 8:30-12 & 2-4:30, Sa 9-12

» *Sharon, CT 06069 (4.7W)*
   ☎860.364.5306, M-F   9:30-4:30,   Sa   9:30-12:30

⊨🛏⚲🍴♨ **Bearded Woods Bunk & Dine** (5.2W) 860.480.2966 Hudson & BIG Lu shuttle hikers to their home. $45PP incl shower w/amenities, clean bunk w/linens, communal laundry, loaner clothes, hearty b'fast, rides to/from trail & local PO. Call or text Hudson for p/u from W Cornwall Rd, Falls Village, or Salisbury between 1p - 6p. Pizza, ice cream, drinks, snacks & resupplies avail for purchase. Free slackpacking between W Cornwall Rd & Salisbury w/2nd night stay. Long distance shuttles anywhere (fee). Not a party place. Reservations recommended. No walk-ins/pets. Open May 1 - Aug 1 (closed Wed). Cash or PayPal. Limited svcs may be avail outside of those dates.⟨beardedwoods.com⟩

🛒 **Sharon Farm Market** (4.6W) 860.397.5161 M-Sa 8-8, Su 8-7.

🍴 **Stacked Kitchen** (4.6W)

➕ **Sharon Hospital** (5.6W) 860.364.4000

💊 **Sharon Pharmacy** (4.6W) 860.364.5105 M-F 8a-6p, Sa 8a-3p, Su 8a-12p.

1491.4   US 7, BRIDGE
         OVER HOUSATONIC RIVER

⊨🛏⚲🍴♨ **Bearded Woods Bunk & Dine** (11.9W) (See info at West Cornwall Rd)

Map labels:
- Iron Bridge (Amesville Bridge) replaced in 2016
- Dugway Rd
- Water St
- Hydro Plant
- Outdoor shower on wall of vine-covered building. There is also a power outlet
- Warren Turnpike Rd
- Railroad St
- Package Store
- Falls Village Inn
- Prospect St
- Main St
- Miner St
- FALLS VILLAGE, CT
- Toymakers Cafe
- 0.4 mi

PO (06031):
860.824.7781
M-F 8:30-1 & 2-5
Sa 8:30-12

Library
860.824.7424
Tu, Th 10-5,
Wed 2-8,
Fri 2-6,
Sa 10-2

1493.4   WATER STREET PARKING AREA

» *Falls Village, CT 06031 (0.5E)*

Falls Village Inn (0.2E) 860.824.0033

Toymakers Café (0.3E) 860.824.8168 B/L Th-F 7-2, Sa- Su 7-4. Free tent sites. No trees for hammocks. Hiker friendly. Knock on upstairs door if closed. Cash only.

1500.7   ★   COBBLE RD
1501.1   UNDERMOUNTAIN RD

» *Salisbury, CT 06068 (0.8W)*

Town Hall (0.8W) 860.435.5170 M-F 8:30-4 Hikers welcome to use bathrooms & phone (local calls only).

Maria McCabe (0.5W) Beds in home $35PP incl shower, use of living room, shuttle to coin laundry. Cash only. Guest Mail: 4 Grove St, Salisbury, CT 06068.

White Hart Inn (0.6W) Rooms $245/up. cafe & b'fast.

Vanessa Breton (0.8W) Beds in home $40PP, no pets, laundry $5. Shuttle avail. Street address is 7 The Lock Up, but send mail to PO Box 131, Salisbury, CT 06068 ($5 for non-guests).

LaBonne's Market (0.9W) 860.435.2559 M-Sa 8-7, Su 8-6p. Grocery, deli, bakery, pizza.

» *Lakeville, CT (2S of Salisbury)*

Boathouse (2.4W) Sports bar/restaurant.

Mizza's Pizza (2.5W) 860.435.6266 Open 11a-10p.

Washboard Laundromat (2.4W) Located behind Mizza's Pizza.

1514.4   ELBOW TRAILHEAD 1.5E TO MA 41

Race Brook Lodge (1.5E) 413.229.2916 Rates lowest off- season (Nov-May). M-Th $85-$160, F-Su $115-170. Stay incl b'fast. Pets $15/night. Stagecoach Tavern on-site open Th-Su for dinner. Visa/MC/Disc ok, open yr-round.(rblodge. com)

1518.1   MA 41

ATC New England Regional Office (0.1W) 413.528.8002 In Kellogg Conservation Center. Water from hose, picnic table, 2 charging outlets, no camping/parking.

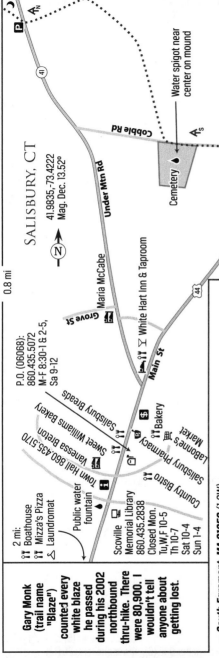

SALISBURY, CT

0.8 mi

41.9835,-73.4222
Mag. Dec. 13.52°

(N)

Under Mtn Rd

(41)

Cobble Rd

A⃗ₛ

Cemetery

Water spigot near
center on mound

P⃗ · ⌒
A⃗ₙ

Maria McCabe

Grove St

⏚ ⫙ White Hart Inn & Taproom

Main St

(44)

P.O. (06068):
860.435.5072
M-F 8:30-1 & 2-5,
Sa 9-12

Salisbury Breads

Sweet Williams Bakery

Vanessa Bréton

Town Hall 860.435.5170

Salisbury Pharmacy

LaBonne's Market

Bakery

Country Bistro

Public water
fountain

Scoville
Memorial Library
860.435.2838
Closed Mon.
Tu,W,F 10-5
Th 10-7
Sat 10-4
Sun 1-4

2 mi:
⫙ Boathouse
⫙ Mizza's Pizza
🛆 Laundromat

Gary Monk (trail name "Blaze") counted every white blaze he passed during his 2002 northbound thru-hike. There were 80,900. I wouldn't tell anyone about getting lost.

» *South Egremont, MA 01258* (1.2W)
⏚⫙ 413.528.1571, M-F 8:15-12 & 12:30-4, Sa 9-11:30

⫙ ⫛ **Mom's Country Cafe** (1.1W) 413.528.2414 B/L restaurant open 7 days
6:30a-3p. B'fast all day, free coffee refills, outdoor water spigot, hikers welcome.
⫙⫛ **Egremont Market** (1.2W) 413.528.0075 Market & deli. Summer hrs M-Sa 6:30a-7p
Su 7a-6p. Ice cream, deli, panini's.

Camping & Campfire Regulations

Many of the camping & campfire regulations along the Appalachian Trail are addressed in The A.T. Guide. However these regulations change frequently. Please visit www.appalachiantrail.org/camping for the most current and comprehensive listing so you may familiarize yourself with the most current regulations for the entire Appalachian Trail.

Seasonal/Regional Droughts, Dry water sources & Fire Danger

Seasonal drought conditions affect water sources. Check the U.S. Drought Monitor for the latest conditions to get general sense of conditions in the area you are planning a hike.

http://droughtmonitor.unl.edu/

677.1	1513.8	**Glen Brook Shelter** (0.1E) 9.7◄8.5◄0.1◄►14.3►19.6►21.4 . . . . 🌙◑◔⊂	1935
676.5	1514.4	Elbow Trail 1.5E to MA 41 near Racebrook Lodge . . . . (pg. 154)	1749
675.5	1515.4	Mt Bushnell	1836
674.4	1516.5	Jug End, view . . . . 📷	1487
673.7	1517.2	Jug End Rd, unreliable piped spring 0.2E . . . . 42.1444,-73.4316 🅿 ◊	878
672.8	1518.1	MA 41, **South Egremont, MA** (1.2W) . . . . (pg. 155)	810
671.8	1519.1	Footbridge, stream (2 close together). ◑	708
671.2	1519.7	Footbridge, stream . . . . ◑	694
671.0	1519.9	Sheffield Egremont Rd, Shays Rebellion Monument . . . . .42.1471,-73.3867 🅿	700
670.2	1520.7	Gravel road	740
669.9	1521.0	West Rd (paved)	703
669.2	1521.7	US 7, RR to south . . . . (pg. 158)	671
		Sheffield, MA (3.0E), **Great Barrington, MA** (3.0W)	
669.0	1521.9	Footbridge, stream . . . . ◑	666
668.3	1522.6	Housatonic River, cross on Kellogg Rd Bridge . . . . 42.144,-73.3595 🅿	650
667.9	1523.0	Boardman St	705
666.5	1524.4	June Mtn	1243
666.3	1524.6	Homes Rd (paved)	1150
665.7	1525.2	Footbridge, spring at bottom of cleft . . . . ◑	1564
665.3	1525.6	East Mountain, view . . . . 📷	1762
664.9	1526.0	Woods road	1811
662.8	1528.1	Ice Gulch, **Tom Leonard Shelter** . . . . 📷 🌙◑◔⊂(10)	1579
		22.8◄14.4◄14.3◄►5.3►7.1►21.1 Campsite overlooking ravine north of shelter.	
		Stream 0.2 on path to left or 0.3 on path	
661.7	1529.2	Lake Buel Rd (paved), parking area with kiosk . . . . 42.1745,-73.294 🅿	1085
660.8	1530.1	MA 23 (paved) . . . . 42.1844,-73.2907 🅿 (pg. 159)	1050
		East Mountain Retreat Center (1.0W)	
659.6	1531.3	Blue Hill Rd (paved), Stony Brook Rd	1550
658.9	1532.0	Beartown Mtn Rd, Benedict Pond, 0.5W on blue-blazed trail to . . . . . ☎◑◔	1602
		Beartown State Forest, beach, picnic area, phone, tent sites $10.	
658.7	1532.2	Benedict Pond Loop Trail to west, footbridge and stream east of AT . . . . . ◑	1623
658.2	1532.7	The Ledges	1820
657.8	1533.1	Stream. . . . . ◑	1630
657.5	1533.4	**Mt Wilcox South Shelters** . . . . 🌙◑◔(5)⊂(6/12)	1787
		19.7◄19.6◄5.3◄►1.8►15.8►24.6 Old shelter 0.1E (6), newer shelter 0.2E (12).	

| 656.6 | 1534.3 | Stream (several) . . . . | ◊ | 1809 |
| 656.5 | 1534.4 | Pond, Swann Brook outlet at south end . . . . | ◊ | 1825 |

656.6 1534.3 Stream (several) . . . . ◊ 1809
656.5 1534.4 Pond, Swann Brook outlet at south end . . . . ◊ 1825

655.7 1535.2 **Mt Wilcox North Shelter** (0.3E) . . . . ☽◊⊏ (10) 2068
    21.4◄7.1◄1.8◄►14.0►22.8►31.6

655.0 1535.2 Motorcycle path 1830
654.9 1536.0 Beartown Mountain Rd, NoBo: turn east . . . . ◊ 1796
654.5 1536.4 East Brook, footbridge, more streams north and south . . . . ◊ 1717

651.9 1539.0 Fernside Rd / Jerusalem Rd (gravel) . . . . ◊ 1200
651.6 1539.3 Shaker Campsite to east; platforms, bear box, water north on AT . . . . . . ☽◊⌂ 934

649.9 1541.0 Cobble Hill 1271
649.7 1541.2 Jerusalem Rd (paved), **Tyringham, MA 01264** (0.6W) . . . . ◊ (pg. 159) 1131
    Water 0.1W on left side of road, water also outside of P.O. 0.6W.
649.2 1541.7 Three streams crossed by footbridges . . . . ◊ 1003
648.6 1542.3 Main Rd (paved), **Tyringham, MA** (0.9W) . . . . 42.2354,-73.1945 🅿 ◊ (pg. 159) 995
    Water, parking to west.

647.0 1543.9 Baldy Mtn 1931
646.8 1544.1 Webster Rd (gravel) 1800

646.2 1544.7 Knee-Deep Pond to west . . . . ◊ 1700

645.2 1545.7 Spring on side trail 0.1W . . . . ◊ 1783

644.4 1546.5 Goose Pond Rd (gravel) . . . . 42.2743,-73.1838 🅿 (0.1E) 1650

644.0 1546.9 Cooper Brook, footbridge . . . . ◊ 1567
643.5 1547.4 Signed trail junction 1705
    ⚠ NoBo: this is not the side trail to Upper Goose Pond Cabin.

642.3 1548.6 Higley Brook, footbridge, Upper Goose Pond to west . . . . ◊ 1495

641.8 1549.1 Old chimney 1476
641.7 1549.2 **Upper Goose Pond Cabin** (0.5W) . . . . ⊏ (pg. 159) 1540
    21.1◄15.8◄14.0◄►8.8►17.6►34.5

640.5 1550.4 MA Turnpike I-90 1400
640.2 1550.7 Greenwater Brook, footbridge . . . . ◊ 1348
640.1 1550.8 US 20, **Lee, MA** (5.0W), hotel 0.1E . . . . . . 42.293,-73.1614 🅿 (0.1W) (pg. 159) 1400
639.7 1551.2 Powerline, stream to north . . . . ◊ 1574
639.3 1551.6 Tyne Rd / Becket Rd, stream to south . . . . ◊ 1781

638.8 1552.1 Becket Mountain 2180

637.8 1553.1 Walling Mountain . . . . 📷 2216

↑ A N

Just North of town:
- Holiday Inn Express,
- Travel Lodge,
- Berkshire South

Mahaiwe
Playhouse

Fairview
Hosp. ✚

Manhattan Pizza ⛽️🍴
Dunkin Donuts

Triplex Cinema 🎬

Bilmar Animal Hospital

The Prairie Whale 🍴

CVS 📷 ✚

Big Y Foods

Guidos Fresh
Marketplace

Auerbuchon Hardware

Great Barrington
Bagel & Deli

Days Inn

Aroma
Bar & Grill

Berkshire
Co-op

← AT to PO 3.1 mi →

Bistro Box

Bogie's Steak & Ale

Brookside Rd

Homes Rd

4.5 mi

GREAT BARRINGTON, MA

Eagle
Boot 🍴

Great Wall Chinese

Berkshire 📷
Rite Aid

🍴 Pizza House

🍴 The Kitchen Table

🍴 Four Brothers Pizza

🍴 Koi Oriental Restaurant

Mountain View Motel

Comfort Inn 🛏

Monument Mountain Motel

Price Chopper, Kmart

🍴 McDonalds

🛏 The Market Place

Ski Butternut

AT from ⑦ to ㉓ is 8.6 mi

Tom Leonard
Shelter

Lake Buel Rd

East Mtn
Retreat Center

← AT to ⑦ 3.1 mi →

P N

Library 413.528.2403
Tu-W 10-7, Th-Fri 10-6, Sa 10-3

P.O. (01230):
413.528.3670
M-F 8:30-4:30,
Sa 8:30-12:30

Downtown restaurants:
20 Railroad St
Allium
Baba Louie's gourmet pizza
Bizen Gourmet Japanese
Castle St Cafe
Fiesta Bar & Grill
Fuel GB: Bistro, Coffee, Spirits
GB Eats
Siam Square (Thai)
SoCo Creamery
Subway
Tangier Cafe
The Well Restaurant & Bar

South on 7:
- 🍴 Sheffield, MA 3.0 mi:
- 🍴 Bash Bish Brew/BBQ,
- 🍴 Market Place Cafe
- 🏪 Dollar General 2.2mi.

1521.7 US 7

🗺 **All Points Driving Service** 413.429.7397 Range: Salisbury-Dalton

» **Great Barrington, MA 01230** (3W from US 7, 4W from MA 23) Resort town; Lodging prices will be steep on weekends & during special events.

🛏🌳💲📶 **Days Inn** (2.7W) 413.528.3350 $79/up. C. b'fast, WiFi, nonsmoking rooms, no pets.

🛏⛱💲📶 **Fairfield Inn & Suites** (4.4W) 413.644.3200 Prices seasonal. Full b'fast, heated pool & hot tub, no pets. Maildrop w/adv reservation: 249 Stockbridge Rd, Rt. 7, Great Barrington, MA 01230.

🛏 **Monument Mtn Motel** (4.4W) 413.528.3272 Su-Th $75S $95D. F-Sa higher. Mail w/reservation: 247 Stockbridge Rd, Rt 7, Great Barrington, MA 01230.

🛏💲📶 **Mountain View Motel** (4.7W) 413.528.0250

🛏🌳💲📶 **Travel Lodge** (4.8W) 413.528.2340 Su-Th $50-89D + tax (ask for hiker rate) $10EAP, cont B, coin laundry, pool.

🏕 **Berkshire South Regional Community Center** (5W) 413.528.2810 15 Crissey Rd north end of town. Free tenting, check-in at front desk. $7PP use of facility (showers, saunas, pool). Free dinner M 5-6p, donations accepted. No smoking, drugs, alcohol, or pets. On BRTA route (tell driver your destination).

🛒 **Guido's** (1.9W) 413.528.9255 M-Sa 9a-7p, Su 10a-6p. Organic produce, cold juices, & more.

✚ **Fairview Hospital** (3.1W) 413.528.0790

» **Sheffield, MA 01257** (3.2E), ☎413.229.8772, M-F 9-4:30, Sa 9-12

🏨🍴💲△🛏🚿🛒☎✉ **Jess Treat** (3.3E) 860.248.5710 jesstrea@gmail.com $40PP or $55 shared bed. Cash, paypal or google wallet. Stay incl p/u & ret, shower, & b'fast. Ask about resupply & maildrops. $15PP tenting incl shower. Clean pvt home, not a party place, reservations appreciated. $5 Laundry. Pets outside only. Convenience store, ATM, PO, restaurant & cafe in walking distance. Shuttles (fee). Slackpacking offered at reduced rates.

🛏🍴🚿△✉ **Moon in the Pond Farm** (6.2E) 413.229.3092 dom@ mooninthepond.org Diverse, small, organic farm. 2 Day adv reservation preferred. WFS Su-Th best, 1 Full work day min. Tentsites, organic meals, shower, $2 laundry. Mail: 816 Barnum St, Sheffield, MA 01257.

1530.1   MA 23

🏨✉ **East Mountain Retreat Center** (1.5W) 413.528.6617 from MA 23 to corner of Lake Buel Rd (there is a blue sign), then 0.5 mi up dirt driveway. $10PP donation. No CC. Shower & hot plate. Check-in by 8p, 8:30a checkout. Quiet after 10p. Open May 15-Aug 15. Mail (FedEx & UPS only): 8 Lake Buel Rd, Great Barrington, MA 01230.

1541.2   ★ JERUSALEM RD (0.6W TO TOWN)
1542.3   MAIN RD (0.9W TO TOWN)

» **Tyringham, MA 01264** (0.9W)
☎413.243.1225, M-F 9-12:30 & 4-5:30, Sa 8:30-12:30

1549.2   UPPER GOOSE POND CABIN (0.5W)

🏕🔥🏠🌙🚿🛶 **Upper Goose Pond Cabin** (0.5W) On side trail north of pond. Fireplace, covered porch, bunks w/mattresses. Swimming & canoeing. Open daily mid May - mid Oct (dates subject to change). When caretaker not in residence, hikers may camp on porch (no cooking) or tent platforms. Please store food in bear box. During summer, caretaker brings water; otherwise, pond is water source. Donations welcome.

1550.8   US 20

🏨🍴🛏🚿 **Berkshire Lakeside Lodge** (0.2E) 413.243.9907 info@ berkshirelakesidelodge.com Wkdays $60-90, wkends $99-175 2-person room, $10EAP. C. b'fast, TV & fridge. No pets. Small motel, reservations recommeded. Hikers welcome to get water. Sodas for sale. No svcs nearby but you can have Italian & Chinese food delivered. Mail (call ahead to arrange p/u): 3949 Jacob's Ladder Rd, Rt 20, Becket, MA 01223.

» **Lee, MA 01238** (5W)
☎413.243.1392, M-F 8:30-4:30, Sa 9-12. *Lodging busy and expensive on weekends and during Tanglewood Music Festival.*

🏨🍴☎ **Pilgrim Inn** (4.8W) 413.243.1328

🏨 **Super 8** (4.8W) 413.243.0143 Call for hiker rates.

🏨☎ **Roadway Inn** (6.1W) 413.243.0813 Jul-Aug Su-Th $99, F-Sa $199 +tax (ask for hiker disc). Other months prices vary. C b'fast.

🏨☎✉ **Econo Lodge** (6.4W) 413.243.0501 gm.ma216@choicehotels.com Apr-May $52-55 Su-Th, $65-75 F-Sa, Jun-Oct $60-79 Su-Th, $110-$195 Fr-Sa, c. b'fast. Oct-Apr $49 Su-Mo. Pet friendly.⟨choicehotels.com/massachusetts/lee/econo-lodge-hotels/ma216⟩

🍴 **Dunkin Donuts, Athena's Pizza House, Friendly's, Joe's Diner, McDonalds,** (4.9W) and many more.

💊🏥 **Rite Aid** (4.9W) 413.243.2402

➕ **Valley Veterinary Clinic** (5.9W) 413.243.2414

△ **Lee Coin-Op Laundry** (4.9W) 413.243.0480

🚌 **BRTA** 800.292.2782 Commuter bus connects Great Barrington, Dalton, Cheshire, North Adams, Adams, Williamstown, Pittsfield, Lee and Berkshire Mall. Buses run M-F 5:45am-7:20pm, Sa 7:15am-7pm. Fare $1.75 for local routes (in-town and adjoining towns), or $4.50 systemwide. "CharlieCard", avail. from drivers for $5, gives you a discount per ride and allows you to make bus transfers. Drivers cannot make change. Flag bus anywhere on route.

| 637.2 | **1553.7** | Finerty Pond . . . . ♦ | 1936 |

635.4	**1555.5**	Washington Mountain Brook . . . . ♦	1762
634.8	**1556.1**	County Rd (gravel)	1849
634.5	**1556.4**	Bald Top	2040

632.9	**1558.0**	**October Mountain Shelter**, intermittent stream, cables . . . . . . ☽ ◊ ⌂ ⊏ (12)	1899
		24.6◀22.8◀8.8◀▶8.8▶25.7▶32.3	
632.2	**1558.7**	West Branch Rd (gravel)	1960

| 630.6 | **1560.3** | AT joins dirt road and crosses . . . . 42.377,-73.1507 ▣ (pg. 162) | 2010 |
| | | Washington Mtn Rd (paved), **Becket, MA 01223** (5.0E) | |

| 628.6 | **1562.3** | Streams . . . . ♦ | 1835 |

| 627.5 | **1563.4** | Blotz Rd (paved), small parking lot on north side . . . . 42.4094,-73.1503 ▣ | 1850 |
| 626.8 | **1564.1** | Warner Hill . . . . 📷 | 2050 |

| 625.2 | **1565.7** | Tully Mountain . . . . 📷 | 2080 |

624.4	**1566.5**	Powerline	1920
624.1	**1566.8**	**Kay Wood Shelter** (0.2E) 31.6◀17.6◀8.8◀▶16.9▶23.5▶33.4 . . . . ☽ ♦ ⊏ (10)	1757
623.8	**1567.1**	Grange Hall Rd	1628
623.6	**1567.3**	Barton Brook, footbridge . . . . ♦	1542

622.2	**1568.7**	Woods road	1324
621.6	**1569.3**	Railroad tracks, Housatonic St + Depot St	1220
621.1	**1569.8**	MA 8 & 9, **Dalton, MA** . . . . (pg. 162)	1145

| 620.1 | **1570.8** | AT on Gulf Rd / High St for 1.0 mile . . . . 42.4818,-73.1783 ▣ | 1180 |

⚠ Many of the water sources listed in this book are springs and small streams that can go dry. Never carry just enough water to reach the next water source.

| 617.9 | **1573.0** | Spring . . . . ♦ | 1920 |

617.0	1573.9	Powerlines		1906
616.9	1574.0	Crystal Mountain Campsite 0.2E, water on AT just north of side trail . . ☽ ♦ ☁ (5)		1950

616.1	1574.8	Gore Brook, outlet of Gore Pond . . . . ♦	2032

615.0	1575.9	Stream. . . . . ♦	1986
614.6	1576.3	Stream. . . . . ♦	1816

613.9	1577.0	The Cobbles, outcroppings of marble with view of Hoosic . . . . ▣	1846
		River Valley, Mt Greylock, and the town of Cheshire.	

612.8	1578.1	Furnace Hill Rd (south end)	1046
612.3	1578.6	Main St + School St, **Cheshire, MA** . . . .(pg. 163)	979
611.8	1579.1	MA 8, **Cheshire, MA, Adams, MA** (4.0E) . . . .(pg. 163)	993

610.7	1580.2	Outlook Ave (paved), stream and powerline to north . . . . ♦	1317

> ✿ Touch-Me-Not – Also known as "jewelweed". Trumpet-shaped flowers with a short curled tail hang horizontally like a bug in flight. Yellow with splotches of orange. Salve from crushed stems is a folk remedy for poison ivy's itch.

608.1	1582.8	Old Adams Rd (dirt)	2342
607.2	1583.7	**Mark Noepel Shelter** (0.2E), spring to right of shelter . . . . . ☁ ☽ ♦ ☁ ⌐ (10)	2823
		34.5◄25.7◄16.9◄►6.6►16.5►23.7 Spring stronger the farther you go.	
606.7	1584.2	Jones Nose Trail to west	3233

604.9	1586.0	Rockwell Rd / Summit Rd to west . . . . 42.6311,-73.1783 🅿	3025
604.5	1586.4	Cross Rockwell Rd twice, side trails to east	3145
603.9	1587.0	Mt Greylock, highest peak in MA. . . . . ⛺(pg. 166)	3491
603.5	1587.4	Thunderbolt Trail and Bellows Pipe Trail, 75 yards apart, both to east.	3104

601.9	1589.0	Bernard Farm Trail . . . . ▣	2780
601.6	1589.3	Mt Williams . . . . ▣	2950
600.8	1590.1	Notch Rd (paved)	2320
600.6	1590.3	**Wilbur Clearing Shelter** (0.3W) On Money Brook Trail . . . . ☽ ♦ ☁ ⌐ (8)	2275
		32.3◄23.5◄6.6◄►9.9►17.1►23.0. Intermittent stream.	
600.3	1590.6	Mt Prospect Trail to west	2505

598.7	1592.2	Pattison Rd (paved) . . . . 42.6876,-73.1598 🅿 ♦	1018
598.1	1592.8	Phelps Ave (south end), on road 0.5 mile	732
597.6	1593.3	MA 2, Hoosic River, ... 42.699,-73.1535 🅿 (0.1E) (pg. 166)	660
		footbridge and RR tracks, **Williamstown, MA** (west), **North Adams, MA** (east)	

1560.3   WASHINGTON MTN RD

▲▼⚡🅿 ⊠ Home of the "Cookie Lady" (0.1E) 413.623.5859
100 yds east. Water spigot near the garage door, please sign register on the steps. Homemade cookies often available. Soda, ice cream, boiled eggs & pick your own blueberries. Camping allowed, ask permission first. Shuttle range from Kent, CT to Manchester Center, VT. Maildrop: Roy & Marilyn Wiley, 47 Washington Mountain Road, Becket, MA 01223.

🅿 ✈ 🅰

🏕 Off-map: (1.4 mi.) to:
Pittsfield Quality Inn,
Walmart, Price Chopper,
Rite Aid,
🍴⚿ Starbucks, Friendly's,
Old Country Buffet,
Applebee's, Wendy's,
■ Home Depot,
Dick's Sporting Goods

■ ✈ Town Garage

Park Ave

⊞ Pittsfield Quality Inn...

🍴 Dalton
Restaurant

Curtis Ave

Hot Harry's 🍴⚿

Dalton CRA
(0.7 from AT)
Free Showers
M-F 5-8,
Sa 7-3, Su 9-1

💲

Carson Ave

📖 Library 413.684.6112
M,W 12-8, Tu 10-4
Th-Fr 12-5:30
Sa 10-2

🏤 PO (01226):
413.684.0364
M-F 8:30-4:30
Sa 9-12 🖂

DALTON, MA
42.4731,-73.1611
Mag. Dec. 13.78°W

N

🍴⚿ Jacob's Pub

⊞ 🍴⚿ Shamrock Inn & Paddy's Restaurant
🍴⚿ Angelina's
Juice & Java
⊞ Cumberland Farms

Daly Ave

Main St
9
North St
8A

Housatonic St

Depot St

🍴⚿ Dewey's
Public House

🍴⚿ Sweet Pea's

Dalton General
Store ⊞

🍴 Manny's Pizza

△ Laundromat

Deming St
8

✈ 🅰 ₛ
L.P. Adams

🎱 Zips Billards

1.1 mi:
Med Express
Urgent Care
413.448.6231
8a-8p, 7 days

8
9

✚

1.4 mi

» *Becket, MA 01223* (5E)
🖂 413.623.8845
M-F 8-4, Sa 9-11:30

⊠ Becket   Motel   (11.6E)
413.623.8888 $65-122+tax, incl
M-F 8-4, Sa 9-11:30

shuttle

🏠🏕🖂⚿📶 ⊠ Shamrock Village Inn (0.4W)
413.684.0860   Hiker rates   Su-Th $85.45
F-Sa $109.57 (incl all taxes, 10% disc.) Well-behaved pets allowed w/$75 deposit. Coin laundry, free use of computer & WiFi.

🏠📶 Econo Lodge (2.6W)
413.443.5661 Prices seasonal.

🍴⚿ Sweet Pea's Ice Cream
413.684.9799 Open M-Sa 1p-9p, Su 3p-9p.

🍴⚿ Berkshire Mall on SR 8, 4 mi. north of Dalton & 7 mi. south of Cheshire. On bus route. Has **Regal Cinema 10** - 413.499.3106, **Sears** - 413.448.9200, & **Target** - 413.236.4210.

🍴⚿ Angelina's Subs (0.3W)
413.684.0414 M-F 9-6, Sa 10-4, Su 10-2.

🍴⚿ Dalton Restaurant (0.8W)
413.684.0025

✈ LP Adams 413.684.0025
On the AT south of MA 8 & 9, look E on Housatonic St. M-F 6a-5p, Sa 6a-1p. Clsd Su. Coleman/denatured alcohol.

△ **Dalton Laundry** (0.7W) 413.684.9702
Tu-F 9a-5:30p, Sa 8a-4p, Su 10a-2p. Clsd M.

1569.8   MA 8 & 9

» *Dalton, MA 01226*
12% Tax on lodging

⊠ Debbie Andrus countrygirl1964&4@gmail.
com. Range: Eastern MA

1578.6   MAIN ST, SCHOOL ST

» *Cheshire, MA 01225*
(pronounced "chesh-er")

St. Mary of the Assumption Church Parish Hall (0.1W) 413.743.2110 fathermatthew@stmaryscheshire.com Outdoor camping on east lawn only. PARISH CENTER (Hall) off back parking lot open until 7:30p daily. No indoor sleeping, laundry, showers, maildrop or cooking avail. No smoking/alcohol/drugs of any kind. No hikers in building if children are in the parish hall. Open May 1 - Sep 30. Hikers should follow guidelines posted in parish hall & are welcome to attend daily or wkend Mass in hiker attire. Donations encouraged to help keep bathrooms stocked & building clean.(stmaryscheshire.com)

HD Reynolds (0.3W) 413.743.9512 M-F 8-5, Sa 8-3. General store, hiker snacks, soda, Coleman fuel/oz.

Diane's Twist Limited hrs, deli sandwiches, soda, ice cream.

BRTA 800.292.2782 (pg. 159) stops at A.T kiosk; ride to outfitter, Adams, MA and to Berkshire Mall (has EMS) $1.75

1579.1   MA 8

Berkshire Outfitters (2.5E) 413.743.5900 M-F 10-6, Sa 10-5, Su 11-4, Full svc outfitter, Coleman/alcohol/oz & canister fuel, frz-dried foods, footwear, minor equipment repairs. Often provides return ride to Cheshire. (berkshireoutfitters.com)

» **Adams, MA 01220** (4E)
413.743.5177
M-F 8:30-4:30, Sa 10-12

Big Y Foods Supermarket (4.4E) 413.743.1941
Rite Aid, Medicine Shop (4.8E) 413.743.4659
Adams Veterinary Clinic (4.9E) 413.743.4000
Thrifty Bundle Laundromat (0.7E) 413.664.9007

Map

CHESHIRE, MA
42.5622,-73.1578
Mag. Dec. 13.8°W
N

Berkshire Outfitters (2.5 mi from AT)
Briggs Dr
Fisk St
Hoosic Rvr
Main St
Main St
(unmarked) Furnace Hill Rd
Diane's Twist
Railroad St
School St
8
Dollar General
Hiker Kiosk
BRTA stop
PO (01225):
413.743.3184
M-F 7:30-1
& 2-4:30,
Sa 8:30-11:30
Shell Convenience Store
Dunkin Donuts (0.2 from A.T.)
North St
Church St
HD Reynolds
Town Hall
Basswater Grill
Italian/Pizza (new 2018)
Cheshire Liquor
South St
Lanesboro Road
Travel Lodge (7.7 mi)
1.0 mi

Check Appalachian Trail (A.T.) guidebooks and maps for guidance and note that camping and campfire regulations vary considerably along the Trail. Travel in groups of 10 or fewer. If you are traveling in a group of more than 5, avoid using shelters, leaving them for lone hikers and smaller groups.

PLAN AHEAD!
Be Aware of Camping & Campfire Regulations

| 597.5 | 1593.4 | Massachusetts Ave / Hoosac Rd. NoBo: east on road for 0.1 mile . . . . . **(pg. 167)** | | 688 |
| 597.2 | 1593.7 | Footbridge, stream . . . . | ♦ | 757 |

| 596.0 | 1594.9 | Petes Spring. Sherman Brook Campsite 0.1W . . . . | ☽♦⌂ | 1352 |

595.3	1595.6	Bad weather bypass trail.		1807
594.9	1596.0	Pine Cobble Trail to west		2113
594.8	1596.1	'98 Trail to west		2127

593.5	1597.4	**MA-VT** border, southern end of Long Trail (LT)		2330
		The AT and LT are concurrent northbound for the next 105.2 miles.		
593.1	1597.8	Spring, stream to north	♦	2154

591.0	1599.9	Stream.	♦	2074
590.7	1600.2	**Seth Warner Shelter** (0.2W) . . . . ☽♦⌂⊏(8)		2229
		33.4◄16.5◄9.9◄►7.2►13.1►21.6 Brook 0.1 left of shelter, known to dry up.		
590.4	1600.5	Country Rd, Powerline		2290

| 588.7 | 1602.2 | Powerline . . . . | | 2894 |

| 587.8 | 1603.1 | Roaring Branch, pond . . . . | ♦ | 2479 |

| 586.6 | 1604.3 | Consultation Peak . . . . | ♦ | 2833 |

585.5	1605.4	Woods road, Stamford Stream	♦	2246
585.1	1605.8	Stream.	♦	2177
584.6	1606.3	Pond.	♦	2191
584.2	1606.7	Woods road		2199

583.5	1607.4	**Congdon Shelter**, creek is water source . . . . ☽♦⌂⊏(8)		2088
		23.7◄17.1◄7.2◄►5.9►14.4►18.7		
582.7	1608.2	Stream.	♦	2223

581.4	1609.5	Stream.	♦	2214
581.0	1609.9	Harmon Hill		2325
580.5	1610.4	Spring	♦	2101

| 579.2 | 1611.7 | VT 9, **Bennington, VT** (5.1W) . . . . 42.8851,-73.1153 🅿♦(pg. 171) | | 1359 |
| | | Bridge over City Stream north of road | | |

| 577.6 | 1613.3 | Brook, **Melville Nauheim Shelter**, stream north of trail to shelter . . . . . ♦⊏(8) | | 2424 |
| | | 23.0◄13.1◄5.9◄►8.5►12.8►17.4 | | |

577.1	1613.8	Powerline		2627
576.7	1614.2	Spring	♦	2570
576.4	1614.5	Stream.	♦	2384
576.0	1614.9	Hell Hollow Brook, footbridge . . . . ⊛ ♦		2350

575.0 1615.9 Porcupine Ridge 2816

572.8 1618.1 Little Pond Mtn (wooded summit) 3306

569.1 1621.8 **Goddard Shelter** 21.6◀14.4◀8.5◀▶4.3▶8.9▶19.3 . . . . ☽ ♦ ☁ ⊏ (12) 3566
Spring 50 yards south on AT, limited tenting.
568.8 1622.1 Glastenbury Mountain, lookout tower . . . . ⊡ ⚲ 3748

SoBo NoBo   1000   3000   5000

564.8 1626.1 **Kid Gore Shelter** 18.7◀12.8◀4.3◀▶4.6▶15.0▶19.9 . . . . . . ⊡ ☽ ♦ ☁ ⊏ (8) 2784
Tenting north of shelter, west side of AT.
564.4 1626.5 Stream. . . . . ♦ 2855

561.1 1629.8 South Alder Brook. . . . . ♦ 2604

560.2 1630.7 **Story Spring Shelter**, spring 50 yards north on AT . . . . ☽ ♦ ☁ ⊏ (8) 2803
17.4◀8.9◀4.6◀▶10.4▶15.3▶18.3

558.6 1632.3 USFS 71 (gravel). . . . . 43.0536,-72.9905 🅿 2499
558.2 1632.7 Footbridge, stream . . . . ♦ 2390

1587.0 MT GREYLOCK, (3,491') is Massachusetts's highest peak. Veterans War Memorial Tower is on the summit. There are views of the Green, Catskill, and Taconic mountain ranges and surrounding towns. No camping or fires on summit.

Bascom Lodge 413.743.1591 On summit pvt rooms \$125/up, bunkroom \$35PP. Bunkroom incl use of shower & c. b'fast. Shower & towel w/o stay \$5, some snacks in gift shop, restaurant serves B/L/D. Open May 19-Oct 21, wkends only in May w/reservation.

1593.3   MA 2

David Ackerson 413.346.1033, 413.652.9573 daveackerson@yahoo.com Range: trailheads from NY to NH, & to/from area airports. Adv notice suggested.

Greylock Community Club (0.1E) Park on grass west of building, leave note w/name & vehicle ID in mailbox, donations accepted. Sign in sheet inside when open.

» **North Adams, MA 01247** (2E) (services spread east of AT)

Holiday Inn (2.3E) 413.663.6500 Summer rates \$169.99/ up. Pool, hot tub. Richmond Grill on-site.

» **Williamstown, MA 01267** (2.6W) All hotels expensive on peak nights, 11.7% lodging tax.

Howard Johnson (1.4W) 413.458.8158 Rates seasonal, c. b'fast. Mail (fee for non-guests): 213 Main St, Williamstown, MA 01267.

Williamstown Motel (1.6W) 413.458.5202 \$69S \$79D wkdays, \$89S \$99D wkends; prices higher on high-demand nights. C. b'fast. Laundry (done for you) \$8. Will p/u at MA 2. Major CC ok. Mail: 295 Main St, Williamstown, MA 01267.

Willows Motel (1.9W) 413.458.5768 Willows Motel, \$58-129, fourth night free, elaborate c. b'fast, free p/u & ret w/stay, discount at adjacent Olympia restaurant. Laundry \$6. Pool, some pets. Mail: 480 Main St, Williamstown, MA 01267.

Maple Terrace Motel (2.1W) 413.458.9677 stay@mapleterrace. com Country charm & warm hospitality, \$79-\$129 wkdys; \$99-\$163 wkds. Heated pool, all rooms non-smoking, C b'fast. CC ok. Mail: 555 Main St,

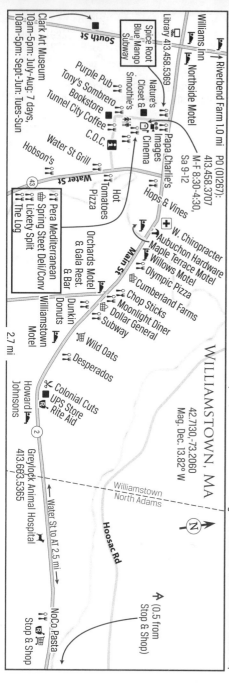

Williamstown, MA 01267.⟨mapleterrace.com⟩

🅿 🏨♨ **Williams Inn** (3.1W) 413.458.9371 $155D/up. Non-guest shower, swim & sauna $8. Restaurant open Su-Th 5p-9p, Fr-Sa 5p-10p. Short term parking $2/day.

🅿 🖂🛒 **River Bend Farm** (4.2W) 413.458.3121 riverbendfarmbb@gmail.com $120D incl b'fast in authentic 1770 colonial farmhouse. Free p/u & ret when avail, short term parking for guests.⟨riverbendfarmbb.com⟩

🖂 **Nature's Closet** (2.8W) Apparel, footwear, canister fuel & consignment sales. Mail: 61 Spring St, Williamstown, MA 01267.

🍴🍺 **Water Street Grill** (2.7W) 413.458.2175 Craft beer, L/D daily.

🍴🍴 **Spice Root Indian Cuisine** (2.8W) 413.458.5200 10% Hiker discount.

🐾 **Greylock Animal Hospital** (0.8W) 413.663.5365 M-F 8-8, Sa-Su 8-4, doctor on call until 11p.

📶 🖥 **Milne Public Library** (3.2W) 413.458.5369 M,Tu,Th,F 10-5:30, W 10-8, Sa 10-4.

🚌 **Peter Pan Bus Lines** (3.1W) 800.343.9999 At Williams Inn

1593.4   MASSACHUSETTS AVE / HOOSAC RD

🛏⛺♨ **The Birches B&B at Steep Acres Farm** (4.3W) 413.281.8510 $150D/up. Free p/u & ret from Massachusetts Ave or MA 2 w/stay. Adv notice req'd. Two night min on wkends Jun- Oct. Swimming pond, laundry, big b'fast. Ask about slackpacking (19.3mi to Bennington).

⚠ **Please be mindful of people's personal property. Do not camp on private land and abide by all "No Camping" signs.**

⚠ **Red-spotted newt** is the slow-moving red salamander that can be seen anywhere along the AT. The newt lives on land for the middle stage of its life, which lasts about two years. During this stage, it's also known as a red eft. It is a tadpole in its first stage. In its last stage it returns to water and turns green, but retains its red spots.

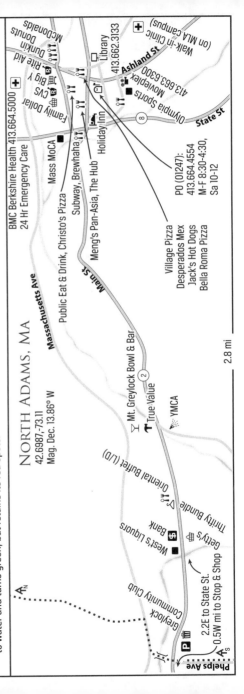

NORTH ADAMS, MA
42.6987,-73.11
Mag. Dec. 13.86° W

BMC Berkshire Health 413.664.5000
24 Hr Emergency Care

Mass MoCA

Public Eat & Drink, Christo's Pizza
Subway, Brewhaha
Meng's Pan-Asia, The Hub
Holiday Inn

Village Pizza
Desperados Mex
Jack's Hot Dogs
Bella Roma Pizza

PO (01247):
413.664.4554
M-F 8:30-4:30,
Sa 10-12

Massachusetts Ave

Main St

Mt. Greylock Bowl & Bar

True-Value

YMCA

Oriental Buffet (L/D)

Thrifty Bundle

Getty's

West's Liquors

Bank

Greylock Community Club

2.2E to State St.
0.5W mi to Stop & Shop

Phelps Ave

Library 413.662.3133

Walk-in Clinic
(on MLA campus)

McDonalds
Dunkin Donuts
Rite Aid
Big Y
CVS
Family Dollar
Movieplex 413.663.6300
Olympia Sports

Ashland St

State St

Williams Inn

2.8 mi

557.5 **1633.4** Black Brook, footbridge. . . . . ♦ 2206

556.6 **1634.3** Stratton-Arlington Rd / Kelly Stand Rd (gravel) . . . . . .43.0611,-72.9681 🅿 ♦ ⌂ 2230
        NoBo: east on road across Deerfield River. Daniel Webster Monument 0.3E.
        Campsite 100 yards north of road to the east.

555.1 **1635.8** Logging road 2584

552.8 **1638.1** Stratton Mtn, lookout tower, caretaker cabin. . . . . ⊗⊗📷 ⋒(pg. 171) 3936
        Side trail Summit on which Benton MacKaye was inspired to propose creation of
        the AT. (0.8E) to gondola

552.6 **1638.3** Spring to east. . . . . ♦ 3817

550.9 **1640.0** Logging road . . . . ♦ 2680
550.3 **1640.6** Footbridge, stream . . . . ♦ 2467
549.8 **1641.1** **Stratton Pond Shelter** (0.2W) . . . . ☽♦⊗⊗⌐(16) 2622
        19.3◄15.0◄10.4◄►4.9►7.9►12.7 Overnight fee, no tenting, no fires.
549.7 **1641.2** Lye Brook Trail to west 2557
549.6 **1641.3** Stratton Pond, North Shore Trail 0.5W to campsite, overnight fee . . . . ♦ ⌂ 2562
548.9 **1642.0** Stream. . . . . ♦ 2498
548.3 **1642.6** Stream. . . . . ♦ 2447
547.8 **1643.1** Winhall River, footbridge, stream . . . . ♦ 2269

546.3 **1644.6** Stream. . . . . ♦ 2209

544.9 **1646.0** **William B. Douglas Shelter** (0.5W) . . . . ☽♦⌐(10) 2286
        19.9◄15.3◄4.9◄►3.0►7.8►15.9 Spring to left of shelter.
544.0 **1646.9** Prospect Rock to west, view. . . . . 📷 2099
        ⚠ NoBo: AT turns east off gravel road.

541.9 **1649.0** **Spruce Peak Shelter** (0.1W) 18.3◄7.9◄3.0◄►4.8►12.9►17.6 . . . . ☽♦⌐(14) 2190
541.5 **1649.4** Spruce Peak 0.1W. 2040
541.1 **1649.8** Stream, powerline . . . . ♦ 1819
540.9 **1650.0** Stream. . . . . ♦ 1839

539.6 **1651.3** Powerline, footbridge, stream . . . . ♦ 1741

539.1 **1651.8** VT 11 & 30 . . . . .43.2068,-72.9707 🅿 (pg. 174) 1840
        Manchester Center, VT (5.4W)

538.2 **1652.7** Footbridge, stream . . . . ♦ 2134

537.1	1653.8	**Bromley Shelter** 12.7◄7.8◄4.8◄►8.1►12.8►14.3 . . . . ♦ ⬥(4)⌐(12)	2535
536.5	1654.4	Ski slope	3090
536.1	1654.8	Bromley Mountain, no tenting or fires, ... ☽ 📷	3260
		okay to overnight in ski warming hut, no smoking, please keep hut clean.	

| 533.6 | 1657.3 | Mad Tom Notch, USFS 21 (gravel) . . . . | 2446 |

| 532.0 | 1658.9 | Styles Peak . . . . 📷 | 3394 |

| 530.3 | 1660.6 | Peru Peak . . . . | 3429 |

529.4	1661.5	Spring . . . . ☽ ♦ ⬥ ⌐ ♦	2801
529.0	1661.9	**Peru Peak Shelter** 15.9◄12.9◄8.1◄►4.7►6.2►6.4 (fee) . . . . . ☽ ♦ ⬥ ⌐(10)	2597
528.7	1662.2	Footbridge, stream (two). . . . . ♦	2570
528.5	1662.4	Griffith Lake Tenting Area, camping only at designated sites within 0.5 mi. . . ♦ ⬥	2600
528.2	1662.7	Old Job Trail to east, Griffith Lake Trail to west . . . . ♦	2612

| 526.4 | 1664.5 | Baker Peak Trail to west, Baker Peak 0.1N on AT . . . . 📷 | 2642 |

| 524.3 | 1666.6 | **Lost Pond Shelter** 17.6◄12.8◄4.7◄►1.5►1.7►5.0 . . . . ☽☽♦⬥⌐(6) | 2192 |
| 523.8 | 1667.1 | Spring . . . . ♦ | 1956 |

522.8	1668.1	Old Job Trail to **Old Job Shelter** (1.0E), Lake Brook is water source . . . ☽♦⌐(8)	1524
		14.3◄6.2◄1.5◄►0.2►3.5►8.3	
522.6	1668.3	**Big Branch Shelter** 6.4◄1.7◄0.2◄►3.3►8.1►13.2 . . . . ☽♦⌐(8)	1492
		Close to road; heavy weekend use. Water source is Big Branch. Privy uphill.	
521.5	1669.4	Danby-Landgrove Rd, ... 43.3727,-72.9627 🅿 ☽ (pg. 175)	1517
		Big Black Branch Bridge, **Danby, VT** (3.5W)	
520.9	1670.0	Footbridge, stream . . . . ♦	1646

519.4	1671.5	Homer Stone Brook Trail to west	1854
519.3	1671.6	**Little Rock Pond Shelter & Tenting Area** . . . . ☽⬥⌐	1835
		5.0◄3.5◄3.3◄►4.8►9.9►13.6 Water source is at the caretaker's platform.	
		Overnight fee. Tenting restricted to designated sites.	
518.3	1672.6	Footbridge, stream . . . . ♦	1938

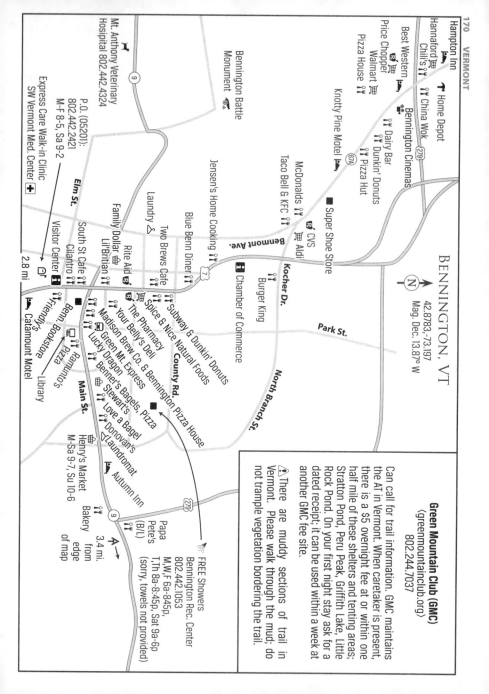

BENNINGTON, VT

(N) 42.8783, -73.197
Mag. Dec. 13.87° W

Hampton Inn
Hannaford 🍴🛒
Chili's 🍴
Best Western 🛏️
Price Chopper 🛒
Walmart 🛒
Pizza House 🍴

🏹 Home Depot
China Wok 🍴
Bennington Cinemas 🎬
Dairy Bar 🍴
Dunkin' Donuts 🍴
Pizza Hut 🍴

Bennington Battle Monument 🗿

Knotty Pine Motel 🛏️

McDonalds 🍴
Taco Bell & KFC 🍴

CVS 🏥
Aldi 🛒

■ Super Shoe Store

Jensen's Home Cooking 🍴

Laundry 🧺

Blue Benn Diner 🍴

Two Brews Cafe 🍴

Bennont Ave.

Kocher Dr.
Burger King 🍴

ℹ️ Chamber of Commerce

Park St.

Mt. Anthony Veterinary
Hosiptial 802.442.4324

P.O. (05201):
802.442.2421
M-F 8-5, Sa 9-2

Express Care Walk-in Clinic
SW Vermont Med. Center ➕

Elm St.

2.8 mi.

Visitor Center ℹ️

South St Cafe 🍴
Cilantro 🍴

Family Dollar
Lil'Britain 🍴

Rite Aid 🏥
Subway & Dunkin' Donuts 🍴

Spice & Nice Natural Foods

The Pharmacy 🏥

Your Belly's Deli 🍴

Madison Brew Co. & Bennington Pizza House 🍴

Green Mt. Express

Lucky Dragon 🍴

Benner's Bagels,
Stewart's 🍴
Love a Bagel 🍴

Donovan's 🍴

Laundromat 🧺

Autumn Inn 🛏️

Benn Pizza 🍴
Ramunto's 🍴

Benn Bookstore 📖

Library

Friendly's 🍴
Catamount Motel 🛏️

Main St.

Henry's Market
M-Sa 9-7, Su 10-6

🔶 Autumn Inn

Papa Pete's (B/L) 🍴
M,W,F 6a-845p,
T,Th 8a-8:45p, Sat 9a-6p
(sorry, towels not provided)

Bakery
3.4 mi.
from
edge
of map

🚿 FREE Showers
Bennington Rec. Center
802.442.1053

County Rd.
Bennington Pizza House

■

North Branch St.

Green Mountain Club (GMC)
<greenmountainclub.org>
802.244.7037

Can call for trail information. GMC maintains the AT in Vermont. When caretaker is present, there is a $5 overnight fee at or within one half mile of these shelters and tenting areas; Stratton Pond, Peru Peak, Griffith Lake, Little Rock Pond. On your first night stay ask for a dated receipt; it can be used within a week at another GMC fee site.

⚠️ There are muddy sections of trail in Vermont. Please walk through the mud; do not trample vegetation bordering the trail.

1611.7 VT 9

» *Bennington, VT 05201* (5.2W)

△ 🄿 🛜 🖥 ⊠ **Autumn Inn Motel** (4W) 802.447.7625 $60S $70D, p/u & ret to trail $10 (each way). Pets $10. Guests only Mail: 924 Main St, Bennington, VT 05201.

△ 🄿 🛜 ⊠ **Catamount Motel** (5.3W) 802.442.5977 $54S, $65D, $5EAP +tax. Laundry $4. One pet room. CC ok. Free shuttle to/from trailhead. Mail: 500 South St, Bennington VT 05201.⟨catamountmotel.com⟩

△ 🛬 🛜 🖥 ⊠ **Knotty Pine Motel** (6.3W) 802.442.5487 $88D/up, $8EAP up to 4. Incl b'fst, pool. Pets free. Close to grocery/Wal-Mart. Guest only mail: 130 Northside Dr, Bennington, VT 05201.

△ 🄿 🛜 🖥 **Best Western** (6.6W) $99/up.

△ 🄿 🛜 🖥 **Hampton Inn** (7.6W) Rates seasonal, hot b'fast.

🍴🥤**Lil' Britain** (5W) Fish & chips.

➕ **SW Vermont Med. Center** (5.9W) 802.442.6361 Hospital, Emg Room, Walk-in Clinic.

➕ **Express Care Walk-in Clinic** (6W) 802.440.4077 No appointment necessary, open daily 8a - 6p.

■ **Bennington Battle Monument** (6.4W) 802.447.0550 7 days 9a-5p. Contains statue of Seth Warner, Revolutionary War leader of the Green Mountain Boys, for whom the shelter is named.

🎬**Bennington Cinemas** (7W) ⟨benningtoncinemas.com⟩

🖥🛜 **Green Mountain Express** (4.8W) 802.447.0477 215 Pleasant St. Free bus route "Emerald Line" passes between Bennington & Wilmington (17E) 3 times a day, M-F. Board at town bus station, or flag the bus down at the trailhead on Route 9. You may also CALL to request an unscheduled ride from trail to town (or reverse) for $3/hiker; M-F 10a-4p only.⟨greenmtncn.org⟩

🖥 **Vermont Translines** 844.888.7267 Routes cover from Albany, NY airport through towns incl Bennington, VT, Wallingford, VT, Rutland, VT & Hanover, NH.

🖥 **Bennington Taxi** 802.442.9052

1638.1 STRATTON MTN,
Side trail (0.8E)
to Gondola

🥾🚠🍴**Stratton Mountain Resort** (2.5E) 802.297.4000 Can be reached by taking side trail from the summit to a gondola ride. Gondola has limited days/ hrs; don't make the walk unless you are certain of gondola operation (or are willing to walk an additional 1.5 miles down ski slopes). Resort has 10 restaurants, rooms in summer at $84/up.

🚿🛁🍴🛜🖥 ⊠ **First Run Ski Shop** (2E) 802.297.4321 tkajah@stratton.com Located at the base of Stratton Mountain VT, 100 yards from the gondola. Fuel, food, footwear, trekking poles, socks, apparel & other simple needs.

Leave What You Find

▲ Leave plants, cultural artifacts and other natural objects where you found them for others to enjoy.

▲ Don't build structures or dig trenches around tents.

▲ Do not damage live trees or plants; green wood burns poorly. Collect only firewood that is dead, down, and no larger than your wrist. Leave dead standing trees and dead limbs on standing trees for the wildlife.

▲ Consider using rubber tips on the bottom of your trekking poles to avoid scratch marks on rocks, "clicking" sounds, and leaving holes along the trail.

▲ Avoid introducing or transporting non-native species by checking your boots, socks, packs, tents, and clothing for non-native seeds that you could remove before hitting the trail.

Read more of the Leave No Trace techniques developed for the A.T.

AppalachianTrail.org/LNT

| 515.1 | 1675.8 | Trail to White Rocks Cliff 0.2W, blue-blazed trail amid stone cairns. . . . . . | 📷 | 2276 |

514.5 | 1676.4 | **Greenwall Shelter** (0.2E) 8.3◄8.1◄4.8◄►5.1►8.8►14.9 . . . . ☽ ◊ ⊏ | 2095
Spring 0.1 mile on side trail behind shelter, prone to fail in dry seasons.
513.8 | 1677.1 | Bully Brook, Keewaydin Trail to west. . . . . ◊ | 1424

513.1 | 1677.8 | Sugar Hill Rd (gravel). . . . . | 1222
513.0 | 1677.9 | VT 140, footbridge, stream . . . . 43.4567,-72.9329 (0.2E) 🅿 ◊ (pg. 175) | 1105
Wallingford, VT (2.8W)
512.0 | 1678.9 | Short side trail to west to Domed Ledge Vista (no longer a view) . . . . | 1674

511.3 | 1679.6 | Bear Mountain . . . . | 2228

510.4 | 1680.5 | Patch Hollow . . . . | 1761
510.0 | 1680.9 | Footbridge, stream (3) . . . . ◊ | 1648
509.8 | 1681.1 | Lake Trail loop to west (yellow blazed), 100 yards north, red-blazed tr to east . | 1652
509.4 | 1681.5 | **Minerva Hinchey Shelter** 13.2◄9.9◄5.1◄►3.7►9.8►14.1. . . . . ☽ ◊ ⚑ ⊏ (10) | 1611
spring 75 yards in front of shelter.

| 507.5 | 1683.4 | View to Rutland Airport. . . . . 📷 | 1424 |

506.8 | 1684.1 | Clarendon Gorge, suspension bridge, swimming holes in Mill River. . . . . . . ◊ | 808
506.7 | 1684.2 | VT 103, restaurant 0.5W . . . . 43.5214,-72.9258 🅿 ◊ (pg. 178) | 860
North **Clarendon, VT** (4.2W) **Rutland, VT** (8.0W)
506.2 | 1684.7 | View, north end of rock scramble . . . . 📷 | 1326
505.7 | 1685.2 | **Clarendon Shelter** (0.1E) 13.6◄8.8◄3.7◄►6.1►10.4►12.9 . . . . ☽ ◊ ⚑ ⊏ (10) | 1244
505.2 | 1685.7 | Beacon Hill . . . . | 1740
504.9 | 1686.0 | Lottery Rd (gravel), powerline . . . . | 1654

504.4 | 1686.5 | Hermit Spring to east (unreliable) . . . . ◊ | 1791

503.3 | 1687.6 | Stream. . . . . ◊ | 1586
503.1 | 1687.8 | Keiffer Rd (gravel). . . . . | 1522
502.8 | 1688.1 | Cold River Rd / Lower Rd (paved) NoBo east on road 75 yards. . . . . 🏛 | 1385
W.E. Pierce Groceries in North Shrewsbury (2.4E)
502.0 | 1688.9 | Gould Brook to west, AT parallel for 0.5 miles. . . . . ◊ | 1480

501.2 | 1689.7 | Upper Cold River Rd (gravel) . . . . | 1630

500.4 | 1690.5 | Gravel road, Robinson Brook . . . . ◊ | 1735

499.6 | 1691.3 | **Governor Clement Shelter** 14.9◄9.8◄6.1◄►4.3►6.8►8.7 . . . . . ☽ ◊ ⚑ ⊏ (12) | 1903
⚠ Shelter's proximity to road makes it prone to use by non-hiking crowd.
499.3 | 1691.6 | AT on gravel road 0.3 miles north of shelter. . . . . | 2049

498.3 | 1692.6 | Ski trail, blue diamond blazes . . . . | 2562

497.3	1693.6	Spring	3321
496.9	1694.0	Shrewsbury Peak Trail to east, signed.	3494

495.3 **1695.6 Cooper Lodge Shelter** 14.1◄10.4◄◄4.3◄►2.5►4.4►16.3 .◙⊗)◀⏝(16)(pg. 178) 3908
Spring 60yds north on AT. Trail behind shelter 0.2 to summit, view, restaurant.

495.2	1695.7	Bucklin Trail to west	3787
495.0	1695.9	Spring	3590

492.8 **1698.1 Pico Camp** (0.5E) 12.9◄6.8◄2.5◄►1.9►13.8►23.7 . . . . ◀⏝(4) 3465
Shelter on Sherburne Pass Tr where it leaves the Long Tr/AT south of Pico summit.

491.6 **1699.3** Spring . . . . ◀ 3133

490.9 **1700.0 Churchill Scott Shelter** (0.1W) 8.7◄4.4◄1.9◄►11.9►21.8►34.1 . . .)◁◀⏝ 2602
Composting privy, unreliable water at southern spur from shelter, no fires.

490.7	1700.2	Stream. . . . . △	2420
489.9	1701.0	Stream. . . . . ◀	2054

489.0	1701.9	US 4, **Rutland, VT** (8.5W). . . . . 43.6666,-72.85 🅿 (pg. 178)	1880
488.9	1702.0	Stream. . . . . ◀	1885

488.0 **1702.9** Maine Junction, Tucker-Johnson camping area (0.4W). . . . . . .)◀◀△ 2239
⚠ The Long Trail is also white-blazed, it turns to the west.

487.8	1703.1	Spring, Deer Leap Trail to east . . . . ◀	2290
487.2	1703.7	Deer Leap Trail 0.3E to view . . . . ◙	2435
487.1	1703.8	Sherburne Pass Trail 0.5E to Inn at Long Trail.	2440

486.3	1704.6	Spring . . . . ◀	1850
485.9	1705.0	**Gifford Woods State Park** . . . . ◀ (pg. 179)	1651
485.7	1705.2	VT 100, **Killington, VT** (0.6E) . . . . .43.6743,-72.8096 🅿 (pg. 179)	1612

485.1 **1705.8** Kent Pond, side trail to **Killington, VT** (0.4E) . . . . ◀(pg. 182) 1554

483.8	1707.1	Thundering Brook Rd (gravel)	1398
483.6	1707.3	Thundering Falls to west.	1232
483.4	1707.5	River Rd (gravel) . . . . 43.6806,-72.7822 🅿	1260

482.1 **1708.8** Quimby Mountain. 2515

481.5	1709.4	Powerline, boulder to sit on, view to Pico slopes.	2329
481.2	1709.7	Gravel road	2325

479.0 **1711.9 Stony Brook Shelter** (0.1E) 16.3◄13.8◄11.9◄►9.9►22.2►31.0 . . .)◀◀⏝(8) 1761
Tent sites behind shelter. Water from stream 0.1N on AT.

478.4 **1712.5** Stony Brook Rd (gravel), Stony Brook and footbridge. . . . . ◀ 1346

Marble Valley Regional Transit District (MVRTA) "the Bus" 802.773.3244, ext 117. Open 7 days. Red & white bus can be flagged down; they will stop if it is safe to do so. **Manchester to Rutland:** ($2PP) Loops from Rutland to Manchester Center, passing through M-Sa 4 times a day. Stops include Rutland Airport, Clarendon, Wallingford, Danby, and Shaws in Manchester Center. (thebus.com)

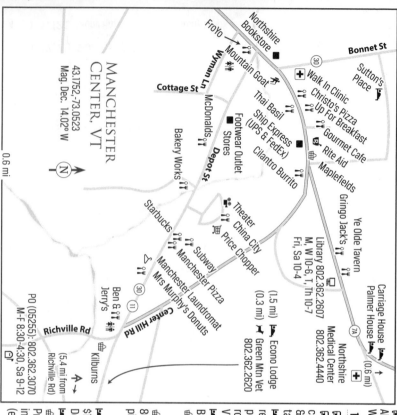

Bonnet St

Northshire Bookstore

Sutton's Place

Walk In Clinic

Christo's Pizza

Up For Breakfast

Gourmet Cafe

Rite Aid

Maplefields

FroYo

Mountain Goat

Wyman Ln

Cottage St

Thai Basil

Ship Express (UPS & FedEx)

Cilantro Burrito

Gringo Jack's

McDonalds

Footwear Outlet Stores

Depot St

Bakery Works

Theater

China City

Price Chopper

Starbucks

Subway

Manchester Pizza

Manchester Laundromat

Mrs Murphy's Donuts

Ben & Jerry's

Center Hill Rd

Richville Rd

Kilburns

(5.4 mi from Richville Rd)

MANCHESTER CENTER, VT
43.1752,-73.0523
Mag. Dec. 14.02° W

0.6 mi

N

Ye Olde Tavern

Library 802.362.2607 M, W 10-6, T, Th 10-7 Fri, Sa 10-4

Northshire Medical Center 802.362.4440

Carriage House / Palmer House (0.6 mi)

7A (0.6 mi)

(1.5 mi) (0.3 mi) Econo Lodge
Green Mtn Vet 802.362.2620

PO (05255): 802.362.3070 M-F 8:30-4:30, Sa 9-12

Vermont Translines 844.888.7267 Routes cover from Albany, NY airport through towns incl Bennington, VT, Wallingford, VT, Rutland, VT & Hanover, NH.

1651.8   VT 11 & 30

Leonards Taxi 802.379.5532

Northshire Taxi 802.345.9333 northshiretaxi@gmail.com All major airports as well as in town (Manchester area) & trail heads from above Rutland to Dalton Mass. Dogs in taxi fine as long as behaved.

The Lodge at Bromley (2E) 802.824.6941 reservations@lodgeatbromley.com $99 hiker rate. No pets. Carlos' Tapas Bar on site w/light menu, game room, ride to/from trail w/stay. Mail (non-guests $10): 4216 VT 11, Peru, VT 05152.

Bromley View Inn (3E) 802.297.1459 522 VT 30, Bondville, VT 05340. (bromleyviewinn.com)

Bromley Market (2.4E) 802.824.4444 7 days, 7a-7p.

» *Peru, VT 05152* (4.2E)

J Hapgood General Store & Eatery (4.2E) 802.824.4800 On Main St. in Peru, next to PO. Wood-fired pizza, beer & resupply. Open 7-7, Th-Su 7-9.

» *Manchester Center, VT 05255* (5W)

Econo Lodge (3.7W) 802.362.3333 $100/D Su-Th, $110/D F-Sa incl c. b'fast. Pets $20. Guest only mail: 2187 Depot St, Manchester Center, VT 05255.

Hapgood House (3.7W) 802.362.3600 Ask for hiker discount, c. b'fast, indoor & outdoor pool. Par-3 golf, tennis courts & trout pond (equipment provided). No pets.

Dutton Farm Stand (3.7W) 802.362.3083 9a-7p, 7 days. Produce, sodas, baked goods, ice cream.

🅟🛏🛜 **1878 Carriage House** (5.2W) \$125PP summer, no pets.

🅟🛏🛜 ⊠ **Suttons Place** (6.1W) 802.362.1165 \$80S, \$95D, \$115(room for 3), no pets. MC/Visa ok. Guest only mail: (USPS) PO Box 142 or (UPS) 50 School St, Manchester Center, VT 05255.

🅟🛏♨⛄🛜 ⊒ **Green Mountain House** (6.6W) 330.388.6478 Jeff & Regina Taussig host hikers at their home. Open Jun 7 - Sep 15. Space limited so reservations are essential. Clean bed w/ linens, shower, free laundry, WiFi, computer & well equipped hiker kitchen. Pvt room for couples. Free b'fast supplies; make your own pancakes, eggs, cereal, coffee. Not a party place, no alcohol. Hikers w/reservations hitch to town, resupply, then call for p/u. Check-in from 1p - 7p. Free morning shuttle back to the trail for guests. CC ok. \$35 + tax pp.⟨greenmountainhouse.net⟩

🥾🔌⊠ **Mountain Goat Outfitter** (5.9W) 802.362.5159 M-Sa 10-6, Su 10-5, Full-svc outfitter, white gas/alcohol/oz canister fuel, footwear. Mail: 4886 Main St, Manchester, VT 05255.⟨mountaingoat.com⟩

✚ **Manchester Medical Center** (5.4W) 802.379.2620

✚ **SVMC Northshire Medical Center** (5.4W) 802.362.4440 Walk In Clinic. M-Th 8-7, R 8-5, Sa 9-5.

🐾 **Green Mountain Veterinary Hospital** (5W) 802.362.2620 M, Tu, Th, F 8-5:30; W-8-6; Sa 8 -1.

1669.4   DANBY-LANDGROVE RD

🚕 **Green Mountain Taxi** 802.282.8826 thegreenmountaintaxi@gmail.com Range: Danby, VT - Killington & Brandont, VT. Pet friendly, local, long distance, airport, Amtrak.

» *Danby, VT 05739 (3.2W),* ⊒802.293.5105, M-F 7:15-10:15 & 11:15-2:15, Sa 7:30-10:30

🏤 **Mt. Tabor Country Store** (3.2W) 802.293.5641 M-Sa 5a-8p, Su 6a-7p.

🏤 🍴🛜 **Nichols Store & Deli** (3.3W) M-Sa 8a-6p.

🏛⊒ **Silas Griffith Library** (3.4W) 802.293.5106 W 2-7, (2-5 summer), Sa 9-12, one computer (Sa 9-12, one computer), Sa 9-12, one computer

1677.9   VT 140

» *Wallingford, VT 05773 (2.8W),* ⊒802.446.2140, M-F 8-4:30, Sa 9-12

🏤 **Wallingford Country Store & Deli** (2.8W) 802.446.2352 M-F 6:30-7, Sa 8-7, Su 8-4

🏤 ⊒ **Cumberland Farms** (2.9W) 802.446.3428 Bus stop for MVRTA (4 times daily) & Vermont Translines (see pg.172)

🍴**Sal's Italian Restaurant & Pizza** (2.6W) 802.446.2935 Dinner.

🛜 ⊒ **Gilbert Library** (2.6W) 802.446.2685 M 10-5; W 10-8; Th-F 10-5; Sa 9-12.⟨ghlib. wordpress.com⟩

Travel and Camp on Durable Surfaces

Read more of the Leave No Trace techniques developed for the A.T. at appalachiantrail.org/LNT

▶ Stay on the trail; never shortcut switchbacks. Take breaks off-trail on durable surfaces, such as rock or grass.

▶ Restrict activities to areas where vegetation is already absent.

▶ If tree branches block the trail, move them off if possible, rather than going around and creating new trails.

▶ Avoid expanding existing trails and campsites by walking in the middle of the trail, and using the already impacted core areas of campsites.

▶ Wear gaiters and waterproof boots, so you may walk through puddles instead of walking around them and creating a wide spot in the trail.

476.1 **1714.8** Streams . . . . ♦ 2013

474.5 **1716.4** Chateauguay Rd (gravel), Locust Creek . . . . ♦ 2003
474.1 **1716.8** Stream. . . . . ♦ 2144
473.6 **1717.3** Stream. . . . . ♦ 2503

> ❉ Clintonia – Foot-tall plant with plastic-looking blue berries atop long stems.

471.6 **1719.3** The Lookout, 0.1W to cabin and tower, no fires . . . . ⌂. 2365

469.1 **1721.8** **Wintturi Shelter** (0.2W) 23.7◄21.8◄9.9◄►12.3►21.1►28.4 . . . . ☽♦◖⌐(8) 2058

468.3 **1722.6** Woods road 1757

466.5 **1724.4** Ascutney Mountain . . . . ◙ 1488

465.3 **1725.6** VT 12, Barnard Gulf Rd (paved) . . . . 43.6552,-72.5662 🅿 ♦(pg. 182) 886
Gulf Stream south of road crossing. **Woodstock, VT** (4.2E)
464.4 **1726.5** Dana Hill. 1550

463.1 **1727.8** Woodstock Stage Rd, Barnard Brook, **South Pomfret, VT** (1E) . . . . . ♦(pg. 182) 820
462.8 **1728.1** Stream. . . . . ♦ 1035
462.3 **1728.6** Totman Hill Rd, footbridge, stream. . . . . ♦ 1007
461.5 **1729.4** Bartlett Brook Rd (gravel), footbridge, stream . . . . ♦ 1001
460.9 **1730.0** Pomfret Rd (paved), Pomfret Brook south of road crossing, powerline. . . . . . ♦ 906
460.5 **1730.4** View . . . . ◙ 1538

459.7 **1731.2** View . . . . ◙ 1713
459.1 **1731.8** Cloudland Rd (gravel), **Cloudland Market** (0.2W) . . . . ⌖(pg. 183) 1370
458.6 **1732.3** Previous AT shelter (Cloudland, 0.5W) now on private land. Owners also . . ⊘⌐ 1617
own Cloudland Market open W-Sa. No camping.

457.3	1733.6	Thistle Hill		1946
456.8	1734.1	**Thistle Hill Shelter** (0.2E), stream 0.1 further. . . . . ☽ ◖ ◗ ⌐ (8)		1754
		34.1◀22.2◀12.3◀▶8.8▶16.1▶25.6		
456.5	1734.4	Dimick Brook . . . . ◖		1504
455.5	1735.4	Joe Ranger Rd (gravel)		1295
454.9	1736.0	Bunker Hill Rd (dirt).		1406
453.1	1737.8	Bench, view to east. . . . . 📷		1134
452.5	1738.4	Stream. . . . . ◖		535
452.3	1738.6	Quechee West Hartford Rd, ⚠ NoBo west on road 0.4 mi, cross White River. . . .		474
452.0	1738.9	VT 14, White River, **West Hartford, VT** . . . .(pg. 183)		392
		NoBo: turn west, on road 0.3 mile.		
451.6	1739.3	Tigertown Rd, NoBo: turn east, on road 0.4 mile		397
451.3	1739.6	I-89 underpass . . . . 43.7208,-72.4132 🅿		559
450.6	1740.3	Podunk Rd (gravel), Podunk Brook. . . . . 43.7168,-72.4002 🅿 ◖		860
450.1	1740.8	Woods road		1048
449.7	1741.2	Woods road, stream . . . . ◖		998
448.0	1742.9	**Happy Hill Shelter** (0.1E) 31.0◀21.1◀8.8◀▶7.3▶16.8▶22.5. . . . . . ☽ ◊ ⌐ (8)		1409
		Brook near shelter, known to run dry.		
447.7	1743.2	Tucker Trail 3.1W to Norwich		1320
446.4	1744.5	Woods road		1131
445.2	1745.7	Powerline		1173
444.7	1746.2	Stream. . . . . ◖		828
444.6	1746.3	Elm Street, NoBo: turn east, on road 1.0 mile		842
443.6	1747.3	Main St + Elm St, **Norwich, VT**, NoBo: turn east, on road 1.4 miles. . . . .(pg. 183)		523
442.7	1748.2	**VT-NH** border, Connecticut River.		380
442.1	1748.8	**Hanover, NH**, Dartmouth College . . . . 43.7065,-72.2776 🅿 (pg. 185)		538
		NoBo: turn east on SR 10.		
441.4	1749.5	NH 120, trailhead near convenience store. . . . .(pg. 185)		506
440.7	1750.2	**Velvet Rocks Shelter** (0.2W) 28.4◀16.1◀7.3◀▶9.5▶15.2▶21.9 . . . ☽ ◗ ⌐ (6)		899
		Spring on northern access to shelter.		
440.1	1750.8	North shelter loop trail . . . . ◖ (0.2W)		953
438.4	1752.5	Pond, boardwalk . . . . ◖		792

1684.2 VT 103

⌂♂¶ **Loretta's Deli** (1W) 802.772.7638 M-F 6a-7p, Sa 10-5. Prepared meals & to-go trail foods. Fuel/oz, water filters. Nearest stop is near Airport Rd & Plus Ln 0.6SE on VT 103.

🚌 **MVRTA** Stops 0.6E of deli 4/day.

» **North Clarendon, VT 05759** (4.2W), ☎802.773.7893 M-F 8-1 & 2-4:30, Sa 8-10

» **Rutland, VT 05701** (8W of VT 103)

1695.6

TRAIL TO KILLINGTON PEAK. (0.2E from Cooper Lodge Shelter)

⌂♂¶🚿💲📶 **Killington Resort** (0.2E) 800.734.9435 Take a break at the Killington Peak Lodge for lunch & drinks or ride the K-1 Gondola to the base into the town of Killington, VT. Hrly bus service avail into Rutland, VT. ⟨killington.com⟩

📶 **Killington Peak Lodge** (0.2E) 800.621.6867 Food svc at the summit lodge, gondola ride ($30 round trip, $24 in adv) to the ski resort. Summer hrs 10a-5p.

1701.9 US 4

⌂♂¶🍴🚿💲📶 **The Inn at Long Trail** (0.9E) 802.775.7181 Hiker rates: walk-in only, space avail, rooms include full b'fast. Limited pet rooms. Reservations (at regular rates only) recommended on wkends in Jul & Aug. Overflow camping across street (no facilities). Coin laundry, outside water spigot. Closed Mid-Apr - Mem Day. Mail: (FedEx/UPS/Direct delivery ONLY, NO packages thru post office) 709 US 4, Killington, VT 05751. ♂¶ **McGrath's Irish Pub** serves menu daily 11:30a - 9p, live music Fri & Sat. Hourly bus svc to Rutland. ⟨innatlongtrail.com⟩

🚌 **Marble Valley Regional Transit District (MVRTA) "The Bus"** 802.773.3244, ext 117 M-F, Red & white bus can be flagged down; they will stop if it is safe to do so. Rutland Killington Commuter (RKC) ($2PP) Loops hourly from 5:15-7:15, 7 days from **Rutland to Killington**, passing AT on US 4. Stops westbound at the Inn at Long Trail. ⟨thebus.com⟩

🚌 **Vt Translines** (pg.174) Stops at Rutland bus station & at Long Trail Inn.

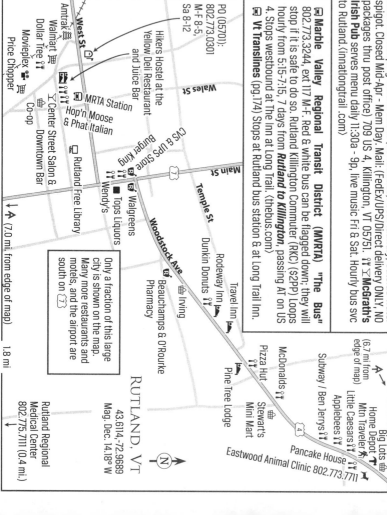

RUTLAND, VT
43.6114,-72.9689
Mag. Dec. 14.18° W

PO (05701): 802.773.0301 M-F 8-5, Sa 8-12

Only a fraction of this large city is shown on the map. Many more restaurants and motels, and the airport are south on [7]

🏕🚿⊠**Mendon Mountain View Lodge** (1.4W) 802.773.4311 Seasonal, ask for hiker rate. B'fast $10. Pets-$25. Pool, hot tub, sauna. Bus stops here. Mail: 5654 Rte 4, Mendon, VT 05701.

🚿**Pico Sports Center** (0.6E) 802.422.1400 $5 hot showers. ⟨picomountain.com⟩

» *Killington, VT 05751 (1.8E from US 4)*

» *Rutland, VT 05701 (8.5W from US 4 trailhead)*

🚕 **Rutland Taxi** 802.236.3133 northeastern cities. ⟨amtrak.com⟩

🏕🛏🍴⊠🚿**Hikers Hostel at the Yellow Deli** (8.5W) 802.683.9378, 802.775.9800 aysh@hikershostel.org Run by a Twelve Tribes spiritual community. Donations accepted (financial or work). Kitchenette, laundry. No alcohol/smoking. Shuttles sometimes avail by donation. Hostel open 24/7 (11p curfew). Stay incl b'fast & 15% off at 🍴**Yellow Deli Restaurant** open Su 12p - Fr 3p. Limited resupply at Hostel. Groc, PO & library 4 min walk. Mail: Hiker Hostel, 23 Center St, Rutland, VT 05701.⟨hikershostel.org⟩

🥾**Mountain Travelers Outdoor Shop** (6.9W) 10-5, Sa 10-4. Full svc outfitter, Coleman/alcohol/oz.⟨mtntravelers.com⟩

🛒**Rutland Food Co-op** (8.8W) 7 days, M-Sa 9-7, Su 10-6.

🐾**Rutland Veterinary** (9.9W) 802.773.2779

🚂**Amtrak** (9W) 800.872.7245 Daily routes Rutland to many

1705.0   GIFFORD WOODS STATE PARK

🏕**Gifford Woods State Park** 802.775.5354 The AT passes thru Gifford Woods State Park. Shelters, discounted tent sites for AT hikers in special hiker section, coin-op showers, water spigot. Open Mem Day-Colum Day. Fills quickly on wkends & in the fall.

1705.2   VT 100

» *Killington, VT 05751 (0.6E from VT 100, 1.8E from US 4)*

🚐 **Apex Shuttle Service "AT Hiker Shuttle"** 603.252.8295 AThikershuttle@gmail.com Steve "Stray Cat" Lake (AT '96). Shuttles, slackpacking options, trail info & support in New England. Shuttles to or from anywhere on the trail if your hike begins or ends in the Hanover, NH area.

🏕🛏⊠**Greenbrier Inn** (0.7E) 802.775.1575 15% Discount for hikers, no pets.

🏕🛏⊠**Killington Motel** (0.8E) 802.773.9535 Call for hiker rate, incl c. b'fast, pool. Next door to PO.⟨killingtonmotel.com⟩

🥾⊠**Base Camp Outfitters** (0.6E) 802.775.0166 Summer hrs: 10-5 daily. Full svc outfitter, alcohol/oz & canister fuel. Also accessible by side trail from Mountain Meadows Lodge. Disc golf. Maildrop $5: 2363 Route 4, Killington VT 05751.

🍴🍷△**JAX Food & Games** (2.3E) 802.422.5334 Eat/drink while-u-wash. M-Sa 3p-2a, Su 12p-2a (laundry downstairs).

🍴🍷**Long Trail Brewing Co.** (12.3E) 802.672.5011 Open 10-7.⟨longtrail.com⟩

KILLINGTON, VT

Map labels:

- Thundering Brook Rd
- Base Camp
- Killington Rd
- Kent Pond
- Pittsfield 7 mi
- Gifford Woods SP
- (100)
- Mountain Meadows Lodge
- Greenbriar Inn
- Killington Deli & Marketplace
- Killington Motel
- The Inn at Long Trail
- Approx. 4.3 mi of the AT are shown.
- PO (05751): 802.775.4247 M-F 6:30 pickup (only), 8:30-11 & 12-4:30 Sa 8:30-12
- Sherburne Pass Tr. 0.5
- Maine Junction
- Inn at Long Trail
- LongTrail
- Tucker Johnson Campsite
- Rutland 11 mi
- Long Trail Brewing Co. 14E →
- Pico Ski Resort
- 2.8 mi

437.7 1753.2 Trescott Rd (paved). 919

436.4 1754.5 Footbridge, stream (2) . . . . ⬥ 849
436.3 1754.6 Etna-Hanover Center Rd (paved), **Etna, NH** (0.8E) . . . . (pg. 185) 845
         ▥ Cell phone reception at cemetery to west.

433.8 1757.1 Three Mile Rd (gravel) . . . . 43.718,-72.176 🅿 1427
433.6 1757.3 Mink Brook, footbridge . . . . ⬥ 1345

432.0 1758.9 Moose Mountain south peak. . . . . 📷 2290
431.4 1759.5 Woods rd ⚠ NoBo stay on AT for another 250 yards to Moose Mtn Shelter 2005
431.2 1759.7 **Moose Mountain Shelter** (0.1E) . . . . ☽ ⬥ ◖ �ᒋ (8) 2111
         25.6◄16.8◄9.5◄►5.7►12.4►17.7 Loop trail to shelter, water at AT and northern
         leg intersection, tenting on northern leg of loop.

430.0 1760.9 Moose Mountain north peak 2297

428.4 1762.5 South fork of Hewes Brook 1039
428.2 1762.7 Goose Pond Rd (paved), parking to east . . . . 43.7528,-72.1233 🅿 958

426.1 1764.8 Holts Ledge, precipitous drop-off, views . . . . 📷 1968

425.5 1765.4 **Trapper John Shelter** (0.2W) ⚠ Side Tr to shelter is white blazed . . ☽ ⬥ ◖ �ᒋ (6) 1467
         22.5◄15.2◄5.7◄►6.7►12.0►27.7 privy behind shelter

424.6 1766.3 Grafton Turnpike(paved), Dorchester Rd . . . . 43.79,-72.1 🅿 ⬥ (pg. 186) 880
         Lyme Center, NH (1.3W), **Lyme, NH** (3.2W) ⚠ NoBo east on wedge of land between
         fork in road.

423.2 1767.7 Grant Brook . . . . ⬥ 1220
422.9 1768.0 Concrete milepost . . . . ⬥ 1124
422.6 1768.3 Lyme-Dorchester Rd (gravel). . . . . .43.79,-72.1029 🅿 1104

421.8 1769.1 Lambert Ridge, multiple views from quartzite ridge . . . . 📷 1921

┌───┐
│ ✻ Queen Anne's Lace – White flower cluster in   │
│   disk shaped doily 3-5" wide on hairy stem.   │
└───┘

419.4 1771.5 Smarts Ranger Trail to east 2681
418.9 1772.0 Campsite, weak spring to east, fire tower north of camp, west of AT . . . . 🏕⬥◖ 3229
418.8 1772.1 Smarts Mountain, **Fire Wardens Cabin** . . . . 📷 ☽ ⬥ �ᒋ (12) 3219
         21.9◄12.4◄6.7◄►5.3►21.0►27.9 Shelter is cabin north of summit,
         west of AT. Spring 0.2 in front of cabin.

414.9	1776.0	South Jacobs Brook	◆	1450
414.3	1776.6	Eastman Ledges	📷	1933
413.9	1777.0	North Jacobs Brook.	◆	1916
413.5	1777.4	**Hexacuba Shelter** (0.3E) 17.7◀12.0◀5.3◀▶15.7▶22.6▶31.6 . . 🌙 ◊ ☁ (2)⌐ (8)		2078

Shelter on steep side trail, unreliable stream at intersection with side trail.

411.9	1779.0	Mt Cube south peak, cross Rivendell Trail to west	📷	2911
411.8	1779.1	Side trail 0.3W to Mt Cube north peak.	📷	2863
410.2	1780.7	Brackett Brook	◆	1462
409.3	1781.6	Stream.	◆	1281
409.1	1781.8	Woods road		1188

408.5	1782.4	NH 25A (paved) NoBo east on road 300 yards . . . 43.9013,-71.9838 🅿 (pg. 192)		909
		Wentworth, NH (4.8E)		
406.7	1784.2	Cape Moonshine Rd (gravel). . . . . 43.9158,-71.9646 🅿 (pg. 192)		1429
		AT northbound joins Ore Hill Trail.		
406.0	1784.9	Ore Hill Campsite . . . . 🌙 ◊ ☁		1876
		Muddy spring 100 yards downhill from tentsites.		
404.0	1786.9	Ore Hill.		1826
403.3	1787.6	Lake Tarleton Rd, NH 25C, **Warren, NH** (4E) . . . . 43.9537,-71.9448 🅿 ◆ (pg. 192)		1542
		AT on road past parking area & power lines, Ore Hill Brook north of road.		
401.3	1789.6	Mt Mist		2200
401.0	1789.9	View	📷	1873
400.7	1790.2	Webster Slide Trail 0.7W to summit, view		1678

⚠️ The notation "AT: Ore Hill Tr ◀▶ Wachipauka Pond Tr" indicates that the AT to the south is coincident with the Ore Hill Tr; the AT to the north joins the Wachipauka Pond Tr.

398.7	1792.2	NH 25, Oliverian Brook north of road. . . . . 43.9899,-71.8995 🅿 (pg. 193)		1043
		AT: Ore Hill Tr◀▶ Wachipauka Pond Tr , **Glencliff, NH** (0.3E), **Warren, NH** (5.0E)		

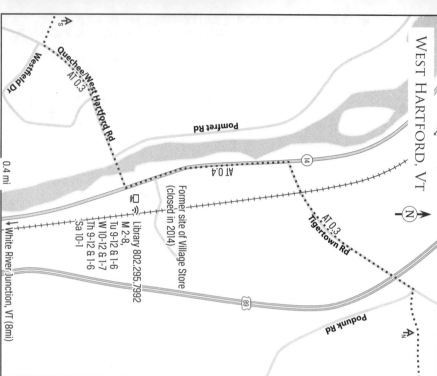

WEST HARTFORD, VT

Quechee/West Hartford Rd AT 0.3

Wesswield Dr

Pomfret Rd

0.4 mi

⌖ White River Junction, VT (8mi)

Library 802.295.7992
M 2-8,
Tu 9-12 & 1-6
W 10-12 & 1-7
Th 9-12 & 1-6
Sa 10-1

Former site of Village Store
(closed in 2014)

AT 0.4

14

AT 0.3

Tigertown Rd

89

Podunk Rd

N

1705.8   KENT POND, A.T. crosses behind lodge near pond, 0.4E trail to Base Camp Outfitters

🅿 ⛽ ☎ ✉ **Mountain Meadows Lodge**   802.775.1010 mountainmeadowsvt@hotmail.com Room $69D, single room $59. Open yr-round, but meals & lodging are not avail most wkends & during events. Ok to charge phones, but please do not loiter when events are held at the lodge. Occasional WFS. L/D sometimes avail. No pets inside. Hot tub, sauna, game room & canoe/kayaks for guests. Parking for section hiking guests. Ask about tenting or the hut. Mail free even for non-guests: 285 Thundering Brook Rd, Killington, VT 05751.(fb.com/Mountain-Meadows-Lodge-1022450683346)

» *Woodstock, VT 05091 (4.2E)*
⊞ ☎ 802.457.1323, M-F 8:30-5, Sa 9-12.
Pricey resort town, several motels, restaurants, & bookstore.

1725.6   VT12, BARNARD GULF RD

⊾ ⊕ **On The Edge Farm** (0.2W) 802.457.4510 Mid May - Labor Day 7 days 10-5:30; rest of year Th-Su 10-5. Pies, fruit, ice cream, smoked meats & cheese, cold drinks.

🛏️ **Shire Woodstock** (4E) 802.457.2211 $138/up, ask for hiker rate.(shirewoodstock.com)

🛏️ **Braeside Motel** (5.2E) 802.457.1366

⊕ **Cumberland Farms, Gillingham & Sons** (3.8E) 802.457.9147

🏪 ✕ **Bentley's** (3.8E) 802.457.3232 Open L/D until 2a.

🍴 ✕ **Pizza Chef** (4.6E) 802.457.1444 11a-9p.

🏥 **Woodstock Pharmacy** (4E) 802.457.1306 M-Sa 8a-6p, Su 8a-1p.

🐾 **Veremedy Vet. Hospital** (4.7E) 802.457.2295 M&W-F 10-6, Tu 10a-8p, Sa 10a-5p.

☎ 📖 **Library** (4.1E) 802.457.2295 M&W-F 10-6, Tu 10a-8p, Sa 10a-5p.

1727.8   WOODSTOCK STAGE RD

» *South Pomfret, VT 05067 (1E)*, ☎ 802.457.1147 M-F 12:30-4:30, Sa 8:30-11:30, located inside of Teago's

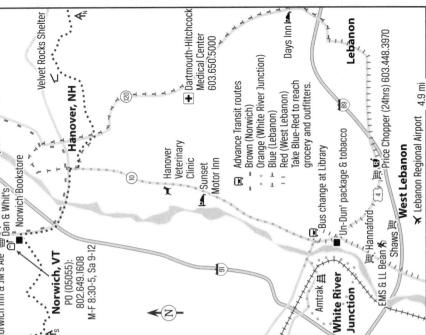

⌂ **Teago's General Store** (1E) 802.457.1626 2035 S. Pomfret Rd. M-Sa 7-6, Su 8-4, B&J ice cream, beer, sandwiches & salads.

1731.8   CLOUDLAND RD (GRAVEL)

⌂ ⚡⛺**Cloudland Farm Market** (0.3W) 802.457.2599 cloudlandvt@gmail. com Farm store w/local ice cream, cheeses, beef jerky, sodas, t-shirts, soap, & occasionally sandwiches or prepared foods. Water avail at outside spigot.

1738.9   VT 14, WHITE RIVER

🚍 **Big Yellow Taxi** 802.295.7878 Also covers Woodstock, Norwich, Hanover, Lebanon & White River Junction

1747.3   MAIN ST + ELM ST

» **Norwich, VT 05055** (more services on map) *Overnight stay may be possible with one of the many trail angels here and in Hanover. Look for list at Norwich Library. (**Norwich, VT services cont'd on pg. 185...**)*

🚗 **Enterprise Rent-A-Car** 800.736.8227 Car rental w/free pickup/ return can be as economical as shuttles. ATC has arranged for hiker discount, use code W15509. Locations include Franklin, NC, Abingdon, VA, Pearisburg, VA, Roanoke, VA, Waynesboro, VA, Front Royal, VA, Charles Town, WV, Carlisle, PA, East Stroudsburg, PA, Warwick, NY, Pittsfield, MA, Bennington, VT, Rutland, VT, Hanover, NH, Gorham, NH.

🚍 **Advance Transit** 802.295.1824 ⟨advancetransit.com⟩ M-F 6-6, offers FREE bus service connecting Hanover area towns. Detailed schedule and stops are avail. on-line and at libraries. The routes are indicated on Norwich and Hanover maps and primary bus stops are:

▲ Norwich-Dan & Whits (Brown).
▲ Hanover-Dartmouth Book Store (Orange/Blue), Hanover Inn (Brown).
▲ White River Junction-Amtrak.
▲ West Lebanon-Main St. (Orange/Red), grocery stores, outfitters.
▲ Lebanon-City Hall (Blue/Red).

See wide-area map on pg. 183

As ↗

Take brown 🚌 route to:
Norwich, VT
1.4 mi. from
Main St. (Hanover)
to Norwich Post Office

PO (03755): 603.643.5201
M-F 8:30-5, Sa 8:30-12
Sat pick-up available until 3

Dartmouth Bookstore (and bus stop)

Maple St

Dartmouth Outing Club (DOC)
Collis Center Student Union 🍴 ⓘ

Thayer Hall 🍴 🍴

Allen St

Stinson's

School St

Baker-Berry Library 603.646.2560 🍴 ⓘ 💻

EBAs 🍴 ⓘ

Dirt Cowboy 🍴

Canoe Club 🍴 🍴

Boloco Burritos 🍴
Mollys 🍴 🍴
Murphys

Moreno Gelato 🍴
Theater 🎭
Zimmermans 🛍

CVS 💊

Irving ⛽

Main St

🛣 10

Currier St

Umpleby's Bakery Cafe 🍴⚡

Salt Hill Pub,
Base Camp Cafe
& Subway

Starbucks 🍴 🍴
Market Table

Lou's (free muffin) 🍴

Hanover Inn

Dartmouth Coach Bus Stop

The Green

Hopkins Center 🎭
🖼 Hood Museum
of Art (free admission)

Hanover Hardware 🔨

Ramunto's Pizza (free
slice for thru-hikers)

South St

C&C Pizza 🍴

Howe Library
603.643.4120
M-Th 10-8, Fri 10-6,
Sa 10-5, Su 1-5

Noodle Station
& Frozen Yogurt 🍴
Jewel of India 🍴

Crosby St

Wheelock St

🛣 10

Take orange 🚌 route to:
Hanover Veterinary Clinic (1 mi from Wheelock)
Sunset Motor Inn (2 mi from Wheelock)
West Lebanon, NH (5 mi from Wheelock)

0.8 mi

Lebanon St (0.7 mi. to Hanover Inn)

🛣 120

🛣 10

Park St

HANOVER, NH

N ↗
43.7022,-72.2892
Mag. Dec. 14.52° W
📶 town-wide WiFi

🅿 Lot A= Call Dartmouth Parking
Operations 603.646.2204 with
vehicle info & dates car will be left.

Take blue 🚌 route to:
Dartmouth-Hitchcock Medical Center (2 mi)
Days Inn (4 mi) 🏥
Lebanon, NH (5 mi)

Richard W. Black
Community Center

Co-op Service Center 🔧
🏪 Co-op Food Store

As ↗

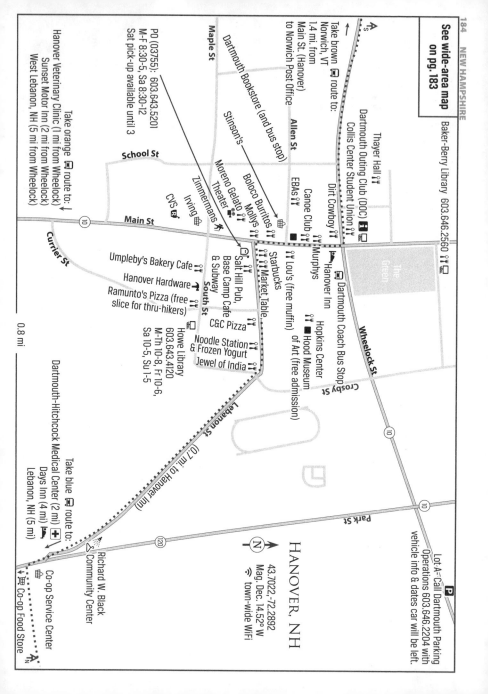

» Norwich, VT

(...services cont'd from pg. 183)

🛏🍴☕🖥📶🗑 **Norwich Inn** (0.1W) 802.649.1143 $129D/up, no smoking, reservations recommended. Rates may vary, subject to avail & black out dates. 🍴🍷**Jasper Murdocks Ale House** W-Su B/L; Dinner daily, microbrewery. Mail for guests: PO Box 908, Norwich, VT 04055, or FedEx to 325 Main St. Will not sign for mail.〈norwichinn.com〉

🍴📶 **Dan & Whit's General Store** (0.2E) 802.649.1602 On Main St. 7 Days 7a-9p. Hikers get free day old sandwiches when avail. Full gear items, canister fuel, batteries, ponchos, hardware & grocery.〈danandwhitsonline.com〉

📶🗑 **Norwich Library** (0.3W) 802.649.1184 M 1-8, Tu-W-F 10-5:30, Th 10-8, Sa 10-3 Open some Sundays.

1748.8   DARTMOUTH COLLEGE

» **Hanover, NH 03755** 🅿 Overnight parking on Wheelock St Lot A, see map. No parking near Connecticut River Bridge.

🔒 **Hanover Friends of the AT** Produce a brochure w/complete list of hiker services, avail at the DOC, P0, libraries, Co-op.〈hanoverchamber.org/appalachian-trail-hikers-guide〉

🚌 **Advance Transit** (see pg. 183)

🚌 **Dartmouth Coach** (3.9E) 603.448.2800 Routes to Boston, Logan Airport & NY. Schedules on website.〈dartmouthcoach.com〉

🚌 **Vermont Translines** 844.888.7267 Routes cover

slackpacking options as well as thru hiker support. Trail info & other support in New England. Shuttles to or from anywhere on the trail, to or from the Hanover, NH. 〈vttranslines.com〉

🚖 **Big Yellow Taxi** 603.643.8294   Pricey, hiker discounts sometimes avail.

🛏🍴☕🖥📶 **Hanover Inn** 603.643.4300 Hanover, NH area.

🛏🍴☕🖥📶🗑 **Sunset Motor Inn** (2.1E) 603.298.8721 Open 8-11, Call ahead for availability; discount for hikers. Will shuttle when bus is not running. Free laundry before 6p, quiet after 10p. $15 Pet fee. Guest only mail: 305 N Main St, West Lebanon, NH 03874.

🍴📶 **Zimmermann's** 603.643.6863 Hiker-friendly, canister fuel, Aquamira, socks & outdoor clothes. Mail (prior approval): 63 Main St, Hanover, NH 03755

🍴📶 **Stinson's** 603.643.6086 Convenience store w/$5 hiker lunch special: deli sandwich, soda & small bag of chips. Good selection of beer & tobacco.

🍴🌶 **Jewel of India** (0.3W) 603.643.2217 Open 7 days. Buffet Su 11:30-2:30.

🐾 **Hanover Veterinary Clinic** (1.3E) 603.643.3313

⛏ **Hanover True Value Hardware** (0.13E) 603.643.2308 7 Days, Coleman/alcohol/canister fuels. UPS shipping.

🔒 📶 **Dartmouth Outing Club (DOC)** (0.1W) 603.646.2428 Unsecured room for pack storage in Robinson Hall & in Howe Library cannot be left overnight. Not avail during Dartmouth orientation (mid Aug - mid Sep). Both places have computers for free internet use. No hiker accommodations on campus.〈outdoors.dartmouth.edu〉

from Albany, NY airport through towns incl Bennington, VT, Wallingford, VT, Rutland, VT, White River Junction, NH, &

» White River Junction, VT (4.5E)

🚆 **Amtrak** (4.5E) 800.872.7245 Vermonter line travels north as far as St. Albans, VT, & south through New York, Philadelphia, Baltimore & Washington, DC. No ticket office at this station. Reserve by phone & pay as you board.〈amtrak.com〉

» Lebanon & W Lebanon, NH, (4.5E) (see map)

🏬 **EMS** (5.1E) 603.298.7716, 🏬 **LL Bean** (5.1E) 603.298-6975, 🛒 **Shaw's** (5.3E) 603.298.0388 7a-10p M-Sa, 7-9 Su.

1749.5   NH 120

🛏🍴📶 **Days Inn** (3.7E) 603.448.5070 4 Mi south of the Co-op on Rte 120 on free bus route. C. b'fast. Pets $20.

🍴📶 **Hanover Co-op Foodstore** (0.1W) 603.643.2667 7a-8p, 7 days

🛏🍴☕📶 **Richard W. Black Community Center** 603.643.5315 M-F 9a-4:30p, Sa Sep-Jun 10a-4:30p. Shower w/soap & towel $3, laundry w/soap $2 (must finish shower/laundry by 4:30p). Pack storage, outside outlet & Trail Angels list.〈hanoverrec.com〉

1754.6   ETNA-HANOVER CENTER RD

» Etna, NH 03750 (0.8E)

🛏🍴📶🗑 **Tigger's Tree House** (3.3E) 603.643.9213 Pvt home; not a party place. No drive-ins. No Cars. Cannot accept mail drops. Advance notice ensures a place to stay. Call from trailhead, Etna General Store (will let you use phone) or Hanover for p/u. Pets allowed. Donations accepted. Buy toilet paper or laundry soap, or WFS. Rides to grocery store, Walmart, EMS.

🍴🗑 **Etna General Store** (0.9E) 603.643.1655 M-F 6-7, Sat 8-7. Deli, hot meals, closed Su.

🔒 **Apex Shuttle Service** 603.252.8295 athikershuttle@gmail.com Steve "Stray Cat" Lake (AT '96) offers hiker shuttles for section hikers, inn to inn hikes,

1766.3 GRAFTON TURNPIKE, DORCHESTER RD., DARTMOUTH SKIWAY

» *Lyme Center, NH 03769* (1.2W)
» *Lyme, NH 03768* (3.2W)

▶🛏🍴🖂🐾🚿⊠ **Dowd's Country Inn B&B**
(3.2W) Call in adv & let them know you are a hiker. PU & ret avail. Rates fluctuate; mid wk starting at $85S, $100D + NH taxes. Wkends thru Sep 20, $125S, $140D + taxes. Incl full b'fast & afternoon tea. Pets $15, allowed in some rooms. Mail: 9 Main St, Lyme, NH 03768.(dowdscountryinn.com)

▶🛏🍴🖂🐾🚿⊠ **Loch Lyme Lodge** (3.9W) 603.795.2141 120 acres & 22 cabins on Post Pond between the CT river & the A.T. - 10 mi North of Hanover - dogs welcome. $49 for one ($59 for a couple), 3rd in cabin $20 add'l. B'fast incl in rate (this rate for A.T. hikers only).(lochlymelodge.com)

⛺🍴 **Lyme Country Store** (3W) ice cream, produce, deli, 7 days.

🍴 **Stella's Italian Kitchen & Market** (3.2W) 603.795.4302 Tu-Fr 10-9, Sa 10-10, Clsd Su & Mo.(stellaslyme.com)

✚ **Lyme Veterinary Hospital** (2.7W) Bear right onto High St & hospital is 50 yds on the left. M-F 8-5, Sa 8-noon.

Appalachian Mountain Club (AMC) 603.466.2727 Maintains AT from Kinsman Notch, NH to Grafton Notch, ME & operates 8 walk-in only huts with space for 30-90 people (no pets). Huts use alternative energy sources and composting toilets. There is no heat or showers. Huts are closed in winter. In spring & fall huts are open to "self-serve" use. Rates (member/nonmember): $28/$34 Su-F; $40/$49 Sa. See White Mtn map for dates. "Full serve" season includes bunk, dinner & breakfast, ranging from $113PP - $135PP. Don't count on Hut stays without reservations, & camping is not allowed near huts, except at Nauman Tentsite. Reservations can be made by phone or with any AMC caretaker. Work-for-stay is available to 2 thru-hikers (4 at LOC), no reservations. Arrive after 3pm and please put sincere effort into your work. WFS hikers get floor space for sleeping, feast on leftovers, and are typically asked to work 2 hours after breakfast. Limit WFS to 3 nights in the Whites to give other hikers the opportunity. Lakes of the Clouds Hut has 4 WFS spots and a $10 thru-hiker bunkroom called **"The Dungeon"**. AMC thru/section hiker pass provides 50% off after first night. 2 free baked goods and one free soup at any AMC Hut. 10% off merchandise.

🛏 **Thru-hikers stop at lunchtime for $2 bottomless bowl of soup.**

🚌 **AMC Hiker Shuttle** (see pg. 193)
(outdoors.org/conservation/trails/appalachian-trail-white-mountains.cfm)

White Mountain National Forest (the "Whites")

Passage through the Whites should be planned carefully. It is one of the more heavily visited sections of the AT, and campsites are limited. The trail is rugged, so your pace may be slowed. Weather is dynamic, adding to the dangers of hiking on stretches of trail above treeline.

Weather changes are very dangerous in the Whites and even in summer, people can die. Take adequate cold-weather gear, check weather reports (NH higher summits forecast, https://goo.gl/4unInv), carry maps, and know your options for overnighting. The AMC and Randolph Mountain Club (RMC) maintain camps, which are detailed in the following pages. Most have fees. Have cash on hand even if you do not plan to use them; your plans may change.

There are many trails in the Whites. The AT is the only white-blazed trail, but blazes are scant. There are no blazes in the Great Gulf Wilderness Area. The AT is always coincident w/ another named trail, & the other trail name may be the one you see on signs. Wherever the AT changes from one trail to another, this book uses the notation: "AT: Town Line Tr(>)Glencliff Tr." This means the AT to the south of this point is coincident w/ the Town Line Trail; to the north, the AT joins the Glencliff Trail.

The area within a quarter mile of all AMC & RMC facilities and everything above treeline (trees 8' or less) are part of the Forest Protection Area (FPA). Trails are often marked where they enter or leave the FPA. Do not camp within a FPA, and camp at least 200' from water and trails. Rocks aligned to form a trail boundary (scree walls) are an indication that you should not leave the treadway. Doing so damages fragile plant life.

🚫 No fires in Forest Protection Areas, at Gentian Pond Shelter, or in Great Gulf Wilderness. Camp at designated sites, or 1/4 mi from roads, facilities & water, 200 ft from trail, below alpine zone (where trees are 8' tall or less).

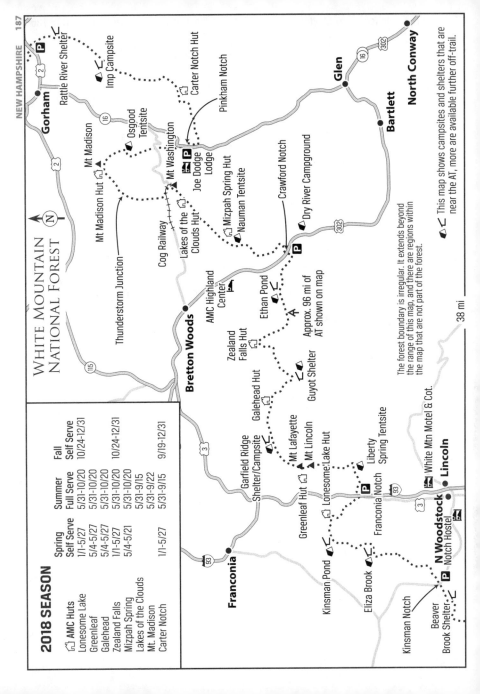

WHITE MOUNTAIN NATIONAL FOREST

N

2018 SEASON

⌂ AMC Huts	Spring Self Serve	Summer Full Serve	Fall Self Serve
Lonesome Lake	1/1–5/27	5/31–10/20	10/24–12/31
Greenleaf	5/4–5/27	5/31–10/20	
Galehead	5/4–5/27	5/31–10/20	
Zealand Falls	1/1–5/27	5/31–10/20	10/24–12/31
Mizpah Spring	5/4–5/21	5/31–9/15	
Lakes of the Clouds		5/31–9/22	
Mt. Madison		5/31–9/15	
Carter Notch	1/1–5/27	5/31–9/15	9/19–12/31

Rattle River Shelter

Imp Campsite

Gorham

Carter Notch Hut

Pinkham Notch

Glen

Bartlett

North Conway

Osgood Tentsite

Mt Madison

Mt Madison Hut ⌂

Mt Washington

Joe Dodge Lodge

Mizpah Spring Hut

Nauman Tentsite

Crawford Notch

Dry River Campground

Thunderstorm Junction

Cog Railway

Lakes of the Clouds Hut ⌂

AMC Highland Center

Bretton Woods

Ethan Pond

Approx 96 mi of AT shown on map

Zealand Falls Hut

Galehead Hut

Guyot Shelter

Garfield Ridge Shelter/Campsite

Mt Lafayette

Mt Lincoln

Lonesome Lake Hut

Liberty Spring Tentsite

Greenleaf Hut ⌂

Franconia Notch

White Mtn Motel & Cot.

Lincoln

Franconia

Kinsman Pond

Eliza Brook

N Woodstock

Notch Hostel

Beaver Brook Shelter

Kinsman Notch

The forest boundary is irregular. It extends beyond the range of this map, and there are regions within the map that are not part of the forest.

◄⌐ This map shows campsites and shelters that are near the AT, more are available further off-trail.

— 38 mi —

397.8	1793.1	**Jeffers Brook Shelter**, Jeffers Brook, footbridge 0.1 south. . . . . . . ☽ ◑ ⊏ (10)	1308
		27.7◄21.0◄15.7◄►6.9►15.9►19.9	
397.7	1793.2	Long Pond Rd⚠ NoBo 0.1E on road AT: Wachipauka Pond Tr◄► Town Line Tr . . .	1329
397.6	1793.3	High St (paved)⚠ NoBo: 0.2W on road. AT: Town Line Trail◄► Glencliff Trail. . . .	1344
397.2	1793.7	Stream. . . . . ◑	1493
396.9	1794.0	Hurricane Trail to east	1661
396.1	1794.8	Stream. . . . . ◑	2484
395.6	1795.3	Spring . . . . ◑	3005

✿ Cattail – A tall (head-high) plant that grows in swampy areas. Characteristic part of the plant looks like a fuzzy cigar impaled lengthwise on a spear.

393.2	1797.7	Mt Moosilauke, Gorge Brook Trail to east . . . . 📷	4802
392.9	1798.0	AT: Glencliff Trail◄► Beaver Brook Trail, Benton Trail to west	4561
391.3	1799.6	Ridge Trail to east	4048
390.9	1800.0	**Beaver Brook Shelter** 27.9◄22.6◄6.9◄►9.0►13.0►28.1. . . . . ☽ ◑ ◖ ⊏ (10)	3732
		Shelter on Beaver Brook trail. Beaver Brook just past shelter.	
389.6	1801.3	Beaver Brook, footbridges, streams . . . . ◑	1880
389.4	1801.5	Lost River Rd, NH 112, Kinsman Notch . . . . . 44.0398,-71.7921 🅿 🏛 ♟ (pg. 193)	1870
		North Woodstock, NH (5.0E), **Lincoln, NH** (6.0E)	
		AT: Beaver Brook Trail◄► Kinsman Ridge Trail	
388.7	1802.2	Dilly Cliff Trail to east	2662
386.1	1804.8	Gordon Pond Trail to east	2682
384.8	1806.1	Mt Wolf east peak, summit to west . . . . 📷	3478
382.9	1808.0	Reel Brook Trail to west.	2624
382.5	1808.4	Powerline	2602
381.9	1809.0	**Eliza Brook Shelter** 31.6◄15.9◄9.0◄►4.0►19.1►24.6 . . . . . . ☽ ◑ ◖ (4) ⊏ (8)	2386
		3 single tentpads, one double. Water source is brook.	
381.1	1809.8	Eliza Brook, parallel to AT for 0.8 mi . . . . ◑	2861
380.5	1810.4	Harrington Pond	3411
379.4	1811.5	South Kinsman Mountain . . . . 📷	4358
378.5	1812.4	North Kinsman Mountain.	4293

378.0	1812.9	Mt Kinsman Trail to west	3842
377.9	1813.0	**Kinsman Pond Shelter** 19.9◀13.0◀4.0◀▶15.1▶20.6▶29.6. . . ☽ ☁ ◆ (4)⌂ (16)	3746

Caretaker, fee $8PP. Treat pond water. Kinsman Ridge Tr to west, Kinsman Pond Tr
to east. AT: Kinsman Ridge Trail◀▶Fishin' Jimmy Trail

377.0	1813.9	Stream. . . . . ◆	2821
376.1	1814.8	Lonesome Lake Hut. . . . . ☽ ◆ ⊨(see AMC notes, pg. 184)	2747

AT: Fishin' Jimmy Tr◀▶ Cascade Brook Tr (east), many other trail intersections

375.1	1815.8	Kinsman Pond Trail to east	2302
374.6	1816.3	Cascade Brook . . . . ◆	2106
373.6	1817.3	Whitehouse Brook . . . . ◆	1649
373.3	1817.6	US 3, I-93, AT underpass. Town east on US 3; better to take side trail (next entry)	1477
373.1	1817.8	Franconia Notch . . . . 44.1002,-71.6825 🅿 (pg. 195)	1432

Paved trail (1.0E) to Flume Visitors Center parking. **North Woodstock, NH** (4.8S)
left from parking area on US 3. Lincoln, NH (1.0E) of North Woodstock.
AT: Cascade Brook Trail◀▶Liberty Springs Trail

372.4	1818.5	Flume Side Trail to east.	1843
371.9	1819.0	Streams . . . . ◆	2067
370.4	1820.5	Liberty Spring Campsite . . . . ☽ ◆ ☁	3905

Overnight fee $8PP, caretaker, 7S and 3D platforms.

370.2	1820.7	AT: Liberty Springs Tr◀▶ Franconia Ridge Tr to west.	4283
368.4	1822.5	Little Haystack Mountain, Falling Waters Trail to west . . . . 📷	4800

NoBo: AT above treeline for next 2.0 miles.

367.7	1823.2	Mt Lincoln, Franconia Ridge . . . . 📷	5089
366.7	1824.2	Mt Lafayette, Greenleaf Hut (1.1W) . . . . 📷 ☽ ◆ (0.2W)⊨	5254

Greenleaf Hut visible from summit of Mt Lafayette. Located down steep Greenleaf
Trail. AT: Franconia Ridge Trail◀▶ Garfield Ridge Trail

365.9	1825.0	Skookumchuck Trail to west	4731
363.6	1827.3	Garfield Pond . . . . ◆	3856
363.2	1827.7	Mt Garfield	4453
363.0	1827.9	Garfield Trail to west	4233
362.8	1828.1	**Garfield Ridge Shelter/Campsite** (0.2W), reliable water . . . ☽ ◆ ☁ (7)⌂ (12)	3923

28.1◀19.1◀15.1◀▶ 5.5▶14.5▶56.5 Overnight fee $8PP, caretaker.

362.3	1828.6	Franconia Brook Trail to east goes steeply down 2.2mi to 13 Falls Campsite..	3427
360.7	1830.2	Gale River Trail to west	3383
360.1	1830.8	Frost Trail to Galehead Hut . . . . ☽ ◆ ⊨	3800

AT: Garfield Ridge Trail◀▶ Twinway Trail

359.3	1831.6	South Twin Mountain, North Twin Spur Trail to west	4902

357.3 **1833.6 Guyot Shelter** 0.7E on Bondcliff Tr, plus 0.3 left on spur trail... ☽ ♦ ◗ (6) ⊏ (14) 4513
24.6◄20.6◄5.5◄►9.0►51.0►57.1 Overnight fee $8PP, caretaker.
357.2 **1833.7** Mt. Guyot, view to east . . . . 📷 4578
356.2 **1834.7** Trail west to summit of Zeacliff Ridge . . . . 📷 4035

354.9 **1836.0** Zeacliff Pond to east 3788
354.5 **1836.4** Zeacliff, Zeacliff Trail to east 3758
354.3 **1836.6** View to east. . . . . 📷 3661
353.8 **1837.1** Whitewall Brook, many streams leading to falls . . . . ♦ 3195
353.4 **1837.5** Lend-A-Hand Trail to west 2667
353.2 **1837.7** Zealand Falls Hut, next to falls . . . . 📷 ☽ ♦ ⊨ 2617
353.0 **1837.9** Ethan Pond Trail to west, AT: Twinway Trail◄► Ethan Pond Trail. 2459

351.6 **1839.3** Zeacliff Trail to east. 2445

350.8 **1840.1** Stream, Thoreau Falls to east . . . . ♦ 2464
350.6 **1840.3** Footbridge, stream . . . . ♦ 2464
350.3 **1840.6** Stream, Shoal Pond Trail to east . . . . ♦ 2509

349.6 **1841.3** Footbridge, stream . . . . ♦ 2626

348.3 **1842.6 Ethan Pond Campsite** (0.2W), Ethan Pond, inlet brook to pond ☽ ♦ ◗ ⊏ (8) 2855
29.6◄14.5◄9.0◄►42.0►48.1►61.8
Overnight fee $8PP, caretaker, 3S and 2D platforms.
347.2 **1843.7** Willey Range Trail to west, stream north on AT . . . . ♦ 2621
347.0 **1843.9** Kedron Flume Trail to west 2457

345.9 **1845.0** Ripley Falls 0.5E 1558
345.7 **1845.2** RR tracks, parking, AT: Ethan Pond Trail◄► road walk . . . . 44.1672,-71.3860 🅿 1436
AT follows paved parking driveway 0.3 to US 302.
345.4 **1845.5** Crawford Notch, US 302. AT: road walk◄► Webster Cliff Trail . . . . . . **(pg. 198)** 1277
345.3 **1845.6** Saco River (treat), Saco River Trail to east, Sam Willey Trail to west. . . . . . ♦ 1261
344.6 **1846.3** Stream. . . . . ◌ 1939

343.0 **1847.9** Webster Cliffs, views from many spots along 0.5 mile traverse . . . . 📷 3288

342.1 **1848.8** Mt Webster, Webster Jackson Trail to west, NoBo: AT to east . . . . 📷 3910

340.7 **1850.2** Mt Jackson, Webster Jackson Trail to west . . . . 📷 4052
⚠ SoBo hikers turn east (left)

339.0 **1851.9** Mizpah cutoff to west, Mizpah Spring Hut to east, Nauman Campsite . . ♦ ◗ ⊨ 3800
Tent site next to hut, overnight fee $8PP.

338.2	1852.7	Mt Pierce (Mt Clinton) . . . . 📷	4312
338.1	1852.8	AT: Webster Cliff Trail ◄► Crawford Path.	4254
337.0	1853.9	Mt Eisenhower Loop Trail west to summit. . . . . 📷	4442
336.4	1854.5	Mt Eisenhower Loop Trail west to summit. . . . . 📷	4480
336.3	1854.6	Mt Eisenhower Trail to east	4499
335.4	1855.5	Mt Franklin . . . . 📷	5004
335.1	1855.8	Mt Monroe Loop Trail west to summit . . . . 📷	5100
334.4	1856.5	Lakes of the Clouds Hut⚠ See map, several trails in area . . . ☽ ♦ ⌷ (pg. 198)	5097
334.4	1856.5	Mt Monroe Loop Trail west to summit . . . . 📷	5041
333.5	1857.4	Davis Path to east, Westside Trail to west	5585
333.1	1857.8	AT: Crawford Path ◄► Trinity Heights Connector	6156
332.9	1858.0	Mt Washington . . . . 📷 (pg. 198)	6288
332.7	1858.2	AT: Trinity Heights Connector ◄► Gulfside Trail	6104
332.5	1858.4	Cross Cog Railroad, stay west on Gulfside Trail	5949
332.0	1858.9	Westside Trail to west	5502
331.7	1859.2	Mt Clay Loop Trail to east. 📷	5432
330.9	1860.0	Mt Clay Loop Trail to east, Sphinx Trail to east . . . . 📷	5021
330.1	1860.8	Mt Jefferson Loop Trail, summit 0.3W . . . . 📷	5402
329.7	1861.2	Six Husband Trail 0.4W to Mt Jefferson . . . . 📷	5334
329.2	1861.7	Edmands Col, Gulfside Spring 50 yards east on Edmands Col cutoff, ... ♦	4959
		Randolph Path & Mt Jefferson loop to west.	
328.6	1862.3	Israel Ridge Path to RMC Perch Shelter (0.9W), $7 fee . . . . ☽ ♦ ⬤ (4) ⌐ (8)	5263
328.5	1862.4	Peabody Spring to east near boulder . . . . ♦	5228
328.1	1862.8	Thunderstorm Junction, RMC cabins to west . . . . (pg. 198)	5500
327.5	1863.4	Airline Trail, King Ravine Trail to west	5148
327.2	1863.7	Madison Spring Hut, Valley Way Trail 0.6W to VW Tent Site, no fee . . . . ♦ ⬤ ⌷	4800
		AT: Gulfside Trail ◄► Osgood Trail	
326.7	1864.2	Mt Madison, Watson Path to west. . . . . 📷	5366
326.4	1864.5	Howker Ridge Trail to east	5113
326.1	1864.8	Parapet Trail to east, Daniel Webster Trail to west	4878

> ⚠ There are no blazes in the Great Gulf Wilderness area, approximately from
> Mt. Madison to Auto Rd. See, "Map of Trail Intersections," (pg. 198)

324.1	1866.8	Osgood Tent Site to west, no fee.⚠ AT: Osgood Trail ◄► Osgood Cutoff. . ☽ ♦ ⬤	2555
323.9	1867.0	Stream. . . . . ♦	2542
323.5	1867.4	AT: Osgood Cutoff ◄► Great Gulf Trail to east . . . . (see map pg. 197)	2341
323.5	1867.4	⚠ Parapet Brook, AT: Great Gulf Trail ◄► Madison Gulf Trail to west. . . ♦	2329
323.4	1867.5	⚠ West branch of Peabody River, suspension bridge. Great Gulf Tr to east . . ♦	2300
322.9	1868.0	Stream. . . . . ♦	2412
322.0	1868.9	Stream. . . . . ♦	2582
321.5	1869.4	Lowes Bald Spot 0.1W . . . . 📷	2849
321.4	1869.5	Mt Washington Auto Rd . . . . 44.2815,-71.2534 🅿	2734
		AT: Madision Gulf Trail ◄► Old Jackson Rd	
321.2	1869.7	Nelson Crag Trail and Raymond Path to east	2679
320.4	1870.5	George's Gorge Trail to west	2570
320.1	1870.8	Peabody River, four other trails cross the AT from here to Pinkham Notch . . . ♦	2271
319.4	1871.5	NH 16, Pinkham Notch . . . . 44.2569,-71.2526 🅿 (pg. 198)	2050
		Gorham, NH (10.7W), AT: Old Jackson Rd ◄► Lost Pond Trail	

1782.4   NH 25A, GOV. MELDRIM THOMSON SCENIC HWY

🏠 **Mt Cube Sugar Farm** (1.9W) 603.353.4111 Hiker Friendly. Owned by the Thomson family. Store is not manned, but caretaker makes frequent stops. Hikers may tent outside or may be allowed to stay in the sugar house. Sometimes more is offered. Open yr-round, pets welcome.

» *Wentworth, NH 03282* (4.3E on NH 25A, then *right 0.5 on NH 25*),
🏪 603.764.9444, M-F 9:30-12:30 & 1:30-4:30, Sa 7:15-12

🏪 **Shawnee's General Store** (5E) Open daily 5-8.

1784.2   CAPE MOONSHINE RD

🏠 ⊕ ♦ **Dancing Bones Intentional Community** (1.4E) 802.440.1612 Water & free camping, composting toilets & good conversation. Residential community. Please be respectful when using shared facilities. Smoking permitted in designated areas. Pets welcome on a case by case basis.(dancingbones.net)

🍴 🍽 **Greenhouse Food & Spirits** (0.7W) 603.764.5708 Th, F: 3-11p, Sa: 12-10, Su: 12-9p. Open mic Th. Band on Fr & Sa.

» *Warren, NH 03279* (4E)

1787.6   LAKE TARLETON RD, NH 25C

🛒 ⊕ 🏕 🍽 🅿 📶 **Scenic View Campground** (4.8E)   603.764.9380 info@scenicviewnh.com Family campground at the base of the White Mountains. Primitive & full hook-up sites avail as well as water & electric. Heated swimming pool in season (mid May - Labor Day). Laundry on site 8:30-8:30.(scenicviewnh.com)

🏪 **Tedeschi Food Shop** (3.7E) 603.764.9002 Open daily 5-11. Grocery w/ produce, deli Su-Th 6:30a-7p, F-Sa 6:30a-8p w/sandwiches & pizza.

🍴 ⊕ 🍦 **Moose Scoops** (3.4E) 603.764.9134 Open seasonally. Ice cream, soda, & hiking shirts. Free WiFi, wireless cell signal extender.

🍴 **Calamity Jane's Restaurant** (3.5E) M, Tu, Th: 6a-2p, F, Sa: 6a-8p, Su: 8a-2p, W: clsd.

📶 📖 **Library** (4.6E) 603.764.9072 M-Tu 10-2, W 3-7, Sa 10-1. No WiFi password, so you can use it after hrs.

🔧 **Burning Bush Hardware** (4.3E) 603.764.9496 Open 7 days.

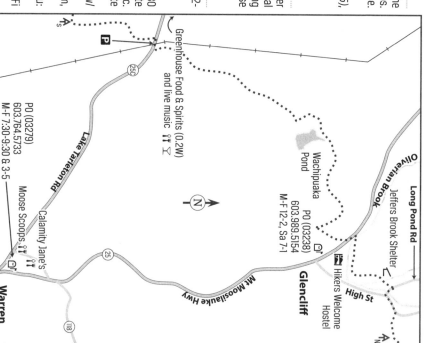

Greenhouse Food & Spirits (0.2W) and live music 🍴 🍽

P

25C

Lake Tarleton Rd

⊗N

25

118

PO (03279) 603.764.5733 M-F 7:30-9:30 & 3-5 Sa 7:30-12

Calamity Jane's 🍴 🍽   Moose Scoops 🍴 🍽   🏪 Tedeschi's

Warren

Mt Moosilauke Hwy

Wachipuaka Pond

PO (03238) 603.989.5154 M-F 12-2, Sa 7-1

Glencliff

High St

🏠 Hikers Welcome Hostel

Oliverian Brook

Jeffers Brook Shelter

Long Pond Rd

⟵ Long Pond Rd

↑N

Randolph Mountain Club (RMC)

Maintains the section of the AT from Edmands Col to Madison Hut and four shelters in the Northern Presidentials. Per-person fees for non-members: Gray Knob or Crag Camp \$20, The Perch or Log Cabin \$10. Fees must be paid in cash for stays at Gray Knob, Crag Camp and The Perch. Persons without cash can stay at the Log Cabin and will receive a receipt to mail in their fee. There is a caretaker year-round at Gray Knob if you need assistance or have questions. During the summer months, a second caretaker is in residence at Crag Camp. A caretaker visits Crag Camp and The Perch every evening throughout the year.

Shelter use is first-come, first-served; no reservations. Weekends are busy. If space is not avail., be prepared to camp. Camping is not permitted within a quarter mile of RMC shelters.

There is no trash disposal. Carry in, carry out. Please keep noise to a minimum after 10pm. The use of cell phones and portable TVs is not permitted. Group size is limited to ten. There is no smoking inside RMC facilities. When a camp is full, all guests are asked to limit their stay to two consecutive nights. Outdoor wood campfires are not allowed at any of the camps. Dogs are allowed at RMC's facilities, but they should be under voice control at all times.

» *Glencliff, NH 03238 (0.3E)*

🛏🏠◐🛍👤⛺🍴🍽🛒🛜 ⊠ **Hikers Welcome Hostel** (0.3E) 603.989.0040 hikerswelcome@yahoo.com Open mid May - Oct 1. Bunk \$25 & Camping \$20 incl shower. Shower only w/towel: \$3, laundry: \$3 wash/\$3 dry. No reservations req'd. Over 30 bunks avail. Snacks, sodas, chips, popcorn, m'wave pizza, & ice cream. HikersWelcome tees for sale. All hikers (even non-guests) are welcome to hang out & enjoy huge DVD library. Slackpacking over Moosilauke daily. Add'l shuttles avail upon request. Coleman/alcohol/oz. Tools to help w/gear repair & selection of used gear avail, particularly winter wear. Pet friendly. Mail for both guests & non-guests. (USPS): PO Box 25 Glencliff, NH 03238. (FedEx/UPS): 1396 NH Rt 25, Glencliff, NH 03238. ⟨hikerswelcome.com⟩

» *Warren, NH 03279 (5E) (see services on pg. 192)*

🚌 **AMC Hiker Shuttle** 603.466.2727 amclodging@outdoors.org Schedule on-line: Operates Jun - mid Sep daily, & wkends & holidays through mid Oct. Stops at Lincoln, Franconia Notch (Liberty Springs Trailhead), Crawford Notch (Webster Cliff Trailhead), Highland Center, Pinkham Notch, & Gorham; \$23 for non-members. Walk-ons if space avail. ⟨outdoors.org/lodging-camping/lodging-shuttle.cfm⟩

🏕🛏⚡👤⛺ **Lost River Valley Campground** (3E) 603.745.8321, 800.370.5678 info@lostriver.com Cabin \$65S, 75D, primitive camp sites \$22. Pets allowed but not in cabins. Showers, coin laundry, & pay phone. Open mid-May to Colum Day 8-9, quiet 10p-8a. Owner, Jim Kelly. Mail: 951 Lost River Rd, North Woodstock, NH 03262. ⟨lostriver.com⟩

🍴 **Lost River Gorge** (0.5E) 603.745.8031 Tourist attraction featuring a boulder jumble similar to Mahoosuc Notch. Gift store w/snacks, coffee, soda. Open early May - late Oct.

» *North Woodstock, NH 03262 (4.8E)*
» *Lincoln, NH (5.8E)*

ℹ **White Mountains Visitor Ctr** (6.8E) 603.745.8720 Area info/maps/snacks. Open 7 days, 8:30a-5:30p. Earlier/later - winter/summer

🛏ℹ🍴🛜 **Woodstock Inn & Brewery** (6.2E) 10% Discount for thru-hikers. Prices seasonal. Stay incl full b'fast. Pet rooms avail.

🛏🛁♿🛜⊠ **Inn 32** (6.4E) 603.745.2416 info@inn32.com \$69/up w/ pool & grills. Laundry, Wayne's Market, bank & Post Office across street. No pets. Walk to restaurants & brewery. Mail: PO Box 198, 180 Main St, N Woodstock, NH 03262⟨Inn32.com⟩

🛏◐🛜⊠ **Autumn Breeze** (6.4E) 603.745.8549 Yr-round. Hiker friendly. \$65 hiker rate incl tax, laundry, shuttle to/fr trail until 5p. Shuttle to town if avail. CC ok.

» *Lincoln, NH (services cont'd on pg. 195...)*

NORTH WOODSTOCK, NH

44.0198,-71.6977

AT crosses at intersection of ③ and ⑨③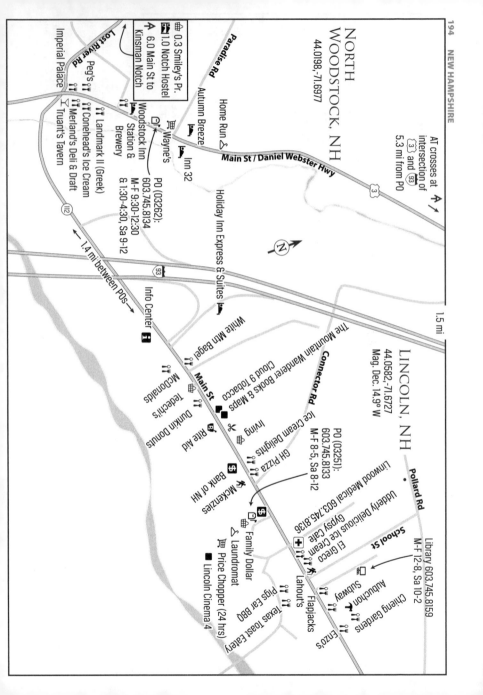
5.3 mi from PO

Paradise Rd

Autumn Breeze

Home Run

Main St / Daniel Webster Hwy

Wayne's

Inn 32

Woodstock Inn
Station &
Brewery

PO (03262):
603.745.8134
M-F 9:30-12:30
& 1:30-4:30, Sa 9-12

⌂ 0.3 Smiley's Pt.
⛺ 1.0 Notch Hostel
Ⓐ 6.0 Main St to
Kinsman Notch

Lost River Rd

Imperial Palace

Peg's

Landmark II (Greek)

Conehead's Ice Cream

Merland's Deli & Draft

Truant's Tavern

1.4 mi between POs →

Holiday Inn Express & Suites

112

93

Info Center

White Mtn Bagel

McDonald's

Tedechi's

Dunkin Donuts

Rite Aid

Irving

Bank of NH

McKenzies

Main St

The Mountain Wanderer Books & Maps

Cloud 9 Tobacco

Ice Cream Delights

GH Pizza

Connector Rd

LINCOLN, NH

44.0582,-71.6727
Mag. Dec. 14.9° W

PO (0325l):
603.745.8133
M-F 8-5, Sa 8-12

Linwood Medical 603.745.8136

Udderly Delicious Ice Cream

Gypsy Cafe

El Greco

Pollard Rd

Library 603.745.8159
M-F 12-8, Sa 10-2

Chieng Gardens

Subway

Audubon

School St

Enzo's

Flapjacks

Lahout's

Family Dollar

Laundromat

Price Chopper (24 hrs)

Lincoln Cinema 4

Texas Toast Eatery

Pigs Ear BBQ

1.5 mi

» Lincoln, NH (...services cont'd from pg. 193)

🏠🏨🅿️🛏️⛺📶🏧🍴✉️ **The Notch Hostel** (5E) 603.348.1483 Bunk in large, white farmhouse on NH 112. Ideally situated for slackpack between Kinsman & Franconia Notch. \$33PP incl bunk, linens, towel, shower, group laundry svc, coffee/tea, make-ur-own pancakes, computer, kitchen, fridge, & large yard. Beer/wine ok in moderation. No liquor. Small store: ice cream, pizza, snacks, soda, & fuel. Rental bikes \$5/day. Check-in 4p-9p, (earlier ok w/text/call: follow welcome sheet if no one home). Open most of the yr; shuttles run Jun 1 - Oct 1, Su-Th for guests w/reserv. For shuttle, send same-day text confirmation w/ reservation name, p/u time, & location. Town & trailhead shuttles depart from hostel 7a, 10a, 3p, 6p; Kinsman Notch (NH 112) p/u +5 min; Flume Visitors Ctr p/u +25min, Town +40min. Mail: 324 Lost River Rd, North Woodstock, NH 03262. Reserve on web, text, or call.(notchhostel.com)

🏠🏨🅿️📶✉️ **White Mountain Motel & Cottages** (7.6E) 603.745.8924 whitemountainmotel@gmail.com Seasonal rates \$69 - \$124. Shuttle to/from Kinsman Notch & Franconia Notch trail heads, & to town center for groceries, lunch, laundromat, internet cafe, ATM, outfitters, & PO... all in the same plaza. Seasonal heated pool, gas grill & fire pit on site is bordered by the Pemigewasset River. Over 500 DVDs w/loaner DVD players for in-room movie viewing. White Mountain trail maps & guide books in stock.(whitemountainmotel.com)

🧖‍♀️📶 **Wise Way Wellness Center** (15.1E) 603.726.7600 Open May-Oct. \$89 for 1-2 persons in cabin, incl light b'fast. Cabin is 10 mi south of Lincoln in Thornton, NH. No shuttle avail. Serene rustic cabin. No TV/ phone. Bathroom & shower inside adjacent building. Pool, mini-fridge & grill. Licensed Massage by appt. Add'l svcs: sauna & outdoor Epsom salt bath. No smoking or pets. Cash/checks/PayPal.

🏪 **Lahout's Summit Shop** (7.6E) 603.745.2882 M-F 9:30-5:30, Sa 9-5:30, Su 9-5, full svc outfitter, packs, Coleman/alcohol/oz, canister, frz-dried food.(lahouts.com)

🏪 **Fadden's General Store & Sugar House** (6.2E) 603.745.8371 Ice cream, fudge & more. Open yr-round, daily 9-5.

🍴🍺🏧 **Wayne's Market** (6.3E) Open yr-round, daily 6a-10p. ATM, large beer selection. Deli closes 9:30p. Cheap sandwiches.

🍴 **Woodstock Station** restaurant, outdoor bar, & a micro-brewery on site.(woodstockinnh.com)

✉️ **Mountain Wanderer** (7.1E) Open most days 10a-5:30p. Book & map store has everything you need to navigate the Whites.(mountainwanderer.com)

1817.8 FRANCONIA NOTCH

» East of Franconia Notch

🅷 🏠🍴🚻✉️ **Flume Visitor Center** (0.5E) 603.745.8391 Cafeteria open daily early May - late Oct, 9-5, serves only pastries at b'fast, hamburgers, hot dogs, pizza remainder of day. Mail (FedEx or UPS ONLY - no USPS): 852 US Rt 3, Lincoln, NH 03251. Mail will be transported from there to Flume Visitor Center.

🚌 **The Shuttle Connection** 603.745.3140 Shuttles between town & Kinsman or Franconia Notch or to bus terminals & airports throughout NH.

🏨🅿️✉️ **Profile Motel & Cottages** (3.1E) 603.745.2759 Fridge & m'wave in room, grills & tables outside, open 7a-10p. Mail: 391 US 3, Lincoln, NH 03251.

⛰️🏨📶✉️ **Mt. Liberty Motel** (3.7E) 603.745.3600 ppeterson@ mtlibertylodging.com Open May-Oct. \$85+ in season, \$59+ off season incl p/u & ret from Kinsman/Franconia Notch & town shuttle. Laundry \$5. No smoking/pets. CC Ok. Mail: 10 Liberty Rd, Lincoln, NH 03251 (mtlibertymotel.com)

» West of Franconia Notch

⛺🏕️ **Lafayette Campground** (2.2W) 603.823.9513 Tent sites \$25D. Limited store. No pets. Quiet 10p. Open mid May-Colum Day. Mail: Franconia State Pk, Lafayette Campground, Franconia, NH 03580.

» Franconia, NH 03580 (11W of Franconia Notch)
📞603.823.5611, M-F 8:30-1 & 2-5, Sa 9-12

🏠🏨📶✉️ **Gale River Motel** (11.6W) 603.823.5655, 800.255.7989 info@ galerivermotel.com \$50-\$200, pets w/approval, laundry wash \$1, dry \$1, Coleman/ oz. Free p/u & ret to trail w/stay, longer shuttles for a fee. Open yr-round. CC ok. Mail (fee for non-guest): 1 Main St Franconia, NH 03580 (galerivermotel.com)

🏪 **Franconia Village Store** (10.1W) 603.823.7782 Open Su-Th 6-9,F-Sa 6-10, deli.

🍴 **Mac's Market** (10.1W) 603.823.7795 Open 7 days 7-8.

📶 **Abbie Greenleaf Library** (9.9W) 603.823.8424 M-Tu 2-6; W 10-12 & 2-6; Th-F 2-5; Sa 10-1.

318.4 **1872.5** AT: Lost Pond Trail◀▶ Wildcat Ridge Trail 2009
318.0 **1872.9** View . . . . 🖽 2860

317.4 **1873.5** Rocky crevasse, stairs 3273

316.7 **1874.2** Wildcat Mountain peak E 4066
316.4 **1874.5** Wildcat Mountain peak D, observation tower, ski gondola 0.1 north . . . . . . 🙥 3990
Gondola rides to/from the AT, $12 round trip, restaurant at base, open Jul-Oct.

315.3 **1875.6** Wildcat Mountain peak C . . . . 🖽 4278

314.4 **1876.5** Wildcat Mountain peak A . . . . 🖽 4422
313.9 **1877.0** Spring . . . . ♦ 3675
313.7 **1877.2** AT: Wildcat Ridge Trail◀▶ Nineteen Mile Brook Trail to east 3401
313.5 **1877.4** AT: Nineteen Mile Brook Trail◀▶ Carter Moriah Trail, Carter Notch Hut (0.1E) ♦🛏 3303
312.8 **1878.1** Spring to west . . . . ♦ 4308

312.3 **1878.6** Carter Dome, Rainbow Trail to east . . . . 🖽 4832
311.9 **1879.0** Black Angel Trail to east, Carter Dome Trail to west 4619
311.4 **1879.5** Mt Hight, view . . . . 🖽 4653

310.9 **1880.0** Zeta Pass, two Carter Dome trailheads to west 3890

308.8 **1882.1** Middle Carter Mountain, view . . . . 🖽 4610

308.2 **1882.7** North Carter Mountain, North Carter Trail to west, just south of summit . . . . 🖽 4539

306.3 **1884.6** **Imp Campsite** (0.2W) 56.5◀51.0◀42.0◀▶6.1▶19.8▶25.0 . . . ♦ ☽ ☁ (5)⌂ (10) 3326
Overnight fee $8PP, caretaker, composting privy.
305.6 **1885.3** Stony Brook Trail to west, Moriah Brook Trail to east . . . . 🅰 3126

304.2 **1886.7** Mt Moriah, summit to west⚠. AT: Carter Moriah Trail◀▶Kenduskeag Trail . . . 🖽 3976
(sparsely blazed for next 3 miles)

302.9 **1888.0** ⚠ AT: Kenduskeag Trail◀▶ Rattle River Trail . . . . ♦ 3369
302.5 **1888.4** Stream . . . . ♦ 2851

301.8 **1889.1** Rattle River . . . . ♦ 2004

300.4 **1890.5** East Rattle River, multiple streams . . . . ♦ 1343
300.2 **1890.7** **Rattle River Shelter** 57.1◀48.1◀6.1◀▶13.7▶18.9▶23.3 . . . . ☽ ♦ ☁ ⌂ (8) 1258
No fee. Water source is Rattle River. Gently sloping trail from shelter to US 2.

298.9 **1892.0** Stream . . . . ♦ 962
298.8 **1892.1** Fork in trail, AT to east (not over bridge) 901

298.3	1892.6	AT 0.1W on US 2, **Gorham, NH** (3.6W) . . . . 44.4008,-71.1098 🅿 (pg. 203)	780
298.2	1892.7	AT east on North Rd. . . . . 44.4064,-71.1168 🅿	794
297.6	1893.3	AT west on Hogan Rd (gravel), parking .25W . . . . 44.407,-71.117 🅿	783

| 296.7 | 1894.2 | Brook . . . . ♦ | 1232 |

> ◤ ME camping: Dispersed camping is permitted except for specific prohibitions. Look for local postings at signposts & shelters; prohibitions listed in this guidebook are not comprehensive. Camping at non-designated locations is prohibited above treeline (where trees are less than 8' tall).

| 294.7 | 1896.2 | Mt Hayes, Mahoosuc Trail to west . . . . 📷 | 2555 |

| 293.1 | 1897.8 | View . . . . 📷 | 2341 |

| 292.5 | 1898.4 | Cascade Mountain . . . . | 2631 |

| 291.4 | 1899.5 | Trident Col Campsite (0.2W), no fee, spring on side trail . . . . ☽♦⌂ | 2020 |
| 291.1 | 1899.8 | Spring . . . . ♦ | 1909 |

| 290.4 | 1900.5 | Page Pond, ⚠ NoBo hikers turn East at Page Pond (NOT marked). . . . . . . ♦ | 2220 |

289.8	1901.1	Wocket Ledge, view. . . . . 📷	2642
289.3	1901.6	Stream. . . . . ♦	2589
288.6	1902.3	Dream Lake, Peabody Brook Trail to east . . . . ♦	2610

286.5	1904.4	**Gentian Pond Shelter/Campsite** (0.2E). . . . . ☽♦⌂⌐ (14)	2162
		61.8◄19.8◄13.7◄►5.2►9.6►14.7 Junction of Mahoosuc Trail (AT) and Austin Brook Trail, inlet brook of Gentian Pond. 3S and 1D platforms.	
285.5	1905.4	Stream. . . . . ♦	2246
285.1	1905.8	Stream. . . . . ♦	2505

| 283.7 | 1907.2 | Mt Success . . . . 📷 | 3565 |

| 283.1 | 1907.8 | Success Trail to west . . . . | 3164 |

> ⚷ Campfires are only allowed along the AT in ME within fireplaces at designated campsites.

281.8	1909.1	**NH-ME** border.	2972
281.3	1909.6	**Carlo Col Shelter and Campsite** (0.3W), on Carlo Col Trail. . . . . ☽♦⌂⌐ (16)	3210
		25.0◄18.9◄5.2◄►4.4►9.5►16.4 Platforms 3S and 2D, bear box, no fee.	
280.9	1910.0	Mt Carlo	3565

279.5	1911.4	Goose Eye Mountain west peak, Goose Eye Mtn Trail to west . . . . 📷	3823
279.2	1911.7	Wright Trail to east on blue blazed trail	3633
279.1	1911.8	Goose Eye Mountain east peak . . . . 📷	3790
278.8	1912.1	Wright Trail to east	3464

1845.5   CRAWFORD NOTCH, US 302

⊞ 🄰 **AMC Hiker Shuttle** (see pg. 193)

🄰 🚿⛺ **Dry River Campground** (1.8E) 603.374.2272 Tent sites $25 for 2 adults & children. Shelter $30D, $10EAP. Pets allowed, coin laundry & showers. Sometimes rides avail. Quiet 10p-8a. Open May-late Oct, reduced svcs through Nov.

⊞🄰⊕ **Crawford Notch General Store & Campground** (3.4E) 603.374.279 Cabins $78-98, tent sites (hold 2 tents) $36. 9% Lodging tax. Store carries hiker foods, ice cream, & beer. Open mid May - mid Oct.(crawfordnotch.com) closes earlier.

⊞🄰⊕🛈📶 ⊠ **AMC Highland Center** (4W) 603.278.4453 Rates seasonal & are highest in summer & on holidays. Lodge $50-$150PP! up incl dinner & b'fast. Shapleigh Bunkhouse $86 w/dinner & b'fast, $58 for bunkhouse only. Rates lower for AMC members. No pets/smoking. AMC Shuttle stops daily mid Jun to Colum Day. Store sells snacks, sodas, some clothing & canister fuel. Mail (include ETA): Route 302, Bretton Woods, NH 03575. Only UPS reliable. USPS & Fedex do not deliver here.

🛈♻ **Willey House** (1W) Snack bar open 9:30-5, 7 days, wkend before Mem Day - wkend after Colum Day. Located in Crawford Notch SP.

» *Bretton Woods, NH* (8W)

🔥 **Drummonds Mountain Shop** (7.9W) 603.278.7547 Open 7 days yr-round 8a-5p. Boots, packs, rain gear, hiking foods, stoves & fuel.

🛈🍴 **Fabyan's Station** (7.8W) 603.278.2222 Open yr-round 11:30-10 (limited hrs in winter).

1856.5   LAKES OF THE CLOUDS HUT

🄰🔶⊕ **Lakes of the Clouds Hut** 603.466.2727 AMClodging@outdoors.org Lodging & WFS (see AMC notes, pg. 186). Also "The Dungeon," a bunkroom avail to 6 thru-hikers for $10PP w/access to hut restroom & the common area. When the hut is closed, The Dungeon serves as an emergency shelter.(outdoors.org)

1858.0   MT WASHINGTON, NH

🚂 **Cog Railway** 603.278.5404 Runs hourly. Wkends only Apr, May & Nov, 7 days Jun-Oct. One-way tickets $48 (if space-avail) sold at summit station. Base station 3 mi away near Bretton Woods, NH.(thecog.com)

⊕🛈🍴 **Sherman Adams Bldg** 603.466.3347 Second highest peak on the A.T., part of Mt. Washington State Pk. Open 8a-5p mid-May to Colum Day, sometimes opens earlier on wkends in season. Snack bar 9a-6p, sometimes

1862.8   THUNDERSTORM JUNCTION

🛖 **Crag Camp Cabin** (1.1W) On spur trail, **Gray Knob Cabin** (1.2W) on Lowe Path, $20 fee for either. If you camp along these side trails, it must be at least 0.25 mi from either cabin.

1864.2 - 1869.5   MAP OF TRAIL INTERSECTIONS

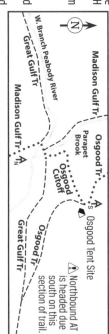

W. Branch Peabody River

Great Gulf Tr

Madison Gulf Tr

Madison Gulf Tr

Osgood Tr

Parapet Brook

Osgood Cutoff

Osgood Tr N

Osgood Tent Site

⚠️ Northbound AT is headed due south on this section of trail.

Great Gulf Tr

1871.5   NH 16, PINKHAM NOTCH

⊞🛈🍴🔥📶⊠ **Pinkham Notch Visitor Center & Joe Dodge Lodge** 603.466.2721 Rates seasonal & are highest in summer & during holidays. Bunkroom starting at $63PP w/o meals; $69 w/b'fast; $89 w/dinner & b'fast. Pvt rooms also avail. Rates on lodging & meals discounted for AMC members. Meals avail to non-guests; AYCE b'fast 6:30-9 daily, a la carte lunch, family-style dinner Sa-Th at 6p, Fr dinner buffet. Open yr-round. Coin-op shower avail 24hrs, $2 towel rental. No pets. Vending machines. Coleman/alcohol/oz, canister fuel. Shuttle 7:30a daily, CC ok. Mail: AMC Visitor Center, c/o Front Desk, PO Box 298 Gorham, NH 03581.(outdoors.org)

» *Gorham, NH 03581* (10.7W) (See services at US 2, Rattle River Trailhead)

National Weather Service Wind Chill Chart

		Temperature (°F)																
		35	30	25	20	15	10	5	0	-5	-10	-15	-20	-25
Wind (mph)	5	31	25	19	13	7	1	-5	-11	-16	-22	-28	-34	-40
	10	27	21	15	9	3	-4	-10	-16	-22	-28	-35	-41	-47
	15	25	19	13	6	0	-7	-13	-19	-26	-32	-39	-45	-51
	20	24	17	11	4	-2	-9	-15	-22	-29	-35	-42	-48	-55
	25	23	16	9	3	-4	-11	-17	-24	-31	-37	-44	-51	-58
	30	22	15	8	1	-5	-12	-19	-26	-33	-39	-46	-53	-60
	35	21	14	7	0	-7	-14	-21	-27	-34	-41	-48	-55	-62
	40	20	13	6	-1	-8	-15	-22	-29	-36	-43	-50	-57	-64

Ways to Give Back
Help Conserve & Maintain the Trail

The most essential service you can perform is to volunteer to maintain the A.T. & overnight sites, or to monitor boundaries and resource conditions. To find out how or where you may assist.

Visit appalachiantrail.org or check with your local trail-maintaining club.

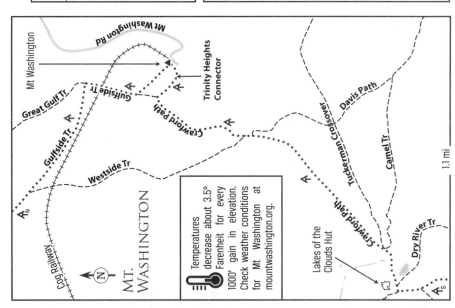

Temperatures decrease about 3.5° Farenheit for every 1000' gain in elevation. Check weather conditions for Mt Washington at mountwashington.org.

277.9 **1913.0** Goose Eye Mountain north peak. 📷 3678

276.9 **1914.0** **Full Goose Shelter and Campsite** 3S and 1D platforms . . . . . . 🌙🌢☁️⌐(12) 2999
23.3◄9.6◄4.4◄►5.1►12.0►15.5 No Fee, stream behind shelter.
276.4 **1914.5** Fulling Mill Mountain south peak 3395

275.3 **1915.6** Mahoosuc Notch south end, Mahoosuc Notch Trail to west 2447
Most difficult or fun mile of the AT. Make way through jumbled pit of boulders.

274.2 **1916.7** Mahoosuc Notch north end, Bull Branch, campsite . . . . 🌢☁️ 2116

273.2 **1917.7** Spring. . . . . 🌢 3265
272.7 **1918.2** Mahoosuc Arm 3770
272.0 **1918.9** Speck Pond brook . . . . 🌢 3420
271.8 **1919.1** **Speck Pond Shelter & Campsite** . . . . 🌙🌢☁️⌐(8) 3429
14.7◄9.5◄5.1◄►6.9►10.4►20.9 Overnight fee $8PP, caretaker. Spring down
Speck Pond Trail just beyond caretaker's yurt. 3S and 3D platforms
270.7 **1920.2** Intersection, AT north on Old Speck Tr., south on Mahoosuc Tr. . . . . 📷🧍 4065
Side Trail 0.3E to Old Speck summit and observation tower.

268.4 **1922.5** Eyebrow Trail to west. 2508
268.1 **1922.8** Stream. . . . . 🌢 2376

267.3 **1923.6** Eyebrow Trail to west. 1522
267.2 **1923.7** Grafton Notch, ME 26. . . . . 44.5897,-70.9467 🅿️🗑️🌙**(pg. 208)** 1495

266.4 **1924.5** Stream, Table Rock Trail to east . . . . 🌢 2106

⚠️ **Two Night Camping Limit from Grafton Notch to Katahdin**

264.9 **1926.0** **Baldpate Lean-to** (0.1E), stream next to lean-to . . . . 🌙🌢☁️⌐(8) 2661
16.4◄12.0◄6.9◄►3.5►14.0►26.8
264.1 **1926.8** Baldpate west peak . . . . 📷 3662

263.2 **1927.7** Baldpate east peak, Grafton Loop Trail . . . . 📷 3810

📶 **(NoBo) Poor cell reception at East B Hill Rd, consider calling ahead if you need ride.**

261.4 **1929.5** **Frye Notch Lean-to**, Frye Brook in front of lean-to . . . . 🌙🌢⌐(6) 2308
15.5◄10.4◄3.5◄►10.5►23.3►31.6

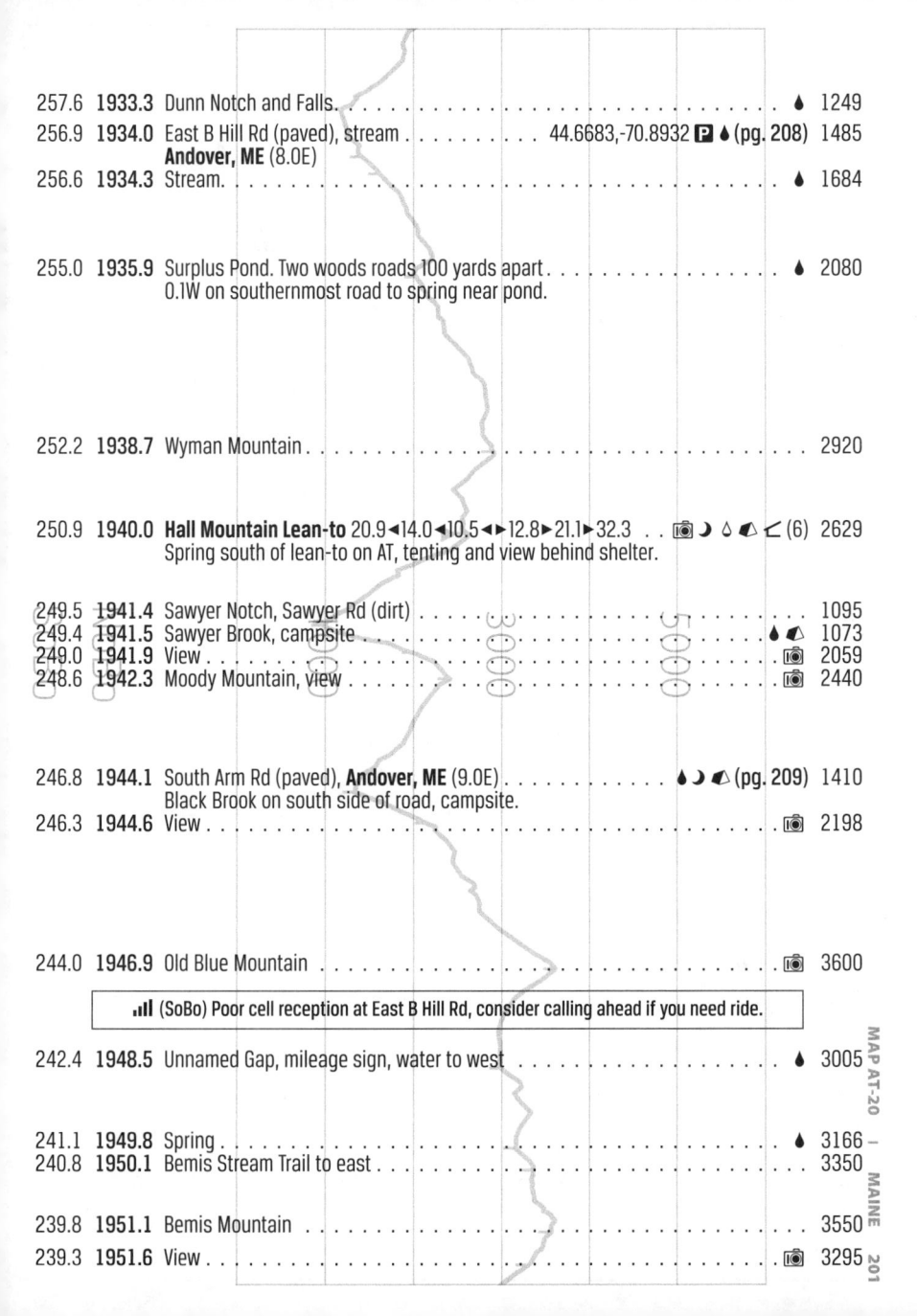

257.6 **1933.3** Dunn Notch and Falls. . . . . ♦ 1249
256.9 **1934.0** East B Hill Rd (paved), stream . . . . 44.6683,-70.8932 🅿 ♦ (pg. 208) 1485
        Andover, ME (8.0E)
256.6 **1934.3** Stream. . . . . ♦ 1684

255.0 **1935.9** Surplus Pond. Two woods roads 100 yards apart. . . . . ♦ 2080
        0.1W on southernmost road to spring near pond.

252.2 **1938.7** Wyman Mountain 2920

250.9 **1940.0** **Hall Mountain Lean-to** 20.9◄14.0◄10.5◄►12.8►21.1►32.3 . . 🎦 ☽ ⬡ ⬢ ⊏ (6) 2629
        Spring south of lean-to on AT, tenting and view behind shelter.

249.5 **1941.4** Sawyer Notch, Sawyer Rd (dirt) 1095
249.4 **1941.5** Sawyer Brook, campsite . . . . ♦ ⬢ 1073
249.0 **1941.9** View . . . . 🎦 2059
248.6 **1942.3** Moody Mountain, view . . . . 🎦 2440

246.8 **1944.1** South Arm Rd (paved), **Andover, ME** (9.0E) . . . . ♦ ☽ ⬢ (pg. 209) 1410
        Black Brook on south side of road, campsite.
246.3 **1944.6** View . . . . 🎦 2198

244.0 **1946.9** Old Blue Mountain . . . . 🎦 3600

   ▪▌ (SoBo) Poor cell reception at East B Hill Rd, consider calling ahead if you need ride.

242.4 **1948.5** Unnamed Gap, mileage sign, water to west . . . . ♦ 3005

241.1 **1949.8** Spring . . . . ♦ 3166
240.8 **1950.1** Bemis Stream Trail to east 3350

239.8 **1951.1** Bemis Mountain 3550
239.3 **1951.6** View . . . . 🎦 3295

GORHAM, NH

(N)

44.3996,-71.18
Mag. Dec. 15.2° W

Walmart
2.2 mi

Sav-a-lot (1.5 mi)

2

16

Bellivue Ave

Mt. Madison Motel

Emergency Medical Services

Fire Dept.

Gorham House of Pizza

Hiker's Paradise /
Colonial Fort Inn

Seafood Delight

Irving Mini Mart / ATM

Gorham Motor Inn
Dynasty Buffet

Northern Peaks

"J"s Corner

Top Notch Inn

Vashaws Beer & Tobacco

Yokohama Restaurant

Wood Fired Pizza

Dublin St

Burger King

North County Animal Hospital 603.466.3800

Pizza Hut

McDonald's

Dunkin' Donuts

Union St

White Mtn Cafe & Bookstore

Main St

Androscoggin River

PO (03581): 603.466.2182
M-F 8:30-5, Sa 8:30-12
ID required; all packages should
include your legal name.

Laundry Basket
7 days 6-11

Mr. Pizza

Saladino's Italian Market

0.8 mi Hikers Paradise to ← PO → to Barn 0.6 mi

Church St

Saalt Pub/Libby's Bistro

Royalty Inn

Scoggins Ice Cream

Library
603.466.2525
M-F 10-6
Sat 10-12

Gorham Hardware & Sports

Welsh's (6am-2pm)

Railroad St

Visitor
Center

16

Subway

Cumberland Farms

The Barn /
Libby House

1.6 mi

10.7 mi. from Main St.

2

3.5 mi. from 16
(inset map covers
area near trailhead)

The section of trail
between roads is 21.1 mi.

This inset is approximately
one-quarter scale of the
larger Gorham Map

0.5mi to Rte 16 in Gorham

Town & Country Inn (2.8 from AT, 0.7 from Gorham)

White Birches (1.7 from AT, 1.8 from Gorham)

2

N

2.8 mi

White Mtns Hostel
(3.5 from Gorham)

Hogan Rd

Androscoggin River

North Rd

P

S

1892.6   US 2, RATTLE RIVER TRAILHEAD

🖵 **Trail Angels Hiker Services** 603.326.6382 Paid shuttle range: NH & ME - Gorham NH.⟨trailangelshikerservices.com⟩

🖦🍴🅿🛏🖵 ⚕🛉 **Rattle River Lodge & Hostel** 603.466.5049 Located on the AT & open yr-round. Clean B&B style rooms, some pvt, starting at $75 w/ fresh linens & towels. Thru hiker bunk rate $35PP incl b'fast, laundry, loaner clothes, showers, fast WiFi, free resupply shuttle to Walmart. Sodas, ice cream, Mr. Pizza delivery avail for guests & non-guests. 21 Mile slackpack free w/2 night stay (Pinkham Notch to US 2). P/U at Pinkham Notch avail at 8a, noon, & 5p for $5 PP, ($20 for unscheduled p/u) based on availability. Parking avail for section hikers. Maildrops free for guests & $5 for non-guests. Label side of box w/last name/eta. Town shuttles for guests $2. Free morning shuttle to PO/gas station 8:30a. Bus p/u & d/o avail. Long distance shuttles avail $2 mile one way. Section hike planning assistance. Late bus p/u fees may apply. Authorized Sierra Madre Research hammock outfitter. Mail: 592 State Route 2, Shelburne, NH 03581. Online booking avail.⟨rattleriverhostel.com⟩

🖦🍴⚕🛏🛉🖵 ⚿ **White Birches Camping Park** (1.9W) 603.466.2022 Bunks $15, tent sites $15PP, pool, air hockey, pool table, pets allowed. Coleman/alcohol/oz & canister fuel. Free shuttle from/to trail & town w/stay. Open May-Oct. CC ok. Guest mail only: 218 US 2, Shelburne, NH 03581.

🖵 **Concord Coach** 800.639.3317 Bus service 7:50a daily from Irving Mini Mart to Pinkham Notch. $7 one-way, $13 round-trip.

» **Gorham, NH 03581** (3.6W from US 2 RR Trailhead)

🖦👤🍴⚕🛏🛉🖵 **Town & Country Inn & Resort** (2.8W) 603.466.3315 Open yr-round. $64-129 seasonal, pets $25. B'fast 6:30-10:30, dinner 5-9, cocktails. Indoor pool, sauna.⟨townandcountryinn.com⟩

🖦👤🍴⚕🛏🛉🖵 **Libby House B&B & The Barn Hikers Hostel** (3.5W) 603.466.2271 Bunks $22, tenting $15PP, B&B rooms avail, Hot country b'fast avail. Fast, free p/u & ret to US 2 trailhead for guests. Shuttle from Pinkham Notch free w/2 night stay to facilitate slackpacking. Celebrating more than 30 yrs of professional svcs. Located w/in walking distance of shops & restaurants. Shuttle to Walmart. Clean beds w/linens, full kitchen w/cookware & refrigerator, lounge w/big screen TV. Laundry $5, No pets.

Visa MC ok. Open yr-round. Mail free for guests, $15 fee for non-guests: 55 Main St, Gorham, NH 03581.

🖦👤🛉 **Royalty Inn** (3.9W) 603.466.3312 Hiker rate $79 wkday, $89 wkend (subject to change). Indoor pool, sauna, A/C. ⟨royaltyinn.com⟩

🖦👤🛉🖵 **Top Notch Inn** (4.5W) 603.466.5496 Guest laundry, pool, hot tub, well behaved dogs ok, no smoking, CC ok. Open yr-round. Guest mail: 265 Main St, Gorham, NH 03581.⟨topnotchinn.com⟩

🛉 **Northern Peaks Motor Inn** (4.6W) 603.466.2288 $70/up + tax. A/C, pets $15, no smoking, all major CC ok, hiker friendly.⟨northernpeaksmotorinn. com⟩

🛉 **Gorham Motor Inn** (4.7W) 603.466.3381 $88-$158 Open May-Oct.

🖦👤🍴⚕🛉 **Hiker's Paradise at Colonial Fort Inn** (4.9W) 603.466.2732 paradise@hikersparadise.com Bunks $25 (incl tax) w/linen, tub/ shower, kitchen. Pvt rooms avail. Restaurants near by. Coin laundry for guests. Coleman/alcohol/oz. Free shuttle w/stay from/to Route 2, other limited shuttles. CC ok. Smoking only on outside porch. No pets or maildrops.⟨hikersparadise.com⟩

🛉 🏛 **Gorham Hardware & Sports** (3.7W) 603.466.2312 Open M-F 8a-5p, Sa 8a-4p, Su 8a-1p. Close Su after ColumDay. Hiking poles, water treatment, hiking food, cold-weather clothes, White gas/alcohol/oz & canisters. Visa/ MC/Disc.

» **Berlin, NH** (10W from US 2)

✚ **Androscoggin Valley Hospital** (12.3W) 603.752.2200

Hiking SoBo?

There is another edition of this book, made specifically for southbound hikers, available from the website:

TheATguide.com

238.1 **1952.8** **Bemis Mountain Lean-to**, small spring to left of lean-to . . . . . . ☽ ◊ ◖ ⊏ (8) 2826
26.8◄23.3◄12.8◄►8.3►19.5►28.4

236.8 **1954.1** Bemis Mountain Second Peak 2905

234.6 **1956.3** Dirt road, campsite and stream north of road . . . . ◊ ◖ 1559
234.4 **1956.5** Bemis Stream (ford) . . . . ◊ 1501

233.6 **1957.3** ME 17, **Oquossoc, ME** (11.0W) . . . . .44.8364,-70.71 🅿 📷 (pg. 209) 2206
Height of Land view, bench and boulder seating

232.5 **1958.4** Woods road 2368

231.9 **1959.0** Moxie Pond . . . . ◊ 2333

229.8 **1961.1** **Sabbath Day Pond Lean-to** 31.6◄21.1◄8.3◄►11.2►20.1►28.1 . . . ☽ ◊ ◖ ⊏ (8) 2377
Pond in front of lean-to. Sandy beach 0.3S on AT, swimming.
229.3 **1961.6** Houghton Fire Rd 2388

228.2 **1962.7** Powerline 2792

225.2 **1965.7** Little Swift River Pond Campsite . . . . ☽ ◊ ◖ 2460
Spring house next to pond.

224.0 **1966.9** Chandler Mill Stream, pond . . . . ◊ 2184

222.9 **1968.0** Stream. . . . . ◊ 2305
222.5 **1968.4** South Pond . . . . ◊ 2174

220.4 **1970.5** ME 4, **Rangeley, ME** (9.0W) . . . . 44.8869,-70.5405 🅿 (pg. 209) 1613
220.2 **1970.7** Sandy River, footbridge . . . . ◊ 1664
219.7 **1971.2** Old County Rd (gravel) 1867

| 218.9 | 1972.0 | Stream. . . . . | ♦ | 1978 |

218.9 1972.0 Stream. . . . . ♦ 1978
218.6 1972.3 **Piazza Rock Lean-to**, stream through campsite . . . . . ꒰ ♦ ◖ ⊏ (8) **(pg. 212)** 2088
　　　　　　　32.3◄19.5◄11.2◄►8.9►16.9►35.5 Two-seat privy and cribbage board.
217.8 1973.1 Ethel Pond. . . . . ♦ 2366
217.6 1973.3 Saddleback Stream. . . . . ♦ 2454
216.8 1974.1 Eddy Pond, woods road passes near north bank, no camping near pond . . . ♦ 2645

214.7 1976.2 Saddleback Mountain, trail 2.0W to ski lodge. . . . . 📷 4120

213.1 1977.8 The Horn. . . . . 📷 3985

212.4 1978.5 Redington Campsite to west, water 0.2W on side trail. . . . . ꒰ ♦ ◖ (8) 3123

211.1 1979.8 Saddleback Junior . . . . 📷 3655
210.7 1980.2 Stream. . . . . ♦ 3266

209.7 1981.2 **Poplar Ridge Lean-to** (1961) . . . . ►.◖.) . . . . . . ꒰ ♦ ◖ ⊏ (6) 2945
　　　　　　　28.4◄20.1◄8.9◄►8.0►26.6►36.8
　　　　　　　Some tenting at lean-to, more on knoll to the north. Stream in front.

207.0 1983.9 Orbeton Stream (ford) . . . . ♦ 1550
206.9 1984.0 Woods road, NoBo: walk a short distance east on road 1623

206.2 1984.7 Sluice Brook. . . . . ♦ 2043

205.6 1985.3 Barnjam Rd, private gravel road 2290
205.1 1985.8 Perham Stream, logging road to north (not accessible by car) . . . . ♦ 2274

203.9 1987.0 Lone Mountain 3260

202.7 1988.2 Mt Abraham Trail, 1.7E to summit above treeline, remnants of lookout tower . . 📷 3245

201.7 1989.2 **Spaulding Mountain Lean-to**, spring on north shelter loop trail . . ꒰ ♦ ◖ ⊏ (8) 3122
　　　　　　　28.1◄16.9◄8.0◄►18.6►28.8►36.5

200.7 1990.2 Crest NW shoulder of Spaulding Mountain 3890
　　　　　　　Side trail 0.1E to summit.
200.0 1990.9 Bronze plaque 3544
　　　　　　　Completion of the last section of the AT from GA-ME.

198.9	**1992.0**	View to east. . . . . 📷	3635
198.6	**1992.3**	Sugarloaf Mountain, stream 0.2E, Sugarloaf Mountain Trail 0.6E to summit . 📷 💧	3637
196.6	**1994.3**	South Branch Carrabassett River (ford), tenting on north side of river . . . . 💧 ⛺	2145
196.5	**1994.4**	Caribou Valley Rd (gravel)	2217
196.0	**1994.9**	Spring . . . . 💧	2439
195.5	**1995.4**	Crocker Cirque Campsite (0.2E), stream. . . . . 🌙💧⛺	2734
194.4	**1996.5**	South Crocker Mountain, summit 50 yards west . . . . 📷	4040
193.4	**1997.5**	North Crocker Mountain	4228
192.3	**1998.6**	Spring . . . . 💧	3365

SoBo   NoBo   1000   3000   5000

188.2	**2002.7**	ME 27 (paved), **Stratton, ME** (5.0W). . . . . .45.1034,-70.3569 🅿 (pg. 213)	1391
187.4	**2003.5**	Stratton Brook Pond Rd	1250
187.3	**2003.6**	Stratton Brook, footbridge . . . . 💧	1206
186.5	**2004.4**	Footbridge, stream . . . . 💧	1283
186.4	**2004.5**	Cranberry Stream Campsite . . . . 🌙💧⛺	1350
185.0	**2005.9**	Bigelow Range Trail 0.2W to Cranberry Pond	2400
183.9	**2007.0**	View to east. . . . . 📷	3354
183.3	**2007.6**	Horns Pond Trail	3147
183.1	**2007.8**	**Horns Pond Lean-tos** 35.5◄26.6◄18.6◄►10.2►17.9►27.9. . . . . . 🌙💧⛺ ⌐ (16)	3158
182.7	**2008.2**	Trail 0.2W to North Horn, small boxed spring just south of this intersection . . 💧	3716
182.6	**2008.3**	South Horn	3831

🚫 No Camping above the treeline in Bigelow Preserve

180.5	**2010.4**	Bigelow Mountain west peak . . . . 📷	4145
180.1	**2010.8**	Avery Memorial Campsite, spring 0.2N on AT, Fire Wardens Trail to east . 🌙💧⛺	3838
179.8	**2011.1**	Avery Peak. . . . . 📷	4090

| 178.6 | **2012.3** | View . . . . 📷 | 2851 |

177.9 **2013.0** Safford Brook Trail to west 2260
177.8 **2013.1** Safford Notch Campsite 0.3E . . . . 🌙 ⬧ ⬧ △ 2254

175.6 **2015.3** View . . . . 📷 2941

174.6 **2016.3** Little Bigelow Mountain, view . . . . 📷 3010

172.9 **2018.0** **Little Bigelow Lean-to** 36.8◄28.8◄10.2◄►7.7►17.7►27.4 . . . . . 🌙 ⬧ △ ⊏ (8) 1795
Plenty of tent sites at lean-to. Swimming in "the Tubs" along AT.

171.5 **2019.4** East Flagstaff Rd, ... 45.1346,-70.1714 🅿 (0.1W) 🌙 1200
AT east on road for 0.1 mile
171.3 **2019.6** Bog Brook Rd, Flagstaff Lake outlet, footbridge. . . . . ⬧ 1198
170.6 **2020.3** Hemlock Trail to east 1246
170.3 **2020.6** East Flagstaff Lake tentpads, 2 beaches, 2 firepits . . . . 🌙 ⬧ △ (9) 1198
169.8 **2021.1** Two intersections with Hemlock Trail 1235

168.7 **2022.2** Long Falls Dam Rd (paved) 1225
168.6 **2022.3** Jerome Brook . . . . ⬧ 1230

> "Carry" ponds are so named because they were used for portage.

165.8 **2025.1** Connector trail to Great Carrying Pond Portage Trail. 1329
165.2 **2025.7** **West Carry Pond Lean-to** 36.5◄17.9◄7.7◄►10.0►19.7►28.7 . . . . . 🌙 ⬧ ⊏ (8) 1325
Swimming in pond. Water at spring house to left of lean-to or at West Carry Pond.
164.5 **2026.4** Unmarked trail 0.5W to Arnolds Point on West Carry Pond. 1325

162.7 **2028.2** Gravel road, AT to west over Sandy Stream . . . . ⬧ 1271

161.8 **2029.1** Gravel road 1282
161.5 **2029.4** East Carry Pond, beach at north end . . . . ⬧ 1261

159.5 **2031.4** Scott Rd (gravel) 1334

1923.7 GRAFTON NOTCH, ME 26

✉ **Rodney Kneeland Shuttle Services** 207.357.3083 fishermanstrio@yahoo.com Serves NH to Rangeley, ME.

⌂♟⛺🅿️❄️🚿⛽✉ **Stony Brook Variety Store & Campground** (13.1E) 207.824.2836 camping@stonybrookrec.com Tentsite $28 for 4, lean-to $33 for 4. Shuttles from Grafton Notch for a fee. Pool, mini golf, zipline, rec room, campstore. 12.0E on Hwy 26, then lft 0.5 mi on Rte 2. Mail: 42 Powell Place, Hanover, ME 04237⟨stonybrookrec.com⟩

» *Bethel, ME 04217 (12E to Rt 2, right 5 mi on Rt 2)*
☎ 207.824.2668, M-F 9-4, Sa 10-12:30

⛺♟⛽❄️🚿 **The Inn at Rostay** (16.9E) 207.824.3111 info@rostay.com Free hot made-to-order b'fast (for guests & seasonal). Rates vary by season/times. Show A.T. Guide for discount. All rooms have fridge/m'wave. Restaurants & resupply nearby.

⛺♟❄️🚿 **Bethel Outdoor Adventure** (17.3E) 207.824.4224 info@betheloutdooradventure.com About 20 min by car from Grafton Notch or US 2 trailheads. $22 Campsites near river w/in walking distance of Bethel stores. Shuttle one-way to/from Grafton Notch tailhead $45/group.⟨betheloutdooradventure.com⟩

⛺🅿️🚿❄️ **Chapman Inn** (18.6E) 207.824.2657 Bunk space $35 incl shower & full b'fast, $25 w/o b'fast. Rooms $89/up incl b'fast. Kitchen privileges, $6 laundry. Mail: PO Box 1067, Bethel, ME 04217.

♟🍴🚿❄️ **Sudbury Inn** (18.6E) 207.824.2174 info@thesudburyinn.com Rooms $89/up, b'fast incl. Dining room open Th-Sa 5:30-9. Seasonal Pub 11:30a till late.⟨thesudburyinn.com⟩

♟⛺⌂♟🚿 **True North Adventureware** (18.9E) 207.824.2201 adventureware@mac.com Full line of gear, footwear, clothing. Open daily. Trekking pole repair, warranty support. Coleman/alcohol/oz & canisters, frz-dried food.⟨truenorthadventureware.com⟩

🛒 **Bethel Shop & Save** (18.8E) 207.824.2121 Su-Th 8-8, F-Sa 8-9. Grocery, deli, wine.

🐾 **Bethel Animal Hospital** (18.9E) 207.824.2212

1934.0 EAST B HILL RD

» *Andover, ME 04216 (8E)*

⌂♟⛺🅿️🚿❄️⛽✉ **Pine Ellis Lodging** (7.9E) 207.392.4161 Bunks $25PP, pvt rooms $45S, $60D, $75T. Incl. shower, lender clothes, kitchen use, laundry, am coffee & muffin. LR w/WiFi & cable. Trailhead p/u for fee-call in adv. Slackpack Grafton Notch to Rangeley, & shuttles to nearby towns, airport & bus station. No dogs. Full resupply. Coleman/denatured/oz & canisters. Guest Mail: (USPS) PO Box 12 or (UPS/FedEx) 20 Pine St, Andover, ME 0426.

⌂♟🚿❄️ **Mountain Village Tiny House** (10.1E) 207.357.7004 moosemountain@rocketmail.com Pvt 1BR cottage w/queen & full futon. $100/night for 4. Full kitchen & bath, A/C. Add'l backyard tent sites $25. Walk to restaurants. Laundry & WiFi nearby.

⛺🚿❄️ **Paul's AT Camp for Hikers** (11.3E) 207.392.4161 Contact Pine Ellis for cabin stay. $60 for 4, 1SEAP incl shower one round trip shuttle from the lodge. Slackpack shuttle svc from the lodge.

⌂♟🚿❄️ **The Cabin** (11.8E) 207.392.1333 Alumni hikers welcome by reserv only. mi from Andover. Great location for slackpacking.

⌂♟🚿❄️ **The Human-Nature Hostel** (16.5E) 207.408.8216 humannaturehostel@gmail.com Large Timber frame Geodesic Dome Hostel on 42 acres. Bunk room, pvt rooms, & tenting space. Great location for slackpacking between Grafton Notch & Rangeley. $30PP incl shuttle, bunk, fresh linens, towel, shower, loner clothes, laundry, kitchen, & WiFi. Pups welcome. $5PP coffee/tea & AYCE Maine Blueberry pancakes! Free shuttle: East B Hill - 9a, 3:50p, 5:50p; South

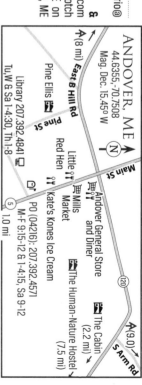

ANDOVER, ME

44.6355,-70.7508
Mag. Dec. 15.45° W

🄽 (8 mi) *East B Hill Rd*

Pine Ellis 🏠

Pine St

Library 207.392.4841 📮
Tu, W & Sa I-4:30, Th I-8

Main St

Andover General Store and Diner

Little 🍴🏪 Mills Market

Red Hen 🍴🏪 Kate's Kones Ice Cream

📮 PO (0426I): 207.392.4571
M-F 9:15-12 & I-4:15, Sa 9-12

🄽 (9.0) 🄽 *S Arm Rd*

(120)

🍴🏪 The Cabin (2.2 mi)

🏪 The Human-Nature Hostel (7.5 mi)

(5) 1.0 mi

Arm Rd - 9:30a, 3:30p, 5:30p. $5PP town resupply, last WalMart on the AT. Call in adv to reserve unscheduled p/u $10PP. Shuttles from Gorham, Grafton Notch, Rangeley (Fees Apply). Beer & Wine ok in moderation. No liquor. Small hiker store: Snacks, hiker meals & fuel. Mail: PO Box 131, Roxbury, ME 04275.⟨humannaturehostel.com⟩

🏚🍴💲Andover General Store (8.1E) 207.392.4172 Short-order food & pizza, ice cream. Open M-Sa 5-8, Su 6-8, in summer until 9p daily.

🏚🍴Mills Market (8.1E) 207.392.3062 Open 7 days 5a-9p.

Little Red Hen (8.1E) 207.392.2253 Summer Hrs: closed M. Tu-Th 6:30a-2p, F-Sa 6:30a-8p, Su 7a-2p. AYCE Italian buffet Sa 5-8. Ask about tenting. Shower & laundry $5 ea. Mail: 28 S Main St, Andover ME 04216.

🍴Kates Kones (8.2E) 207.357.3268 Ice cream. Summer hrs 1-8:30.
■Donna Gifford (8E) 207.357.5686 Massage therapist, call for rates. Free p/u $ ret to Andover.

1944.1   SOUTH ARM RD

South Arm Campground (4W) 207.364.5155 camp@southarm.com Tent sites, store, hot showers, privy. No CC, checks ok. Pets ok. ADA comp. Open May 1-Oct 1.⟨southarm.com⟩

» *Andover, ME 04216 (8E from South Arm Rd)*

1957.3   ME 17

» *Oquossoc, ME 04964 (11W)*
✆207.864.3685, M-F 11:30-3:30, Sa 9-12

🏚🍴Oquossoc Grocery (10.9W) 207.864.3662 Su-Th 6-8, F-Sa 6-9 pizza, deli, bakery, wine, Coleman fuel.
🍴Four Seasons Cafe (10.9W) 207.864.2020 7 days 7-9 B/L/D extensive menu, full bar.
🍴Gingerbread House (10.9W) B/L/D, vegetarian specials.

1970.5   ME 4

🏚The Hiker Hut (0.3W) 207.670.8095 hikerhut@gmail.com A restful sanctuary along the Sandy River w/flower gardens, hummingbirds & our pet chipmunks. $25 Stay incl bunk w/ mattress & pillow, hot shower, snacks on arrival, & tea, coffee, pastry on departure. $7 Hot meals & $3 laundry avail. Pvt huts $50/D, $40/S. Pet friendly. Fuel & denatured alcohol avail. Slackpacking by experienced mountaineer. Sports massage therapist on site. Open May 15-Sep 15. Mail ($5 non-guest): C/O Steve Lynch, 2 Pine Rd, Sandy River Plantation, ME 04970.

» *Rangeley, ME 04970 (9W),* Safest to hitch from end of guardrail (0.3W), in front of Hiker Hut. Rangeley is halfway between equator and north pole (3107 miles from either).

🛏Rangeley Saddleback Inn (9W) 207.864.3434 $135D, pets $10 incl c. b'fast. Rides sometimes avail. 🍴Twisted Willow Pub onsite.

» *Rangeley, ME* (services cont'd on pg. 212...)

158.7 **2032.2** North branch of Carrying Place Stream . . . . ◆ 1200

> Trails to Harrison's, before and after the dam, can be used to bypass the dam.

155.2 **2035.7** **Pierce Pond Lean-to**, 27.9◄17.7◄10.0◄►9.7►18.7►22.8 . . ☽◆⊏ (6) (pg. 213) 1174
Blue-blazed loop trail west to lean-to. From north end of loop, Harrison's is 0.3E.
155.1 **2035.8** Wooden dam, outlet of Pierce Pond . . . . ◆ 1140
154.8 **2036.1** Trail 0.1E to Harrison's Pierce Pond Camps, boat landing to west . . . . .(pg. 213) 1100
154.6 **2036.3** Otter Pond Rd (gravel) 1070
154.1 **2036.8** Pierce Pond Stream Falls 0.1E 999
154.0 **2036.9** Waterfall 0.1E 989
153.5 **2037.4** Otter Pond Stream, footbridge . . . . ◆ 864

> 🚫 Camping on either shore of Kennebec River is prohibited.

151.6 **2039.3** Kennebec River. Do not ford. Use ferry service . . . . ◆ (pg. 213) 484
151.2 **2039.7** US 201, **Caratunk, ME** (0.3E) . . . . 45.2384,-69.9963 🅿 (pg. 213) 520
150.9 **2040.0** Woods road 679

148.6 **2042.3** Holly Brook . . . . ◆ 896

147.2 **2043.7** Grove Rd (gravel) 1234
146.7 **2044.2** Holly Brook . . . . ◆ 1300

146.0 **2044.9** Boise-Cascade Logging Rd to west (gravel), Pleasant Pond Rd to east. 1426
145.5 **2045.4** **Pleasant Pond Lean-to** 27.4◄19.7◄9.7◄►9.0►13.1►22.0 . . . . ☽◆⊏ (6) 1370
Stream left of lean-to. Beach 0.2 on side trail beyond lean-to.
145.3 **2045.6** Pleasant Pond Beach to east. Private property open for public use from 1334
May 15 - Oct 1 from 8a-8p. No camping, no fires. High quality water source.
144.2 **2046.7** Pleasant Pond Mountain . . . . 📷 2470

> ❋ Blueberries – Abundant on open summits like Pleasant
> Pond Mountain and north peak of Moxie Bald.

139.7 **2051.2** Stream. . . . . ◆ 1040

139.3	2051.6	Moxie Pond south end, road, powerlines . . . . .45.2497,-69.831 🅿 ⬥	970
139.1	2051.8	Baker Stream (ford) . . . . ⬥	975
138.8	2052.1	Powerline	1019

| 136.5 | 2054.4 | **Bald Mountain Brook Lean-to** (0.1E) . . . . 🌙⬥⊏(8) | 1314 |

28.7◄18.7◄9.0◄►4.1►13.0►25.0 Bald Mountain Brook in front of lean-to.
""AT Road" (gravel) 75 yards north of shelter.

135.1	2055.8	Summit bypass trail to west	2154
134.5	2056.4	Moxie Bald Mountain . . . . 📷	2629
134.2	2056.7	Summit bypass trail to west . . . . 🌙	2409
133.5	2057.4	Trail to Moxie Bald north peak (0.5W) . . . . 📷	2216

| 132.4 | 2058.5 | **Moxie Bald Mountain Lean-to** . . . . 🌙⬥⊏(8) | 1217 |

22.8◄13.1◄4.1◄►8.9►20.9►28.3
Bald Mountain Pond in front of lean-to.

131.3	2059.6	Gravel road	1256
130.8	2060.1	Gravel road	1232
130.4	2060.5	Bald Mountain Stream (ford) . . . . ⬥	1213

| 128.5 | 2062.4 | Bald Mountain Rd (gravel) . . . . .45.2762,-69.6885 🅿 ⬥ | 1117 |

bridge and stream to west

| 127.0 | 2063.9 | Marble Brook . . . . ⬥ | 979 |
| 126.5 | 2064.4 | West Branch of Piscataquis River (ford) . . . . ⬥ | 965 |

River normally knee-deep. During heavy rain periods, fording can be dangerous.

| 123.5 | 2067.4 | **Horseshoe Canyon Lean-to** 22.0◄13.0◄8.9◄►12.0►19.4►24.1 . . . . 🌙⬥⊏(8) | 822 |

On blue-blazed trail. Stream at northern AT junction or river in front and below.

| 123.1 | 2067.8 | Stream. . . . . ⬥ | 730 |

121.2	2069.7	East Branch of Piscataquis River (ford) . . . . ⬥	599
120.9	2070.0	Gravel road	744
120.8	2070.1	Shirley-Blanchard Rd (paved) . . . . .45.2845,-69.5871 🅿	850

| 119.7 | 2071.2 | AT on woods road for 0.5 mile . . . . | 975 |

» **Rangeley, ME** (services cont'd from pg. 209...)

Fieldstone Cottages (9.3W) 207.670.5507 Hiker bunkroom for $30PP, incl shower w/towel & ret to ME 4 trailhead. Pvt rooms avail. No parties. Laundry $5. Slackpacking. Clean facility w/use of a kitchen. Quick walk to town. Unscheduled shuttle for fee. Shuttle range Gorham to Monson & to airports, train, bus & car rental hubs in Portland, Bangor, Farmington, Augusta & Waterville. 0.5 S of IGA. Mail: 2432 Main St, Rangeley, ME 04970

North Country Inn B&B (9.6W) 207.864.2440 info@northcountrybb.com $99-149 incl. b'fast. Multi-night discount. (northcountrybb.com)

Town & Lake Motel (9.9W) 207.864.3755 Hiker rates $65/1, $75/2, $10EAP. No discount on wkends Jul/Aug. Pets $10. Canoes for guest use. Mail: PO Box 47, Rangeley, ME 04970. (rangeleytownandlake.com)

Alpine Shop (9.5W) 207.864.3741 info@alpineshoprangeley.com M-Su, 9a-8p. Full outfitter, fuel oz. (alpineshoprangeley.com)

Ecopelagicon (9.5W) 207.864.2771 Seasonal hrs. Gas/alcohol/oz & canisters. Frz-dried food, water filters, clothes, Leki poles & warranty work. Ask about shuttles. Mail: PO Box 899, 7 Pond St, Rangeley, ME 04970

IGA Supermarket (8.7W) 207.864.5089 ATM 7 days 7-8, 9 in summer.

Rangeley Inn (9.3W) 207.864.3341 Rates start at $140 in the Summer. 5% Direct booking discount. Complimentary c. b'fast, use of kayaks/canoe, WiFi, domestic phone calls. (therangeleyinn.com)

Moose's Loop Cafe (9.3W) 207.864.3000 W-Sa 7a-3p, Su 7a-1p. Clsd M-Tu

Sarge's Sports Pub & Grub (9.4W) 207.864.5616 L/D & bar, daily 11a-10a, house bands F & Sa.

Moose Alley (10.1W) 207.864.9955 Bowling, billiards, darts, dance floor, food. Just west of The Shed BBQ on Main St.

Rangeley Family Medicine & Wellness Center (8.8W) 207.864.3303 (RFM), 207.864.3055 (WC) On Dallas Hill Rd south of IGA. Wellness Center $5 shower, towel provided. M-Th 5a-8p, F 5a-7:30p, Sa-Su 8-2.

1972.3   PIAZZA ROCK LEAN-TO

» Two side trails north of shelter; 100 yds north: west to Piazza Rock, 0.1 north: To "The Caves", blue-blazed trail through boulders & caves.

2002.7   ME 27

Mountainside Grocers (2.7E) 207.237.2248 Open M-Sa 7:30-8, Su 7:30-6.

STRATTON, ME
45.1408,-70.4436
Mag. Dec. 15.73°W

Stratton Motel & Hostel
White Wolf Inn Restaurant & Bar
Fotter's Market
Stratton Plaza
Old Mill Laundry
Flagstaff General Store
Main St
Library M,W,F 10-5; Tu,Th 1-5; Sa 9-1
PO (04982): 207.246.6461 M-F 8:30-1 & 1:30-4, Sa 8:30-11
Limited cash-back
School St
Sargent Ave
0.8 mi
Spillover Motel (0.6 mi from PO)
N
(5.0 mi from PO)
Looney Moose
(5.0 mi from PO)

» **Stratton, ME 04982** (5W)

Spillover Motel (4.3W) 207.246.6571 $89/up. Pets $15, c. b'fast, full kitchen for use by guests. Gas grill. Shower $5. Guest Mail: PO Box 427, Stratton, ME 04982. (spillovermaine.com)

Stratton Plaza Hotel (5.1W) 207.246.2000 Dining, lounge, some rooms. Closed Su-M.

White Wolf Inn (5.1W) 207.246.2922 $69D, $79D on wkends, $10EAP + tax. A/C, refrig & m'wave in all rooms. Pets $10. Visa/MC ok ($20 min). Restaurant (closed Tu & W) serves L/D. Home of the 8 oz Wolf Burger; Fish Fry Friday; Wolf Den Bar onsite. Mail (non-guest fee): Main St, PO Box 590, Stratton, ME 04982.

Stratton Motel & Hostel (5.2W) 207.246.4171 thestrattonmotel@gmail.com $30 bunk, pvt room avail. Complimentary shuttle from trailhead (when avail). Same owners as

Three Rivers (4.0 from AT) 🚶
Northern Outdoors (2.0 from AT) 🏠

Caratunk House B&B 🏠

PO (04925):
207.672.3416
M-F 2-4
Sa 7:30-11:15
(0.3 mi from AT)

Main St

School St

201

Kennebec River

CARATUNK, ME

Sterling Inn (1.4 mi from AT)

Fieldstone Cottages of Rangeley who facilitate supply bumps from town to town & slackpacking in area. Shuttle for fee, Gorham to Monson & to airports, train, bus & car rental hubs in Portland, Bangor, Farmington, Augusta & Waterville. Mail: PO Box 284, Stratton, ME 04982; FedEx & UPS 162 Main St,Stratton, ME 04982⟨thestrattonmotel.com⟩

🏠🍴▣ 🛜 Flagstaff General Store (4.9W) 207.246.2300 Deli, pizza, subs, sodas, coffee, protein bars, beer, fuel. M-F 5:30-9, Su 7-7.

🏪▣ Fotter's Market (5.1W) 207.246.2401 M-Th 8-7, F-Sa 8-8, Su 9-5. Coleman, alcohol/oz
🍴▽Coplin Dinner House (4.3W) 207.246.0016 Fine food & pub food. Open W, Th, Su 5p-9p, Fri & Sa 5p-9:30p.

» Kingfield, ME 04947 (17.9E from both rds)
☎207.265.4122
M-F 7:30a - 3:45p; Sa 8a - 11:45a; Su Closed

🏠▣🛜⊠ Mountain Village Farm B&B (18.3E) 207.265.2030 Kingfield is a designated AT Community. Thru-Hiker rate of $60PP for room, pvt bath, incl b'fast. Round-trip shuttle $40 for up to 4 persons from either trailhead. Pets welcome. Bed & b'fast on an organic farm; inquire about WFS. Town center w/in walking distance has grocery, laundry & restaurants. Slackpack the Bigelows (Stratton to East Flagstaff Rd, either direction) $50/carload. Mail: PO Box 216, Kingfield, ME 04947.

🏠 Sillanpaa's Trading Post (17.2E) 207.670.5500 Hiking gear, trail food.

2035.7, 2036.1   TRAILS TO CAMP, DAM BYPASS

🏠🍴⚓ Harrison's Pierce Pond Camps (0.1E) 207.672.3625, 207.612.8184 May-Nov, 7 days. Bed, shower & 12-pancake b'fast for $40. For b'fast only, ($9-12 served 7a), reserve a seat the day before. Cash only, no reservations taken by phone. Pets welcome. Ok to get water at camp & dispose of trash. Shortest route to camp is west from the north end of blue-blaze shelter loop trail.

2039.3   KENNEBEC RIVER

» Kennebec River, The ferry is the official A.T. route. Do not ford; current is unpredictable due to an upstream dam.

🚣Cheryl Anderson 207.672.3997 Privately run ferry service $30. Can take up to 4.
🚣The Kennebec Ferry 207.858.3627 Free ferry svc provided seasonally by the ATC & MATC. Ferry holds 1-2. Reservation req'd & signed release form req'd. Scheduled hrs: May 26 - Jun, 9a-11a; Jul 1-Sep 30, 9a-2p; Oct 1-Oct 8, 9a-11a. $50 fee for on call ferry svc outside of scheduled hrs, weather permitting. Provided by Maine Guide Services.

2039.7   US 201

🏠🚻♿🍴▣🛜⊠ Three Rivers Trading Post (4.4W) 207.663.2104 info@threeriversfun.com Store open yr-round until 6-8p. Carries variety of pkgd food, beer & wine. Lodging & restaurant open May-mid Sep. Tenting $12PP, bunk houses, cabins & Inn avail too. Rafting trips by reservation, tube, kayak, & SUP rentals. 🍴▽Boatman's Bar & Grill on-site open 4p-1a. Mail: PO Box 10, West Forks, ME 04985.⟨threeriverswhitewater.com⟩

» Caratunk, ME 04925 (0.3E)

🏠🚻♿🍴🛜⊠ The Caratunk House B&B (0.04E) 207.672.4349 (2017 rates & dates) Jun 1 - Sep 30. Close to ferry 150 yds from trail. Beds: $20/T rooms, $25 to $40/pvt rooms. No tenting. Family style b'fast, $7. Shuttle svc, WiFi. CC ok. Pet friendly. Laundry $5, Shower $5 for non-guests. Long term resupply. All fuels, homemade baked goods, milk shakes. A quiet, non party house. Free Mail: 218 Main St (PO Box 98) Caratunk, ME 04925.

» (Caratunk, ME services cont'd on pg. 220...)

119.3	**2071.6**	Gravel road		896
117.8	**2073.1**	Historic AT route near Lake Hebron. . . . . 45.2907,-69.5333 🅿 (pg. 220)		900
		0.2E on woods road to Pleasant St & parking, then left 1.6 mi to **Monson, ME**.		
117.4	**2073.5**	Dirt road.		1026
115.9	**2075.0**	Side trail to Doughty Ponds (0.1W), 180' footbridge built in 2014	♦	1220
115.8	**2075.1**	Stream.	♦	1241
115.2	**2075.7**	Gravel road		1385
114.5	**2076.4**	ME 15 (paved), **Monson, ME** (3.6E) . . . . 45.3309,-69.5354 🅿 (pg. 220)		1215
		South end of 100-Mile Wilderness.		
114.4	**2076.5**	Spectacle Pond outlet	♦	1178
113.6	**2077.3**	Old Stage Rd (dirt) once a stagecoach road and part of the original AT.		1282
113.3	**2077.6**	Bell Pond	♦	1278
112.6	**2078.3**	Lily Pond.	♦	1130
111.5	**2079.4**	**Leeman Brook Lean-to**. . . . . ⏾♦⊏ (6)		1060
		25.0◄20.9◄12.0◄►7.4►12.1►16.1 Stream in front of lean-to.		
110.7	**2080.2**	North Pond outlet	♦	1016
110.4	**2080.5**	North Pond Tote Rd		1082
109.3	**2081.6**	Mud Pond		1014
108.9	**2082.0**	Bear Pond Ledge		1190
108.5	**2082.4**	James Brook	♦	944
108.1	**2082.8**	Woods road		937
108.0	**2082.9**	Little Wilson Falls, west 30 yards	♦	862
107.7	**2083.2**	Little Wilson Stream (ford), campsite	♦⌂	750
107.3	**2083.6**	Follow gravel road for 100 yards, pond		917
105.4	**2085.5**	Big Wilson Tote Rd		571
105.2	**2085.7**	Thompson Brook	♦	570
104.8	**2086.1**	Big Wilson Stream (ford)	♦	600
104.5	**2086.4**	Railroad tracks		882
104.1	**2086.8**	**Wilson Valley Lean-to** (1993) . . . . ⏾♦⊏ (6)		963
		28.3◄19.4◄7.4◄►4.7►8.7►15.6 Spring on opposite side of AT.		
103.4	**2087.5**	Woods road		1181
102.1	**2088.8**	Stream.	♦	935
101.8	**2089.1**	Stream.	♦	931
101.0	**2089.9**	Wilber Brook	♦	608
100.8	**2090.1**	Vaughn Stream	♦	632
100.3	**2090.6**	Bodfish Farm/Long Pond Tote Rd (gravel), ford Long Pond Stream north of road	♦	636

99.4	2091.5	**Long Pond Stream Lean-to** 24.1◄12.1◄4.7◄►4.0►10.9►20.8 . . . . . ☽ ◊ ⊏ (8)	909
99.2	2091.7	Trail 0.8E to Otter Pond parking . . . . .45.4184,-69.41023 🅿	1041
98.2	2092.7	Barren Slide to east, view . . . . 📷	1976
98.1	2092.8	Barren Ledges . . . . 📷	1999
96.3	2094.6	Barren Mountain, remnants of tower	2660
95.4	2095.5	Side trail to **Cloud Pond Lean-to** (0.4E) . . . . ☽ ◊ ⊏ (6)	2467
		16.1◄8.7◄4.0◄►6.9►16.8►24.0 Cloud Pond is water source.	
93.9	2097.0	Fourth Mountain Bog	1946
93.3	2097.6	Fourth Mountain	2380
92.1	2098.8	Mt Three and a Half	1966
91.7	2099.2	Third Mountain Trail to west	1807
90.8	2100.1	Third Mountain, Monument Cliff . . . . 📷	2100
90.2	2100.7	Trail 0.1E to West Chairback Pond, stream crosses AT north of side trail . . . . ◊	1770
89.3	2101.6	View . . . . 📷	2150
89.2	2101.7	Spring . . . . ◊	2237
88.9	2102.0	Columbus Mountain	2325
88.5	2102.4	**Chairback Gap Lean-to** 15.6◄10.9◄6.9◄►9.9►17.1►20.7 . . . . ☽ ◊ ⊏ (6)	1960
		Spring on AT north of shelter.	
88.0	2102.9	Chairback Mountain . . . . 📷	2180
85.9	2105.0	0.2W to East Chairback Pond . . . . ◊ (0.2W) ⌂	1709
85.3	2105.6	Spring . . . . ◊	1460
84.7	2106.2	Katahdin Ironworks Rd (gravel) . . . . 45.4772,-69.2851 🅿 (0.4E)	783
84.2	2106.7	West Branch Pleasant River (ford) . . . . ◊ ⌂	663
		Wide ford with slick rocky bottom. Campsites to south; no camping/fires for 2.0N.	
83.3	2107.6	Stream . . . . ◊	748
82.8	2108.1	Gulf Hagas Trail to west, 5.2 mile loop trail whose ends intersect the AT . . . . ◊	875
		0.7 mile apart. Features narrow, deep gorge with many waterfalls.	
82.1	2108.8	Gulf Hagas Trail to west . . . . ◊	1050

⚠ All 100 M.W. roads are privately owned, gated, and have fees. Road names vary on maps and in local use. Both roads that pass by Logan Brook & Cooper Brook Shelters may be referred to as "B Pond Road". If getting shuttles or drops be clear about the destination.

MAP AT-22 — MAINE

78.6 2112.3 **Carl A. Newhall Lean-to** 20.8◄16.8◄9.9◄►7.2►10.8►18.9 . . . . ☽ ♦ ◗ ⊏ (6) 1923
Gulf Hagas Brook, south of shelter, is water source.

77.7 2113.2 Gulf Hagas Mountain 2681

76.8 2114.1 Sidney Tappan Campsite, water 0.1E . . . . ♦ ◗ 2434

76.1 2114.8 West Peak 3178

74.5 2116.4 Hay Mountain 3244

73.7 2117.2 White Brook Trail to east 3004

72.8 2118.1 White Cap Mountain . . . . 📷 3650

71.9 2119.0 View of Katahdin from north side of mountain . . . . 📷 2730

71.4 2119.5 **Logan Brook Lean-to** 24.0◄17.1◄7.2◄►3.6►11.7►23.1 . . . . ☽ ♦ ◗ ⊏ (6) 2386
Some tent sites; better sites 0.1N on AT. Logan
Brook in front of lean-to; cascades upstream.

69.8 2121.1 Logan Brook Rd (dirt) . . . . ♦ 1602
Piped spring 50 yards south of road, west of AT

67.8 2123.1 **East Branch Lean-to**, Pleasant River in front . . . . ☽ ♦ ⊏ (6) 1242
20.7◄10.8◄3.6◄►8.1►19.5►29.6
67.5 2123.4 East branch of Pleasant River (ford) . . . . ♦ 1208

65.9 2125.0 Mountain View Pond outlet . . . . ♦ 1574
65.6 2125.3 Spring to east . . . . ♦ 1561

64.3 2126.6 Side trail 100 yards to Little Boardman Mountain 1980

63.0 2127.9 Kokadjo-B Pond Rd (gravel) 1222
62.7 2128.2 West to beach on Crawford Pond (no camping) . . . . ♦ 1249

62.1 2128.8 Cooper Brook . . . . ♦ 1206

60.2 2130.7 Stream . . . . ♦ 1000

| 59.7 | 2131.2 | **Cooper Brook Falls Lean-to** 18.9◄11.7◄8.1◄►11.4►21.5►29.6 . . . ☽ ♦ ⚫ ⊏ (6) | 928 |

Brook, falls, swimming hole in front of lean-to. Privy across trail and up hill.

| 59.1 | 2131.8 | Large tributary to Cooper Brook . . . . ♦ | 821 |

| 56.0 | 2134.9 | Jo-Mary Rd . . . . 45.6515,-69.0317 🅿 ♦ (pg. 222) | 625 |

| 54.6 | 2136.3 | Footbridge, snowmobile trail. . . . . ♦ | 585 |

| 53.5 | 2137.4 | Side trail 0.2E to north shore of Cooper Pond. . . . . ♦ | 516 |
| 53.1 | 2137.8 | Mud Pond to west, footbridge over Mud Brook . . . . ♦ | 508 |

| 51.8 | 2139.1 | Antlers Campsite . . . . ☽ ♦ ⚫ | 500 |

Campsites on edge of Jo-Mary Lake. Fort Relief two seat privy.

| 50.3 | 2140.6 | Potaywadjo Ridge Trail 1.0W . . . . | 514 |
| 50.1 | 2140.8 | East to sandy beach on lower Jo-Mary Lake . . . . ♦ | 499 |

| 48.3 | 2142.6 | **Potaywadjo Spring Lean-to** (1995) . . . . ☽ ♦ ⚫ ⊏ (8) | 637 |

23.1◄19.5◄11.4◄►10.1►18.2►29.7 Potaywadjo Spring to right.

| 48.0 | 2142.9 | Tirio Access Rd (gravel). . . . . | 555 |
| 47.7 | 2143.2 | Twitchell Brook, footbridge, east to Pemadumcook Lake, view of Katahdin. . 📷 ♦ | 493 |

| 46.5 | 2144.4 | Deer Brook . . . . ♦ | 502 |

45.8	2145.1	Woods road	510
45.7	2145.2	Mahar Tote Tr, Blue-blazed tr 0.2E **White House Landing** pickup	510
45.6	2145.3	Tumbledown Dick Stream (ford) . . . . ♦	501
45.1	2145.8	High water trail to west	496
44.5	2146.4	Ford branch of the Nahmakanta Stream . . . . ♦	512
44.0	2146.9	Nahmakanta Stream Campsite . . . . ☽ ♦ ⚫	520

> ✿ Indian pipe - A plant without chlorophyll that grows in moist soil. Translucent white candy cane shape 3-4" tall, grows in clusters. Scale-like leaves/petals.

| 42.0 | 2148.9 | Stream. . . . . ♦ | 616 |

| 41.2 | 2149.7 | Gravel Road near south end of Nahmakanta Lake . . . . . . .45.736,-69.1035 🅿 | 638 |

Camping on shore of Nahmakanta Lake is prohibited.

| 40.0 | 2150.9 | Prentiss Brook . . . . ♦ | 661 |

38.6	**2152.3**	Side trail east to sand beach on shore of Nahmakanta Lake	◊	657
38.2	**2152.7**	**Wadleigh Stream Lean-to**, stream can be dry during summer . . . . . ☽ ◊ ⊏ (6)		685
		29.6◄21.5◄10.1◄►8.1►19.6►33.0		
37.2	**2153.7**	Spring	◊	819
36.3	**2154.6**	Nesuntabunt Mountain, short side trail east to view of Katahdin, ...	📷	1520
		16 mile line-of-sight distance to Katahdin summit from here.		
35.7	**2155.2**	View	📷	1181
35.1	**2155.8**	Wadleigh Pond Rd (gravel)		1022
34.3	**2156.6**	Crescent Pond west end	◊	1000
33.6	**2157.3**	Pollywog Gorge, side trail overlooking gorge	📷	891
32.6	**2158.3**	Pollywog Stream . . . . 45.7796,-69.172 🅿 ◊		668
		Cross stream on logging road bridge.		
30.6	**2160.3**	Outlet stream from Murphy Pond	◊	954
30.1	**2160.8**	**Rainbow Stream Lean-to**, baseball bat floor . . . . ☽ ◊ ◖ ⊏ (6)		1002
		29.6◄18.2◄8.1◄►11.5►24.9►0.0		
		Tenting on hill behind lean-to. Excellent swimming hole upstream.		
28.2	**2162.7**	West to Rainbow Lake dam	◊	1100
28.0	**2162.9**	Stream.	◊	1062
26.3	**2164.6**	Rainbow Lake Campsite, spring west 30 yards . . . . ☽ ◊ ◖		1100
25.1	**2165.8**	Stream.	◊	1079
24.8	**2166.1**	Unmarked trail leads 0.2W to Rainbow Lake Camps (private)		1125
24.5	**2166.4**	Trail 0.7E to Rainbow Mountain		1145
22.9	**2168.0**	Side trail 0.1E to Little Beaver Pond, 0.7E to Big Beaver Pond	◊	1085
21.1	**2169.8**	Rainbow Ledges, view of Katahdin	📷	1517

18.6	2172.3	**Hurd Brook Lean-to**, baseball bat floor . . . . ☽ ◦ ⊏ (6)	701
		29.7◄19.6◄11.5◄▶13.4▶0.0▶0.0	
18.1	2172.8	Small spring. . . . . ◦	774

15.9	2175.0	Bog bridge	606
15.4	2175.5	Golden Rd (paved), NoBo east on road, **Millinocket, ME** (19E) . . . . . (pg. 222)	591
15.1	2175.8	Abol Bridge crosses west branch . . . . . . 45.8352,-68.9693 🅿 📷 (pg. 222)	560
		of Penobscot River. Parking on east side of road between bridge and trailhead.	
14.7	2176.2	End of Golden Rd, NoBo veer left on dirt road	603
14.6	2176.3	Abol Stream Trail to east, footbridge, Baxter State Park Boundary . . . . . . ◦	589
14.3	2176.6	Information board, Abol Pond Trail east, registration for The Birches Campsites. .	577
14.0	2176.9	Footbridge, Katahdin Stream, Foss and Knowlton Trail to east . . . . ◦	573
13.2	2177.7	Foss and Knowlton Brook, footbridge . . . . ◦	580

> ⚠ Baxter State Park - Fires & other cooking/heating devices permitted only in
> designated campsites & picnic areas. Camping at designated campsites only.
> Camp/Shelter reservations strongly recommended for those starting SoBo from Baxter,
> flip-flop thru-hikers, & NoBo hikers who started less than 100 mi from Baxter.

10.5	2180.4	Lower fork of Nesowadnehunk Stream . . . . ◦	606
		Both forks of this stream may require fording. There is a highwater bypass.	
9.5	2181.4	Upper fork of Nesowadnehunk Stream . . . . ◦	790

| 8.7 | 2182.2 | Short side trail to view of Big Niagara Falls . . . . 📷 | 930 |
| 8.4 | 2182.5 | Side trail west to Toll Dam and Little Niagara Falls . . . . ◦ | 1042 |

7.7	2183.2	Daicey Pond Nature Trail to west, parking area and privy north of trailhead	1078
		45.8809,-69.0318 🅿 ☽	
6.9	2184.0	Tracy and Elbow Pond Trails to west, Daicey Pond Nature Trail to east . . . . . ◦	1100
6.2	2184.7	Grassy Pond Trail to west (two intersections).	1063
5.8	2185.1	Footbridge, stream . . . . ◦	1040
5.3	2185.6	Perimeter Rd	1073
5.2	2185.7	Katahdin Stream Campground . . . . ◦ ◭ ⊏ (12) (pg. 222)	1088
		The Birches Lean-tos & Campsite (0.2E) thru-hikers only, $10PP pay at KSC	
		ranger station or info board. 1 Night limit (9.1S) 33.0◄24.9◄13.4◄▶0.0▶0.0▶0.0	
4.0	2186.9	Owl Trail to west, footbridge, stream . . . . ◦	1548
3.9	2187.0	Katahdin Stream Falls. . . . . ☽◦	1634

| 3.0 | 2187.9 | Spring . . . . ◦ | 2392 |
| 2.6 | 2188.3 | Pass "The cave" small slab cave . . . . | 2842 |

| 1.6 | 2189.3 | The Gateway, The Tableland . . . . | 4522 |

| 1.0 | 2189.9 | Thoreau Spring, Abol Trail to east . . . . ◦ | 4620 |

| 0.0 | 2190.9 | **Katahdin,** Baxter Peak, Northern Terminus of the AT . . . . (pg. 223) | 5268 |

» *Caratunk, ME (...services cont'd from pg. 213)*

maineskeptsecret@yahoo.com Bunk $30, pvt $455, $64D (shared bed), $108/4. All incl shower, laundry, b'fast & tax. CC/debit/pets OK. Open yr-round. Free shuttle to/from trail, P0 & nearby restaurants. Resupply, shower, laundry & free mail drops even for non-guests, incl fuel/oz, canister fuel, batteries, first-aid, hygiene, food, drinks, cook-yourself options, & more. Address: 1041 US Route 201. Mail & shipping: P0 Box 129, Caratunk, ME 04925.⟨maineskeptsecret.com⟩

⊞**The Sterling Inn** (1.4E) 207.672.3333

⊞**Caratunk Country Store** has everything a hiker needs, incl fuel/oz, canister fuel, first-aid, hygiene, food, drinks, call for rates. No pets in campground. Coin laundry, hot tub, free WiFi, restaurant open daily 7a - 9p, beer avail from onsite ▽**Kennebec River Brewery**, Mail: C/O Northern Outdoors, 1771 Route 201, The Forks, ME 04985.⟨northernoutdoors.com⟩

⊞**Berry's General Store** (7.6W) 207.663.4461 5a-7p daily, yr-round. Open till 8 in summer.

2073.1   HISTORIC AT ROUTE, *side trail 0.2E to Pleasant St, then left 1.7 to Monson*

⊞**Monson AT Visitor Center** (1.9E) Downtown Monson. Open daily Jun 5 - Oct 14 (dates & hrs may change in 2018) from 8a-11a & 1p-5p (hrs subject to adjustment). The Visitor Center is a critical source of info for all hikers on the trail in Maine. NoBo hikers should stop in & make plans for entering & staying in BSP, permits, climbing Katahdin & leaving the trail.

Northern Outdoors (2W) 207.663.4466 info@ northernoutdoors.com Free shuttle (coincides w/ferry schedule). Use resort facilities w/ or w/out stay. Hikers receive 30% lodging discount; prices vary, call for rates.

2076.4   ME 15

» *Monson, ME 04464* **ME 15**

⌂**John Baptist Mission** (3.6E) *Strictly enforced: No stealth camping in town.* Mission house on Main St. Shower, laundry, use of kitchen. Donation req'd. No drugs/alcohol.

Shaw's Hiker Hostel (3.6E) 207.997.3597 shawshikerhostel@gmail.com Thru hiker owned & over 40 yrs of continuous operation. Per Bryson's, A Walk in the Woods, "The most famous guesthouse on the A.T." Mid-May thru Oct, bunks $25, pvt room $50S $60D, $12 tent/hammock. P/U & ret w/stay. $9 B'fast, $5 laundry, $5 shower(w/o stay), high speed WiFi. Kayak & canoe. Food drops, licensed/insured shuttles-slackpacking all over ME. ⚲**Poet's Gear Emporium** onsite (8a-11a, 2p-5p) extensive ultralight gear & full resupply. Hyperlite, ULA, Big Agnes, Darn Tough, Leki, etc. Gear repair & shakedowns. CC ok. Mail (nonguests $5) USPS: P0 Box 72, Monson, ME 04464. For UPS/Fed Ex only: 17 Pleasant St.(shawshikerhostel.com)

Lodging & Pub (3.8E) 207.997.7069 (try 1st), 207.343.5033 (Owner, Rebekah Anderson's mobile) thelakeshorehouse@ yahoo.com Lakefront, kayaks, swimming, walking distance to all svcs, dog friendly, fun-but-not-party-crazy, at home feeling, house quiet by 10p. CC ok & ATM on premise. Bunks $25 pp/semi pvt $35pp/pvt $50 pp plus tax incl: shower, early check-in, WIFI, loaner laptop, mail drops, cable in most rooms, fans, clean loaner clothes, trailhead p/u & ret, use of boats, epic VHS collection & a free cold non-alcoholic beverage upon arrival. Fees for non-lodging guest: Shower, trailhead p/u or ret & laundry $5 each (all goes to charity). Pub w/homemade eclectic food & full bar/draught beer, open daily except Mo 11:30a -9p. Open Mic Night Th 6-9, Live music

LakeshoreHouse

MONSON, ME
45.2864, -69.5006
Mag. Dec. 16.12° W

(3.5 mi.)
Greenville Rd
Center St
Pleasant St

Shaw's Hostel &
Poet's Gear Emporium

1.7 to trailhead
parking area

Monson
General Store
7a-7p, 7 days

Spring
Creek BBQ

P0 (04464): 207.997.3975
M-F 9:15-12:15 & 1:15-4:15
Sa 7:30-11

Library
(no phone at library,
call Town of Monson:
207.997.3641)
M,W,F,12-4

Water St

0.4 mi

Lake Shore House ⌂

Pete's Place

Robinson's

Guilford Rd

Su 3-6. Hiker friendly. Mail: 9 Tenney Hill Rd, PO Box 215 (Use full address for mail drops & deliveries), Monson, ME 04464. ⟨thelakeshorehouse.com⟩

▲◎🛏🍴⛺ **Pete's Place** (3.8E) 207.997.3400 Open May 1 - Oct 31; Su - Sa 6-12. Lodging (pvt bunks) up to 4 in home. Small bakery w/a big b'fast & ice cream. Resupply: hiker foods, small gear items, dog food. Coleman/denatured/oz, canisters.

Spring Creek BBQ (3.6E) 207.997.7025 Th-Sa 11a-8p, Sunday 11a-5p, or until the food runs out!

🍴🛏 **A.E. Robinson's** (3.9E) 207.997.3700 3a-10p 7 days. ATM fee $2. **Country Cafe Deli** inside serves burgers, pizza, b'fast.

» *Greenville, ME 04485 (10W from ME 15)*

» *Kineo View Motor Lodge* (7.7W) 207.695.4470 $99-$109D, $10EAP incl c. b'fast. Clean, quiet motel w/view, 7.5mi from trailhead. ⟨kineoview.com⟩

▲🛏🍴 **Kelly's Landing** (12.2W) 207.695.4438 Lake Resort. Call for rates, Restaurant 7 days 7a-9p, Su AYCE b'fast.

🐾🛒 **Indian Hill Trading Post & Supermarket** (9.9W) 207.695.2104 Open M-Th 7-8, Fr 7-9, Sa 7-8, Su 8-9

🐾🍴📶🖥 **Northwoods Outfitters** (10.6W) 207.695.3288 Full svc outfitter w/dehyd meals, fuel/oz, canister fuel. Espresso bar, pastries. 7 Days 8-5. ⟨maineoutfitter.com⟩

🏛🍴 **Jamieson's Store / Jamo's Pizza** (10.7W) 207.695.2201

🍴 **Dairy Bar** (10.6W) Ice Cream

🍴📶 **Kineo Coffee Station** (10W) 207.695.2167 Open Tu-Sa 7a-1p. Baked goods, B'fast sandwiches, Paninis, coffee, cold brew.

➕ **Charles Dean Memorial Hospital** (11.5W) 207.695.5200

🍴💊 **Harris Drug Store** (10.6W) 207.695.2921 Ice cream counter inside.

🏧 **Two Banks w/ATMs in Greenville** (10W)

2134.9   JO-MARY RD

» *(little traffic on road) 12.0E to ME 11*

Manufacturers & Retailers

AntiGravityGear	910.794.3308	LL Bean	206.292.2210
Arc'Teryx	866.458.2473	Marmont	800.441.8166
Asolo/Lowe Alpine	603.448.8827	Merrell	800.349.1835
Backcountry.com	800.409.4502	Montbell	800.800.1020
Big Agnes	877.554.8975	Mountain Hardwear	800.953.1020
Black Diamond	801.278.5552	Mountainsmith	877.927.5649
CamelBak	800.767.8725	Mystery Ranch	800.551.5889
Campmor	888.226.7667	NEMO	877.477.4292
Camp Trails	345.5622	North Face	740.445.4327
Cascade Designs	800.531.9531	Osprey	800.521.1698
(MSR/Therm-a-Rest/Platypus)		Outdoor Research	800.464.9208
Cedar Tree (Packa)	276.780.2351	Patagonia	757.643.8908
Coleman	800.835.3278	Petzl	855.818.5966
Columbia	800.547.8066	Photon	800.572.8822
Danner	877.432.6637	Primus	
Eagle Creek	800.874.1048	Princeton Tec	800.755.6701
Eastern Mtn Sports	888.463.6367	REI	866.676.5336
Elemental Horizons	919.280.5402	Royal Robbins	800.535.3589
Etowah Outfitters	678-767-8051	Sawyer Products	800.255.9982
Ex Officio	800.644.7303	Salomon	828.552.4578
Feathered Friends			603.356.5378
First Need		Sierra Designs	800.441.5713
Frogg Toggs		Sierra Stove	888.357.3262
Garmin		Sierra Trading Post	800.288.3124
Gossamer Gear	512.374.0133	Six Moon Designs	503.430.2303
Granite Gear	218.834.6157	Slumberjack	800.233.6283
Gregory	877.477.4292	SOTO Outdoors	877.927.5649
Hammock Gear	740.445.4327	Suunto	503.314.5119
Hi-Tec	800.521.1698	Tarptent /	833.548.1999
Hyperlite Mtn Gear	800.464.9208	Henry Shires	800.997.9301
Jacks 'R' Better	757.643.8908	Tecnica	888.863.1968
JanSport	855.818.5966	Teva	866.284.7830
Johnson Outdoors	800.572.8822	Trail Designs	855.967.8197
(Eureka/Jetboil)		Caldera Stove	800.638.6464
Katadyn/PUR	800.755.6701	ULA	877.807.3805
Keen	866.676.5336	Vasque	877.584.6898
Kelty	800.535.3589	Warmstuff	800.443.4871
Leki	800.255.9982	Western	800.257.9080
LightHeart Gear	828.552.4578	Mountaineering	800.426.4840
Limmer	603.356.5378		800.587.9044

2145.2 MAHAR TOTE TR, BLUE-BLAZED TRAIL

White House Landing Camps (0.2E) 207.745.5116 Call/text. Reservations highly recommended. Arrival date flexible. P/U & ret at boat dock incl 1 mi boat ride. Open May 15- Oct 15. Bunk $35PP, semi-pvt 45, $85 double bed +tax. Shower, towel & pillowcase incl. Linens extra. Resupply. Dinner menu for overnight guests incl burgers, pizza & more. AYCE b'fast. Device recharge. Free use of canoes. CC ok. All amenities require overnight stay. Mail (allow 7-10D for arrival): PO Box 1, Millinocket, ME 04462.

2175.5, 2175.8 GOLDEN RD, ABOL BRIDGE

Abol Pines 207.287.3821 Abol Pines $12+tax ($6+tax ME residents) self-register tent sites & shelters across the street from Abol Bridge Store, south of Golden Rd. Provided by Maine Dept. of Conservation.

Abol Bridge Campground & Store 207.447.5803 Store hrs 7a - 7p. Summer camping season: May 25-Oct 15. Campsites $25pp/night +tax. Bunk cabins $75/night 1-2 people, $140/night 3-4 people, $195/night 5-6 people +tax. Showers & b'fast incl w/stay. Showers $5 w/o stay. Scheduled shuttle svc between Abol, Katahdin Stream Campground & Millinocket, coin-op laundry on site. Visa/ MC ok. Subs, sodas, ice cream, long-term resupply. $10 Maildrop fee. *Please call/ email beforehand, send at least 2 wks in adv Mail: PO Box 536 Millinocket, ME 04462.

The Northern Restaurant 207.447.5803 Adjacent to Abol Bridge Store. Food & full bar w/local & micro-brewed beer. Restaurant open Jun 15-Sep 15, 11a-7p daily. B'fast buffet 7a - 9a daily, free w/stay, $10 w/o stay.(greatnorthernvacations.com)

CPM PetCare (20.7E) 207.723.6795, 207.731.3111 cpmpetcare@hotmail.com In house, privately run kennel svc. P/U & d/o at Millinocket, Abol Bridge & other campgrounds.

2185.7 KATAHDIN STREAM CAMPGRD & THE BIRCHES

» *Millinocket, ME 04462 (25E from KSC) Trail's End Festival (25E)* 207.723.4443 *Sep 14-16, 2018. Vendors, food & entertainment/live music. Hardcore trail work on Friday. (trailsendfestival.org)*

Pamola Shuttle Service 207.731.6663 Serving the Katahdin region since Dec 2017. Will take you where you want to be. Fast, friendly, & reliable. Reservations welcome.

Big Moose Inn (16.4E) 207.723.8391 info@ bigmoosecabins.com Open Mem Day - Colum Day, prices listed incl tax. Rooms w/shared baths for $65.40PP. Suites w/pvt baths $163.50/up. Cabins $119.90/up. Tenting $13.08PP. Lean-to $16.35PP. WiFi in lobby, pets allowed at campsites only & must be attended at all times. **Fredericka's Restaurant** on-site open W-Sa 5:30p-9p. B'fast avail for Inn guests daily. **Loose Moose Bar & Grill** open every night 5p-10p.(bigmoosecabins.com)

Wilderness Edge Campground (23.6E) 207.447.8485 Tent site $12PP, up to 4/cabin, incl free hot shower & swimming pool. Cabin tents $17PP, up to 4/cabin. Open May 11-Oct 15. Shuttle to trailheads & Medway bus depot avail, coin laundry, store: coleman/cannister fuel, soda, candy, ice cream.(wildernessedgecampground.com)

The Appalachian Trail Lodge (25.2E)Paul (OleMan) & Jaime (Navigator) Renaud 207.723.4321 provide svcs from Mem Day - Oct 24. CC ok. Bunkroom $25, pvt room $55, family suite $95D +$10EAP. Showers for nonguests $5. Coin laundry. Free daily guest shuttle ($10 non-guest) from Baxter SP from Sep 1 - Oct 15, between 3:30p-4:30p. Licensed & insured shuttle service for hire to & from bus in Medway, into 100-Mile Wilderness or Monson, food drops, slackpack in 100-Mile Wilderness, other shuttles by arrangement. Free parking. No pets. SoBo special: p/u in Medway, bed in bunkroom, b'fast at **AT Cafe**, & shuttle to KSC, $70pp, by reserv. Guest mail (they DO NOT sign for mail: 33 Penobscot Ave, Millinocket, ME 04462. **Full line of gear:** ULA & Hyperlite packs, bags, fuel, stoves, poles, Southbound A.T. Guide, etc. Limited clothing, no shoes. Serves B/L,.(appalachiantraillodge.com)

Parks Edge Inn (25.3E) 207.447.4321, 207.227.2692 Hiker discounts. Suites from $65 to $125. All rooms have kitchen, bath, TV & DVD players. Guest Mail: 19 Central St, Millinocket, ME 04462.

Hotel Terrace & Ruthie's Restaurant (25.6E) 207.723.6305 Rates subject to change. Ruthie's serves B/L/D.

Katahdin Cabins (25.9E) 207.723.6305 Skip Mohoff run eco-friendly cabins, b'fast, TV, DVD, fridge & m'wave. $65 up to 3

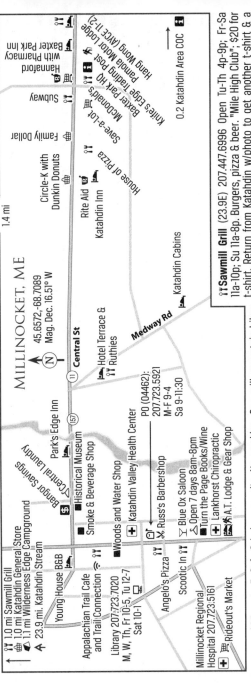

MILLINOCKET, ME

45.6572, -68.7089
Mag. Dec. 16.51° W

N

Central St

Medway Rd

1.4 mi

0.2 Katahdin Area COC

Baxter Park Inn
Pamola Motor Lodge (AYCE 11-2)
Hang Wong
Hannaford with Pharmacy
Knife's Edge Trading Post
Baxter Park HQ
McDonald's
Subway
Save-a-Lot
Family Dollar
House of Pizza
Circle-K with Dunkin Donuts
Rite Aid
Katahdin Inn
Katahdin Cabins

Hotel Terrace & Ruthies

Park's Edge Inn

PO (04462):
207.723.5921
M-F 9-4
Sa 9-11:30

Historical Museum
Smoke & Beverage Shop
Woods and Water Shop
Katahdin Valley Health Center
Russ's Barbershop
Blue 0x Saloon
Open 7 days 8am-8pm
Turn the Page Books/Wine
Lankhorst Chiropractic
A.T. Lodge & Gear Shop

Bangor Savings
Central Laundry

Appalachian Trail Cafe and Trail Connection
Library 207.723.7020
M, W, Th, Fr 10-5, Tu 12-7
Sat 10-1
Millinocket Regional Hospital 207.723.5161

Young House B&B
Angelo's Pizza
Scootic In
Rideout's Market

1.0 mi Sawmill Grill
1.0 mi Katahdin General Store
1.1 mi Wilderness Edge Campground
23.9 mi. Katahdin Stream

Katahdin Cabins

persons, $85 up to 5. Cafe & bakery on-site. Gas grill, mountain bikes & fishing tackle free for use. Community room. Accepts CC/cash/checks. Mail: 181 Medway Rd, Millinocket, ME 04462.⟨katahdincabins.com⟩

Katahdin Inn & Suites (26E) 207.723.4555 Cont b'fast. Indoor heated pool & hot tub.⟨katahdininnandsuites.com⟩

Baxter Park Inn (26.4E) 207.723.9777 $104.99D + tax, $10EAP, pets $25, sauna, pool.

Pamola Lodge (26.5E) 207.723.9746 pamolalodge@ ymail.com Affordable, pet friendly, knowledgeable staff.⟨pamolalodge.com⟩

Maine Quest Adventures (35.2E) 207.447.5011 P/U at Medway. D/0 at Katahdin Stream or Abol Bridge. Shuttles to Monson, 100-Mile Wilderness, & throughout ME. Food Drops possible.⟨mainequestadventures.com⟩

North Woods Trading Post (16E) 207.723.4326 Open Mem Day - mid Oct. 8-8 most days; hrs vary. Good selection of trail foods, many gear items. Sandwiches & pizza made onsite.

Sawmill Grill (23.9E) 207.447.6996 Open Tu-Th 4p-9p; Fr-Sa 11a-10p; Su 11a-8p. Burgers, pizza & beer. "Mile High Club"; $20 for t-shirt. Return from Katahdin w/photo to get another t-shirt & a free meal.

Turn the Page Bookstore and Wine Bar (25.4E) Offers healthy food, great wines, used books, comfortable loungy atmosphere. Pet friendly.⟨fb.com/read.dine.wine⟩

Katahdin Kritters Pet Resort (32E) 207.746.8040 Kennel free w/24 hr supervision. Rabies, distemper & kennel cough vaccine req'd. Register online. P/U possilbe.⟨katahdinkritters.com⟩

Katahdin Air (16.3E) 866.359.6246 fly@katahdinair.com One-way flights to 7 trailheads in ME's 100M wilderness. Flights from base on Ambajejus Lake w/free shuttle from Abol Bridge. $85-$140.⟨katahdinair.com⟩

Millinocket Municipal Airport (26.4E) 207.731.9906 Roundtrip car rentals avail from airport on Medway Rd, 1.0S of Central St.

2190.9   KATAHDIN, BAXTER PEAK, (See pg. 224)

Baxter State Park

baxterstatepark.authority.com | facebook.com/baxterstatepark

H All AT hikers (northbound, southbound, section and flip-flop) must secure a AT Hiker Permit card at the **Katahdin Stream Campground (KSC)** ranger station prior to their summit hike. Hikers must also sign in and out on the Trail head register on their way up/down Katahdin. For park information and reservations call 207.723.5140 or visit the website. Mem Day - Colum Day 8-4 x 7D, Colum Day to Mem Day 8-4 M-Fri. When driving, tune to AM 1610 for recent reports. Dates vary based on weather, but the hiking season is approximately May 15 - October 22. Weather conditions may prompt trail closure at any time to protect alpine habitat or other Park resources, subject to Park Director's approval. Weather reports are posted at KSC at 7am daily, along with "Trail Status and Alerts." Consequences for hiking when the trail is closed include fines, eviction, loss of park visitation privileges and reimbursement of search and rescue costs. Daily recommended cut-off times for starting hikes to Baxter Peak are noon in June and July, 11am in August, 10am in September, and 9am in October. Overnight camping is allowed in designated sites only. Hikers are welcome to leave their backpack at KSC; loaner daypacks are available at no charge from the ranger's station. Northbound thruhikers completing their hike in late summer or early fall usually have an easy time hitching from KSC into Millinocket. There are fees for nonresidents entering the park by car and fees for campsites that also apply to residents. Fees must be paid in cash; no credit cards and no work-for-stay. Campsites at KSC or Abol Campground can be made in advance by phone or online. Pets are not allowed in the park. Cell phone reception is unlikely anywhere in the park other than on Katahdin. Please do not place calls from the summit or within earshot of other hikers. Please use a cell phone only if there is an emergency. Maine law prohibits the drinking of alcohol or the use of marijuana in public places.

◁⌂ The Birches The Birches near KSC has 2 shelters and one tent site, open to northbound long distance hikers who have hiked a minimum of "the 100 mile wilderness" immediately prior to entering the Park. Stay is limited to a single night, is limited to 12 persons (combined tenting and shelter)

and the fee is $10 per person. All other hikers, including flip-floppers and southbound thru-hikers, who wish to overnight in the Park should make reservations in advance. Common options, listed in order of their proximity to KSC are Abol Campground, Daicey Pond Campground (cabins $57D/up) & Foster Field Group Area, north of Katahdin. Note that Abol Campground in the Park, Abol Pines at Abol Bridge and privately run Abol Bridge Campground are three distinct entities. Please note that Abol Bridge does not have an ATM, you must have cash prior to entering the 100 mile wilderness.

P Baxter gates open at 6am. Maine residents enter for free; $15 per vehicle for non-residents. KSC parking is limited and you will not be allowed to enter if the lots are full. Day-use parking reservations are highly recommended and can be obtained for KSC, Abol or Roaring Brook Campgrounds by phone up to 3 weeks in advance, for a $5 fee. The reservation expires after 7AM. There is no long-term parking in Baxter. Check with local taxi and shuttle services for info on long term parking outside the Park. Park Fees expected to increase slightly.

Getting to Katahdin

Most routes to Katahdin are through Bangor, ME, 91 mi from Baxter SP. Bangor has an airport & bus terminal. Shuttle services will pick you up in Bangor, but it is more economical to take **Cyr Bus Lines** to Medway, 31 mi from Baxter. Hikers often take layover in Millinocket, 24 mi from KSC, the closest parking area to Katahdin.

⊞ Cyr Bus Lines Cyr Bus Lines 800.244.2335 (cyrbustours.com) One-way routes 7D $12. Cash & CC accepted. Routes below are to Concord Hub near airport; bus also stops at Greyhound station 20 min later on arrival, sooner on departure.

▼ Medway 9:30am (station at Irving store) to Bangor 10:50
▼ Bangor 6:30pm to Medway 7:40pm

⊡ Concord Trailways 207.945.4000 Bangor airport hub, svc to South Station in Boston (concordcoachlines.com)

⊞ The Appalachian Trail Lodge, Maine Quest Adventures, & Bull Moose Taxi, all listed in Millinocket, provide transportation from Medway Millinocket & Katahdin.